Santa Fe, N.M.
Jan. 13, 1994

to her more than
through it all.
all the best,

Jack Samon

CHENNAULT

ALSO BY JACK SAMSON

Line Down! The Special World of Big Game Fishing   1973

The Best of Corey Ford (edited)   1974

The Sportsman's World   1976

The Worlds of Earnest Thompson Seton   1976

Falconry Today   1976

A Fine and Pleasant Misery (edited)   1978

Successful Outdoor Writing   1979

The Bear Book (edited)   1979

The Pond   1979

The Grizzly Book (edited)   1981

The Great Fish   1983

Modern Falconry   1984

Hunting the Southwest   1985

Chennault

by JACK SAMSON

Doubleday
NEW YORK   1987

ACKNOWLEDGMENTS

From *China—The Remembered Life* by Paul Frillman and Graham Peck. Copyright © 1968 by Paul Frillman and Graham Peck. Reprinted by permission of Houghton Mifflin Company.

From *Way of a Tiger* by Claire L. Chennault, edited by Robert B. Hotz. Copyright © 1949 by Claire L. Chennault. Reprinted by permission of Anna Chennault.

Library of Congress Cataloging-in-Publication Data

Samson, Jack.
  Chennault.

  1. Chennault, Claire Lee, 1890–1958. 2. United
States. Army Air Forces—Biography. 3. Generals—
United States—Biography. I. Title.
UG626.2.C48S26 1987   358.4'0092'4 [B] 86-24404
ISBN 0-385-23171-7

To the memory of those young men whose dreams
came to an end in China, Burma, and India.

FOREWORD

As always, on those rare occasions when I have been asked to write a Foreword for a book, particularly a book concerning the life of a man whom I had a great interest in and great respect for, I approach the problem with somewhat a degree of temerity.

I never had the pleasure of knowing General Chennault personally, although I served in the China-Burma-India Theater and although in my job in the early part of World War II of training young cadets to shoot their weapons at aerial targets and ground targets, I grew to realize that this was the one man in our whole aviation effort who had dedicated any really large degree of interest in the subject of hitting a target by bullets fired from one aircraft at an enemy trying to get away. He had developed what later became known as "the curve of pursuit" [the continually changing angle of deflection a fighter pilot must keep in mind when firing at a moving enemy plane], and although his teachings were not as detailed as we were ultimately able to provide after consultation with the Royal Air Force, he was able to impart enough of this knowledge to the Air Force that he commanded in China to allow them to shoot down many Japanese aircraft. He was, as this fine book will tell you, commander of the Fourteenth Air Force in China, and later he retired in 1945 as a major general and as president of a large airline in China.

At the outbreak of the war following the Japanese attack on Pearl Harbor in 1941, the Asian Theater's elite fighter squadrons, organized and commanded by Claire Chennault, became known as the Flying Tigers. Their missions were grimly simple: to impede the Japanese advance over the vast area of China and Burma while the global war against the Axis was fought and won elsewhere. But for these men, the real war was right overhead—their American P-40s against the Oscars and Zeros of Japan. They were desperately short of munitions and material and almost constantly short of gasoline and even short of aircraft. But these men continued to fly from very crude front-line airfields over practically unmapped territories, where a parachute jump from a stricken plane would probably end in death.

The general was a flying product of World War I, having received his wings in 1918, then having flown in the Mexican Border Patrol, later with the Hawaiian Pursuit Squadron, was an instructor at Brooks Field, and a member of the United States Army Pursuit Development Board. After retiring from the Air Corps and going to China as an adviser to the Chinese Air Force in 1937, his was the professional background one is going to sense throughout this book, the background of a man newly embarked upon a new aerial mission of armed forces without anybody at that time really having a great knowledge of how to go about it.

I would go back to my first words of this Foreword and point out that it was his fundamental grasp of the theory of "the curve of pursuit" that, in my opinion, enabled him to achieve the successes that he achieved in China, that, plus a driving determination to properly equip his men, feed his men, and take care of them. These latter facts I knew, because I flew a few missions myself of supplies to his bases, and I could tell immediately the great respect that the men had for this commander, a respect that grew in me.

Claire Lee Chennault was a fascinating man in a fascinating time in history. This book will go a long way toward ensuring him his deserved place in that history.

Barry Goldwater
United States Senate

PREFACE

I first encountered the highly controversial Claire Lee Chennault when—as a young second lieutenant navigator/bombardier in the 425th Bomb Squadron of the 308th Bomb Group in Kunming, China, in 1944—I suddenly realized the pitcher on our softball team was the famed head of the "Flying Tigers" himself. Several of my squadron mates—supposedly in the know—said he was part Cherokee Indian. I bought that story at the time because he certainly looked like an Indian chief. Wearing a baseball cap and dressed in a sweat shirt and suntan pants, he didn't look a bit like a two-star general, nor did he act like one.

It was not until I returned to the Far East in 1950 to work as a public relations director for Chennault's civilian airline, Civil Air Transport (CAT), that I got to know the "Old Man" personally. I loved to hunt and fish and so did Chennault. It was only natural that the two of us ended up hunting pheasants and ducks together on the south tip of Taiwan in the 1950s. He was a warm and generous man who never forgot any of his "boys"—as he called those men who had served with him in the American Volunteer Group (AVG), the China Air Task Force (CATF), or the U. S. Fourteenth Air Force in China.

He was a simple, straightforward man and—if there is such a thing—a pure patriot. He never had any doubt about his role in life. It was to serve his United States as a military man against her enemies. He fought the Japanese with a curious intensity, and when they were defeated he turned his attention toward the Chinese Communists. While he must have known Generalissimo Chiang Kai-shek had faults as a ruler of China, he never abandoned the Nationalist regime on the mainland, and he continued to support it on Taiwan as long as he lived. He had considered Chiang a friend and his military commander since the days when they fought together against overwhelming odds in 1937. Loyalty, to Chennault, was not just a word. It was a way of life.

There are a number of people to whom I am indebted for help in regard to this book. I owe a special thanks to Professor William Leary of the University of Georgia for turning over to me much declassified material from the CIA about the formation and operation of Civil Air Transport. His research was invaluable.

To Cindy Bellinger, who laboriously typed and edited this unwieldy manuscript, my everlasting thanks.

To my old cronies of the Fourteenth Air Force, who reached back into the dim recesses of memory for events long past, my deepest appreciation.

To my associates of the CAT Association, for patience in putting up with my interminable questions, more thanks.

To the members of the Flying Tiger Association—the AVG—my gratitude for their help in keeping the record, long blurred by time and misinformation, straight.

Many individual people helped more than they perhaps will ever know and to them my special thanks—Bill Leary, P. Y. Shu, Tex Hill, Sebie Smith, Joe and Lil Rosbert, Louise Willauer Jackson, Lilian Finnerty, Max Chennault, Peggy Chennault, Anna Chennault, and my old CAT associate Malcolm Rosholt.

In researching this project, I ran up against many differences of opinion. Even Chennault's age was a matter of controversy. On his tombstone appears the date of his birth and death—the birthday 1893. I found that Chennault himself, in his autobiography and on his personal records, used 1890 as the year of his birth. His widow, Anna, who had the 1893 date put on his tombstone, told me his father changed Chennault's age so that his son might join the United States Army in World War I.

I asked the United States Air Force and this is the official answer I received in 1979:

> According to official military sources, research of a military historian, and logic, Claire Chennault was born on September 6, 1890. The *Army Registry* for 1929, 1937, and 1945 (a random sampling) lists 1890 as the year of his birth. The retired list also indicates Chennault was born in 1890. Additionally, Dupre's biographies of Air Force leaders indicates that his birth took place in 1890. Furthermore, Mr. James Eastman recently researched Chennault's papers. According to Mr. Eastman, Chennault's personal records indicate he was born in 1890.
>
> Logic would favor the 1890. Chennault joined the Army in 1917 at the age of twenty-seven. He was older than the average recruit and it would not have made sense for him to give 1890 as his birth year (if he wanted to be accepted into the Army) if he had, indeed, been born in 1893. Logically, he would not have lied to make himself older.

Given the official military records . . . and the thrust of logic . . .
Claire Chennault was born on September 6, 1890.

> Earl H. Tilford, Jr.
> Captain, USAF
> Historian

I am inclined to agree.

> JACK SAMSON
> *Santa Fe, New Mexico*

LIST OF ILLUSTRATIONS

CHENNAULT

PART I

One

As the U.S. Dollar Line's *President Garfield* knifed into the Pacific swells thirty miles out of San Francisco on the afternoon of May 8, 1937, the dark, stocky man at the rail glanced upward at the flock of hovering sea gulls that had followed the liner since it passed beneath the awesome span of the nearly completed Golden Gate Bridge several hours earlier.

There was a stiff wind blowing out of the southwest and the man buttoned up the collar of his light jacket and turned, making his way unsteadily to a row of wooden deck chairs lined against the white bulkhead. Unused to the motion of a ship at sea, he felt slightly queasy as the big liner slowly rolled on its way out to sea.

There was the quick feeling of annoyance as he lowered himself into the chair and slid the folded San Francisco *Chronicle* from beneath his arm. After all the years of flying, how could he let the roll of a ship bother him?

He shook out the folds in the newspaper and looked again at the front page. Terrible. What a tragedy. The headlines read: HINDENBURG BURNS IN LAKEHURST CRASH: 21 KNOWN DEAD, 12 MISSING; 64 ESCAPE. He read the subheads in the single column below. "Ship Falls Ablaze—Great dirigible bursts into flames as it is about to land—victims burn to death—some passengers are thrown from the blazing wreckage, others crawl to safety. Sparks from engines or static believed to have ignited hydrogen gas. . . ."

He slowly lowered the paper to his lap. God, what a miserable way to die. There had never been any sense in flying lighter-than-air balloons filled with such highly flammable stuff. The Germans had been warned over and over that one day they were going to have a hell of an accident. He reached into a left shirt pocket and slid a package of Camels out through the opening of the jacket. Flipping open the lid of his battered silver lighter, he lit the cigarette and inhaled deeply. The smoke filled his lungs and he grimaced as he expelled it, the sea wind whipping it away as soon as it left his lips. Maybe the voyage would be good for the cough. The damn chronic bronchitis had been with him almost as long as he could remember. It—as much as the deafness —was the reason the Army Air Corps had insisted on the early retirement. Retired. Forty-six years old. Twenty years as a fighter pilot and now— washed up. Now that he was officially out, at least he could look at it clearly —from a distance. It was while he lay in bed all those months in the hospital at Hot Springs, Arkansas, that the defeat had eaten at him. Bitterness can be tasted when a man thinks he has wasted his life.

There were all those years—when he had first gotten the wings and the commission, when he and Nell had first been married and the children had come along—when he had thought he could make a difference. It had seemed possible at first that he could make a name for himself in the Air Corps—especially in the mid-twenties when so much was new about avia- tion. There had been such promise for a fighter pilot who was good. At the very least, he could have made the permanent rank of colonel. That would have ensured security for the family and a respectable position. But captain —not much to show for twenty years, even if he had, in the last few months, been made temporary major.

He flipped the cigarette butt out and over the rail and rested his head back against the metal bulkhead. God, what was he doing here—on this strange ship headed out across the Pacific to China of all places? Nell and the kids would be safe and happy at the house in Waterproof, Louisiana, for the three months, but still it was a crazy idea to take the job. Adviser to the Chinese Aeronautical Commission. The pay—a thousand dollars a month—was a fortune. It would come in handy for the farm when he got back, but this was sure not what he had planned. The bass would be spawning in the Tensas River, hungry to hit almost any lure at this time of year. The buds would be green and the fields ready for planting. There would be broods of young waterfowl in the sloughs and bayous and the redwing blackbirds would be making their rusty-gate calls as they swung from the bent cattails along the river.

He grunted and got to his feet, picking up the newspaper as he did. He walked along the rail for a dozen yards until he came to a heavy metal door and pulled it open. His leather heels thudded against the steps of the metal stairway. Making his way along a dark corridor, he finally came to a state- room door with the number 12 on it and turned the brass knob. Inside, he tossed the newspaper on the lower bunk and, shrugging out of the light jacket, hung it on a hook behind the door.

He slid the heavy leather suitcase out from beneath the bunk and opened it in the middle of the faded blue rug. Reaching inside one of the deep side pockets, he dug out a bottle of bourbon and set it carefully on the small wooden desk. He reached up and took a glass from the metal medicine cabinet above the small metal sink and splashed several inches of the amber bourbon into it. Raising the glass to his lips, he drained it with a quick toss of his head. He slid the suitcase back beneath the bunk and sat down at the desk. He flipped on the switch of the desk lamp and unbuckled the straps of a scarred and battered leather briefcase. Opening the flap, he leafed through the contents, then slid a packet of papers onto the desktop.

It was going to be a long trip—a week to Honolulu and another ten days or so to Shanghai. There would be ample time to work out all the plans. He had purposely not done much paperwork on the train to San Francisco, preferring to save it for the isolation of the sea voyage.

He flipped open the new green passport and stared at the print. "I, the undersigned, Secretary of State of the United States of America, hereby request all whom it may concern to permit safely and freely to pass, and in case of need, to give lawful aid and protection to Claire Lee Chennault, a citizen of the United States."

Below it added: "Given under my hand and seal of the Department of State at Washington, March 26, 1937." It was signed by Cordell Hull.

On the facing page he continued to read: "Description of bearer: height 5 feet 9½ inches, hair black, eyes brown. Distinguishing marks or features: scar on forehead. Place of birth: Commerce, Texas. Date of birth: September 6, 1890. Occupation: farmer." Following that was his signature. He smiled, thinking of the occupation. Hell of a place for a farmer.

He folded the passport and slipped it inside the briefcase. He took the pile of papers and began to sort through them. When he found the one he was seeking, he rested his elbow on the desk and frowned as he read. The handwriting across the top of the first page was that of Roy Holbrook, a former Air Corps pilot who had been with him at Brooks Field and who was now a confidential adviser to the Central Trust Company of China.

"The blank spaces are for your name, Maxwell Field, etc. I have written in some of them. This is the copy of my letter to the Generalissimo."

There followed five sheets of paper. Holbrook had filled in the blank spaces with Chennault's name where it was needed. The letter was really a long recommendation for him to serve as an adviser. Roy had gone to great lengths to outline Chennault's qualifications and said it just might be possible to convince Major Chennault to resign his commission to the U.S. Army Air Corps if satisfactory arrangements could be made. Chennault and Holbrook had discussed the possibility of his taking the advisory position some time before, so the conditions had been worked out ahead of time. Chennault wanted full control and responsibility for advanced pursuit training and a voice in determining the selection of all armament, accessories, and instruments of all pursuit planes and equipment. He had asked for two old Maxwell Field cronies, W. C. ("Billy") McDonald and John H. ("Luke") Williamson, as his assistants. He asked for the organization of an aircraft reporting service for the collection and transmission of information to pursuit and bombardment headquarters and he wanted authority to issue all training manuals, textbooks for students, squadron commanders, tactical units, and pursuit units. In addition, he wanted authority to organize, when the proper time arrived, an advanced school for Chinese senior officers, similar to that of the Army Air Corps.

If he were granted these provisions, he would then consider a contract with the Chinese government to serve for two years with terms for renewal at the end of that time.

His salary was to be at the rate of twelve thousand dollars (U.S.) per year and he was to be guaranteed passage to China and back to the States at the completion of his contract. In case of disability or death, one year's salary was to be paid to his family. In case of death, his body was to be returned to his family.

This three-month survey trip was being paid for by the Chinese government and, supposedly, if Chennault agreed to serve as an adviser after that, he would take retirement from the U.S. Air Corps. As far as the Chinese knew, Chennault was on leave.

The letter went on and on and Chennault smiled as he put it down. Good old Roy. Always thinking of a pal. He had no intention of seriously considering a two-year contract. He was sure he could give the Chinese all the advice they needed for the fighter plane division of their Air Force in three months.

He leaned back on the straight wooden chair and smiled. Well, at least he wouldn't be alone. Luke Williamson and Billy McDonald, with whom he had been stunt flying for years in the Air Corps, had taken jobs as flying instructors the year before and had been teaching Chinese students to fly at Hangchow, south of Shanghai. McDonald was to meet him at Kobe, Japan, on this trip. Together they were to go on to China.

He took a swallow of the bourbon, then reached for a cigarette. The three months would not seem long. It would be good to see Luke and Billy again. All he had to do was to get the paperwork done on this ship and the rest would be easy. After all, this was May. Three months from now it would be August and he could start back to Louisiana. The dove season started September 1 and after that the duck season would begin. He smiled, stuffed the papers back into the briefcase, and took a long drag on the cigarette. The big liner shuddered a bit as her bow bit into the long swells of the Pacific.

By the third day out, he had got used to the slow roll of the ship and was able to walk around the decks without the stagger that had bothered him the first few days. His years of acrobatics in fighter planes had given him a strong stomach when it came to motion.

Though the seas were moderate, some of his fellow passengers did not fare as well. There were perhaps a dozen people in cabins near his and not many of them came to meals at first. It was only on the third day that he began to notice a few of them on deck and in the dining room. Several men in Navy uniforms accompanied by their wives were en route to duty at naval bases in Hawaii.

He was assigned to table 16 in the dining room and to lifeboat number 4. The significance of the boat assignment did not dawn on him until the captain called a boat drill at 3:30 P.M. on the third day. He felt a bit foolish donning the bulky life preserver and sitting in the boat with other passengers but was enough of a military man to appreciate the need for readiness.

For years, as an Army Air Corps officer, he had played cards. There had been long hours of waiting to take off and the time had been passed by playing poker, bridge, cribbage, or keno. He and Nell had got into the habit of playing bridge at the officers' clubs over the years and he loved the game. By the fourth day of the cruise he had met some of the Navy personnel and played bridge with Lieutenant and Mrs. Sanchez and another officer named Shantz.

Always athletic, Chennault yearned for some form of vigorous exercise on the ship but had to settle for brisk deck walks. Shuffleboard did not interest him much. Ever since he was a small boy in the woods and bayous of Louisiana he had been a dynamo of activity. Along the Tensas River he had fished for bass and catfish, trapped raccoons and muskrats, hunted squirrels with a single-shot .22 rifle, and stalked waterfowl with a shotgun. As he grew older, he hunted deer in the thick cover of the river bottom and was never happier than when on his own. Blessed with a hard, compact body and fine reflexes, he was good at all sports. In school he excelled at baseball and later became a coach. After graduating from Louisiana State Normal School in 1907 he taught in a rural school in Gilbert, close to Waterproof.

The weather grew worse as the ship approached Hawaii and on May 13 he slept late. Getting up about noon, he made his regular rounds of the deck, dressed in a pair of corduroy trousers, tennis shoes, a sweat shirt, and a cap. Stopping off at the radio room, he scanned a bulletin board in the hallway on which was posted the news of the day on typewritten sheets. On this Thursday, the media were mostly concerned with the coronation of King George VI and Queen Elizabeth of England. The ceremony in Westminster Abbey had caught the attention of most of the world. A big CIO labor strike had shut down two plants of the Jones & Laughlin Steel Corporation in Pittsburgh, idling twenty-seven thousand workers. John L. Lewis had begun his drive to organize the nation's steelworkers into one big union. On another sheet of paper was a story about the Spanish rebels beating back an attack by Loyalists on the city of Toledo, while insurgent planes dropped more than a hundred bombs into the suburbs of Bilbao. Chennault shook his head as he read. The plane was coming into its own as a weapon of war.

On the last day before arriving in Hawaii, it rained continuously and the seas were up. He was invited to the captain's dinner that night and enjoyed meeting Navy Commander and Mrs. Knox and Lieutenant Commander and Mrs. O'Connell. There were mechanical horse-race games and he won two dollars. There was dancing to the ship's orchestra, but, as he wrote in his diary later that night, "Tried to dance in the evening, but ship rolled too much." He had never kept a diary before, but the thought of all he might encounter on this trip had led him to purchase a small pocket notebook in which he jotted down a few details each day.

The stay in Honolulu was uneventful. It was good to revisit the scene of his earlier days as commanding officer of the 19th Fighter Squadron at Luke Field in late 1923, and he had a chance to visit with some old cronies. Hume Peabody came down to the boat and they had a drink at the Young Hotel. The ship left for Japan at 6 A.M. in a driving rain squall.

Knowing he had at least ten days ahead before the ship reached Kobe, he decided to submit to the Chinese a tentative outline of pursuit tactics based on his twenty years of experience in the Air Corps. He had no idea what sort of an air force the Chinese had—except for the sketchy information given him by Holbrook, McDonald, and Williamson—but he figured anything he submitted to them about fighter plane tactics would be new to them.

He dug out his dog-eared copy of *The Role of Defensive Pursuit,* which he had written in 1933 while a tactical air instructor at Maxwell Field, Alabama. It had been finished and turned over to his superiors in 1934, but nothing much had ever come of it. The brass at that time—as later—were convinced the future of air warfare lay with the heavy bomber. It was the fashion of the times to be a disciple of General Giulio Douhet, the Italian military theorist. His writings on the need for saturation bombing by heavy bombers—*Probable Aspects of Future War, Master of the Air,* and *The War of 19 . .*—had been translated into French and published in one volume by the journal *Les Aigles* under the title *La Guerre de l'air,* which, in time, was translated into English under the title *The Command of the Air.* The volume was taken so seriously in Europe that Douhet's strategy had been followed to the letter by the Italians in their air maneuvers in 1931 and 1932 and by the British in the same years. The French had revised their military aviation completely. As a result, nobody was interested in reading about fighter plane tactics by an obscure captain—especially when they pertained to defense against heavy bombers.

In brief, what Douhet advocated was the accumulation of huge concentrations of heavy bombers with considerable range and a great bomb-load capacity. These planes were to be arranged on a number of airfields so that, when hostilities began, they could be sent out in columns. The columns would be aimed at strategic targets and wave after wave of bombers would move down those columns. Douhet theorized that ground weapons would not be geared to a defense against wave after wave of bombers any more than would defensive pursuit aircraft. Both the ground defense and the defensive pursuit would soon be exhausted and unable to offer further resistance to the bombers. It was assumed that after three or four days of this constant bombardment the people of the besieged nation would sue for peace at any cost. Apparently European military experts had decided that bombers, once in the air, could not be stopped.

For years Chennault had been saying this was nonsense. His superiors had grown tired of hearing him claim that fighter aircraft would play as important a part in future wars as the bomber. His years of experience in teaching fighter tactics and flying fighters convinced him of two things: fighter aircraft must fly and fight as a team, and the biggest problem was the lack of an intelligence network. He knew that, without a continuous stream of accurate information as to where high-speed bombers were, attempts at fighter interception would be useless.

He had experimented with fighters in pairs, in trios, and in elements of four planes. His research into World War I fighter battles had taught him the old military formula that the difference between the firepower of two opposing forces—all other factors being equal—is not the difference in number of fire units but the *square* of the difference of the number of fire units. That meant a two-plane team of fighter planes attacking a target represented not odds of two to one in its favor, but of four to one. He decided the two-plane team was the most easily maneuvered and could concentrate the most firepower on a bomber or enemy fighter plane and at the same time offer the most protection to each attacking pilot.

The old dogfight concept of World War I—in which each fighter peeled off and began a one-on-one battle—was still being taught in some Air Corps schools. When Chennault was a student at tactical school in 1931, his instructor, Clayton Bissell, a World War I ace, was still teaching the old Western Front tactics of the dawn patrol and the dogfight.

Chennault, participating in air maneuvers in the 1930s, was so convinced of the fallacy of this teaching that he became a thorn in the side of high-echelon brass. After writing an eight-page rebuttal to the conclusions reached by a lieutenant colonel, commenting on the reasons for fighter failure to intercept bombers during a 1931 maneuver, Chennault's school received a letter. "Who is this damned fellow Chennault?" wrote General Henry H. ("Hap") Arnold, who was later to be commanding general of the Army Air Corps in World War II.

Chennault never succeeded in convincing the upper echelon of the Air Corps of the wisdom of his theories. As late as October 1941, Arnold told a class of West Point cadets, "Frankly, fighters have been allowed to drift in the doldrums."

Now, aboard the *President Garfield* in the spring of 1937, Chennault returned to writing. At least he could attempt to sell his theories on fighter plane warfare to the Chinese, who would soon have a need for them, the way the Japanese occupation of Chinese territory was progressing.

He knew what to advise the Chinese on pursuit flying. He knew what sort of warning net was needed to give advanced signals of the approach of enemy bombers, but he had no real knowledge of the size or readiness of the Chinese Air Force.

While at Maxwell Field, he had organized an acrobatic team called "Three

men on a Flying Trapeze." His wing mates had been two sergeant pilots—
Billy McDonald and Luke Williamson. Flying the high-wing Boeing P-12E
fighter plane, they were recognized as the best stunt team in Air Corps
circles. At the Pan-American Air Maneuvers in Miami in 1936 some visiting
Chinese aviation experts saw them perform. One of the visitors was Mow
Pan-tzu, a Moscow-trained pilot who later commanded the Chinese Air
Force under the name Peter Mow. The Chinese were impressed with the
Americans' flying and later offered them contracts to come to China to
teach.

Both McDonald and Williamson accepted and, after resigning from the
Air Corps, sailed to China from British Columbia aboard the Canadian
Pacific liner *Empress of Russia* on July 11, 1936. With them went a number
of ground crew personnel—among them Sterling Tatum, Rolfe Watson, John
Holland, and Sebie Biggs Smith, an instrument specialist. Chennault, uncertain of his status in the Air Corps at the time, had declined the offer. But in
the next year, as his health deteriorated and Army doctors grounded him, he
began to think seriously about taking up an offer to become an adviser. Luke
and Billy had kept him informed of the situation at the training school—the
Central Aviation School at Shien Chiao, an old air base a few miles east of
the city of Hangchow. Their information, in addition to that of Roy Holbrook, who had gone over in 1935 to join retired Colonel Jack Jouett, had
given him a rough idea of the situation. Jouett had done a credible job of
setting up the training school at Shien Chiao, modeling it on United States
training schools. By the time his contract ran out in 1935, he had taught
several hundred Chinese pilots. His Chinese counterpart at the school was
Peter Mow.

Chennault had an idea that the entire Chinese Air Force did not number
much more than several hundred aircraft—both bombers and fighters—but
he could not be sure. There was no official estimate of military air strength.
So he had to assume, from his recommendations to the Generalissimo, that
there were at least that many or more. Now, as the liner bore toward Japan,
he began his tentative proposal for a modern fighter plane air force for the
Chinese.

It was Thursday, May 27, when the liner pulled into the harbor of Kobe
under darkness and it was 10 P.M. before it docked. There was little reason to
go ashore at that time of night, so he watched the activity of the docks from
the railing for an hour, then turned in. The weather had been humid and
rainy all the way from Hawaii. The monsoon season was just beginning and
veteran travelers on the ship told him the wet weather would last right up
through September.

In the morning Chennault went ashore and drove up to Kyoto with Lieutenant Commander and Mrs. Ralph. He was awed by the size of the shrines
and temples at Nara, founded as Japan's first true capital in 710. The small

group walked about in the warm May sunshine and visited Horyuji, Japan's oldest temple and the site of the world's oldest wooden structures. The Great Buddha at Todaiji seemed to dwarf everything around it and Chennault stood quietly for a long time, looking at the serene face of the huge statue. Towering pines lined the gravel walks and he was fascinated by the tame deer that meandered everywhere. Kyoto was a much larger city than he had imagined. His image of Japan had been of a rural land with farmers in conical hats tending rice paddies. The busy city streets of the beautiful city that had been the imperial capital for nearly eleven hundred years almost seemed out of place. He was also surprised to see so many Japanese men dressed in black business suits. He had thought they would all be wearing kimonos. A number of the older men and all the women did wear kimonos, forming a sea of color on the crowded sidewalks. There were bicycles, pedicabs, and automobiles everywhere. Never had he seen streets so heavy with humanity. Schoolchildren trooped by in navy blue—the boys in uniforms with visored caps and the girls, walking apart from the boys, in dark blue dresses.

They drove back to Kobe in the rented car and he went aboard ship to shower and change before meeting Billy McDonald. He had worn a white linen suit bought years ago in Hawaii for wear off the base, but the heat and humidity had caused it to wilt considerably during the day, so he dressed in a fresh pair of slacks and a clean white shirt after the cool shower.

It was good to see Billy again. His smiling face and stocky build stood out on the dock among the Japanese. He arrived at the ship at five-thirty and they had a drink on board before deciding to see the sights of Kobe. Billy said he was traveling with a passport that listed his occupation as the assistant manager of a troop of acrobats. Chennault almost choked on his bourbon. McDonald reminded him that the occupation "farmer" on his own passport wasn't much better. He said that as an instructor for the Chinese Air Force he would never have been able to get a visa at the Japanese consulate in Shanghai, so he had to think of something.

They left the ship and walked down the crowded streets of the harbor city. Chennault was amazed at the tiny stores packed tight along each side street that joined the main thoroughfare. There were a number of other foreigners interspersed with the hundreds of thousands of Japanese on the streets. Wineshops and small sushi bars were everywhere, as were small restaurants with white rice paper serving as panes in the wooden squares of latticework. Most of the establishments had flat, polished stones set in the floors. Everything was spotlessly clean. They went into a small dark restaurant that had an inner courtyard just off the dining area. They took off their shoes and sat on the tatami-covered floor with their legs folded beneath a black lacquer table. Chennault had his first taste of saki and found it bland: he had thought it would taste like some sort of whiskey. They ate sashimi, a raw fish that Chennault found delicious. It tasted more like raw beef than fish and was

seasoned with green horseradish and soy sauce. Both ordered Japanese beer
and found it quite good, although it was served warm.

After dinner they walked the streets, looking into small shops and larger
stores. Chennault bought a set of black lacquer bowls for Nell and two tiny
porcelain dolls dressed in kimonos for his daughters Peggy Sue and Rosemary. The six boys would have to do without gifts. Boys didn't need them
anyway.

Chennault had been taking photographs of everything he had seen so far
in Japan. No police stopped him and no one seemed to care, though the
Japanese police were notorious for interrogating strangers in those days.
Perhaps the officials simply assumed both were harmless tourists.

Returning to the ship, the two men had a nightcap in Chennault's state-
room and Billy left for his own room shortly after midnight. The ship sailed
at 2 A.M. while they were both asleep.

The following day was a wonder of sights. The ship made its way through
the Inland Sea, passing innumerable islands in the mist and skirting the
shores of both Honshu to the west and Shikoku to the east. There were
fishing boats everywhere. Near Hiroshima Bay the sun came out and they
were able to see the great red wooden tori of the Itsukushima Shrine, dating
from 593 and dedicated to the three goddesses of the sea. Shimmering bright
red in the distance, it rose out of the tidal waters of the bay. Looking at tiny
villages perched on points of land, both men agreed that it would not take
much to burn down most of the cities of Japan with incendiary bombs because the majority of buildings were constructed of pine and rice paper.

By 8 P.M. the ship passed by Shimonoseki at the western end of the Inland
Sea and nosed into the East China Sea.

The two friends played Ping-Pong and deck tennis in the morning, but the
waves began to build up later in the day as the liner sailed into the Yellow
Sea. By evening the ship was rolling considerably and they went to bed early.

The next day the *President Garfield* nosed up to the docks of one of the
most cosmopolitan cities in the world—Shanghai. Chennault was intrigued
by the busy docks and fascinated by the thousands of rickshaws and the
throngs of people. There were naval vessels anchored in the river—British,
American, French, and Japanese. Tall buildings lined the Whangpoo River
and a smoky haze hung over the huge city. At the end of the day, he wrote in
his diary: "At last I am in China, where hope to be of service to a people who
are struggling to attain national unity and a new life." He could scarcely
have guessed how much service he would be called upon to give.

There was quite a reunion at the dock. No sooner had Chennault and
McDonald walked down the gangplank than they were greeted by Luke
Williamson, the third member of the old "Men on the Flying Trapeze"
acrobatic team.

Sterling Tatum, another pilot Chennault had recommended, and Colonel
Eddie Yen of the Chinese Air Force were also at the dock. The welcoming

committee whisked the two off to the Metropole Hotel, a meeting place for foreigners, and proceeded to celebrate. The party went on well into the night.

The following morning, slightly hung over, Chennault was taken by the Chinese on a sightseeing tour. In typical Chinese fashion, Colonel Yen, his brother-in-law, and his sister drove him around the city and then out to Hungjao Airfield, where they visited the home of General Yow. The whole party took their guest to the famous Sun Ya Restaurant for dinner.

The partying went on the following day, Wednesday, and Chennault wound up the day at the Park Hotel, where he met a number of American businessmen and learned at first hand how discouraging business conditions in China were for foreigners. Having performed admirably as a host for several days, Colonel Yen departed for the capital city of Nanking, leaving Chennault in the capable hands of McDonald and Williamson.

On Thursday he was granted an interview with Madame Chiang Kai-shek —a meeting that was to change his life. Roy Holbrook, who had been delayed getting down from Nanking to greet Chennault, arrived and called the hotel to announce that he was coming over to pick him up.

They drove to the high-walled French concession west of the Old City and Roy knocked on a massive gate. A guard let them in and a servant ushered them both into a dim, cool interior room to wait. It was suffocatingly hot and humid outside and the wait in the cool room was pleasant. As they talked, a youngish girl in a light print dress swept into the room. Thinking she was a friend of Roy's, Chennault remained seated. He was shocked and embarrassed when Holbrook said, "Madame Chiang, may I present Colonel Chennault."

As he recalled later: "It was the Generalissimo's wife, looking twenty years younger than I had expected and speaking English in a rich Southern drawl. This was an encounter from which I never recovered. To this day I remain completely captivated."

That night he wrote in his diary: "Granted interview by Her Excellency, Madame Chiang Kai-shek, who will hereafter be 'The Princess' to me."

Mayling Soong had been educated—along with her two sisters—in the United States, her sisters at Wesleyan College for Women in Macon, Georgia, and Mayling at Wellesley College in Wellesley, Massachusetts. Her father, Charles Jones Soong, a former Southern Methodist Episcopal missionary and later a successful Bible manufacturer and salesman in Shanghai, had wanted his daughters to be educated abroad. He had been educated at Trinity Methodist college in Durham, North Carolina, and at Vanderbilt University in Nashville, Tennessee. Mayling spoke English like any other Southern girl. She lived in Georgia from the age of nine until she went to Wellesley and had years to grow up with her American classmates—mostly all Southerners. And like most Southern women, she considered Southern men, and especially military officers, "gentlemen."

She and Chennault struck up an immediate and lifelong friendship. While attracted by her femininity, Chennault was nevertheless impressed by her directness and grasp of military matters. She had recently shouldered tremendous responsibilities as head of the Chinese Air Force and she wanted professional advice. They talked for several hours and he told her as much as he could about his ideas for a modern fighting air force. She asked him to put his ideas in the form of a report and he promised to have it for her in three months. They discussed his role as an adviser and she promised to make that job official if he would send a letter to the Senior Secretary of the Aeronautical Commission, outlining his duties.

She suggested that the first item on his agenda be a survey of the Chinese Air Force facilities. She would want to know everything about the Air Force's status and capabilities. She asked that he begin at Nanking. He was given the use of two BT-13 trainer planes and asked to pick his own survey team. He picked Billy McDonald to fly the other plane and chose Sebie Smith as expert mechanic. The other member of the team was Po Yen Shu, a major in the Chinese Army who was assigned to Chennault as a personal interpreter.

"P.Y.," as he was to be called by everyone who knew him, was a civilian aviation enthusiast who had been assigned to help Colonel Jack Jouett with the translation of Chinese textbooks. He had attended the University of Michigan and was a native of Changsha. He was to remain with Chennault throughout his nine-year stay in China and was to remain a close friend for the rest of his life. A small, smiling man with a black mustache, P.Y. was never at ease in aircraft—though he was forced to fly in them most of his life. He had a tendency to airsickness and, unfortunately for him, flew over China for years with Chennault in small planes. Dressed in flying overalls and wearing a bulky parachute, P.Y. always looked like an unhappy urchin when he climbed down from a plane.

The following day Chennault took care of some details before starting on the inspection tour. He opened an account at the Chase Bank, took the first of his cholera and typhoid shots from Dr. W. T. Gardiner at 17 Canton Street, wrote a letter to Nell and the children, and later that afternoon was invited for a drink with W. H. Donald at his flat in the Broadway Apartments.

He was fascinated with this ruddy, sandy-haired Australian newspaperman who was reputed to be a power behind the Generalissimo. He had been in China for years and had served as an adviser to a number of warlords. He had moved over into the Gimo's camp after spending some time with the Young Marshal, Chang Hsüeh-liang, the Manchurian warlord. Donald had gained the confidence of the Young Marshal after getting him off drugs and seeing to it that he was restored to power. He knew everything and everyone in the inner circle of Chinese power and politics. He was convinced China needed an air force and was thoroughly in favor of Chennault's plans to build one. He was a close confidant of Madame Chiang and served as go-between in many negotiations for her, although he spoke not one word of Chinese. Another one of those strange foreigners who was fascinated by China, Donald had never developed a liking for Chinese food and made no attempt to learn the language. But he was to aid Chennault over and over again in the months and years to follow, and Chennault once again said that if it had not been for Donald's help and encouragement he might have quit and sailed home any number of times. By the time he left Donald's flat, he was beginning to have a severe reaction to the shots. He needed to get back to his hotel and rest.

On Tuesday, June 8, Chennault and Holbrook flew up to Nanking to meet with the Aeronautical Commission. Along with five Chinese generals, there was an Italian adviser, General Scaroni, in attendance. The talk was very general and Chennault came away with the feeling that nobody was very sure about the organization of the Air Force.

The following day he conferred with Colonel Chow—head of the Medical Section—and that afternoon visited Nanking Air Base, which had been laid out in 1928–29, shortly after Chiang Kai-shek decided upon Nanking as the capital of China. The runway had been lengthened by Colonel Jouett in 1933 but it was still dirt and, like most Chinese airfields, unusable in wet weather. Jouett had established the beginnings of an air force by 1934, but the American government was only able to support him to a limited extent. When Chiang's government asked Jouett to help bomb some rebels holed up in several towns in Fukien Province, the colonel had to refuse. Though his was an unofficial mission, he still needed permission from the American government for such actions and the government denied it. General Peter Mow, commander of the Chinese Air Force, went anyway and blasted holes in the thick earthen walls of the towns so that the infantry could get through. Chiang, not stupid about military matters, immediately saw what aircraft were capable of doing.

The American refusal to become involved in China's internal affairs coincided with an Italian push to gain a hand in China's young military aviation program and they moved in quickly as advisers. Dr. H. H. Kung, the Finance Minister, had been in Italy about that time on one of his innumerable missions to raise foreign capital and had been wined and dined by Mussolini. In exchange for some financial aid to help refinance the Italian Air Force, Il Duce offered to send some of his Italian "advisers" to China. The advisers soon grew to a force of more than fifty military pilots headed by the Italian general whom Chennault had met the day before. As a result, the Chinese Air Force, he was to discover, was a confused mess of training techniques and odd equipment.

The Chinese cadets were flying a mixture of Italian BR-3s, Boeing P-26s, and Curtiss Hawks brought out by Colonel Jouett. These Curtiss biplanes were powered with 715-h.p. Cyclone radial-cooled engines. Each had twelve cylinders and was armed with two .30-caliber machine guns—one in each lower wing. They had been purchased from the United States at a cost of $12,000—minus the engines. For primary training planes the cadets had been flying the Consolidated Fleet trainer with a 125-h.p. Kinner engine. About a hundred and twenty of these had been purchased from the States in 1933. For bombers, the Chinese had a combination of Russian, Italian, and American planes.

But the real trouble with the Italians lay in their training—or the lack of it. Their basic flight training was poor and they taught only a few of the rudimentary lessons of flying. As a result, the pilots who graduated—and nearly all the students graduated—were unable to do much more than land and take off. Face—always a problem in the Orient—played a big part in it. At the Italian flying school in Loyang, all the cadets who took the course were graduated as flying officers. Chinese aviation cadets were carefully chosen from the upper strata of Chinese life and it would have been a great loss of face to the families if the cadets had been washed out. The American system in China was the same as it was in the States: cadets who were not suited were weeded out in training and only the best graduated. The Italian system suited the Central Government because Chiang Kai-shek did not have to make excuses to wealthy families when a student did not meet the standards. The trouble was that cadets who graduated from the Italian school were not qualified to fly either fighters or bombers and were a menace to themselves and others.

Nanking was filled with Italian officers walking the streets in full-dress uniforms. General Scaroni roared through the streets in an open touring car, wearing a uniform covered with medals and dripping with gold braid. The Chinese liked the pomp and circumstance, but the Chinese Air Force was being shortchanged because of the Italians' sale of inferior equipment. Also an Italian assembly plant at Nanchang turned out a Fiat fighter that proved to be a firetrap in combat, and the outmoded Savoia bomber assembled there was so old it had to be used as transport rather than as a bomber. Also the Italians insisted that no plane turned over to the Chinese Air Force was ever to be removed from the official rolls. It could crash or be damaged but it remained on inventory forever. As a result, when war broke out with Japan in July, the Chinese Air Force officially consisted of five hundred planes. In truth, only ninety-one were fit to fly in combat.

This was the situation Chennault found after a week of inspection. He was not only disgusted but despondent. "I am appalled by situation here and would go home if I did not want to serve China," he wrote in his diary. "The Air Force is terribly unprepared for war. I'll do what I can to aid them."

Chennault was inspecting flying cadets at the Italian school at Loyang when word of the Japanese attack at the Marco Polo Bridge near Peking on July 7 reached him. It was to prove the beginning of China's war with Japan. Chennault immediately cabled Chiang Kai-shek that he was offering his services in any capacity to the Central Government.

Two

While Chennault's background and training made him ideally suited for a combat role in China, he was totally inexperienced in politics. He had no great knowledge of geography and was no student of history. Born in Texas and raised in rural and small-town Louisiana, his early career had been in teaching. He was a simple, straightforward man who attacked problems directly. His friends knew him as generous and warm, totally honest, and stubborn to a fault when he thought he was right. He was loyal to friends and expected loyalty in return. He was fearless in a fight and, in truth, liked a good battle—whether personal or professional. He was highly literate and very expressive, both vocally and with the written word. He was a "loner" and resented pressure from superiors he thought either ill equipped or ill informed.

He understood the military and tactical problems China faced in her conflict with Japan and thought he knew what to do to solve them. But in the intricate maze of Chinese politics, particularly those of the Central Government of Chiang Kai-shek in 1937, he was a babe in the woods. He had been exposed to the relatively simple politics of the U.S. Army Air Corps in his twenty years as an officer. But that had just been a matter of survival. Any man can learn the politics of military survival within a rigid system. What he faced in China was utterly baffling to him. If it had not been for the briefing and advice of W. H. Donald, it is doubtful he would have survived the test. In the days after the outbreak of the war with Japan, Donald took him aside and explained the facts of Chinese political life as it pertained to the world of 1937, Shanghai, Nanking, and the existing power structure.

He began with the republic founded by Dr. Sun Yat-sen. He explained how Chiang had come to power and where he had come from. He went into detail about the family of Charlie Soong: his son T.V. and his three daughters, Ai-ling, Ching-ling, and Mayling. He told Chennault where T. V.

Soong's money came from and also how the fortune of Dr. H. H. Kung, the
present Finance Minister, had begun in a string of pawnshops in Shensi
Province. He described the marriages of Ching-ling to the then aging Sun
Yat-sen; of Ai-ling to the extremely wealthy "Daddy" Kung; and of the
youngest daughter, Mayling, to Chiang Kai-shek. He dwelled upon the various warlords and which ones would most likely be faithful to the Central
Government. He spoke briefly about the kidnapping of Chiang by the Young
Marshal, Chang Hsüeh-liang; Chiang's later release; and the Young Mar-
shal's political exile.

In summing up, he said, "The Generalissimo is power-hungry and can be
very brutal when it is necessary. But he is a true patriot. He would do
anything for China and especially to win the war against Japan. Communicate with him as a military man—just as you are. Always be honest with him
and you will do fine. Madame, for all her femininity, is as hard as steel. She is
politically ambitious and as power-hungry as the Generalissimo. But there
again," he added, "winning the war is everything to her. Deal only with the
Generalissimo and Madame. The rest will all take orders from them." It was
excellent advice and Chennault followed it throughout his entire stay in
China.

His first test of dealing with the Generalissimo—or the "Gimo," as Donald called him—came a few days later. He and Peter Mow, commanding
general of the fledgling five-year-old Chinese Air Force, were summoned to
the resort of Kuling for a conference. It was necessary for visitors to be
carried in sedan chairs by coolies several hours up a mountain to the
Chiangs' summer hideaway. The Gimo received the two men on the screened
porch of his bungalow. Madame Chiang was with him. Wasting no time,
Chiang began to speak rapidly in Chinese to Mow. Madame translated.
Mow, sweating profusely, stood at rigid attention. It seemed the Generalissimo wanted to know how many first-line aircraft the Air Force had ready
for combat. Records of the Aeronautical Commission showed a total of five
hundred combat-ready planes.

"Ninety-one, Your Excellency," said Mow.

Chiang turned beet red and began to stride up and down the veranda,
spitting curses as he walked. Madame stopped translating.

"The Generalissimo has threatened to execute General Mow," she finally
whispered to Chennault.

The Generalissimo eventually stopped pacing and turned to Chennault.
"What does your survey show?" he asked in Chinese with Madame translating.

"General Mow's figures are correct," Chennault said quietly.

The Generalissimo stared at him.

"Go on," Madame urged. "Tell him what you have found out."

Chennault began to talk, telling the Gimo what he had discovered on his
recent inspection trip. He spoke of the damage the Italians had done and the

poor shape of the Air Force. He spoke of the need for pilot training based on the American system and what types of planes were needed to fight the Japanese. He talked of the need for a ground warning net and new airstrips. He never took his eyes from those of the Generalissimo. When he had finished, the Gimo stood looking at him, then nodded slowly and left the porch to enter the small house. Madame also nodded and smiled.

"Thank you," she said. "That was well done."

General Mow was spared the execution and Madame gained the power she needed to oppose and revamp the Aeronautical Commission. Chennault earned the respect of Chiang—a respect he never lost during his many years of close association with the ruler.

Chiang came down from his summer palace a few days later and delivered a speech that was more conciliatory than his followers would have welcomed. He knew he was not ready for all-out war with Japan and perhaps never would be, but he knew he had to stall for time. Perhaps he could encourage foreign intervention. At the very least, he could hope to buy arms and perhaps mercenary troops to help out. The people were enraged at Japan's actions. Nanking was a beehive of demonstrations. Buildings and buses were being painted gray. Chiang's lukewarm speech was bringing its hoped-for results. Leaders were flocking to the capital to see him. Each day newspapers called for war and students demonstrated in favor of a strong stand.

Chiang knew he had no navy to compare with the mighty Japanese imperial fleet. His armies were ill equipped, except for a crack force of eighty thousand German-trained soldiers who had kept warlords from any open break with Chiang for years. They had been trained by officers in the German Mission in Nanking under the command of General Ludwig von Falkenhausen. But Chiang knew even that powerful force would only hold the many divisions of Japanese infantry, artillery, and tanks for a short time. One by one the leaders came to see him with their pledges of personal troops. Many of these warlords had been bitterly opposed to Chiang's battles with the Communists, but they were united in their hatred of the Japanese. It was the only time in modern history that the various factions of China stood united.

Chennault had finally got his contract ideas together and mailed them to the Aeronautical Commission. Before posting it, on July 26, he read it over one more time.

Subject: Terms of contract between the Aeronautical Commission and Col. C. L. Chennault.

To: The Senior Secretary, Commission on Aeronautical Affairs.

1. Upon returning here from Nanking, I had a conference with Mr. Holbrook with regard to the terms of my contract with the Aeronautical Commission. He informs me that he forwarded the terms agreed upon

before my departure from the United States to you by letter dated May 27, 1937, copy of which he furnished to me. These terms were accepted by me and approved by Madame Chiang Kai-shek and Dr. Kung.

2. The only features of the contract which are not definitely stated are included in paragraph 6 of Mr. Holbrook's letter: "Other features of contract satisfactory to both parties which are included in contract with American Aviation Advisers." While I am not acquainted with the features referred to in above quotation, I would like to have the following additional terms definitely included in the contract:

a. Salary to be paid by the rate of U.S. $1,000.00 per month, exclusive of all taxes or deductions. Monthly payments to be made on the first day of each month following the last day of the month during which salary is unpaid. Payments to be deposited in the Chase Bank, Shanghai, to the credit of the account of C. L. Chennault. Salary to begin on the date of sailing from the United States and to terminate on date of departure from China. In this case, the date of sailing was May 8, 1937, via *President Garfield* from San Francisco, and receipt of first month's salary, U.S. $1,000.00, and travel expenses, U.S. $600.00, is acknowledged.

b. The Chinese government shall provide an airplane of the type specified by Col. Chennault for the purpose of making flights on official business, flights for demonstration and instructional purposes, and flights for the maintenance of flying proficiency. This airplane shall be serviced and maintained by the Chinese government without cost to the party of the first part, and he shall not be held liable for its damage or loss while being employed for the purposes named.

c. The party of the first part shall be entitled to the travel allowances authorized for foreign aviation advisers when required to travel from his usual place of duty by official orders or instructions. This provision shall apply from date of arrival in China to date of departure from China, travel allowance from U.S. to China and from China to U.S. having been agreed upon in paragraph __ of this contract.

d. This contract shall be subject to cancellation by either party upon ninety days written notice. In case of cancellation by either party, the party of the first part shall be paid in full to the last day of the notice period and shall then be paid the travel allowance agreed upon in paragraph __ of this contract. (Allowance for return to the U.S. from China.)

NOTE. The provision exempting my salary from income tax or other deductions is included because I accepted the salary offered, U.S. $1,000.00 per month, as the minimum net offer which I could consider. This agreement was reached before the passage of the Income Tax law and the payment of the tax will result in a considerable reduction from the net terms agreed upon. If payment of the tax cannot be waived, my salary should be increased by an amount equal to the tax.

3. After considering the matter, I have come to the conclusion that this contract should be drawn and signed immediately so that there can be no possibility of a misunderstanding by either party. If cancellation is desired by either party at the end of the period agreed upon for making my survey of military aviation in China, it can be obtained by exercising the cancellation option. It is requested that you have the contract drawn, submitted to the Aeronautical Commission for approval, and forwarded to me for signature without delay.

4. My address until further notice is: Central Aviation School, Hangchow.

Thank you and the members of the Aviation Commission for the courtesies extended to me during my recent visit. I am

Most sincerely,
C. L. Chennault
Colonel, Aviation

He knew Madame Chiang would approve of it, as she had already made it clear he could have all he asked for in the contract, but he wanted it on paper. He was too new to China to trust anything to the spoken word. Besides, he needed something concrete to refer to in case of any tax claims on his salary by the United States Government. Roy had been a big help to him in writing up the terms of the contract, but Roy had left for home aboard the *Scharnhorst* in late June. His wife Mary wanted no part of a war.

By August 6 the Gimo had indicated there would be war. Chiang's German-trained troops were fighting the Japanese near Peking in the north and the small Air Force was ordered to move up from Nanchang to the town of Kaifeng on the Yellow River—the only natural barrier between Peking and Nanking. Chennault had planned to move there himself but was diverted on August 10 to Shanghai by Madame to warn foreign nationals to evacuate Shanghai and take precautions concerning their people. He found every foreign embassy and legation—except the Swedes—completely unconcerned about the fighting to the north. He went over to the China National Aviation Corporation—the government-owned civilian airline—to see if any of the pilots were interested in volunteering for military service. H. N. Bixby, the manager, and Ernie Allison, the chief pilot, who had once been an instructor of Chennault's, gave him permission to recruit pilots from CNAC in case of war but laughed at his fears.

But the Chinese knew. Mobs of Chinese were storming the foreign concessions—seeking shelter in case of a Japanese attack. Chennault took a train for Nanking that night, but the train was commandeered by the military. All passengers were taken off and the train turned and headed for Shanghai, loaded with Chinese troops. Several trains were stopped and taken over before Chennault was able to get back to Nanking.

The next day the Japanese struck Shanghai. The first shells landed in the huge city and civilians began to die by the thousands. It was Friday the thirteenth.

On Saturday Madame Chiang asked Chennault what he could do. The Air Force planes had flown back from Kaifeng to help guard Nanking. Chennault knew the shelling was coming from Japanese warships anchored in the Whangpoo River. They were providing supporting fire for advancing Japanese infantry. Madame had asked her Chinese Air Force officers for plans, but none of them knew how to organize a combat mission. Chennault—with twenty years of U.S. Army Air Corps tactical training—was in the right spot at the right time.

He decided to send his Curtiss Hawks as dive bombers against Japanese light cruisers and the Northrop light bombers against the Japanese naval headquarters aboard the heavy cruiser *Idzumo*—all anchored in the Whangpoo.

As he stood looking at a situation map of the city and the riverfront, he thought of his poorly trained young air crews. None of them had seen combat. A few had been trained by Colonel Jouett, but most of them had been trained by the Italians. They were all eager to fight, but they were so totally unprepared. It was one thing to go into battle as a trained, seasoned fighter pilot. It was a different story when one had to send youngsters to die. It was only the first of many times he would be forced to do that.

August 14 in Shanghai was later remembered as "Bloody Saturday." The inexperienced pilots Chennault sent to bomb Japanese shipping in the Whangpoo River caused complete havoc instead. Pilots flying the Northrop 2E bombers had been carefully trained to bomb at an altitude of 7,500 feet and at a fixed airspeed. They were not experienced enough to realize that changes in both altitude and airspeed would drastically change the impact point of their bombs.

It was a hot, humid, and overcast August day and the overcast made it difficult for the pilots to see the city well. The *Idzumo*—their intended target —was anchored in the river off the Japanese Sector of the International Settlement on the eastern edge of the vast city.

The International Settlement also included the French Sector to the southwest, the British Sector to the west, and the small Italian Sector on the northwest edge. The U. S. Marine Sector was in the west-central part— below the Chinese community of Chapei, which was a municipality but not officially part of the International Settlement. In the center was Shanghai proper, where the United States and British troops were stationed and which bordered the river. To the south was the Old City and south of that the suburb of Nantao. Besides the *Idzumo,* there were other Japanese light cruisers in the river and such foreign naval vessels as the British cruiser *Cumberland* and the American cruiser *Augusta.*

The bombers came in over the city from the northwest, hoping to avoid ground antiaircraft fire from the Japanese Sector and from the naval vessels in the river. But because of the overcast the pilots decided to drop lower and make a dive-bombing attack. Releasing their bombs while in a glide, they struck far short of the intended targets. The bombs hit just off the customs jetty and struck the Cathay Hotel and the roof of the Palace Hotel, both at the corner of Nanking Road and the Bund. Those killed were mostly refugees trying to escape into the International Settlement. Estimates were that about a hundred and fifty people were killed by the first bombs. The smoke, debris, and flames from those bombs set off a panic in the crowded streets. The bombs had been 1,100-pound general-purpose ones and the damage was considerable. A few other bombs had shattered glass aboard the *Augusta,* but the *Idzumo* was not touched.

Chennault—flying a Hawk 75 monoplane fighter that had been purchased for him by the Madame—came down the river from Nanking to watch the raids. He was delayed by rain squalls upriver and arrived late. He could see heavy smoke climbing into the leaden sky above the Bund area but could see no signs of damage to the *Idzumo.* As he put the fighter into a steep bank over the city, he saw a large naval vessel under way downriver. It was churning up a considerable wake in the muddy water and throwing up a dense smoke screen. Needing a better look at it, he dove through the smoke and pulled out just over the decks. Through the gray he saw the Union Jack painted on her afterdeck and the winking of countless bursts of gunfire from her many turrets. Pulling the Hawk into a vertical climb, he got out of range quickly, but not before he had taken a number of hits through his fuselage and wings. He could see no other planes in the air and assumed they had gone back to the base. God, he thought as he leveled off over the city, this is sure to cause an international incident.

Later in the day another Chinese bomber flew over the city at an altitude of 5,000 feet and dropped two bombs on a traffic circle at Avenue Edward VII and Race Course Road. They too were large demolition bombs and killed three thousand people in and around the most heavily congested intersection in Shanghai. By this time Chennault was back at the field in Nanking —sick at the results of the raids. The Chinese fighters, on the other hand, had not done badly.

The Japanese Navy had at least three aircraft carriers operating off Chungming Island in the mouth of the Yangtze River. They were the *Kaga,* the *Soryo,* and the *Ruyjo.* They were equipped with Nakajima A2Ms and A4N biplane fighters, as well as Yokosuka B4Ys and Aichi D1A bombers. They had just arrived from Sasebo and were intent upon avenging the attack on the *Idzumo.* Their bombers could not reach Hankow, Changsha, or Nanchang—where most of the Chinese Air Force planes were based—but they could reach Shanghai, Nanking, and the Central Aviation School at Shien Chiao, south of Shanghai near Hangchow.

That night at Nanking, Chennault wrote in his diary: "Aerial attacks very poor. V Group, led by Ding, almost sunk British cruiser *Cumberland,* which had no business up Yangtze River. II Group dropped two more bombs on International Settlement. Honkew set on fire though. IV Group shot down a number of Jap bombers near Hangchow. Japs lost twelve ships on raid."

The next day the Japanese attacked Nanking for the first time. Chennault had moved in with Royal Leonard at the Metropolitan Hotel. Leonard, who had been a student of Chennault's at Kelly Field early in 1923, had left the Air Corps and had gone on to make a name for himself in commercial aviation. A handsome, dark-haired pilot who had flown almost everything flyable over the years, Leonard had come to China in 1935 at the invitation of an old Kelly Field classmate, Julius Barr, then the personal pilot for the Young Marshal, Chang Hsüeh-liang. After arriving in China, Leonard accepted the job of personal pilot to Chiang Kai-shek and had been flying the Generalissimo all over China. He had been reunited with Chennault a few weeks earlier and their room at the Metropolitan Hotel quickly became the general headquarters for all the American pilots and the Chinese Air Force officers. Leonard had been flying the Gimo about in a Boeing 247 that was kept at Nanking and he remained on standby at all times. On any night in their room one could find Billy McDonald, Luke Williamson, Sebie Smith, Sterling Tatum, and Julius Barr, besides a number of CNAC pilots staying the night in Nanking.

The morning following the raids on Shanghai, a group of pilots and mechanics were outside the hotel in Nanking when the attack began. Sebie Smith later recalled the attack.

"It was one of those summer days—hot, soggy, low ceiling—and all of a sudden it seemed like all hell had turned loose. The Japanese formation slipped down from out of the clouds, slipped underneath, while all the machine guns, with tracer bullets firing and all the antiaircraft from all around Nanking were firing at them, and everything was bursting in the sky. And bombs started falling on the airport. The thunder from exploding bombs and all the antiaircraft shells and the light from all this fireworks was really an impressive deal. I saw Chennault run—for the first time—to a dugout. I had a motion picture camera and I was behind, running and trying to make a picture of him. All other times it seemed Chennault would just dare anything to happen to him."

Chennault was to live through many an air raid in the years to come, but he remembered his first vividly. It was so new to everyone. Nanking was a large city, filled with hundreds of thousands of people. The downtown section was modern, for China, and the sprawling suburbs spread for miles on the outskirts. There had been preparations for an air raid, as there had been in most cities along the eastern seaboard of China in those first days of the war, but nobody really expected the Japanese to bomb.

Chennault, crouched in the slit trench near the Metropolitan Hotel, watched in awe as the drama unfolded before him. Everywhere air raid alarms were being sounded. Sirens blew all over the city and gongs echoed from every direction. Hundreds of automobile horns were being blown and thousands of voices shouted that the enemy planes were approaching. The panic was contagious. Pigeons flew from the rooftops, dogs ran barking in all directions, chickens flapped and screeched beneath the feet of madly running people. Horses, mules, pigs, burros, and cattle stampeded. Rickshaws careened down the narrow streets, their owners apparently trying to find someplace to hide them. Old women and young girls carrying babies ran on bound feet, trying to find shelter in dugouts and trenches. On each face was an expression of deep concentration.

Overhead there was the steady drone of Chinese pursuit aircraft high above the clouds—waiting for enemy bombers. Mixed with the sound of fighter planes was the deeper roar of the bomber engines as Japanese planes, in tight formation, came across the airfield and dropped their loads. There was the steady *pop, pop, pop* of machine-gun fire from the bombers, the blast of antiaircraft fire from the big guns all around the city, and the high, thunderous reports of antiaircraft shells bursting in the air near the enemy planes. The explosion of bombs as they hit came as a surprise to Chennault. He had not realized they would sound so deafening, nor had he expected the sudden impact that expelled air from the lungs and pushed at the chest cavity.

He saw a plane suddenly peel off from the formation near the airfield, twisting slowly as it fell and trailing a long black tail of smoke. Where the bombs hit he could see columns of fire, black smoke, and debris rise into the air as if in a slow-motion movie.

A parachute appeared from the low-hanging clouds and the pilot drifted slowly to earth. It was impossible to tell from a distance whether it was a Japanese or Chinese pilot.

Gradually the din subsided as the enemy bombers circled and climbed into the overcast. Silence settled over the landscape; only the baying of a lone donkey out in the rice paddies, the barking of dogs, and the grunting of a pig nearby could be heard. Slowly the people crept out of holes, trenches, and from doorways. They looked numb from the noise and concussion. At first they stared at one another, then a few laughed nervously. Soon all were chattering and waving arms as they told one another what had happened— as if each one did not know.

Chennault climbed out of the trench and shook the dirt from his clothing. He looked at the others getting to their feet near him and slapping the mud and dust from themselves. He reached for the package of Camels in his shirt pocket and carefully lit one with his silver lighter. His hands were shaking. He inhaled and slowly blew the smoke from his lungs. So this was war.

The Japanese—now that their undeclared war was heating up—shifted into high gear and began to bomb in earnest. Their bombers, based on the island of Formosa, could and did reach Nanking, Changsha, and Hangchow regularly. The bombers that flew from Formosa were the heavy twin-engined Mitsubishi Ki.21s. With the landing of the Shanghai Expeditionary Army at the mouth of the Whangpoo River on August 23, the Japanese Imperial Naval Air Force began to attack Chinese bases from its three carriers on a regular basis.

The Chinese fought back as well as they could with the limited air strength at their disposal. In spite of the odds against them—both in numbers and in the types of aircraft—Chinese fighter pilots gave a good account of themselves as long as they lived.

The Japanese, at first, attacked with bombers only. The Chinese fighters—diving from above as Jouett and Chennault had taught them—knocked a number of them out of the skies until the enemy caught on. While the Chinese were flying outmoded Curtiss Hawk IIs and IIIs, and Boeing P-26s, the Japanese soon began sending bombers escorted by the latest Navy carrier fighters, Nakajima Type 90 and the Mitsubishi A5M2 with open cockpits, far superior to the Chinese planes.

Chennault threw himelf into the defense of the Chinese airfields as well as the cities. He organized a ground warning net of telephones in the Shanghai–Hangkow–Nanking triangle, based upon his old Maxwell Field plan. He, Billy McDonald, and Luke Williamson picked the best Chinese fighter pilots to learn special tactics against intruding bombers. One fighter was to dive from above, another would climb from below, while the third plane would wait in reserve to make the final attack. In three successive days of attacking Nanking without fighter escort, the Japanese lost fifty-four bombers before it dawned on them that flying unescorted bombers was suicidal—a fact Chennault had known for years.

As the planes of Nippon began bombing at night, Chennault started to teach his fighter pilots the complicated techniques he had laboriously perfected in the many hours of flying fighters against the old Keystone bombers over Alabama while Coast Artillery searchlights probed the skies. Searchlights were arranged in a grid pattern so that their lights could pick up an intruding bomber as it approached the target from some distance out. Then the plane, or formation of planes, would be passed from one searchlight to another, always keeping it in the lights. It was impossible for a pilot to see anything by looking downward into the brightness of the searchlight. He was unable to determine whether or not he was bombing correctly and he couldn't see attacking fighter planes from below. Chennault taught his Chinese pilots to dive for maximum airspeed quite a distance from the attacking bomber formation, then to come screaming up out of the searchlight in a vertical climb—blasting away at the vulnerable underbelly of the bomber as they closed in.

The third night the Japanese tried night-bombing Nanking, the Chinese pilots shot down seven out of thirteen Japanese bombers. They never tried night bombing again over Nanking.

In addition to the help Chennault and his Americans were giving them, the Chinese were being assisted by the Russians. Stalin had entered into an agreement with the Chinese in early 1937 to supply planes and instructor pilots in exchange for metals and other commodities. While these pilots were officially listed as "instructors" to the outside world, the Russian squadrons were Red Air Force units commanded by their own officers, complete with ground crews and Russian supplies. There is no official record of how many Russian pilots flew against the Japanese in those years, but the Russians gave China a $20-million credit, about four hundred combat planes in addition to the Russian squadrons, and antiaircraft artillery. The aircraft were trucked from Soviet railheads across Central Asia and unloaded and assembled at Lanchow in southern Kansu Province. The planes were two kinds of fighter aircraft—the single-seater open-cockpit biplane Polikarpov E-15 and the two-seater low-wing monoplane Polikarpov E-16—and a number of Tupolev SB-2 twin-engine bombers. All in all, in the period from 1937 to 1939, the Russians probably sent as many as a hundred and twenty combat planes and as many pilots to help the Chinese in their war against Japan. Stalin wanted China to keep the Japanese from becoming too interested in Siberia. The Russians were excellent pilots and fearless in combat. Chennault was interested in their operations and commented on their behavior more than once in his diaries.

They were a rowdy bunch when off duty, but when on duty they hardly ever went more than twenty feet from their aircraft—some spending almost the entire tour sitting in the cramped cockpits of their stubby fighter planes. In the air they were more than a match for the Japanese and in battles around Nanking shot down any number of Japanese fighters in dogfights. Chennault commented in his diaries that it seemed ironic that Japan tended to ignore the fact that Red Air Force squadrons fighting them in China were in violation of diplomatic relations. On the other hand, he wrote, the aid the Americans were giving the Chinese was a constant cause of diplomatic protests to the Chinese and United States embassies. The American consul general in Shanghai, Clarence Gauss, was constantly threatening Americans with deportation for aiding the Chinese.

Chennault wrote that the Russian pilots seemed to be older than the Americans who were teaching the Chinese. He said they could combine twelve-hour alerts and strenuous air battles with all-night carousing in a way he had never seen before—and he had been around pilots all his professional life. The Chinese students loved the E-16, with which they were able to loop and get on the tail of a Japanese fighter. It was the only fighter of its day in China that could do that. The Russians kept to themselves in their own quarters and in separate compounds, but there were never any incidents between the Americans and the Soviets, since they were all fighting toward the same end. Chennault worked with them on many bombing missions and found them easy to get along with.

In addition to the Soviets, there were a number of other foreigners in China who wanted to help out against the Japanese. Some were American pilots, and others who wanted to fly were an assortment of Frenchmen, Germans, and Dutchmen. While long on enthusiasm, most were short on flying time and combat experience. As the Chinese pilots were rapidly being killed by the better-equipped Japanese fighter pilots, both the Generalissimo and Madame turned to foreign volunteers. Chiang asked Chennault to take charge of the foreigners and try to whip them into some sort of an effective fighting force. The biggest problem, Chennault later wrote, was in getting bomber pilots and long-range planes that could hit Japanese supply depots and vital bridges in China.

William D. Pawley, an aircraft salesman for the Curtiss-Wright Company, had come to China in 1932 to help the government build a repair facility at the Central Aviation School at Shien Chiao. He had expanded into all sorts of commercial enterprises by the time Chennault met him in 1937 and at that time had managed to bring in some Vultee II attack bombers for the Chinese government. They were slow but had a range of more than two thousand miles and were just what Chennault needed.

As a start, he borrowed Julius Barr and Royal Leonard from the CNAC and the Generalissimo to help recruit pilots, and with the help of Billy McDonald, Sebie Smith, and armament specialist Rolfe Watson, he set out to try to organize a bombing force. Luke Williamson—at the urging of his wife —had decided to return to the States and had left by ship in late summer.

There were a few good pilots in what was called the 14th Volunteer Bombardment Squadron or the 14th International Volunteer Squadron, but not many. One American, Jim Allison, had flown against the Germans and Italians in Spain. Elwyn H. Gibbon had been trained in the States and had taken a discharge from the Army Air Corps, and another American, George Weigle, was what Chennault called "an enthusiastic graduate of a cow-pasture flying school." Vincent Schmidt, a New Yorker, had flown in World War I and in Spain. Another American, Dudley Long, was assigned to the squadron as a mechanic. Two others—Tommy Allen and Herbert Walker—were made gunners on the bombers. The Chinese officers—pilots and bombardiers —were not enamored of the idea of following foreigners into combat. Loss of face again. But the enlisted gunners had no such qualms and did not mind at all. It was better than being in the infantry.

Training of the squadron began inauspiciously. One of the French pilots— on his first attempt to fly—stalled out while attempting to land and was killed. Sebie Smith described the accident:

"He came in with full flaps down, landing gear down, the carburetor heat on, and the prop in high pitch. He almost fell on me trying to go around and, after overshooting the field, he stalled out, winged over the edge of the field, and spun in."

Chinese consulates around the world had been quietly attempting to recruit foreign volunteers for the squadron and—much to Chennault's annoyance—a steady stream of unqualified pilots trickled into Nanking. Both Barr and Leonard had managed to recruit a few good pilots from the United States and Manila, but most were totally unfit.

Chennault made Schmidt a squadron commander. Both Jim Allison and another American, Lyman Woelpel, had been commercial pilots in Seattle and were qualified to fly the bombers. So were Elwyn Gibbon and George Weigle, but that was about all.

Whatever usefulness the volunteer squadron might have attained in the air was offset by the behavior of its members on the ground. The group was moved from Nanking to Hankow early on and most of the pilots spent their off-duty time in the bars and whorehouses along "Dump Street"—the red-light district. The place was a nest of Japanese agents and the enemy often knew more about the bombing missions to be run than did the Chinese.

Malcolm Rosholt, in his excellent book *Flight in the China Air Space,* says the pilots were paid a thousand a month, but that was in Chinese dollars, which at the time amounted to about three hundred in American money.

Stories about the volunteer squadron must have filtered back to the States, and the State Department probably received some stiff protests from the Japanese. Secretary of State Cordell Hull was interviewed on the subject and remarked that such activity was against United States law and said the penalty for enlistment in foreign armies for pilots would be a fine of two thousand dollars and up to three years in prison, plus loss of citizenship. The American pilots in China, however, paid little attention to such warnings.

Chennault was never very impressed with the potential of the 14th Volunteer Bombardment Squadron, although he did what he could—at the orders of the Gimo—to make it an effective force. To an old military man, the majority of the pilots were civilians without much military training. Their behavior off duty did not amuse him, although he was certainly no prude. He simply believed in sticking by the rules when working. The squadron flew a number of missions—all in China—and did hit some bridges and railroad yards. But they were more of a token force than any real threat to the Japanese.

The final straw came when Chennault organized a raid against troop depots at Tsinan in Shantung Province. The Vultee bombers were gassed up the afternoon before to save time for an early predawn takeoff. The pilots must have talked about the coming raid along Dump Street that day because the Japanese came in low at sundown and blasted the lined-up bombers to bits. As Chennault wrote: "What was left of the Chinese bombing force vanished in five seconds of flame and dust. With it went the jobs of the International Squadron pilots."

As the summer passed into fall, Chennault realized that his three-month contract had already expired. So wrapped up had he been in the bitter fighting that he had hardly thought of home, although he had continued to write to Nell. He was already discouraged by the terrible losses to his young Chinese pilots. Facing far superior numbers and better planes, they fought bravely but died by the hundreds. Many refused to bail out of crippled planes because they felt to do so would be to lose face. The air battles over Nanking decimated the pilots trained by Colonel Jouett and by Chennault's people. What was left was a handful of seasoned veterans, who became aces, and the rest were youthful cadets just out of flying school.

It became obvious—because of the constant air raids and the rapidly approaching Japanese divisions—that Nanking would have to be evacuated soon. The Central Government planned to move to Chungking, far up the Yangtze River above the Gorges, where the Japanese Navy could not penetrate. The Air Force would then pull out and move to Hankow, several hundred miles upriver, and try to hold out there. It would give the bombers and fighters a distant base from which they could hit the approaching Japanese for as long as possible.

Chennault was sitting at his desk in his room at the Metropolitan Hotel, writing a letter home, when Royal Leonard came in. He tossed a copy of the *South China Morning Post* on his bunk and slid into a chair. He had returned that night from Hong Kong.

"Might want to read that." He waved at the newspaper. "The U.S. finally got around to calling the Japs what they are."

Chennault got up and retrieved the paper from the bunk. He spread it out on the desktop. It was the October 8, 1937, issue. The headline read: U.S. CONDEMNS JAPAN AS INVADER OF CHINA: DROPS NEUTRALITY POLICY TO BACK LEAGUE; GENEVA CALLS MEETING OF 9-POWER NATIONS.

He read the story slowly. "About time," he grunted. Secretary of War Henry L. Stimson had urged a joint move by the United States and Britain to stop supplying war goods to Japan. The Japanese Foreign Office had called an emergency meeting in Tokyo to discuss the condemnation. He put the paper down. "Looks like they finally realized what's going on out here," he said.

Royal got up and moved to his wall locker, where he kept his liquor. "Calls for a drink." He smiled as he brought the bottle to the desk. He poured some whiskey into two glasses and filled them with water from a glass pitcher. "To the geniuses who finally realized there is a war on."

Chennault grinned back and they both drank.

"Royal," Chennault said, returning his glass to the table, "what are you going to do about this business over here? You going to stay?"

The dark-haired pilot took another sip from his glass and looked at Chennault. "Why? You thinking of going home?"

Chennault sat in the chair and lifted his legs to the desk. "Hell," he said,

"I don't know. I'd like to go home—on one hand. I've got a wife and eight kids. I'd kinda like to get back to my farm in Louisiana and do a little hunting this fall. On the other hand"—he took a slow sip—"there is so much to do here. I'd feel as though I was quitting if I let these people down after all the work we've put into training and all. My contract ran out a couple of months ago and I haven't done anything about it. What did you do about yours?"

Leonard smiled. "I'll tell you," he said. "The day after the raid on the *Idzumo*—when the Chinese planes dropped the bombs on Shanghai?"

Chennault nodded.

"Madame called me up and asked me to come over to their place. When I got there she asked me one thing: 'Will you stick with us through the war?' I said yes. We shook hands and that was the end of that. We never even talked about extending my contract and I've been getting paid regularly every month."

Chennault shook his head. "I guess that's what I'm doing," he said. "I'm still getting paid each month."

"You will be," Leonard said. "That's the way things work out here."

They were both silent for a moment. Then Chennault turned to the other pilot. "Thanks. Guess I'll stay awhile." He reached for the letter he had been writing and slowly tore it up.

Three

By the time the weather began to turn clear and cold in mid-October the Japanese were bombing almost at will. On the twelfth Chennault lost a pilot and three planes. On the following day there were five air raid alarms at Nanking and his outnumbered pilots tried to fight off the incessant formations of bombers plastering the city and airfield. He lost two more fighter pilots that day.

On Thursday, October 14, Chennault tried to get a mission together with the aircraft he had left. When he finally assembled four Martin bombers, five Northrop light bombers, six Douglas attack bombers, and three Hawk fighters, he mounted a mission to the Japanese Sector of Shanghai. It was an evening raid and all the planes returned safely late that night.

The following morning, attempting to bomb the same docks and troop depot area, two of his Martin bombers crashed on takeoff, killing all on board but one pilot. The weather clouded up again and Chennault came down with a bad cold and bronchitis. With the combination of his cold and fever, the weather, and the losses of so much life and aircraft, he hit a new low. He seldom lost hope about the outcome of the war, but this was perhaps the most despondent he ever became. On October 16 he wrote in his diary: "Am greatly discouraged over my inability to hit the Japs. Every plan is upset by lack of training, indifference, or stupidity of Chinese pilots and mechanics. I seem to be the only aviator desirous of operating against the Japs. Received a $10,000 bonus from the Generalissimo, but do not feel I am earning it."

The following day he made the last Nanking entry in his diary. It was Sunday, October 17, 1937. "Too much trouble to report a diary of continued trouble."

A week later he was ordered by the Generalissimo to evacuate Nanking and set up the headquarters of the rapidly dwindling Chinese Air Force at

Hankow. There could be no doubt about the fate of Nanking. Japanese naval vessels were just downriver, having blasted their way through the barricades of sunken ships the Chinese had placed in the river to slow their advance. Infantry and artillery divisions were within shooting distance of the capital. The retreating Chinese Army was taking everything it could carry from the city before surrendering it.

Nanking fell in mid-December, with rapings, massacres, and pillage—all of which shocked an outside world not yet familiar with the Japanese style of occupation.

Chennault moved his personal belongings from Nanking by car. He had been given a black Hupmobile for his personal use by the Central Government and it came with a driver. The car was worth its weight in gold, as transportation was very difficult to come by. It became a familiar sight to the flying personnel around the airfields and in Nanking. The only problem with having a car and driver, Chennault once said, was that everyone he knew wanted to borrow it at all hours and it was either out on loan or in the repair shop when he needed it most.

He loaded his personal footlockers and other gear into the car and the driver took his and some of Leonard's belongings on the crowded road to Hankow. The rutted roads were clogged with refugees making their way west from the besieged cities and towns in the path of the advancing Japanese. In Hankow he took up quarters in the Terminus Hotel, where he had stayed while visiting Hankow on several occasions over the past six months.

Hankow was now a refugee city—although far quieter than the frantic streets of Nanking. It was several hundred miles upriver from Nanking, and the winding river would keep the Japanese naval vessels from getting to it for some time—as would the sunken wrecks put in the way by the Chinese. But it was only a matter of time before the Japanese captured the city, as Chennault and the rest of the foreigners knew.

The field at Hankow was a vast stretch of mud, snow, and standing water, with stretches of gravel for runways and taxi strips. The main runway was about ten thousand feet long, but not very wide. Sebie Smith, who was in charge of the mechanics at the field, said the conditions were miserable that winter. He said the days and nights were cold and the windswept field made conditions unlivable for mechanics trying to service the planes. Water stood ankle-deep most of the time and the planes constantly sank in the mud as they were being moved from one spot to another. He said the Vultee bombers were the easiest to move about because they had large balloon tires. The mechanics were responsible for starting the engines of both bombers and fighters, and it was a terrible task to start cold engines early in the morning. The Chinese were still flying sporadic bombing missions at that time and Sebie and his Chinese mechanics devised a system of building vertical wooden boxes around the engines and installing kerosene heaters in each box. With the heaters running all night and with quilts wrapped about the cowlings, the engines could be started. It was probably the first preheating system invented for the Chinese Air Force.

The Japanese bombers were hitting Hankow in force at every opportunity. They were now accompanied by first-line Japanese fighter aircraft, which took a terrible toll of the remaining Chinese fighter pilots.

There was also on the field at the time a Chinese squadron of Gladiators, that had been purchased by the Chinese Central Government from the British. Chennault tested one of the unwieldy planes against the Russian E-15s and E-16s and found it inferior for combat.

During January and February the Chinese continued to lose valuable pilots. On February 18, in one big battle, Chinese squadrons took off to intercept a formation of twelve Japanese bombers escorted by twenty-six fighters. Chinese fighters were stationed at three cities along the Yangtze River: Hankow, Wuchang, and Hanyang. The area was known collectively as Wu-Han. Most of the Hawk fighter planes had been destroyed by this time and the Chinese were flying Russian E-15s and E-16s. The Japanese were using the carrier fighter Type 96 (known to the United States later as Claude).

The Chinese sent up twenty-nine fighters—the entire strength of the Chinese Air Force's IV Group. They spotted the enemy about twelve thousand feet northwest of Hankow and the fight began. Four enemy fighters were shot down, but the battle cost the Chinese their group commander, Captain Li Kwei-tan, the 23rd Squadron commander, Lieutenant Pa Tsing-chen, and two other pilots—Lieutenant Wang I and Lieutenant Li Pong-chiang. The fighter leader, Lieutenant Wang Ku-kin, was wounded. The Chinese Air Force could not stand such losses for very long and still survive. One of the men fighting in these battles was Art Chen, a Chinese-American from Portland, Oregon, who was made an ace in the dogfights over Hankow. He was shot down twice—the last time in flames—and spent months in a hospital but returned later in the war to fly for Chinese commercial aviation.

Chennault went up on many of these days in his personal Hawk 75, watching the dogfights and debriefing Chinese pilots after the battles. The Hawk returned from many of these fights with holes in the fuselage and wings. Since the Hawk 75 was the fastest plane in the China skies, both Chennault and Billy McDonald used it frequently for reconnaissance. Both men agreed they would never talk about their combat experiences of those days because the penalty of fighting for a foreign power was severe. Neither man ever publicly admitted fighting the Japanese in the skies over China in 1937–38, but Chennault wrote to the widow of Rolfe Watson, who was killed in the Korean War in 1951, and said:

"Rolfe was a great fellow—generous, hard-working, and liked by his associates. I will always be grateful to him for the excellent work he did with me in China. In addition to training Chinese gunners and armament mechanics, he kept the guns of my personal plane in the finest condition. My guns never failed to fire when I needed them. At the same time, Sebie Smith kept my engines in top shape. I am certain that the work of the two men, Rolfe and Sebie, saved my life several times in 1937 and '38."

Considering Chennault's nature—volatile, quick-tempered, and fearless—it is difficult to believe he did not fire back when fired upon. And with his experience as an acrobatic stunt pilot in Air Corps fighter planes, it is equally hard to believe he did not engage in combat against the Japanese fighters.

As late winter and early spring arrived in Hankow and the Japanese drew ever closer the mood grew more despondent. The Chinese Air Force was almost nonexistent and only the Russians were left to guard the city from the air. The bitter nights were given up to card games and drinking parties in hotel rooms, barracks, and private homes. Most of the single men found their entertainment on Dump Street, where Chinese girls and White Russian women were employed in the bars and dance halls. Sebie Smith told how the men would purchase rolls of tickets from the attendant at the door and then use them up one by one for dances. The Russian girls were some of the most attractive in the world and had fled Russia with their families following the Revolution. Many of them managed to survive the occupation days in Shanghai, Nanking, and other cities by their wits. All spoke fluent Chinese and were a constant source of joy to foreign servicemen because of their striking occidental features.

While Chennault, because of his position, was unable to patronize the dance halls openly with his men, he did not suffer for female company. A healthy forty-seven-year-old with a love of action, he did not find it difficult to attract the attention of both Russian and Chinese girls in Hankow. Handsome, with black hair and black piercing eyes, he was particularly fond of oriental women and during his many years in China became close friends with a number of them.

As he had in Nanking, he entertained friends both at his hotel quarters and in various restaurants in the city. Though most of his friends were American airmen and Chinese members of the Air Force, he enjoyed many pleasant meals with W. H. Donald and James M. McHugh, an American who had earlier spent years in China and had returned the previous November as assistant naval attaché—although he was a captain in the Marine Corps. McHugh, an expert in naval intelligence, spoke excellent Chinese and liked Chennault for his directness, honesty, and grasp of the military situation in China. While Chennault did not play politics, he was nevertheless interested in what was going on in the military and political circles of the Nationalist Government. Between Donald and McHugh, they knew just about everything a foreigner could. At Donald's residence on the Hankow side of the river the three men would spend nights over after-dinner coffee and drinks. It was one of the few places in Hankow where one could get decent foreign food.

McHugh had known Donald since 1925. He had been sent out as a new graduate of the Naval Academy in 1922 and Donald had just arrived as a newspaperman and was working for a paper in Hong Kong. From their bantering conversations Chennault gathered that McHugh did not always agree with Donald's theories.

Donald admired Madame Chiang to the point of idolatry. He was totally captivated by her charms as well as her politics. While not as devoted to the Generalissimo, he was a staunch defender of him as a leader. McHugh was more of a cynic and more apt to look at the Chiangs and their Nationalist circle of officials as opportunistic politicians rather than patriots. Chennault learned much that was helpful to him later through their late-night discussions.

Donald talked about the founding of the Communist Party in Shanghai in 1921 and how it began to have considerable influence by the late 1920s. He said that when Chiang started out from Canton on his Northern Expedition in 1926 to overthrow the warlords who had been bringing misery to the people, he had not been particularly anti-Communist. He had sided with the Russians in the early 1920s and had visited Russia for four months in 1923. There were also Communists on the faculty of the Whampoa Military Academy in Canton when Chiang was named to head it in 1924 by Dr. Sun Yat-sen. Some of the faculty—Chou En-lai, Yeh Chien-ying, and Lin Piao—were to become prominent in the Communist state later.

But by 1927 the Communists and the more conservative members on the Northern Expedition began to have problems and the expeditionary forces finally split up into two sections with headquarters in different cities. The anti-Communists set up their base in Nanking, while the Communist headquarters was in Hankow.

Chennault asked when the final break came between Chiang and the Communists and Donald said it was probably in 1927, when the city of Shanghai was captured after the Communists had stirred up labor strikes and other disturbances. Chiang had been forced to decide then whether he would side with the bankers and the conservative elements who supported him financially or whether he would side with the Communists. He chose the conservatives and never changed after that, Donald said.

The Communists gradually gained power, however, and by 1930 had been able to muster considerable strength in Kiangsi Province. Chiang's Nationalist Government continued to campaign against them but was never able to make any sizable dent in the Communist power structure until Chiang's German military advisers devised a plan to blockade the Communist strongholds and supply routes.

Unable to hold out against the blockade, the Communists began their Long March to the west in 1934—under attack most of the way by Chiang's forces. Biographers of Chiang later wrote that he apparently did not wish to destroy the Communists so much as he wanted simply to drive them away from east and central China. Because of the slowness with which the Communists moved west, and the number of noncombatants who traveled with them, it would have been easy to destroy them with a well-equipped military force. Chiang probably did not want to be blamed for killing many of his countrymen and merely harassed them until they reached the remote province of Shensi, where they were allowed relative peace.

The Communists grew in strength in the Shensi–Kansu–Ninghsia border area near the Yellow River in northern China and the Nationalist Government meant to keep them there. Periodic attacks were made against them. In 1936, Chang Hsüeh-liang, son of the late Manchurian warlord Chang Tso-lin, was in command of one of these Nationalist armies. He felt that Chiang Kai-shek—with whom he had sided—should not be fighting his own countrymen but should be concentrating on preparing to resist the Japanese, who were at that time getting ready to invade China.

In December 1936 the Young Marshal—after trying in vain to convince Chiang that he should stop fighting the Communists—kidnapped the Generalissimo while he was in Sian, the capital of Shensi Province, on an inspection trip. Madame Chiang immediately called upon Donald and the two of them flew to Sian to see what they could do about freeing the Gimo. The Young Marshal tried a number of times to get Chiang to change his views but finally had to give up when Chiang's temper tantrums convinced him it was no use. On Christmas Day, 1936, Donald said, the Generalissimo returned to Nanking with the Young Marshal, who was immediately arrested. He had been kept under house arrest ever since.

But while in Sian, Chiang had conferred—at the insistence of the Young Marshal—with representatives of the Communists, among them Chou En-lai. The result of the talks, never put in writing or made public, was the formation of what was called the United Front Against Japan. Both sides agreed, at least for the time being, to put aside their differences until Japan was forced out of China. The Communists agreed to recognize Chiang as their leader and three divisions of Communist troops—about forty-five thousand soldiers—were incorporated into the Nationalist Government as the Eighth Route Army. However, the Communists still had a number of troops of their own. Chiang also agreed to give some representatives of the Communists official seats in his Nationalist government. Chou En-lai later became Vice Minister of the Political Affairs Department of the Military Affairs Council.

The agreement—shaky at best—held up for a while but soon began to show signs of strain. Chiang had stationed large numbers of his best-equipped and most loyal forces around the Communist-held area and maintained a blockade there. Foreign observers were discouraged from entering the region and not much was known about the Communists or their strength. Chiang felt that they were his real enemies—perhaps more so than the Japanese.

The subject at Donald's one night was the bitter family fight going on in Hong Kong between T. V. Soong and two of his sisters, Madame Chiang and

Madame H. H. Kung. The argument, which had been going on for years, concerned the terms under which T.V. might make peace with his family and accept a post in Chiang Kai-shek's government. It had reached a point where the family—slyly referred to in many Chinese circles even in 1938 as the Soong Dynasty—had to make some sort of concession because of the war effort. It was well known that T.V. and Chiang Kai-shek were bitter rivals and had disliked each other for years. T.V. had been fired as Finance Minister—a post he had held for nine years until 1933. The post had then been taken over by his brother-in-law, H. H. Kung, a soft, easygoing man whom Chiang could and did control. Chiang had gradually taken away all of T.V.'s power in financial circles except for his post as the head of the Bank of China. His sisters were at the point of threatening that if he did not give up his opposition to Chiang he would also lose this last job, all that remained of his former financial prestige in the country. For the sake of a unified front against the common enemy, Japan, the family wanted T.V. to join the government.

Donald was of the opinion that Kung, because of his immense wealth and his loyalty to Chiang, was more valuable to the government than T. V. Soong. McHugh, mindful of the scandals in financial circles caused by the heavy-handedness of Kung, his wife, and son David, and the shaky condition of China's finances, was in favor of putting T.V. back in power, so that he could restore China's reputation in international financial circles. The argument went on into the early morning hours, much to Chennault's amusement and interest.

Just about the only ray of light Chennault had in the spring of 1938 in Hankow was a solid defeat of the Japanese on Hirohito's birthday on April 29. The Russians had been hitting the Japanese planes hard for weeks, and even though Chennault knew the Japanese might pull off a raid on the Emperor's birthday, he made sure of it. The Chinese and Russian planes together appeared to evacuate Hankow the day before, circling the city at a low altitude so that all who were interested could see they were leaving. Later that evening the planes slipped back one by one at treetop level and loaded up with gas and ammunition for the next day.

Early the following morning the air raid sirens warned of approaching planes and soon a formation of fifteen bombers, escorted by a large force of fighter planes, showed up. The Japanese had been basing their fighter aircraft at Wuhu, a forward base in east China. But they usually had just enough gas to get to Hankow and back.

Chennault sent up twenty Chinese pilots in Russian fighters to patrol the air south of the city with orders to engage the fighters long enough to burn up a lot of their gas. East of the city a force of forty Russians waited high in the sky for the Japanese to start back toward their base at Wuhu. The Russians timed it perfectly. They quickly separated the fighters from the bombers and systematically began to shoot the bombers down. The Japanese fighters didn't dare turn and defend the bombers because of their shortage of gas. Then the top cover of Russians dove down on the retreating Japanese fighters. A total of twelve bombers and all the fighters were shot down, thirty-six of the thirty-nine Japanese planes. The Russians lost only two planes, while the Chinese lost nine planes and four pilots—but the cost was well worth it in terms of morale. The Chinese papers played it to the hilt—a birthday present for Hirohito.

But that was the last great victory. By early summer the end was almost in sight. The best troops the Chinese had were fighting near the town of Hsüchow, about three hundred miles northeast of Hankow. Throughout the spring they had faced a force of about a hundred thousand fresh Japanese troops near the city. After some skirmishes, the Japanese finally took the town in June and that was the last barricade between them and Hankow, the temporary capital. Retreating Chinese troops blasted the dikes of the Yellow River, keeping the Japanese troops from following but causing a mind-boggling disaster as the river raged and flooded through heavily populated farmlands.

By August the Japanese divisions were threatening Hankow. A two-pronged attack, aided by the Japanese Navy, which finally pushed through the mines and scuttled wrecks in the huge river, sealed the fate of the city. Both the Nationalists and the Communists joined in a united front against their common enemy, but they could not hold back the infantry and armored divisions much longer.

By September most of the occupants had left the stricken city. The soldiers were ordered to strip Hankow of everything made out of metal—manhole covers, water pipes, iron fences, and gates—whatever could be made into weapons. The refugees left by road or on trains to Hong Kong and the docks alongside the river were awash with thousands waiting for ships to carry them upriver to cities in the interior. The capital was officially moved to Chungking, a fog-enshrouded city far inland past the Yangtze Gorges.

Chennault was ordered to set up new flying schools for Chinese pilots far back in the paddy fields of Yunnan Province, almost at the foot of the Himalayas. The ancient city of Kunming was to be his home for many years to come.

Madame Chiang, in the face of defeat, still hoped to salvage something of her Air Force. At least a continuous training program could be maintained in the interior of China to fight the swarm of Japanese aircraft. She ordered Chennault to drive to Chihkiang in western Hunan Province and attempt to set up a training school with the few Hawks remaining. There was a small dirt field there and Chennault, with P. Y. Shu along as his interpreter, made the long drive in the Hupmobile in late October.

P.Y. remembered the field: "We only stayed a few weeks there. The General and I were all alone—with just a few Chinese cadets to train and only three Hawk planes. We had no bathroom facilities, no electricity, and just country Chinese food, but the General always liked that kind of food, so he didn't go hungry. We played cards at night by the light of a lantern—not much to do but work and sleep. Pretty soon the cadets crashed two of the Hawk planes and we had to give up and move on to Kunming."

Chennault telephoned Madame, who was in Hong Kong at the moment, and she ordered him to proceed to Kunming and do what he could about building up the flying schools he had started back in August. The schools were to train as many young Chinese cadets as could be recruited. The war was to be fought at any expense, she said.

This was another low point in Chennault's life in China. It looked as if everything he tried was doomed to failure. He knew he could fight and beat the Japanese if he had the right training, equipment, and raw materials, but there was such a shortage of everything that he became quite discouraged. He applied to the U.S. Army Air Corps by mail, hoping to be allowed to return to active duty. The reply was that there were no funds available for the return to duty of retired officers. This was at a time when people in the States were desperately hoping that Neville Chamberlain's appeasement policy would put an end to Adolf Hitler's relentless aggression. The military in the United States had not yet realized that war—both in Europe and the Pacific—was imminent and that they would need all the retired officers they could get.

When he received the answer from the Air Corps, Chennault resigned himself to doing what he could do best—teach others how to fly and fight.

He and P.Y. piled their gear into the black car and instructed the chauffeur to head for Kunming. It was October 27, 1938, and in his diary that day Chennault wrote: "Left Chihkiang at 10:30 A.M. in light drizzle. Late start due to failure to get gas yesterday. Lost temper, but will find it somewhere on the road, no doubt. Stopped at Chengyuan at 5 P.M. for night. Road long and rough."

The trip didn't get any easier the following day, as evidenced by the next diary entry: "Left Chengyuan at 6:30 A.M. Arrived Kweiyang at 5 P.M. after breaking spring 65 kilometers east. Haven't found temper yet. Stopped at government inn. Met Capt. Kwok, station manager. Fine fellow. Telegraphed Gen. Chow for MacDonald and N.A." (North American aircraft)

Finally having enough of driving, Chennault decided to fly to Kunming. He left P.Y. to continue the trip with the chauffeur and flew on ahead the following night.

Training was at a low ebb when he arrived. The Chinese apparently had decided it was no use. Chennault, his resolve back, pitched in with his usual vigor to get the training program back on its feet. The first barrier in his way was the attitude on the part of Chinese officers at the school as to the authority of Americans at Kunming. It was necessary to get Madame Chiang on the phone and have her straighten out the misunderstanding. The director of the training school was Wang Hsu-ming, later to be better known to Americans as "Tiger" Wang.

Chennault's American instructors, mechanics, armament men, and other ground personnel began to arrive. Already with him was Billy McDonald who, along with Sebie Smith, had been to the States to get married. They had both sailed in the *Scharnhorst* in late summer via Europe and had returned by ship with their new brides via Hong Kong. Billy agreed to teach in Kunming, while Sebie was hired as an instrument specialist and mechanic by CAMCO—Central Aircraft Manufacturing Company—an agent for Curtiss-Wright in China. Headed by William Pawley, the company moved its assembly and repair facility from east China down to Loiwing on the Chinese border with Burma. It was thought to be safe from Japanese bombs there. Both McDonald's and Sebie's wives were to join them by train from Indochina.

In addition to McDonald, Chennault had Boatner Carney, an American, as an instructor, and Rolfe Watson as an armorer. Also serving as American instructors were reserve officers Frank Higgs, Skip Adair, Willie Heston, Jr., Bill Cherymisin, Harold Mull, Jim Bledsoe, and Emil Scott. A Swiss named Harry Sutter, a marvelously bilingual man, and his part Indian, part Chinese wife Kasey were also there. Boatner Carney and his wife Rose, also a Chinese girl, had been with Chennault at Hankow. The four often dined with Chennault.

Chennault managed to have his favorite shotgun, a Winchester 12-gauge pump gun, shipped over to him from Louisiana. He had been told there was excellent hunting in Yunnan Province and decided to find out for himself. His pilot friends from CNAC managed to find him several cases of bird shot in Hong Kong. The British—bird shooters at home and abroad—always had guns and shells. Chennault went hunting out on Gallifu Road with McDonald and a couple of other instructors. The rice paddies were filled with teal and mallards, visible from the road, but the men wanted to get a bit farther out from the city.

When they reached the shores of Tienchich Lake, ducks were everywhere. The small hunting group walked along the edge of the lake, jump-shooting ducks that took off from the sheltered coves. The day was cold and clear, with the mountains beyond the lake shining hard and bright in the early November sunlight. Doves flew past as they walked, and in an hour they bagged several dozen doves and eleven ducks. The chauffeur laid all the ducks out on the floor of the car trunk and Chennault smiled as he looked at the several rows of blue-wing teal, widgeon, mallard, and gadwall glistening in the afternoon sunlight. His homesickness for Louisiana—for the first time in months—vanished; he turned to McDonald.

"This makes up for a lot," he said, looking at the nearby range of mountains. "As long as there is bird hunting like this, I can put up with all kinds of inconveniences."

Chennault, McDonald, and another instructor, Johnny Preston, rode back to the field beneath rows of ancient eucalyptus trees, planning to eat the birds that night. It had been one of the few relaxing days for Chennault since leaving Hankow.

The Japanese Army Air Force in China at this time had at least twenty-four squadrons. Fourteen of these were stationed in north China, while ten squadrons were stationed in central China—at Hankow, Nanchang, and Changsha. They were able to reach most of the Chinese cities of the west with heavy and light bombers. The Japanese Navy Air Force also had a number of squadrons based where they could reach west China and in November they began to bomb Chihkiang, Kweilin, Chungking, and Chengtu. By the end of October the Japanese had captured Canton and stationed a large force of planes at White Cloud Airport. In December they began to hit the Chinese air base at Liuchow with devastating results. Kunming had air raid alerts several times a week, but the enemy had not yet hit the big city. Chennault came down with a bad cold and flu and was in bed with a high fever and a painful cough for a week. On the day that he finally was able to get up and sit in the sun, there was an air raid alarm, but the planes bombed Poseh—far east of Kunming.

In December life began to settle down to a round of social events—including dinner with American Ambassador Nelson Johnson—in Kunming. There were dinners at the French Club with his fellow pilots. Under orders from the Generalissimo, Chennault made occasional flights to Chungking, where he was able to dine with Donald again. Chungking was being bombed fairly regularly, but his Chinese students were hardly qualified to fly combat —even if they had had late-model fighters.

As Christmas approached and the cold and flu gradually left him, he was able to go hunting—and in the afternoon of December 24 he shot a dozen sandhill cranes. The training squadron had a feast that night. The following day he went hunting again and caught a chill, but he still went to a Christmas party at the American consulate that night.

On the twenty-seventh Harold Johnson, one of the pilots flying the Gimo's Boeing aircraft, failed to report back from a flight. It was unusual, so the entire training school entered into the air search. It was not until December 31 that they discovered Johnson and his crew had been killed instantly when the Generalissimo's plane hit a mountain at Wenshan.

Harvey Greenlaw, a representative for North American Aviation, was forced to evacuate Hengyang, where he had planes that were to be sold to the Chinese. He was a West Point graduate of the class of 1920 and had been a pilot with Colonel Jack Jouett's school in 1935. He and his wife Olga, a Californian, who traveled with him wherever he went, stayed in Kunming for several days and had dinner with Chennault. Greenlaw remained in China for years as an aviation representative.

Even at this coldest time of the year, Kunming had a pleasant climate. Nestled on a large plateau, the sprawling old city had long been considered a vacation paradise by the French who had colonized the hot, humid jungles of Indochina to the south. They had built a narrow-gauge railroad to the city from Haiphong and Hanoi and for centuries had enjoyed the vacation atmosphere of Kunming. The quiet city had been the terminus of an age-old trade route for tin, salt, and opium—all of which had come to China from Burma and India since the days of Marco Polo. Yunnan was an agricultural province and Kunming was surrounded by miles of rice paddies and fields of wheat, soybeans, and mustard. The city rested at the base of foothills to the west. Northwest, the foothills rolled up to the base of the most spectacular mountain range in the world—the Himalayas—topped by magnificent Mount Everest.

Most of the buildings in Kunming were one- and two-level mud and stone structures. Their red roof tiles were laboriously made of native clay pressed over the thighs of workmen. The houses squatted by the thousands beneath pepper and eucalyptus trees which lined the cobblestone streets. The airfield —about eight miles away—stood between Kunming and Tienchich Lake, a huge shallow body of water lined with marshes and formed by a serpentine river. The range of mountains to the east of the lake was topped by a red rock cliff on the face of a mountain the airmen renamed "Old Baldy."

The climate of the area was dry and cold in the winter, but when the monsoon season began in June, the fields and roads turned to deep mud and mildew grew on shoes and clothing stored in closets. The crops thrived on the moisture, but the city's inhabitants grew weary of the rain and mud by the end of the monsoon season in September.

Like every other large Chinese city, the streets of Kunming swarmed with humanity. Thousands of people jammed the thoroughfares, which were lined with stalls of every conceivable type of business. Vendors hawked vegetables, meats, and dry goods on the narrow sidewalks. Merchants displayed their wares on rickety wooden tables set up alongside the curbs and on carts parked beneath the ancient trees. The stores were narrow and dark and filled with the odors of spices, fragrant woods, and exotic foods. Meat, hanging on poles in front of the stores, was covered with flies most of the time—a fact that never seemed to bother the Chinese. It did bother foreigners, though, even those who had lived in China for years. Most foreigners never became used to eating in the open with flies buzzing constantly over their food. The Chinese seemed to ignore the insects as if they did not exist.

Rickshaws moved through the crowd of pedestrians, jostling each other on the rutted cobblestones. Countless children in faded blue denim clothing played on sidewalks and in the gutters, many with the seats of their trousers cut away, which saved their mothers the task of pulling down and raising the garments. The level of voices in the streets was always somewhere above a din; automobile horns, bicycle bells, the shouts of vendors, the barking of dogs, and the wail of Chinese music mingled with the reverberations of innumerable gongs. Farmers led bullocks through the crowds and everywhere there were herds of cattle and pigs wandering about beneath the trees.

Chennault loved the city. The constant furor exhilarated him and the color and mystery intrigued him. Long a devotee of hot, spicy French food in his native Louisiana, he loved the hot Szechwan food that was served in so many restaurants in Kunming. The stinging hot peppers held no fear for him and the torrid sauces delighted him. He and many of the pilots occasionally had wonderful meals at the Kunming Café.

The training went on. The Americans were dealing with a totally different class of cadets in the Yunnan flying school. While many of the earlier Chinese cadets had been trained by the Italians or by Colonel Jouett in the Shanghai and Hankow areas, the new ones had survived the long evacuation from the eastern cities and were war babies by now. They had no illusions about being pilots for social reasons—as had the earlier pilots of the well-to-do families. They flew because they had been told they were the only hope of stopping Japanese in the air—the enemy that was beginning to bomb Chungking daily.

When the first class of flying officers flew their Hawks to Kunming for training under Chennault, they cracked up six of the thirteen planes on landing. Chennault, furious at the loss of aircraft, grounded the entire class. General Chow, then head of the Chinese Air Force, questioned Chennault's authority to take such action. When the Generalissimo answered his telegram with a reply that Chennault was in charge of all training, Chow became a convert and a devoted fellow worker.

While the Chinese Air Force had no planes with which to oppose the Japanese bombers plastering the cities of western China, it could at least see to the building of airfields for the time when new planes arrived. In the spring and summer of 1938 and on into the following winter, hundreds of thousands of coolies were put to work building all-weather airstrips. Up to that time all Chinese airfields had consisted of turf or dirt. The rains turned them into long strips of mud that were useless for training. Chennault had taught the Chinese how to build proper runways at Nanking, but the field had to be abandoned to the Japanese. They started all over again at Hankow, but that too was lost. Now they began building airstrips with crushed rock and broken tiles all across eastern and central China. It was in those days that the long, hard runways of Hengyang, Liuchow, Kweilin, and Lingling were built by men, women, and children carrying wicker baskets of broken stone to dump on the fields. Giant steel rollers were pulled by hand to pack down loose rock. Work was also begun late in 1938 on the fields at Paoching and Chihkiang—later to be of so much value to the American Air Force.

Under Chennault's direction, the Chinese began to construct an intricate network of a ground air raid warning system stretching from the Japanese-occupied areas of the east to the remote parts of western China. Besides people, it involved the use of radios, telephones, and telegraph lines. The system was based upon Chennault's early Maxwell Field warning net and was the most efficient method yet invented to warn of approaching enemy aircraft. It also served to locate downed fliers and get them back to friendly lines. The most sophisticated net was constructed around the Kunming area and was set up by John Williams, an American communications expert. Williams was helped by Harry Sutter and a Chinese staff that was particularly worried about attacks from Hainan Island to the south. When an enemy plane left its base, Chinese agents close to that base would either pick up a telephone and call the takeoff time and direction headed or would report the same information by portable radio. The plane's passing would then be picked up by the next spotter and so forth all across China. Fighter aircraft could be warned well in advance, and by the time the enemy was within interception range the fighters would know the number of planes, the type, the altitude, and the heading. It was this net that made the American Volunteer Group (AVG) so successful later in the Kunming area and was also of such great help to the U. S. Army Air Force when it came to China in 1943.

To Chennault, the warning net and the airfields were as much a part of the coming air war as the planes he hoped to get from America. He thought in terms of air warfare in a part of the world where even air transportation was so new that almost no one in China ever thought of traveling by plane. He was thinking of fighter and bomber tactics at a time when most military planners thought in terms of land armies and navies.

In 1939 the airplane was just beginning to play its role in war. It had been intended primarily as an observation tool for the infantry in World War I, but soon the early fighter plane dogfights had developed. The war in Spain had seen the bomber come into its own, but even those planes were experimental compared to the waves of bombers and the groups of fighter aircraft that were soon to be used in the Battle of Britain. It was not until America entered the war that air warfare began on a large scale—in Europe and the Pacific. A few Chinese generals had learned the value of the bomber in blasting the mud-walled defenses of Chinese cities, but most still thought in terms of infantry, artillery, and tank warfare.

The Chinese were beginning to learn the devastating power of bombs against undefended cities. Europeans would soon learn the same hard facts of life. It is to Chiang Kai-shek's credit that he saw the potential for air power as early as he did. It made sense to him when the war finally reached a stalemate on the ground.

The Japanese Navy was unable to sail up the Yangtze River because of the Gorges. The Gorges and vast mountain ranges protected the wartime capital of Chungking from ground attack. The vast interior of China itself was a natural defense against Japanese infantry. Tokyo had no desire to extend its already long supply lines far into the interior just to defeat Chinese ground forces. The Japanese in the north were dug in across rivers from Chinese infantry and neither side was doing much more than exchanging desultory shots. In the south the Japanese had captured Canton and held the south China coast. They had no desire to waste troops on the mountains of Kwangsi Province in an effort to take more of the interior. Planning to take all of southeast Asia, they were saving the ground armies for those campaigns. They were content to send their bombers against Chungking from White Cloud Airport in Canton and the airfields on Hainan Island to the south, hoping to wear down Chinese morale from the air. The Japanese knew the Chinese had no potential to rebuild an air force in the vast regions of western China. They were content to bomb until the weary Chinese were ready to sue for peace.

Chennault was enough of a military strategist to understand the Japanese master plan. Like the Japanese minds that had built up the massive navy and army air forces, he knew air power was the answer to war over vast regions of a country which had few railroads and almost no paved roads. Its few navigable rivers were far to the north and only a few of those could be utilized by naval craft.

Military experts in Europe and America were just beginning to realize that the plane was an awesome new weapon. The German Stuka dive bomber and the heavy bombers of the Third Reich would soon be blasting European cities to rubble and parts of inner London were to be almost totally leveled before the end of the war. It was yet to be shown that there was almost no defense except fighter aircraft against heavy bombers.

In China in 1939—and in India and Burma—conventional minds still thought war must be waged on the ground.

Four

In October 1939, Chennault finally took a month's leave—provided for in his contract—and flew back to the States to spend Christmas with his family. He departed from Hong Kong by Pan American Clipper and arrived in the United States five days later. There were no nonstop flights in 1939 and the huge Martin M-130 set down in the Philippines, Wake Island, Guam, and Hawaii, droning along for hours between stops. From San Francisco he flew to Houston and then took a train to Beaumont, where he was met by his daughter Sue and his son Bob. Sue drove him to Kinder, Louisiana, where Nell met them. They made the long drive to Waterproof by six that evening. It was October 30 and late fall had set in. Chennault was struck by the beauty of his homeland. The leaves had turned and the big cypress trees along the bayous stood silver against the black water. Flights of waterfowl crisscrossed the skies over the Tensas River. Ever since arriving in San Francisco, he had been aware of the emptiness of America as compared to the Orient. Where were all the people—the walking masses, the people on bicycles, the rickshaws?

Nobody seemed to be *walking* in the United States. They drove down to the corner store for what they needed. And the fresh air smelled so—*clean*—with none of the human waste odor he had lived with for so long in China.

He was startled at the way his children had grown. His oldest, Jack, was now twenty-six, Max was twenty-four, and the other two "boys"—Charles, twenty-one, and Claire, eighteen—were almost grown up.

Jack was a second lieutenant in a fighter group that was based in Michigan at Selfridge Field. Chennault flew up to see him and his wife Irene and his first grandchild, twenty-month-old Claire Lee, for several days. Then he and Jack took a commercial DC-3 flight from Selfridge to Detroit, where they spent a day with Max and his wife Anne. Max was a station agent for Penn Central Airlines and Anne was six months' pregnant with their first child. It was a festive visit and Max cooked some venison that turned out to be tough, but nobody really cared. Chennault and Jack flew on to Buffalo, New York, to visit the Curtiss-Wright plant that was manufacturing the new P-36 fighter plane.

By the time he returned to Waterproof, the rest of the family was in a holiday mood. Sue and her husband Bob Lee had been married since 1937 and were spending the holidays with the Chennaults. They had one son, fourteen-month-old Bobby Pat Lee, who was a terror around the place and a source of great amusement to Chennault. Charles—or "Pug" as he was called by the family—was home from Auburn University in Alabama. When Chennault had last seen Pug, he was a gawky eighteen-year-old and his father was amazed at what a serious student he had become.

His fourth son, Claire Patterson, or "Pat," was also visiting, with his wife Hilma. Pat, now just eighteen, worked for the Armstrong Rubber Company in Natchez, Mississippi, and he and Hilma had been married since the previous May when they had both graduated from Waterproof High School. Chennault remembered the pretty girl from Pat's high school dating days and was pleased at the marriage, as was Nell, although he had some reservations about the boy getting married that young and giving up college.

The younger children were still in school. David Wallace, sixteen, seemed to think of nothing but hunting. His family had nicknamed him "Dink" and he was a pleasant, stocky boy with a freckled face and wide smile. His plans after graduation seemed a bit vague to Chennault but, remembering his own childhood along the Tensas River, he decided it was too early to worry about Dink's plans. There would be plenty of time after high school. The days in the swamps and bayous passed all too quickly as it was.

Young Robert Kenneth, was fourteen and at that awkward age when he was neither child nor adult. Bob was not making good grades in school and that worried Nell. Chennault had a long talk about study habits but had the feeling his words were not making a very deep impression. Bob's greatest ambition seemed to be to own his own car—a not too radical ambition, Chennault finally decided.

The baby of the family, Rosemary Louise, was eleven and the brunt of all the family teasing. She was a mischievous child and Chennault could see she would have no trouble making friends with her twinkling eyes and ready smile.

Nell seemed to have taken the long separation well. Having her large family around her obviously seemed to have kept her busy, and her many civic activities—from church matters to the PTA—had not left her much time for loneliness. Chennault was a bit surprised at the weight she had put on during the two years he had been gone. Priding himself on always keeping fit, he was intolerant about others letting themselves get out of shape. He mentioned it to her once, but she simply shrugged it off and he saw no point in spoiling the vacation by pursuing the matter.

He went over to see his father one day and found him quite healthy for his seventy-seven years. The old man kept up his house fairly well, with the help of an elderly housekeeper, and still got around easily. He talked about the recent fishing in the river and how he had managed to go duck hunting twice in the fall. He listened intently when told about China, but Chennault felt he did not quite grasp the meaning of it all.

He went hunting with old friends in the marshes and bayous around Waterproof and down along the Mississippi. There were thousands of ducks and geese and the men had fine hunts, spending the evenings in the hunting camps with drinks and hot, spiced Louisiana food. The friends were fascinated by Chennault's tales of hunting in China and particularly by the numbers of birds he could keep. Seasons and bag limits were strictly enforced in the United States in the late 1930s after the unregulated market-hunting days at the turn of the century.

At the end of November he and a friend, Bill Croswell, flew a Stinson to Nashville and Cleveland and on to Maxwell Field, Alabama, where Chennault met with old Army Air Corps friends. On December 6 he showed some movies he had taken in China to the Air Corps Training School and gave a talk on the air war in the Far East. He and Croswell then flew back to Waterproof that night.

Christmas was a festive affair, with all the children gathered around and friends dropping in from all over the state. Still, in the midst of the holiday celebrations, he kept thinking of China. Several times—with a big fire burning in the huge living-room fireplace and the laughter of family and friends in the big house—Chennault found himself thinking of burning cities and Chinese student pilots falling from the skies in their riddled obsolete fighter planes. In the midst of the plenty he saw piled on the tables he thought of the peasants and their meager fare. He found himself becoming annoyed at comments from friends on the futility of trying to help "a bunch of Chinamen" fight the Japanese half a world away. Most Americans were concerned far more about the war in Europe. The newspapers were filled with stories about the Russians, who had marched into Poland in September and were in the midst of their invasion of Finland, and about the Germans, who seemed to be hell-bent on conquering Europe. Most Americans Chennault talked with were hoping that the United States could avoid being dragged into the war. His insistence that the United States get into the war right away and help our European allies—before the war spread to our shores—did not earn him many friends. His warnings that Japan intended to start a war in the Pacific and would eventually attack U.S. bases there was received with laughter or with silent disbelief. By the first of the year Chennault was ready to return to China. Nell seemed to have made a life for herself in Waterproof with her bridge club and work with the schools. After the novelty of having their father home had worn off, his children had plunged back into the world of their friends and activities, jobs and school. The hunting seasons were over and he suddenly began to itch for action of some sort.

Toward the end of January, Chennault said good-bye to his family and friends and took off for Los Angeles. While in the city, he visited the Lockheed, North American, and Vultee aircraft plants and traveled down to San Diego to look at the Ryan and Consolidated aircraft factories. A few days later, on February 1, 1940, he flew up to San Francisco on a commercial flight. The following day he got a new Chinese visa at the Chinese Embassy, another visa for Hong Kong at the British Embassy, and had his passport updated at the American consulate. After a round of cocktail parties with friends, he took off for Honolulu on February 5.

The trip back was uneventful and Chennault read during the long hours over the ocean. By the time he left Midway, however, he felt a rising excitement. The vacation had been fine, but it would sure feel good to get back to China and to work. By Saturday, February 12, the big flying boat reached Portuguese Macao and it was only a half-hour flight from there to the British crown colony at Hong Kong. It was cold and gray when the plane docked at 3 P.M. By the time he finally got a room at the Ammex Hotel, Chennault was ready for a drink and a change of clothes. He was pleased and flattered to get a message at the Pan Am office that Madame Chiang and W. H. Donald would meet him that night at the Kai-Tak Airport to bring him up to date on what had happened during his absence.

When he met them at 8:30 P.M., Madame looked her usual beautiful self, wrapped in a long black cloth coat with a mink collar. Donald said little as Madame told him about the Air Force training program, which was not going well, owing to a lack of pilots and planes. On the brighter side, the Chinese Air Force had received a shipment of Hawk 75s, which were deployed at various bases in China. They had also come because he was their friend and in the hope that he might have some encouraging news from the States, but, there was nothing Chennault could tell them to comfort them.

The Japanese were using saturation bombing on Chungking and the huge city had been taking a terrible beating on days when the cold and damp winter mists lifted, allowing the Japanese pilots a clear view of their targets. Regular bombing had also begun on Kunming and Chinese training flights had to be restricted to early morning and late afternoon hours—before and after the raids.

Chennault shopped for a day and paid a visit to T. V. Soong before booking himself on a CNAC DC-3 flight to Kweilin and Chungking on Thursday, February 15. The wartime capital was cold and damp, wrapped in the winter mists that made Chungking so uncomfortable yet protected it a bit from the Japanese bombers. As he drove from the airport to his hotel he looked at the fire-blackened houses and the jumble of rubble along the road. Rain-soaked coolies plodded alongside the car, their tree-bark raincoats pulled over their shoulders and the water running from their wide rice-straw hats. His quarters were cold and it took an hour to warm them up with a fire from a metal stove in the center of the room. The houseboy unpacked his bags and hung his clothes in a closet. The rain was still falling heavily as he washed and changed his shirt and pants. The boy brought him his mail and he read it by the stove and the light from a naked light bulb above.

It was several hours later—after dinner and a rendition of Handel's *Messiah* by the Chengtu Chorus at the home of New York *Times* correspondent Tillman Durdin and wife Peggy—that he finally felt that his journey had ended. As the voices lifted in harmony in the long room and the flames from a fireplace sent shadows flickering over the white plaster walls and the light played on the shining youthful Chinese faces of the chorus, he sipped his drink and smiled. He was back where he belonged—with an important job to do.

Chennault's professional duties at that time consisted of operating the tiny flying school in the rice-paddy fields of western China. It was maddeningly dull work. The training field at Kunming, unlike the newer airstrips in eastern and central China, was built on sod and dirt. Whenever it rained—which it did frequently—the runways and taxi strips turned into clinging mud. The small Fleet trainers could not take off or land in the morass and flying had to be canceled for the day—sometimes for several days. Chennault's responsibilities were administrative, which meant overseeing the paperwork of twelve classes of Chinese student pilots—all the way from primary flight school up through basic and into advanced flying school. He had a number of American flight instructors to train the students, so he was not concerned with the actual flying, though he did have to supervise the instructors.

He taught courses in navigation to the advanced students, as well as courses on the theories of gunnery and bombing. The classes were held in a small mud house at the edge of the field where Chennault would draw trajectories of machine guns and bombs on a blackboard.

There were approximately forty students to a class and they moved inexorably up through the training, with many dropping out on the way. There was plenty of time to teach them—as the war was far away at the moment—but many of the students had neither mechanical ability nor the reflexes needed to fly a plane or simply could not grasp the essentials of flying. It was Chennault's job to inform the students who had flunked out.

He had to maintain a liaison with the Chinese Air Force, which was headquartered at Chungking to the north, but the communication was perfunctory at best. General Mow came down occasionally to inspect the graduating classes, but that was about the only official connection between the Air Force and the training school.

When they graduated, the students had no planes to fly. Two Hawk 75s at Kunming, purchased by the Madame from Curtiss Co., were too valuable to trust to the inexperienced pilots. Only Chennault, McDonald, and a select few of the American instructors were allowed to fly them.

Life settled down to a round of frustration on the teaching and flying side, hunting on the off days, and a fairly busy social life. Boatner and Rose Carney had a house near Chennault's and invited him often for dinner. In addition, there were Harry and Kasey Sutter. When Harry was away on communications business, Kasey made a good fourth for dinners, lunches, or picnics. John Williams and the other married Americans had Chennault over frequently for home-cooked meals. James McHugh often came through Kunming from Chungking and Chennault was sometimes able to get away on business to Chunking, where he would have lunch or dinner with Donald. Another of his instructors, Skip Adair, and his wife were close friends and he played tennis regularly at the French Club with them. He also played badminton now and then but never grew to like the game. Evenings were mostly devoted to cards—poker being the favorite—although Chennault liked almost any card game and was good at most. He finally tried mah-jongg, starting out with P. Y. Shu and his wife and finally graduating to games in which he took on all-Chinese groups of Air Force officers and their wives—no mean task.

His circle of Chinese women friends widened that spring and he was frequently seen at the Carneys', at cocktail parties in Kunming, at the movies, or on picnics with either Kasey Sutter, Fay Tseng, Lilliann Leung, or Sophie Tsu. He loved parties and attended American movies at the local theater as often as he could. He enjoyed good food and liked to drink—particularly bourbon. Many a night after dinner he would start games—any games—just to compete. His black eyes snapping and a wide grin across his face, Chennault would wrestle any man who was willing. They would twist and grunt on the living-room floor, to the accompaniment of shouts and applause from the other after-dinner guests until one of the wrestlers won. Chennault was usually the victor—being in excellent shape and highly competitive. He particularly liked to outdo the younger men and many times would challenge them to hold out a wooden chair by the bottom of one leg. It took exceptional strength of the forearms—a trick he had mastered years before. If there were no physical games in which he could interest anyone, Chennault would fetch a battered fedora from a closet and set it upside down in the middle of the floor. Then, sitting in a chair along one wall, he would flip playing cards into it. With a cigarette hanging from the corner of his lips, the smoke curling up into his squinted eyes, he would flip cards against anyone —for bets—for hours. He particularly enjoyed challenging women to this game and several of his Chinese women friends became so good at it that they beat him frequently—much to his amusement—but he was never amused by being beaten at any game by a man. Wrestling, tennis, baseball, volleyball, and shooting—all were serious sports to Chennault. No one ever beat him at hunting, although a few men shot almost as well as he did. However, he lost at tennis and baseball now and then and never thought it funny.

But on most nights he played cards. He would sit up until the small hours of the morning playing mah-jongg or poker. He drank steadily while playing poker but never enough to cloud his judgment—unlike some of his poker-playing friends. When he played John Williams and Tom Gentry—a doctor friend—who drank slowly like Chennault, the games would go on. But when Boatner Carney and some of the other Americans who drank too much played, many a game would be broken up by an argument. Chennault never got into a serious fight with anyone because of these drinking bouts and poker games. It was necessary to calm Carney and some of the others down now and then and it usually fell to the gentle giant John Williams to walk them home in the darkness.

Chennault met a number of interesting people in Kunming and Chungking during those years. Colonel Joseph Warren Stilwell was a visiting U.S. military attaché and he had first met Chennault on an inspection trip to Yunnan the winter before. They had dinner at the Hotel du Lac in Kunming, a most pleasant dinner during which the two discussed the Chinese Air Force—or lack of it. Chennault's recollection of the man was summed up later as "a gaunt, leathery man with a perpetual squint through his steel-rimmed glasses."

In May 1940, Colonel David Barrett called on him. Barrett was a short, rotund, ruddy-faced man with an almost bald head, a jolly man who loved parties, girls, and jokes. He and Chennault became friends almost immediately. Barrett had been in China for years—first as a Chinese-language student in Peking and later in the same city as a military attaché for three years. Then he was assigned to duty as a regimental intelligence officer with the U. S. 15th Infantry at Tientsin—where George Marshall and Joseph Stilwell had both served. During the Japanese occupation of Peking, Barrett had served as assistant attaché, a difficult job at best. By 1940 he was assigned to Chungking as military attaché. He spoke beautiful, fluent Mandarin Chinese —perhaps the best Chennault had ever heard—and had a wonderful sense of humor. He was especially irreverent about his military superiors and politicians, as Chennault had been throughout his own military career, and that no doubt contributed to their almost instant friendship. Barrett was a frequent companion at Chennault's dinner parties during that winter, spring, and summer.

The Japanese planes were coming ever closer to Kunming. The Japanese had no intention of letting the Chinese train an air force and were prepared to bomb the training school off the face of the earth. On April 10 a few Japanese planes got as far as the border between Burma and China, but no farther. On April 25 forty-eight bombers were reported near Foochow and on April 26 eighteen Japanese bombers hit Mengtzu just north of the Indochina border south of Kunming. These planes probably came either from the big Japanese base at Sama Bay on Hainan Island or from White Cloud

Airport at Canton. Several Hawk 75s took off from Kunming at the air raid alerts, but no contact was made.

On May 9 an air raid signal was sounded and the first ball of the "Jing Bao" alert was hoisted. The Jing Bao was a system of boosting red paper balls high in the air on some tree or tower—one ball signifying the first stage of an alert, two the second, and the third the final stage. It became a familiar sight to American airmen later in the war. By the third alert, it was assumed everyone was well protected in a slit trench or cave. As the war went on, everyone took the first ball rather calmly. The second ball would cause some hurrying and scurrying on the part of both Chinese and foreigners. The third ball caused considerable fast movement.

On this day the Japanese sent a force of twenty-seven bombers over the training field at Kunming at 3:05 P.M. Chennault sent all planes into the air at 1 P.M. when the alarm first went off. By the time the Japanese bombers arrived, the Chinese pilots were almost out of gas and no combat was reported. Thirty people were killed and fifty were wounded on the outskirts of the field in that first big raid.

The monsoon season gradually crept in from the jungles of Burma and Indochina that spring. It became warm and muggy, and flying each day was restricted to the hours when the rain stopped and the field was not too muddy. Chennault had his eleventh class soloing by this time in the Hawk IIIs and fewer students were killing themselves on landings and takeoffs. Spins continued to take a big toll, however, as students waited until the last minute to jump from the spinning planes and parachutes failed to open.

In early July a bubonic plague scare broke out at Loiwing and Bill Pawley came through Kunming with five doctors on the way down to the CAMCO repair facility there to see what they could do to stop the disease. One death had already been reported and more were feared. Chennault had been down to the facility a month earlier and found the repair depot on the Burmese border in excellent shape. The shops were sending his damaged Hawks back to him as fast as anyone could expect in such a remote land.

As the weather grew hotter and more muggy the air raid alarms went off less frequently at the airfield. The Japanese preferred to wait to bomb Kunming until the weather cleared. However, they were trying to force the French in Indochina to the south to let them land troops—a prelude to invasion.

On days when the weather was reasonably good, Chennault would take up one of the planes to keep in practice. His battered logbooks totaled almost ten thousand hours of flying time. But, like most experienced flying men, he knew that only constant practice and mastery of the latest technology would ensure flying proficiency.

So he would take up one of the Fleet trainers for simple takeoffs and landings and a few basic aerobatics. In good weather he would take the cumbersome biplane trainer high over the lake and do loops, lazy eights, and

1. Graduating officers of the Air Corps Training School, Maxwell Field, Alabama, 1930–31. Chennault is fourth from the right of the next to last row. (U.S. Air Corps Photo)

2. Billy McDonald, Chennault, and Luke Williamson in front of a P-12 at Maxwell Field, 1935. (Courtesy of John Williams)

3. A rare photo of the Generalissimo, Madame, and Chennault about the time the AVG was organized. (Courtesy of P. Y. Shu)

4. A group of AVG pilots at Loi-wing, late April 1942. *(Left to right)* H. G. Cananah, Tex Hill, Bill Reed, Arvid Olson, Moose Moss, Parker Dupouy, Bob Prescott, and Cliff Groh. (Courtesy of Tex Hill)

5. Pilots of the AVG 2nd Squadron, "Panda Bears." *(Back row)* Buster Keeton, Frank Lawlor, Freeman Ricketts, Bob Layher, Hank Geselbracht, Tom Jones, Frank Schiel. *(Front row)* Ed Rector, Pappy Paxton, Pete Wright, Jack Newkirk, Tex Hill, Gil Bright, and Ed Conant. (Courtesy of Tex Hill)

6. AVG flight nurses Red Foster and Jo Stewart. (Courtesy of John Williams)

7. Arvid Olson, Chennault, and Jack Newkirk, Kunming, 1942, discussing an AVG mission. (Courtesy of John Williams)

8. A shark-nosed AVG P-40, with an auxiliary fuel tank below. (U.S. Air Corps Photo)

9. Chennault discusses plans with AVG pilots, with Arvid Olson leaning over his shoulder. (Courtesy of Malcolm Rosholt)

10. Brigadier General Chennault with his new star. He still wears his AVG blouse and cap. (Courtesy of Max Chennault)

FIFTEEN CENTS

DECEMBER 6, 1943

TIME

THE WEEKLY NEWSMAGAZINE

CHENNAULT OF THE FOURTEENTH AIR FORCE

VOLUME XLII

(REG. U.S. PAT. OFF.)

NUMBER 23

11. Chennault becomes a world figure after being the subject of the cover story in the December 6, 1943, issue of *Time.*

spins in the calm spring sky. The feel of stick, rudder, and throttle had become second nature to him and he would hang upside down in his safety belt at the top of a loop, then relax as the force of gravity flattened him in the seat at the bottom of the dive. As in the early days of his Air Corps career, Chennault flew for the sheer love of it and the feeling of well-being he got from being detached from the earth.

On days when he felt the need to hurl himself through the skies—as he had done for years with the Air Corps acrobatic team—he would take up one of the Hawk 75s and put it through a series of maneuvers. The high whining roar of its engine rattled windows and made walls vibrate near the field as he took the sleek fighter high overhead and dove it toward the earth —pulling out at the last minute and snap-rolling it across the field, much to the amusement of the Chinese students and his American instructors. He would pull the fighter straight up into the blue of the spring sky over Yunnan and let it fall backward in a dead-stick stall that finally ended in a spin. The silver plane would fall for several thousand feet until he pushed the opposite rudder and flattened out into an almost vertical dive toward the green rice paddies. As a finale he would fly the Hawk 75 upside down just over the runway, pulling up into a slow roll.

"Nobody flies a fighter," Boatner Carney once said, "like the Old Man."

Chennault kept up his tennis at the French Club, where talk of the Japanese problem was uppermost. On August 15 journalist Theodore White came through Kunming and he and Chennault had dinner together. White was convinced that the Japanese invasion of Indochina was only days away and that Burma would be next. His prophecy came true when the Japanese invaded Indochina on the twenty-third. The fall of Paris in June had visibly shaken the French in Kunming. The Japanese—seeing the Axis victories in Europe as even greater justification for their Greater East Asia Co-Prosperity Sphere—had stepped up their demands in the Far East. They were pressuring the French to close the railroad from Hanoi to China and were leaning on the British to close the Hong Kong frontier and the Burma Road. The Chinese government had been keeping a wary eye on the British in India, lest they give in to the demands and close China's last land supply road in the west. The road was not bringing in any substantial amount of supplies at the moment, but the fact that it was there—having been scraped out of the mountainsides by the hands of two hundred thousand laborers—was important to them. When the British gave in to the Japanese demand on July 12 and closed the road, Chiang Kai-shek was furious.

Chennault—far removed from all the politics—read the newspapers from Hong Kong and Rangoon that came in on each CNAC flight and listened to the radio each day. The news was not good. As a military man, he saw the threat from Indochina and Burma on the ground, but he was really only concerned with the air war that he knew was coming. He had no way of knowing about the wave of pessimism that struck the government at Chungking when the Burma Road was closed or the intricacies of political pressure being put on U.S. officials in Washington by representatives of the Nationalist Government. His talks with the Generalissimo had been only of military needs and in his talks with Madame Chiang they had stressed only the need for his training program. Chennault had talked about general foreign affairs with T. V. Soong when he had dined with him in Hong Kong the previous February, but Soong had not discussed financial affairs or international politics. Chennault's only other connection with the Central Government was through Dr. H. H. Kung—and that was mostly on a social level. He knew Dr. Kung was the man who paid all the bills as Finance Minister, but since the Shanghai and Hankow days Chennault had known him only socially as a member of Madame's family—a friendly man who seemed to like foreigners who were trying to help China. Chennault's grasp of international affairs was still a bit vague, and apparently he was not fond of the French, in spite of his Huguenot ancestry—as evidenced by a letter he wrote to Nell on October 9, 1940, from Kunming:

"The Japs got the airdromes they demanded in Indochina (which is French territory and should be neutral) and now they send pursuit planes of the very best quality to support their bombers. They've bombed the city twice but haven't done much damage yet. Both times the bombers were above 20,000 feet and bombed cross-wind. However, the city will eventually be badly damaged, as they will come down to lower altitudes soon. When the French let the Japs into Haiphong and Hanoi they found and took great stores of gasoline, oil, trucks, and other war supplies which the French had held up there during the past two years. They (the Japs) are now using this stuff against the rightful owners. If nothing else results from this war, I certainly hope the French are driven out of Indochina."

Apparently he was referring to himself and the Chinese as the "rightful owners."

As the weather began to clear up and the rains lessened, the Japanese came back to Kunming with a vengeance. They hit the airfield on September 30 with twenty-seven bombers, flying in three waves of nine planes each. The Chinese and Chennault had nothing to oppose them with but trainers. On the following day the Japanese returned with eighteen planes and caused considerable damage. On October 7 twenty-five Japanese bombers, accompanied by half a dozen of the latest fighters, plastered the field—shooting down four Hawk III trainers and an E-15 pursuit plane. "The I-98 is far superior," Chennault noted in his diary about the sleek Japanese fighters.

On October 12 he received an urgent summons to Chungking to talk with the Generalissimo. Chennault had no idea it was to be anything other than a progress report on the training schools. The following day, as he was trying to book a flight on CNAC to Chungking, the Japanese hit the Kunming training field in earnest—eight dive bombers and twenty-seven more bombers, escorted by the deadly I-98 fighters. The dive bombers blasted hangars and repair facilities and several bombs shattered the house where Chennault and John Williams shared quarters. They were forced to move their gear to the Carneys' house while Chennault's house was being repaired.

His trip to Chungking was marred by a devastating raid by Japanese bombers and it took him hours to reach the Generalissimo's house. Scores of houses were burning and fire fighters were engaged in a losing battle to put out the flames. Chennault was forced to wait on one street while volunteers attempted to put out a building fire with buckets of water. A low cloud of acrid smoke covered the city and flickering fires could be seen in every section. The city was suffering from the many air raids—the Japanese had been using from ninety to two hundred bombers a night. The Gimo had decided that something drastic needed to be done. He was concerned that the morale of the people of Chungking would not stand up to much more of the saturation bombing.

He and Madame were waiting when Chennault finally arrived. Through Madame, he heard the Gimo ask him what he thought of the possibility of obtaining American pilots and planes to fight in China. When Chennault asked how many he had in mind, the Gimo said he thought five hundred would do. After a few moments of silence Chennault said he thought it would be impossible to get that many. The Gimo sat impassively while Chennault explained why he thought that the planes would be difficult to get. It had to do with the commitments to America's European allies. He had visited the various aircraft plants in Southern California, Chennault said, and found they were already far behind on orders to the British alone. The only possible chance, he explained, would be in getting some slightly out-of-date or obsolete fighter and bomber aircraft, but that would certainly be better than what they had now. The meeting broke up with nothing settled and Chennault returned to Kunming after having dinner with Barrett and Donald.

It was five days later—on October 20—that he received the second summons to return to Chungking to see the Generalissimo. Chennault was ill with a recurrent case of bronchitis and Kasey Sutter flew back to Chungking with him. He was running a fever when he met with the Gimo. He was startled when Chiang handed him a set of written orders to proceed to the United States and report to T. V. Soong in Washington. T.V. was the administrative officer of an organization called China Defense Supplies and was doing what he could to get as much of everything possible for China. Chennault's job, as expressed by the Gimo through Madame, was to get as many American planes—fighters and bombers—and as many American pilots as he could to fly them. He was to travel with Peter Mow and they were to leave immediately. It was quite a surprise to Chennault, but he managed to conceal it. There was no doubt that the only way to defeat Japan in the skies over China was with American men and equipment. He had been training Chinese pilots long enough to realize that.

After saying good-bye to Kasey, he and Peter Mow left the following morning for Hong Kong and two days later they climbed aboard a Pan American Clipper for the long flight across the Pacific.

As the flying boat droned on for the seemingly endless hours between Pacific island stops, Chennault nursed his congested chest, fever, and a cough that cut through him like a jagged knife. He could not help feeling that he was deserting his friends and the Chinese people when they needed him most. The thought of how little he had been able to accomplish over the past three and a half years depressed him. For all his teaching and all his work, the Chinese Air Force was almost nonexistent. Hundreds of his students had either been killed by the Japanese or had died in training accidents. Chennault felt he had not earned his salary. He knew that Chiang was right to send him to the States to get American planes and pilots, but he was not confident that he knew enough people in high places to pull it off. The war in Europe had first priority and Chennault knew it would take a near miracle to get aircraft companies to divert fighter planes to China. For all the death and devastation taking place in China, hardly any Americans in authority knew what was going on there.

The Chinese were discouraged with the progress of the war. For years they had watched the Japanese slowly grind up the best Chinese armies in their inexorable march inland from Manchuria and east China. They had watched their industries crumble, their commerce come to a halt, and their government vacate the big eastern capital and flee to the shelter of fog-shrouded Chungking, far in the interior. They had seen the invaders—with a vast modern navy and an armada of efficient planes—gradually take the seaports of Shanghai, Wenchow, Amoy, Swatow, and Canton and occupy Hainan Island. They had watched helplessly as the modern armies of infantry, artillery, and tanks swallowed up five provinces and installed puppet governors to carry out Japanese orders. Millions of Chinese soldiers had died so far in what seemed a useless war to the average peasant farmer. Hundreds of thousands of helpless women and children had perished in the horror of constant Japanese bombardment.

While the hundreds of millions of surviving Chinese patiently rebuilt the blasted cities, airfields, railroads, and highways in the wake of Japanese bombs, their foreign allies seemed indifferent. Only a small trickle of supplies had reached them from the three routes to the outside world. Meager supplies came into Chungking from Russia via the railroad from Sergiopol in Chinese Turkestan. Foreign aid had been reaching Kunming and Nanning— prior to the Japanese invasion of Indochina—from Haiphong, where foreign ships had been able to dock. The supplies had been moved by truck to Hanoi and then by railroad to the two Chinese cities, but all that had stopped now. The last supply route was via Rangoon, where supplies had been sent by rail up to Mandalay and then to Lashio, from where they were offloaded onto trucks and moved 688 miles to Kunming on the tortuous Burma Road. The

British had reopened this vital supply link on October 18; it had been closed long enough for the Chinese to realize their only supply route to the outside world was subject to the political whims of a foreign government.

With no air force, no navy, and their armies dug in and pinned down by the Japanese in the north and east, the Chinese were constantly bombarded by Japanese propaganda leaflets dropped on their cities and by radio broadcasts. They were always reminded that their so-called foreign allies were in reality their enemies. The Japanese had begun a propaganda drive of "Asia for the Asiatics"—stressing that for years the foreigners had only exploited China. They reminded the Chinese that the British had colonized Hong Kong and pointed to the lack of aid to China by her allies in her time of war. Tokyo hinted at graft in the Chungking government and dissension in the ranks of Chiang's party, and puppet Chinese voices predicted that the government would soon collapse. Inflation had already set in and the prospect of starvation was not attractive to millions of Chinese. It was a low point in the war and the future looked hopeless. It was a depressing point in Chennault's life also. And now—as he looked from the plane window down to the vast surface of the Pacific—he knew that he would need some sort of miracle to help these long-suffering people.

Five

One of the first things Chennault did when he got to Washington was to turn over what he could of intelligence material on Japanese fighters to Army intelligence. In 1939 the Chinese had captured a Type 97 Japanese fighter intact and had brought it to Chengtu, north of Chungking. Chennault had gone to the field and put the fighter through flight tests. Impressed with the plane's capabilities, he had painstakingly, with the help of Chinese mechanics, noted all the specifications and photographed it thoroughly.

A forerunner of the Oscar, which was a first-run Japanese fighter for years in the Pacific theater, the Type 97 was a top-notch fighter in 1940. It was some months before Chennault heard anything from the War Department. By then he was back in China and the letter said the material had been turned over to "aeronautical experts," who had informed the War Department that a fighter plane with such a performance could not possibly be built with the specifications submitted. This was the first model of the Zero—the fighter that was to cause so much death and destruction later in the war. Chennault knew this model had a top speed of 322 m.p.h., a range of over a thousand miles equipped with a belly tank, could climb to 16,000 feet in six minutes, and was armed with a 20-mm. cannon and four 7.7-mm. machine guns. Apparently, the Air Corps never got a copy of the dossier Chennault turned over to Army intelligence, as the Air Corps manual in use at the time of the attack on Pearl Harbor contained a blank page on the Zero.

On November 1, 1940, Chennault reported to T. V. Soong at the China Defense Supplies offices on Washington's V Street. T.V.—because of his vast wealth and international banking expertise—was well acquainted with U. S. Secretary of the Treasury Henry Morgenthau, Jr., and with Secretary of the Navy Frank Knox. Both men proved to be valuable allies.

Chennault's instructions from Chiang were simple but sweeping: get as many fighter planes, bombers, and transports as possible, plus all the supplies needed to maintain them and the pilots to fly the aircraft. He was assigned a desk in a small office at China Defense Supplies and began the incredibly difficult—and, for him, dull—task of making up lists of equipment needed to maintain a small air force.

Some spadework had already been done in a few circles on the need to supply China with air defense. Bruce G. Leighton, a former naval officer and vice-president of Intercontinent Corporation—a jointly owned Chinese and American company that owned CAMCO, Pawley's repair facility at Loiwing —had been quietly working on some high Navy brass in Washington. Leighton presented some arguments for air power in China to the Chief of Naval Operations. His thoughts were that it was to America's interests that Japan be prevented from gaining control of China and that this could only be done by establishing an effective air force there. Leighton suggested that the United States send a hundred pursuit aircraft, a hundred bombers, ten transports, and perhaps fifty American pilots to help the Chinese fly them. He estimated the cost to be about $50 million—to be obtained from American banks and secured by the Chinese government. Leighton also suggested that American Army and Navy fliers could be, if not actively recruited, not discouraged from going to China to help. Leighton's plan was not wholly patriotic, although his was certainly the first plan submitted. He did it for business reasons too, suggesting that Intercontinent should handle the job under contract with China and "without any direct participation by the United States Government."[1]

In January 1940, Leighton said the Loiwing factory in Yunnan employed fifteen American experts and about fifteen hundred Chinese. He planned to expand that force to three thousand Chinese and employ ten more Americans. He estimated the plant could turn out two hundred planes per year— assembled from parts shipped to Loiwing from the Curtiss plant in America. The Loiwing factory was well situated, he argued, connected by seventy-five miles of road to Bhamo in Burma. From there, ships could move up and down the Irrawaddy River towing barges capable of lifting two thousand tons. His argument carried some weight as a money-making proposition. The previous year William Pawley had transacted about $11 million (Chinese) worth of business with the Chinese government. All this had not fallen on deaf ears. Frank Knox had been made aware of the plan and was not against it.

T. V. Soong told Chennault that he would worry about the money problems and instructed Chennault to concentrate on compiling a supply list. China Defense Supplies would purchase all the materials Chennault ordered, but they needed a comprehensive breakdown of all the essentials. As the long, cold, damp, and gray Washington winter wore on, Chennault worked at his cluttered desk, making up long requisitions for everything from oxygen masks and machine-gun barrels to toilet paper and paper clips. He made trips to aircraft factories from coast to coast in an effort to find planes.

Almost all were consigned to Europe. The British were in desperate need of fighters and bombers—any the Americans could build. His social life was almost nonexistent and he fell asleep at night exhausted after the hours of travel or paperwork. One evening he dined with Soong and two journalists who were anxious to hear about conditions in China—Edgar Ansel Mowrer of the Chicago *Daily News* and Joseph W. Alsop, Jr., of the New York *Herald Tribune.* Both were sympathetic to his views on the need to help China, but both realized the odds against the United States doing anything about it. All eyes were on the war in Europe.

While Chennault had been sent to Washington as Chiang's military representative, his duties were really more of a civil and administrative than diplomatic nature. As a retired captain, he carried no weight with the United States military. General Hap Arnold, head of the U. S. Army Air Corps, had never been friendly to him when he was on active duty and did not agree with his pursuit theories. U.S. Army Chief of Staff General George C. Marshall in all probability had never even heard of Chennault or his air warfare theories. Chennault's only connection with the military was through Frank Knox, a civilian, who was interested in the war in China primarily because of his friendship with T. V. Soong.

President Roosevelt had a genuine interest in China through his family. He never tired of telling friends that the Roosevelt family fortune had been tied to the Shanghai opium trade. This, he felt, gave him a connection to the Orient. There was a wooden Chinese junk on his desk, a present that T. V. Soong and H. H. Kung had sent him years earlier from the capital at Nanking. Long a supporter of the Soong family, Roosevelt was predisposed to help China, though his Oval Office was not open to T.V. Although the President himself never went to visit T.V. and his attractive wife Laura at their suburban Chevy Chase, Maryland, home, many of his Cabinet members and associates were entertained there. Among them were Secretary of Commerce Jesse Jones, Morgenthau, Frank Knox, Warren Pierson of the Export-Import Bank, and Thomas J. ("Tommy the Cork") Corcoran—a high-level influence peddler and lawyer who had been with the Roosevelt administration for years as a speech writer and confidant. He had since gone into private practice.

Others who could be found at T.V.'s table, or with him at social events, included future OSS Chief William Donovan and Dr. Lauchlin Currie, an economist and aide to Roosevelt. Currie had been unofficially asked to handle the "China problem" as a coordinator and expediter. Also observed around T.V. in those days was John F. Fairbank, who had been born in China of missionary parents and who would help Dr. Currie with his China affairs in the years to come. Other frequent dinner guests included Special Assistant Harry Hopkins and Assistant Secretary of War John J. McCloy.

Therefore, the real work of getting money, planes, and supplies for China was being done by T.V. in the behind-the-scenes area of cocktail and dinner parties. It was largely T.V.'s doing that Congress had approved a loan of $25 million to China that September. After Roosevelt's reelection in November, F.D.R. asked Congress for and got, in December, an additional $100 million from Morgenthau's Treasury Department. One half was to stabilize China's currency and the other half was to purchase food and war supplies. Some of this money was used to set up T.V.'s Universal Trading Corporation—headquartered in New York's Rockefeller Center—and the Washington headquarters of China Defense Supplies. Tommy Corcoran's brother David headed China Defense Supplies, while Tommy served as the general counsel. The company secretary was Whiting Willauer, a behind-the-scenes man who would have intelligence connections to the OSS. Another officer of the company was Frederic Delano, an uncle of President Roosevelt's who had connections to the Far East.

Chennault, in consultation with T.V., had come up with a practical plan to get the planes, supplies, and materials needed by China. He argued that an effective air force in China could operate on the flank of any Japanese attack on Singapore. The British were particularly worried about a Japanese attack on that crown colony in the winter of 1940–41 and were putting considerable diplomatic pressure upon the United States to prevent it. As Chennault saw it, attacks on Japanese in China could be achieved by a force of three hundred and fifty pursuit aircraft and a hundred and fifty bombers flown by Americans. T.V. had previously asked Morgenthau for five hundred planes, but the Secretary of the Treasury had indicated that they would cost far too much money. The government saw no possibility of allocating the fighters and bombers to Chennault either—although many in positions of authority agreed that Chennault's requests were not excessive.

In the meantime, Lauchlin Currie had been invited to China by Chiang Kai-shek to make a survey for Roosevelt on the condition of China's air force and the status of China's ground war against the Japanese. He took official leave from his duties at the White House and his travel expenses were paid by the Chinese government at T.V.'s suggestion. He was to be an adviser on economic matters. Currie took General P. T. Mow with him on a Pan American Clipper flight on January 28, 1941. Chiang asked Currie to transmit to the President a request for an American political adviser and Owen Lattimore was later dispatched to Chungking. Chiang then asked for an economic adviser and Manuel Fox was sent to China a few months later. When Chiang requested a technical adviser for the Burma Road, two veteran transportation experts, Dr. John Baker and Daniel Arnstein of the Chicago Trucking Authority, were sent. Upon his return to the States on March 11, Currie's report to Roosevelt suggested that the United States supply China with a force of American planes, including American crews, equipment, and supplies, under the provisions of the pending Lend-Lease program—in other words, financed by Lend-Lease funds. If there was an official response to Currie's report, it was never published.

While Currie was in China in early February 1941, Chennault and an old friend at the Curtiss-Wright Aircraft Company in Buffalo, New York, Burdette Wright, who was vice president, came up with a scheme to procure some of the badly needed fighter planes. Wright said that if the British would waive their priority on a hundred P-40C aircraft currently in production, the company would later produce a hundred later-model P-40s for them. The British, it turned out, did prefer to have the later models and agreed to Wright's offer. The Universal Trading Corporation in New York secured the release of the hundred Curtiss-Wright Tomahawks from the British and plans were quickly made to ship them to China.

There were a few problems with the P-40C, but Chennault was so desperate for late-model fighters that he agreed to take them anyway. He was sure he could modify them later. They had already been fitted with British .303-caliber machine guns instead of American .30-caliber guns. There were no military radios in them—as the British had planned to equip them with VHF radios in England—so it was necessary for China Defense Supplies to purchase general aviation radios, not the best equipment for fighter aircraft. In addition, the planes were not equipped with gunsights, bomb racks, or any system of attaching belly tanks.

Efforts to get ammunition for the guns turned into a nightmare. The British were to supply the .303-caliber ammunition, while the .50-caliber and .30-caliber ammo was to be supplied by the War Department. The bickering went on from March until late August before both T. V. Soong and Lauchlin Currie finally managed to get the ammo—in two lots—from General Leonard Gerow of the War Plans Division. One lot of 900,000 rounds was made available under Lend-Lease procedure from the Raritan Arsenal in New Jersey. The U. S. Maritime Commission made the USS *Warrior* available to transport the ammunition to China via Rangoon, Burma, sailing on August 14.

The second lot—.50 and .30-caliber ball, armor-piercing and tracer ammunition—was finally sent to Rangoon from Manila on September 16, 1941, on the steamer *Iran.*

General Marshall, who had been cool to the program from the beginning, had been little help in obtaining the ammunition. The need for ammo for the P-40s had been explained to Marshall by Dr. Currie in a letter dated June 3. General Marshall's reply, dated June 16, to Currie stated that "A study of the ammunition requirements to meet the minimum needs of the Army and Navy, including certain special requirements, indicates the inability of the War Department to fulfill your requests."[2]

Similar difficulty was experienced in supplying the P-40s with spare parts. Since the Universal Trading Corporation had been very anxious to get the aircraft when offered, they were bought and shipped without spare parts. The Chinese purchasing agents were slow about placing orders for parts and the manufacturers were even slower to fill them. One of the problems was that Curtiss-Wright had ceased production of the P-40C. Pressure from T.V., Lauchlin Currie, Harry Hopkins, and finally from the Army resulted in the Chinese obtaining the remainder of the original promised equipment. But the Army authorities took no direct responsibility for helping to supply the spare parts for the planes that had been purchased by the Chinese—right up until Pearl Harbor. Even though the purchase had been approved by the White House, the Army continued to feel it was being imposed upon each time it was asked to help the Chinese with a supply problem.

Upon his return from Chungking in late February, Lauchlin Currie told the President that Chiang had requested that a "high-ranking aviation officer" be sent to assess the potential of the Chinese Air Force and the quality and tactics of the Japanese Air Force. The President passed on his approval of the mission through Currie to Secretary of War Henry Stimson. On March 29 the Secretary ordered General H. B. Clagget to proceed to China. Clagget was preparing to assume his duties as commanding general of the U. S. Army Air Forces in the Philippines when he received the order. He took General Harold George with him and they finally arrived in Chungking on May 17—arriving back in the Philippines on June 7. Clagget assumed the mission was a political one and instead of giving Chiang any objective criticism on the condition of the Chinese Air Force (which by then was practically nonexistent), he reported that the Air Force was in good shape. The only plus about the mission that Currie could find was a report to him by Commander Edward O. McDonnell, U.S.N., on Japanese effectiveness in the air and on the means of strengthening the Chinese Air Force by sending American aid through what he termed an "American Volunteer Group." This was the first mention by anyone of such an organization.

The recommendations from Clagget's mission were as follows:

1. That a direct service from Chungking to Manila be established by CNAC (China National Aviation Corporation), so as to familiarize both Chinese and American pilots with the route.

2. That a total of 100 members of the Chinese Air Force—pilots, navigators, bombardiers, radio and armament mechanics—should be sent for training in the United States, where they should concentrate upon heavy bombardment operations and be ready to fly American bombing planes to China.

3. That groups of 20 or 25 Chinese pilots should be sent in relays for a period of three months' training in the Philippines, where the United States Army Air Force would train them in medium bombardment.

4. That groups of 15 Chinese pursuit pilots, each forming one pursuit squadron, should be sent to the Philippines for training by the United States Army Air Corps after they had each received fifty hours' further instruction in China.

5. That graduates of Chinese primary training schools should be selected and sent to the United States for further instruction.

It was also requested that additional American air attachés should be permitted by the Chinese government to be stationed in China and accorded all the facilities that had been extended to General Clagget's mission.

It was a case of being in the right place at the right time again for Chennault. Commander McDonnell had first suggested the idea of organizing an American Volunteer Group in early 1940. That idea became the central part of the American Lend-Lease program to help China, although it was never formally expressed. Shortly after his return from Chungking, Currie went to Roosevelt to talk about the program for American volunteers. The President at that time gave Currie verbal assent to the idea of "loaning" reserve officers and enlisted men on a volunteer basis from the Army, Navy, and Marines to the Chinese, with the provision that the men could return to the various services later—if they could still pass the physical exam.[3]

Soon Bill Pawley got into the act with a demand that Curtiss-Wright pay him $4.5 million on the sale of the hundred P-40Cs to China. Pawley produced a signed contract that stated that he was to receive a 10 percent commission on all planes sold to China by Curtiss-Wright. It took the combined talents of T. V. Soong, Lauchlin Currie, and Tom Corcoran to settle the problem. Pawley was finally awarded $250,000 and an agreement that the Central Aircraft Manufacturing Company would assemble, test-fly, and service the P-40Bs in Burma. The agreement between the Chinese government and CAMCO was signed on April 15, with the stipulations that:

CAMCO was to engage the personnel for "three advanced training and instruction units," hiring them by contract and paying them.

CAMCO was to be reimbursed from a revolving fund of $700,000, which would be replenished when it fell below $250,000.

CAMCO was to furnish technical assistance for assembling, maintaining, and repairing equipment of the units, receive material shipped to Rangoon, and was to "send technical personnel to assist in operations of the 'training and instruction units.' "

CAMCO was to accept the instructions of the "American supervisor" of the units.

CAMCO was not allowed to break any laws of any country in which it operated. This new contract was signed by T. V. Soong and Bruce G. Leighton.

The contract form for CAMCO employees, as drawn up on April 15, provided that:

Employment was to be effective and salary begin when the employees reported at the port of embarkation; they were to continue for one year from the date of arrival at the port of entry into China (to be designated) and thereafter until terminated by either party on thirty days' notice.

The employee would receive travel expenses and five hundred dollars at the end of the contract. Employees were to receive a month's leave per year, six months' salary for total disability or death, and be dischargeable for various causes.

As a possible legal basis for the program, on May 31, Oscar Cox of OEM, Division of Defense Aid Reports, gave Currie the draft of an amendment that could be used to arrange to detail American Army, Navy, or Marine officers to China. The amendment, to an act of 1926, revised in 1935, allowed the President to detail such officers, on application, to assist the governments of the American hemisphere and the Philippines, simply by adding the word "China" to the list of governments. But Cox judged it would be better not to try to get it through Congress and to rely instead on the President's power as Commander in Chief of the armed forces. Roosevelt agreed that he had the authority.

On May 31 the State Department denied that American service pilots were being released to fight for China, but George Bookman of the Washington *Post* published a story on June 1 that stated that a Chinese recruiting agency had been set up in Washington and that American pilots who signed up for duty in China would not lose their citizenship. The War and Navy Departments also denied the arrangement.

The President issued verbal instructions to all the military bases in the country that civilian recruiting personnel were to be allowed to interview pilots and ground personnel for possible employment with CAMCO. Richard Aldworth, an agent for CAMCO, then toured these bases to interview and hire pilots. Anyone who signed up for duty in China was required to take out a $10,000 government life insurance policy.

The active recruiting of volunteers began in April after orders from Navy Secretary Knox and General Hap Arnold went out to all the military bases. Arnold was actually opposed to the plan but was told by Secretary of War Stimson to send the orders. These orders authorized the bearers of "certain letters" complete freedom to talk to all military personnel. Despite these orders, the commanders of the bases, Chennault said later, were appalled when civilians came to interview their personnel. The base commanders became enraged when they found out why the interviewers were really there— to steal experienced pilots. Several of the commanders angrily called Washington to demand that the interviewers leave—only to be told to go along with the project.

Aldworth was helped in the recruiting by Chennault's friend Skip Adair; Rutledge Irvine, a retired Navy commander; Harry Claiborne; and Seton L. Brown. They interviewed Marines at Quantico; Navy personnel at Norfolk and San Diego; and Army personnel at McDill, March, Mitchell, Langley, Hamilton, Eglin, Craig, Maxwell, Barksdale, and Randolph fields.

The contract called for volunteers "to manufacture, repair, and operate aircraft" at salaries ranging from $250 per month to $750—from technical, administrative ground personnel to pilots. Travel expenses would be paid by CAMCO, thirty days' leave a year would be given, and the recruits would be provided with quarters and given an additional thirty dollars per month for rations. By the beginning of May the recruiters had received a total of 243 applications—from which 18 pilots and 58 ground personnel were accepted. The medical personnel—7—were recruited by June 21; 55 administrative people were accepted by September; and by October 18 a total of 289 persons had been inducted into the program.

Meanwhile, the first group had already sailed on June 9 aboard a transport and the second contingent of 123 people left on July 10 on board the Dutch ship *Jaegersfontaine.* Currie suggested that the President order some protection for the ship, as about a hundred AVG pilots and mechanics would be aboard. Word was passed on to Secretary of the Navy Knox. The *Jaegersfontaine* was picked up off Hawaii by the U.S. cruisers *Salt Lake City* and *Northampton* and escorted until a Dutch cruiser took over near Australia.

Chennault was beginning to feel the excitement after the long months of desk work. His dream was beginning to come true and he couldn't wait to get started on the actual training program. On July 8 he flew from Washington to San Francisco and met with Aldworth and Tom Gentry—who was to be flight surgeon for the AVG—and inspected the *Jaegersfontaine* before she sailed. At 4 P.M. he took off on the China Clipper. Owen Lattimore, bound for China as political adviser, was a fellow passenger. As Chennault wrote of that late afternoon takeoff:

"For the first time in my battle against the Japanese . . . I had everything I needed to defeat them."

Six

By July 14, 1941, the United States consul at Rangoon reported that a total of sixty-eight P-40s had arrived and that thirty American airmen were about to arrive. Thirty-two of the Tomahawks were equipped with general aviation radios and only about half with machine guns. While these small general aviation radios might have been fine for flying a Piper Cub in the United States, they could not stand the strain of combat operations and repeatedly failed at critical times. The Chinese Aeronautical Commission received the shipment and negotiated with the British for the use of an airfield at Toungoo in Burma—166 miles from Rangoon by rail. Ten of the planes were assembled by mechanics from the Loiwing factory, who had been sent up to the field at Rangoon. It was closer to Toungoo than Loiwing and had better facilities for general aircraft maintenance.

The first group of thirty airmen arrived on July 28. They had been aboard an ancient Dutch freighter that had crept up the western side of the Malay Peninsula. They were under the command of Paul Frillman, a Lutheran minister who was fluent in Chinese. Chennault had first met Frillman in Hankow in 1937 and had suggested that he would be an excellent chaplain to the AVG. Frillman had already begun to earn his pay aboard the troopship that took the group from San Francisco via Australia to Rangoon, acting as liaison between the military and the noisy bunch of hard-drinking and irreverent fighter pilots. By the time they sailed into Rangoon Harbor he was a seasoned administrator. Chennault, William Pawley, and Pawley's brother Ed were waiting at the dock when the ship arrived in the suffocating heat and high humidity. Frillman later described the event:

"I don't suppose anyone could have called Chennault 'glamorous' to his face without being punched. But he was a vain man, and obviously relished making an impression. Like MacArthur, he had immense natural magnetism on which to base his public figure. That day on the docks he was wearing some slapdash adventurous costume as usual—mosquito boots, officer shirt with Chinese insignia, beat-up Air Force cap—which emphasized his gamecock look. Watching him for only a few minutes, anyone would get the impression of informality and lack of military pomp, plus a quick, sure air of decisive authority. I don't think any of the men on our ship had ever seen him before, and I looked down the rail where they were lined up, staring silently at him. I could see that, for the time being anyway, Chennault had them all in his pocket."

Chennault had a threefold task ahead of him: to ready the hot, humid, and bug-ridden base at Toungoo for fighter training and combat operation; to find enough spare parts to keep the P-40s flying; and to train the odd assortment of men to operate as a unit.

The intrusion of the Americans was a bit of a thorn in the side of the British—who had awarded Burma quasi-dominion status in 1937 after it had been annexed to British India in the nineteenth century. The British were doing all they could to avoid a war with Japan—having enough military problems with the Nazis in Africa, the Atlantic, and at home. They were trying to be as helpful to the Americans and the AVG as they could without intimidating the Japanese any more than they already had. Back in April, the British had told the Chinese, through T. V. Soong, that, while the AVG might assemble their planes at the recently completed but unmanned RAF Kyedaw Air Base, six miles from Toungoo, they could by no means engage in any combat training. Chennault, General P. T. Mow, and the Pawleys met with the British in Rangoon to try to resolve the issue. Present were the governor of Burma, Sir Reginald Hugh Dorman-Smith, his military commander, Lieutenant General D. K. MacLeod, and the senior air officer, Group Captain E. R. Manning. While both Dorman-Smith and MacLeod were quite willing to bend the rules a bit, Manning remained adamant that no such combat training or flying be permitted in his theater, probably because he feared that his command was being invaded by people over whom he might not have any control.

Peter Mow had a unique argument to offer in favor of the Americans being allowed to practice combat: that Japan had never formally declared war on China and therefore the Americans could not be considered belligerents and would not be violating any neutrality. It was no use. The Americans had to be content with the assembly of the aircraft and simple flight training until something could be worked out. Later in the fall the British relented and allowed the Americans to begin full combat training, provided they not use the base as a springboard to attack the Japanese.

The original plan had been to ship the Tomahawks to Kunming, where they would be assembled and made ready to attack the Japanese bombers expected to hit Chungking when the monsoons lifted in late September. But the red tape and wrangling in Washington and the late shipment of the P-40s made it necessary to carry out the assembly and flight training in Burma.

Besides, the Chinese had not got the runways and quarters ready at Kunming in time and the monsoon rains had turned the Kunming runways into a quagmire. At least at Toungoo there was a four-thousand-foot asphalt runway on which to train the pilots on the "hot" P-40s.

The question as to who was to control the activities of the AVG had been shuffled around for months. Originally, Currie had been guided by a memorandum from Commander McDonnell, who stated: "The American Volunteer Combat Unit in China should be commanded by an experienced American aviation officer accountable only to Chiang Kai-shek. The staff and key positions should be manned entirely by Americans. Colonel Chennault is the best available officer."

Apparently this view was also shared by the Generalissimo. On his return to China, Chennault went directly to Chungking for a series of meetings with the Gimo and Madame, who was head of the Chinese Aeronautical Commission. Also in attendance were General Mow, General Chow, and other military leaders of the Chinese Air Force. Finally it was agreed:

1. That the American Volunteer Group should be an independent unit within the Chinese Air Force. This was in accordance with the conditions laid down before the men and materials were released for the Group in Washington—under which the Group was not to be sent on any mission not fully approved by the Group commander.

2. That the AVG and the Chinese Air Force would cooperate on all matters, but in areas where the AVG was predominantly operating the Group commander would be the senior authority.

3. That all material coming in from the United States—Air Corps equipment and supplies—would go to the AVG.

Obviously, to the Chinese government, Chennault was the boss of the American Volunteer Group and it was clear that Currie, as aide to President Roosevelt, meant this to be so.

However, Chief of Staff General George Marshall—ever the political strategist—had no intention of letting any air units commanded by American civilians, whether Chinese or not, get out from under his control. In a letter of July 15 to Currie, which set up the Chinese pilot training program, Marshall added certain provisions that referred only to the American Volunteer Group, not to pilot training.

"It is recommended that State Department action be initiated to secure, first, guarantees from the Chinese Government which will insure that the American Volunteer Air Unit is commanded and staffed by experienced American aviators; and second, the Chinese Government to agree that the Chief of the American Air Mission to China will be the sole judge of the readiness for combat of the American Volunteer Air Unit."[1]

The combat pilot training program for Chinese pilots had been approved by the President on July 2, with the added provision, desired by General Marshall on July 15 but in a slightly different form, that the AVG be "commanded and staffed by experienced American aviators, and that the Chinese Government agree that the readiness for combat of the AVG be determined by the appropriate American Government representative."

This was sent to T. V. Soong on July 23, with the added statement that the proviso would be taken up through diplomatic channels. In this way the AVG program was linked directly with the Lend-Lease program by Marshall and the other authorities involved.

The State Department, having been asked by Marshall for its opinion, released an unsigned memorandum on August 5 suggesting that guarantees be sought "by process of direct conference between appropriate authorized representatives" of the respective services, and stating that it would not be "appropriate or practicable" to ask the Chinese government formally to agree that the chief of the American Air Mission be the sole judge of combat readiness. Instead, this precaution should be achieved by "conference, continuous cooperation, and effective liaison." These matters might be taken up by General John Magruder, head of the Military Mission, answering directly to General Douglas MacArthur in the Philippines—and from there, obviously, to Marshall.

On August 6, Currie informed Marshall of this State Department view. "Will you let me know if this suggestion is satisfactory? I will then take up with the appropriate officers in your department the question of the initiation and prosecution of the project."

On August 30, Marshall held out for his original stipulation that assurances be obtained from the Chinese military that: (1) readiness of the AVG for combat should be judged solely by the chief of the American Military Mission or another mission specifically designated; (2) the AVG should be commanded and staffed by experienced American aviators. Magruder would be instructed to discuss this with the Chinese to be sure no safeguards were lacking.[2]

Chennault's authority was already being limited—even before the AVG was fully operational. Military observers of the American Military Mission in Chungking would watch him—and the AVG—like hawks.

The second contingent of men arrived in Rangoon on August 15 while Chennault was in Chungking meeting with members of the Chinese Air Force, the Generalissimo and Madame, Donald, Barrett, and McHugh. The Japanese had begun to hit Chungking with a steady stream of bombing attacks. It was the worst bombing Chennault had seen in a little over four years in the Far East. Apparently the Japanese were using the wartime capital as a practice exercise for their graduating bomber crews. Wave after wave of bombers—some escorted by fighter aircraft—swept over the battered city from dawn to dusk. It was necessary for Chennault to take a Yangtze ferry from the airfield to the city and there were many times when he was caught in midriver during a raid. There was nothing he could do but hang on until the ferry hit shore. Whenever the air raid sirens sounded the entire population would run for cover. They had been blasted and pounded for so long and so hard that they now knew the true meaning of bombardment. Hundreds of thousands of people had been killed so far and the bombings threatened to become worse as the monsoon rains lessened. There were no Chinese planes to oppose them and Chennault contained his seething rage as best he could while the bombers calmly banked over the city after releasing their loads. All he could do was tell Chiang and Madame that the day of retribution was coming—if they could just hold on a while longer. Madame seemed to believe him. The Gimo—with all his other military problems—did not appear as confident.

On August 21, Chennault finally managed to get back to Toungoo—via a CNAC flight to Rangoon and then by a twin-engine Beechcraft to the jungle base. The ground crews and pilots had been sweating and stewing in the heat and humidity and were all in a foul mood. Toungoo, a shabby little Burmese town alongside a railroad track and bordering the Sittang River, was lined with the corrugated tin-roofed shops of Chinese and Indian merchants. Except for a dirt road—which alternated between being mud and dust—down the center of the town, Toungoo was surrounded by steamy jungles and teak plantations. The heat soared over 100 degrees at noon and the humidity on most August days was stifling. It was literally like living in a goldfish bowl filled with warm water.

The British had recently completed barracks of solid teak and they were well constructed, but there were no screens and at night all sorts of insects flew in. Burmese cooks served up food that was almost indigestible for Americans. On most days there was some species of warm fish and rice for breakfast—hardly what the Americans were used to. A warm rain fell for hours each day and the entire field and town became a sea of sticky mud. The electricity for the camp was intermittent and usually went off at night when the men wanted to play cards or read.

The pilots were about equally divided between Navy and Army Air Corps, with a few Marines thrown in. They had been told that they were to train in China and were disgusted when they found they were to train and fly in this Burmese pesthole. Only a few P-40Bs had been assembled and most of the men had not had the opportunity to fly them yet. Although a number of the men had flown fighters—some for the Army and others on Navy carriers— the great majority of them had twin-engine experience and a few were ex-Navy flying boat pilots; most had had no time in the P-40. The mechanics discovered that the P-40s had no bomb racks, no facilities for attaching belly tanks, and no gunsights. They were discouraged about the prospects of being able to install this equipment. There were no spare parts available and no indication they would get any soon. Since arriving at Toungoo, the ground personnel and the pilots had been hanging around the barracks, drinking too much, and griping almost constantly. Frillman had done what he could to maintain discipline but he did not have the rank or authority to enforce anything. Old-timers like Boatner Carney did what they could to perk up morale, but nothing seemed to help. They were all waiting for Chennault to get back from Chungking.

When he arrived on the twenty-first he found morale at a new low and was immediately handed resignations from five pilots and several ground crewmen—all wanting to return to the States and citing misrepresentation as the reason. To forestall a mutiny, Chennault sensibly accepted, signed the resignations, and sent the men packing. He then called for a meeting of all personnel. Reverting to his old Army Air Corps days, he became a hard-nosed commanding officer. With his battered face chiseled in anger, he reminded the rest of the men that there were provisions in their contracts for fines and dishonorable discharges for failure to carry out their duties. He said that all pilots would take sixty hours of flight training beginning immediately and everyone would attend ground classes—two courses of seventy-two hours each—beginning the following morning at 6 A.M. Staring down the disgruntled volunteers with his snapping black eyes, Chennault told them there would be calisthenics, a regular routine, and fines for misbehavior. Meals would be served at regular hours and the men would be fined for being late for anything. They were to shape up. There was a sullen silence as they filed out of the hall, but no one had any doubt who was in charge.

The RAF had abandoned Toungoo during the rainy season—May, June, July, and August—because the British felt that Europeans could not survive the jungle monsoons. They were close to being right. It is doubtful that, without the iron will of Chennault, anyone could have driven the young Americans to become a fighting force of any kind. Where mad dogs and Englishmen might have failed, several hundred American youngsters succeeded.

The P-40C was not the most ideal fighter plane to fly in such jungle conditions. It was heavy and unwieldy. It landed at 100 miles per hour and scared the hell out of most of the pilots at first. Because of its weight, it was an unforgiving craft and tended to fall out of a stall like a brick. The War Department, with uncharacteristic efficiency, had supplied Chennault with a secret document on the difficulties likely to occur in the operation of the P-40. It was dated August 1, 1941, and was sent to him from Lieutenant Colonel J. S. Winslow, chief of the Military Attaché Section. It was hardly reassuring—in light of the weather, inexperienced pilots, and a complete lack of spare parts. It read:

Subject: Difficulties Likely to Occur in P-40 Airplanes
To: Military Attaché,
           American Embassy,
           Chungking, China

1. Please make the following data available to Colonel Chennault. They have been compiled at the request of Mr. Lauchlin Currie.

2. The following are the known difficulties which may occur in the P-40 airplanes, with any remedies which may have been used to correct them.

*a. It has been reported that the personnel of British assembly stations in Africa have been very lax in their work. This was partially due to improper instruction, lack of enthusiasm for American-made airplanes, and not having the proper tools or instruction manuals.

The planes when first shipped from America arrived in Africa without assembly or maintenance instructions and consequently were assembled more or less haphazardly.

The men working in the assembly plant did not care particularly about working on American-made planes and therefore paid little attention to details, such as removing heavy protective grease from pulleys, solenoids, and particularly guns; so that when assembled there were many minor malfunctions.

American-size tools were lacking for a long period and this hindered the assembly considerably.

b. The ferrying personnel that were sent to the assembly station were pilots with little experience, some having only 150 to 200 hours, and to be given an airplane like the P-40 to fly without very much ground instruction, resulted in many accidents, which gave the airplane a bad name. Consequently, some British pilots even refused to fly them. This was finally straightened out after some of the planes were put into operation in squadrons with more experienced pilots, who after a short time admitted the airplane was better than the Hurricane in nearly all respects.

The report went on to list difficulties found in engine operation—the most serious being bearings that tended to freeze when excessive manifold pressures and high r.p.m.'s were used at low altitudes and a tendency for the engine to cut out at altitudes from 15,000 to 25,000 feet when the throttles were opened to full.

Difficulties had cropped up with the machine guns, which had not been properly adjusted when leaving the factory, such as improper head space. Some synchronizers were found to be faultily shimmed at the factory. Most of the other problems were minor, but there were a lot of them.

Tight-lipped, Chennault finished reading the letter, then folded it and slipped it into the top drawer of his desk. There was little sense in showing this to the mechanics. He would discuss it with his line chief and let him pass the word down as he saw fit. Morale was low enough as it was.

Seven

As the first September days of 1941 arrived, matters settled down a bit and training began in earnest. CAMCO hired a test pilot named Byron Glover to try out the P-40s as soon as they had been assembled at Rangoon. When Glover finished testing a plane at Mingaladon Airfield in Rangoon he would telephone Chennault at Toungoo and a pilot would be sent by train to pick up the plane and fly it to the jungle base.

The monsoon was slowly moving back down south and the field dried up a little more with each passing day. Chennault insisted on changing cooks after sampling the swill the Burmese turned out and several Chinese restaurant cooks were hired away from local establishments—a great improvement in the meals. The men protested bitterly at first at the stringent regulations on the use of vehicles. There were only a few available and they were to be restricted to use by the top officers. Chennault—knowing the men were badly in need of physical exercise—didn't want them riding to town in cars. A stock of cheap Japanese bicycles was discovered in a store in Toungoo and from that time on bicycle races to and from town were common. There were daily calisthenics, with Chaplain Paul Frillman in charge, and on dry afternoons there were softball games—sometimes with Chennault pitching. As the weeks wore on the men—who had been soft, pale, and overweight after the months at sea and loafing about Toungoo—became tanned, hard, and slimmed down. All felt better and they worked hard at classes and flying. In the evening many of them went into town, where they looked into the small shops that sold leather goods, semiprecious stones, and the excellent cashew nuts of the area. When not flying or in class, others biked out to the teak plantation to watch elephants moving the huge logs about. However, most pilots preferred to stay at the field at night and either drink in the small thatched bar or play cards. Chennault would join them for poker or a game of cribbage—though he did not drink with them—and enjoyed the easy banter of his men. They called him "Colonel" or "Sir."

Many of the young pilots had been in awe of him. His age, his lined face, and his reputation had made them timid and uneasy in his presence and it was not until they saw him on the ballfield or at the card table in the evenings that they began to relax in his presence. A few never did warm up to him personally, however—referring to him as "a washed-out ex-Army captain that had been hiding out in China all these years." Usually they were ones who did not make the grade in training and later resigned. Pilots who did not measure up in flight training or who resigned for personal reasons were given dishonorable discharges from the Group.

In the first few months of training twenty-three men resigned—not only pilots but ground personnel as well. Some were fired for insubordination, drinking too much, or failing to fulfill their duties. Some pilots could not or did not want to fly the P-40s. Some could not adjust to the climate or the life in a strange land. Some were simply afraid of combat. Others missed their homeland and families. Chennault's feelings were summed up in a letter to the Navy requested by Lauchlin Currie. Apparently word had reached the President about resignations and he wanted documentation.

                                                        Toungoo, Burma
                                                        21 October 1941

The Chief of Naval Operations
The Navy Department
Washington, D.C., USA

Sir:

The enclosed forms cannot, unfortunately, tell the precise story behind the broken contracts of the men who have left the Group. Generally speaking, these fall into two classes. The first, and in my opinion the smaller class, is made up of men either too sanguine or too shortsighted to envisage the conditions of the service for which they were volunteering, although these were carefully explained to them. On their arrival in Burma, such men lost morale so completely that they became worthless, and I was glad to let them go. It would hardly be necessary for me to point out that this loss of morale in unfamiliar surroundings seriously reflects on these men's military usefulness.

As for the second class, in which I would include all the more intelligent contract-breakers, and especially the pilots, their motives appear to me to have been more various but generally discreditable. Several are believed by me, on good evidence, to have used the AVG as an avenue of escape from military service at home. At least one, on his own testimony, enlisted with the AVG in order to pay his debts, and appears to have returned home as soon as he had accumulated sufficient cash to relieve his embarrassment. Still others, when finally faced with the prospect of actual combat, could not bring themselves up to scratch.

Among the men who have broken their contracts with us, there are, of course, one or two honestly moved by family troubles or ill health. But everyone who joined the AVG was quite clearly told what he was joining, and what the service would be like; so that after making all allowances it is hard to find excuses for men who took AVG salaries, when they found the venture not wholly to their tastes.

Very sincerely yours,
C. L. Chennault

In his daily training classes at Toungoo Chennault was at last able to utilize some of the vast store of information he had gathered on the Japanese fighter and bomber tactics he had observed for years. He had been taking detailed notes on both since the days of the first Shanghai bombings and while at Kunming had managed to obtain Japanese flight and staff manuals. These he had translated into English by the Chinese Air Force. In addition he had carefully noted all the details of each captured Japanese bomber and fighter plane. Now he went over each detail carefully on a blackboard. He had personally flight-tested two captured fighters and was impressed with their performance. Unlike many Stateside Air Force officers who thought the Japanese built cheap, flimsy aircraft, Chennault was fully aware that their first-line fighters and bombers were deadly efficient machines and in many cases far superior to American equipment.

In the muggy heat of afternoon, when flying was impossible because of the buildup of clouds and high thermal currents, he taught his classes of young pilots the strengths and weaknesses of each type of enemy aircraft. He went over and over the vulnerable spots on each plane and would circle the areas and then erase them. Then he would ask a pilot to come up and redraw the areas. He went over the arcs of fire of each enemy plane and how best to avoid them. He described the formations of bombers that had attacked Shanghai, Hankow, Chungking, and Kunming and explained how they would fly in a loose formation to lure fighters into range, then suddenly tighten up to give all their gunners a concentrated field of fire. He described how a single fighter would drop from a three-plane element in order to draw an enemy away from the others—and then how the other two would dive on the attacker's tail.

Pilots were awakened each morning at 5 A.M. and after a light breakfast were sent aloft in the still, cool air to engage in hour-and-a-half dogfights. Chennault, in shorts, a short-sleeved shirt, and wearing a pith helmet, would climb into a rickety bamboo control tower. There, with a pair of binoculars in one hand and a microphone in the other, he would instruct the pilots as they dove, rolled, and climbed in the morning sky. A secretary, ex-Navy man

Tom Trumble, employed by CAMCO because of his shorthand and typing skills, would take down all Chennault said, to be used later in classes.

Many of the pilots were leery about the P-40. Scuttlebutt in the States had it that the plane was a pilot-killer and hard to handle at low speeds. To make matters worse, almost none had flown one, so it was easy to find oneself believing the Stateside rumors—which were not true. All fighter planes had their detractors. The Republic P-47, or "jug," was also considered a killer at low altitudes when an engine failed, but then all such aircraft were danger-ous under such conditions. The P-39 Bell Airacobra was thought to tumble over and over—though it was difficult to find an eyewitness to such a manuever. Most of the pilots recruited had been either multi-engine pilots or had flown dive bombers. By the time these youngsters began flying the P-40B at Toungoo the plane had already been relegated to the status of a training plane at home. The P-40 was so obsolete that it was being used in secondary theaters of war, such as Libya. The Curtiss-Wright plant was turning out the P-40E and F. The B model was a low-wing, single-seater fighter made of aluminum and steel with a 12-cylinder, liquid-cooled Allison engine, rated at 1,040 h.p. It had a pointed spinner ahead of the three-bladed electrically controlled propeller. It was an extremely heavy plane—owing mostly to two heavy slabs of armorplate that protected the pilot's back and head from the rear. The armament consisted of six machine guns—two heavy .50-caliber guns mounted on the front of the fuselage and synchronized to fire through the whirling propeller and four .30-caliber machine guns mounted in the wings. All were sighted to converge their fire at 250 yards. It was a lot of firepower compared to the Japanese planes, which had much lighter machine guns and therefore less firing range. Loaded with gasoline and ammunition, the P-40B had a top speed of about 300 m.p.h. at 10,000 feet and about fifteen miles per hour less at 20,000 feet. The Allison engine was not super-charged and the P-40 ceiling—in Burma at least—was between 25,000 and 30,000 feet. The Tomahawk—the model name given it at the plant—had a stalling speed of 87 m.p.h. and landed at 100 m.p.h. It was the landing speed that gave most pilots trouble—especially on the hot, black asphalt of the 4,000-foot runway. The heat formed a cushion close to the asphalt and it was difficult to get the speeding plane down before running out of strip. As a result many of the pilots either dropped the plane in from too much height, causing landing-gear damage, or tried to land it tail up, resulting in ground loops. Its chief advantage was that its weight gave it an incredible diving speed in excess of 500 m.p.h., making it easy for the pilots to dive away from pursuing Japanese aircraft. In addition, the sturdy construction and fire-power—plus its protection for the pilot—made it a good plane for the job for which it was chosen. It might have been obsolete for any other theater of war, but because of the peculiar set of circumstances—enemy planes and jungle terrain—it turned out to be a good fighter plane for the time it was used in Burma.

When the flying sessions were over for the day it was back to the chalk and blackboard for the pilots. Chennault stressed teamwork above everything else.

"In combat you are part of a team," he said over and over in the muggy heat of the classroom. His teaching was based on the idea that two planes fighting together were far more effective than three or four planes fighting alone. Two fighter planes, boring in on an enemy, would have twelve guns firing instead of six. Two planes together would allow one plane to dive in and fire while the other could drop back and watch the first one's tail in case of enemy fighter attack.

Using the Japanese flight manuals he had had translated, he showed the pilots the battle plans the Japanese had for both bombers and fighters. He told them Japanese pilots were superbly trained but lacked initiative when it came to improvising on their own.

"They have been drilled for hundreds of hours in flying precise formations and rehearsing set tactics for each situation they may encounter," he said. "Japanese pilots fly by the book, and these are the books they use. Study them and you will always be one step ahead of the enemy.

"Bombers will hold their formations until they are all shot down. Fighters always try the same tricks over and over again. God help the American pilot who tries to fight them according to their plans. The object of our tactics is to break up their formations and make them fight according to our style," Chennault instructed. "Once the Japanese are forced to deviate from their plan they are in trouble. Their rigid air discipline can be used as a powerful weapon against them."

He went on to explain to them how the P-40 and their flying skills could be used against the Japanese.

"You must use the strong points of your equipment against the weak points of the enemy," he said. "Each type of plane has its own strength and weakness. The pilot who can turn his advantage against the enemy's weakness will win every time. You can count on a higher top speed, faster dive, and superior firepower. The Jap fighters have a higher rate of climb, higher ceiling, and better maneuverability. They can turn on a dime and climb almost straight up. If they get you into a turning combat they're deadly.

"Use your speed and diving power to make a pass, shoot, and break away. Close your range, fire, and dive away. Never stay within range of the Jap's defensive firepower any longer than you need to deliver an accurate burst. You need to sharpen your shooting eye. Nobody ever gets too good at gunnery. The more Japs you get with your first burst, the fewer there are to jump you later. Accurate fire saves ammunition. Your plane carries a limited number of bullets. There is nothing worse than finding yourself in a fight with empty guns.

"Fight in pairs," he would say to the jammed classroom in the jungle shack. "Make every bullet count. Never try to get all the Japanese in one pass. Hit hard. Break clean. And get in position for another pass. Keep looking around . . . follow them home. They are usually low on ammunition and gas when they break off and head for home. If they maneuver or open full throttle they will not get back.

"All Japanese pilots are good gunners," Chennault warned. "They use deflection shots almost exclusively. However, their guns don't have the range or destructive power of American aerial guns. The Japanese 20-mm. cannon is heavier than any of the guns we carry out here, but it lacks the range of our .50-caliber guns due to a low muzzle velocity. Japanese aerial armament is generally not effective at a range of over two hundred yards."[1]

Into the last weeks of October, pilots practiced until they began to get the feel of their olive-drab fighter planes. Not every day, however, was a triumph. On one day in early November seven P-40s were damaged through improper landings, accidents while taxiing, ground loops, and tire blowouts. When an eighth plane was damaged by a mechanic riding a bicycle Chennault, in disgust, called a halt to the day's flying.

The spare-part problem became a nightmare. Ground crews did their best to improvise parts but some parts were beyond them. Tail-wheel tires, electric switches, radio tubes, gun solenoids, oxygen bottles, carburetors, spark plugs, batteries—all had to be sent from the States or scrounged from other sources in the Far East. Supply was to be a problem for Chennault during his entire professional life in the Orient, but at this moment it was almost literally a matter of life and death.

By this time Joseph Alsop had become actively involved in the war. With his Groton and Harvard background and as a distant cousin of President Roosevelt, he had many friends in high places. Leaving his job as columnist for the North American Newspaper Alliance, he had been sent to India with a Navy mission, then had resigned from the Navy and had managed to get himself hired by CAMCO and to join Chennault as an aide—with no military rank. A tireless worker with all sorts of connections to the military as well as to the countless correspondents then moving about the world, Alsop was a friend in need to the AVG. He was able to help set up a workable office system, with the help of Tom Trumble, who had been a yeoman first class in the Navy and understood the Navy's system of filing.

When the spare-parts problem became acute Alsop volunteered to try to get parts from the British in Rangoon and Singapore. Air Chief Marshal Robert Brooke-Popham and his aide, Air Vice Marshal Pulford, were helpful, offering Chennault tire wheels from the Brewster Buffalos, but they would not fit. Other parts they did not have. CAMCO agents and representatives of the AVG were all over the Far East trying to get parts for the P-40s. Chennault bombarded CAMCO and Washington with requests for parts and Lauchlin Currie was doing his best to get them shipped. Gunsights were a problem, as the reflector sight that came with the P-40s were too bulky for the quick sighting required by Chennault's special training. They could not be adjusted because the tools and spare parts for them had never been sent from the States. One of the engineering officers, Charlie Mott, using the tools at hand, modified the sights until the pilots were able to aim them in split seconds. The fighter planes were dragged about by ground crews until they were in the target revetments—U-shaped earthen shelters—with their tails propped up. Then all six machine guns were sighted in and fired until their murderous fire was concentrated on the target 250 yards away. Chennault, observing from a truck nearby, smiled grimly as the .30- and .50-caliber slugs spewed mud and dirt high in the air above the targets.

Harvey Greenlaw had arrived at Toungoo and Chennault, remembering his long service in China and his knowledge of the land and its people, made him executive officer of the Group. Harvey had brought his wife Olga, an attractive, shapely brunette, with him and they set up house in Toungoo. Chennault was leery of having an American woman that close to a combat base—especially one who had no official duty with the Group. Finally, at the urging of both Harvey and Olga, he condescended to make her Group war diary statistician. Not the only woman at the base, she was the only one with time on her hands. Two American nurses who had been employed by CAMCO had arrived the month before the Greenlaws. They were Jo Stewart of Dallas, Texas, and Emma Foster of State College, Pennsylvania. Both were under the command of Chief Flight Surgeon Dr. Tom Gentry. "Red" Foster was a very tall, redheaded girl with bright blue eyes and a mass of freckles, while Jo Stewart was considerably older—a matronly gray-haired woman whom most of the personnel called "Mrs. Stewart." They, Gentry, and two other American doctors—Sam Prevo and L. J. Richards—plus a Chinese doctor, C. V. Lee, comprised the medical staff. E. W. Bruce was the dental surgeon.

Also assisting Chennault at headquarters was Boatner Carney, his long-time friend and pilot instructor from Kunming days. John Williams was named commanding officer for the Kunming detachment and left shortly for that city. It had been planned from the start to base the AVG in Kunming, but the construction of hostels, offices, hangars, and other repair facilities, plus hard-coated runways, was continually being delayed. Madame Chiang promised Chennault they would be completed shortly and that he could soon move the entire Group. It was not as simple as it sounded. She was attempting to expedite the building program from Chungking but, with constant bombardment and her many other problems of state, things were progressing slowly.

On October 31, disgusted with the slowness of construction at the base in Kunming, Chennault wrote one of his periodic progress reports to Madame Chiang. He pointed out that nearly two months earlier he had been promised it would only take ninety days to complete the work and he could then move the AVG there. He reminded her that no wiring had been installed at the site and no dugouts had been constructed for safety in case of air raids. (Madame had inquired a short time before about when he could be expected to move the three squadrons there. She was anxious to have him try to stop the incessant bombing of Chungking and Kunming.)

He reminded her that the temporary quarters at the university near the airfield, which they would have to occupy if they moved now, would be a conspicuous target for the Japanese planes. In hopes that she could build a fire under the Chinese construction crews and other workmen, he told her there was also discouraging news about the progress of the radio and airplane reporting nets. Owing to nondelivery of essential parts, the airplane reporting net would not be fully completed for another two months. The command net, however, could be put in working order in three weeks.

Chennault finally managed to get a personal plane from Chungking—a battered twin-engine Beechcraft that was put in flying condition by the mechanics at Toungoo. One of the props was five inches shorter than the other, but spare parts were so scarce that the plane was flown with it anyway. Now he had some mobility. Before, he had been at the mercy of CNAC schedules when he had to fly to Kunming or Chungking. He was flown alternately by a handful of pilots, including Bert Christman, Bob Little, Ed Goyette, and Ben Foshee.

The P-40s were simply olive-drab-painted fighter planes with few distinguishing characteristics. One evening a group of the pilots asked Chennault what he thought of painting leering sharks' mouths on the noses of the planes. In Rangoon, Erik Shilling, Lacy Mangleburg, and George McMillan had got a magazine, the *Illustrated India Weekly*, in which was an illustration of a P-40 in North Africa painted with the sharks' teeth. The men were enthusiastic and wanted to see how they would look on their planes. Chennault saw no harm in the idea and thought it might aid morale. The mechanics painted a leering tiger shark grin, complete with a baleful eye, on each plane.[2]

Security was a constant problem. The Toungoo air base was technically under British command but there was constant friction between the military and the civilian government of Burma. No American guards were permitted and native Burmese swarmed over the base at all hours of the day. Since it was suspected that many of them—particularly a sect of yellow-robed monks —were Japanese agents, it was necessary to get some sort of protection. Chennault found it necessary to shoo Burmese from the doorway of his office, where they stood watching him at work. The British finally assigned armed Gurkha guards to the base and that settled the problem.

The training flights took their toll as the days crawled past. Jack Armstrong of Hutchinson, Kansas, was the first pilot killed when his plane collided in midair with one flown by Gil Bright. Bright bailed out and was not badly hurt. Max Hammer of Cairo, Illinois, died when he became lost in a monsoon over Toungoo and crashed into a mountain. Pete Atkinson of Martinsburg, West Virginia, was killed when the propeller governor failed on his

P-40 and he plowed into the ground after a screaming dive at over 700 m.p.h. Chaplain Paul Frillman conducted the funerals and tried his best to raise the dampened spirits of the pilots and ground crews alike.

Paperwork was taking up most of Chennault's time as a commander, and he found himself at his desk most of the day. He worked far into the night on correspondence with John Williams in Kunming and with Madame Chiang, trying to settle the interminable problems of red tape between the Group and the British. Group Captain Manning was particularly irritating as he was a stickler for detail and did things "by the book." Nothing could be done physically to alter conditions at the base under the contract the AVG had with the British, and no action could be taken without written permission from Manning. Sighting-in and firing the machine guns on the fighter planes was a ticklish subject with him as he considered firing the guns the next thing to entering into combat with the Japanese—unthinkable under RAF peacetime regulations. He refused to give Chennault the Royal Air Force Code Book and as a result the AVG was never in contact with the RAF by radio during the five months it operated out of Toungoo. This forced Chennault to rely on telegraph lines or long-distance public telephones when attempting to contact British authorities—uncertain communication at best and certainly unsatisfactory for sending any classified messages.

Information gleaned from correspondents, such as Ed Mowrer and Vincent Sheean, who had completed a tour of Singapore, Bangkok, Rangoon and Toungoo and had stopped over to visit with Chennault and their longtime associate Joe Alsop, indicated that all was not sweetness and light within the British ranks. The newsmen also brought unofficial reports of developments in Indochina and Thailand. Over drinks in Chennault's quarters they reported that, according to combined intelligence—established in Singapore by Americans, British, Chinese, and Dutch—the Japanese were making obvious preparations for an invasion of Yunnan from northern Indochina. About nine hundred trucks were reported to have been landed at Haiphong and large quantities of steel rails—obviously intended to bridge the gap in the Hanoi–Kunming Railroad, torn up by the Chinese—had been offloaded and concentrated at Lao-kai. Reports had it that from 18,000 to 30,000 new Japanese troops had been sent into the region. Both Mowrer and Sheean were of the opinion that Thailand would fold up immediately if attacked. It seemed the young Thais wanted to fight but they had no weapons and a fifth column had been established by one of the Thai princes.

As far as British strength in Singapore was concerned, reports were that it was garrisoned by a mixed force of 50,000 troops. One Indian Army corps was stationed to the northwest, guarding the land approaches to the Malay Peninsula, and about 18,000 Australian troops occupied the Sultanate of Johore, against which lay Singapore Island. It was estimated that perhaps 6,000 British troops were in the British crown colony. Naval strength was estimated at practically nothing and the rumor was that the base was being kept in the hope that the U. S. Navy would eventually occupy it.

Neither correspondent was able to supply much information on British air strength. Although the only field they had visited was well supplied with Brewster Buffalos and Lockheed Hudson bombers, they had the feeling that air strength was weak. The most discouraging information concerned the lack of cooperation on the part of the British military and the colonial government. Organization in Singapore was confused, they reported. Admiral Sir Geoffrey Leighton, commander-in-chief of the China Squadron, was in command of all British vessels between the east coast of Africa and the west coast of North America; Lieutenant General Percival had control of all troops east of India; Air Vice Marshal Pulford had a tenuous control over the Air Force in India as well as Burma and Malaysia; and Sir Robert Brooke-Popham was technically commander in chief of the Far East. The areas of command were vague and in many cases overlapped. Leighton's and Brooke-Popham's feuding had become rather public knowledge in military circles. (Leighton referred to Brooke-Popham as "Old Pop-off" because of his habit of traveling continuously throughout his command in a plushed-up Blenheim bomber.) Rumor also had it that Admiral Thomas C. Hart, the U.S. commander in chief of the Asiatic Fleet, had not got on well with Brooke-Popham at their meeting in Manila and had been saying so ever since. The scuttlebutt was that Brooke-Popham was to be replaced. This was unpleasant news to Chennault, as he *had* got on well with the man. There were also reports that Prime Minister John Curtin was demanding that all Australians in the RAF be separated from it and attached to the new Australian RAF. This pointed to the possibility of more confusion, which would result in mixed squadrons and of staffs like Group Captain Manning's.

Both correspondents were pessimistic about the news at home. They talked about confusion and lack of direction in Washington, indicating that America was by no means planning to enter a war in the Pacific. While both admitted to some improvement in defense production, they were not optimistic on foreign policy. Mowrer said he knew for a fact that after the inner Cabinet and all the principal White House advisers had fully approved the midsummer speech in which the President took a strong line on the Far Eastern question, Secretary of State Cordell Hull's entourage of appeasers had worked on him so successfully that Hull spent the whole morning before the speech was delivered pleading with the President to water it down.

Mowrer had some disquieting things to say about General Magruder and the China Mission. He had just come over on the Pan Am Clipper with Magruder and said he had asked him what he thought of releasing bombers to Chennault and the Chinese Air Force. According to Mowrer, Magruder argued that only a few bombers were available to China, that a few bombers could not materially affect the war's outcome, and that release of them might rouse Japan to further aggression. He also said that, as the bombers would need American pilots, their release would not fit into the "defensive theory" of American policy. Pursuit planes, he said, were permissible as defense, but bombers, as offense, were questionable to say the least. The evening broke up in the small hours. Both correspondents were due to leave the next day for Rangoon and from there on to Chungking.

By late November the Group was organized into three squadrons on a combat basis. The 1st Squadron was composed mostly of ex-Army pilots and was headed by Squadron Leader Robert J. Sandell of San Antonio, Texas. He was a small, dark, and wiry pilot who had spent most of his flying time in aerobatics. This squadron was named the "Adam and Eves" and on each plane was painted a large apple around which Adam chased Eve.

The 2nd Squadron was named the "Panda Bears" and was commanded by Jack Newkirk, a twenty-seven-year-old fighter pilot from Scarsdale, New York. No bears were painted on their planes but Bert Christman painted a caricature of each pilot.

The 3rd Squadron was composed of Army, Navy, and Marine pilots and was named "Hell's Angels." It was led by Arvid ("Oley") Olson, a tall, thin, twenty-five-year-old from Los Angeles, California. Each of their planes carried a painting of a nude red angel in a different pose.

Chennault, watching them dive and roll in the late autumn skies over the jungle base, felt they were ready for combat. If all went well they would be transferred to Kunming in a few weeks and he could ambush the Japanese bombers that were daily blasting Chungking into crumbling ruins.

That afternoon a radioman handed him a dispatch that had just come in from RAF headquarters in Rangoon. It was dated December 8, 1941—Pearl Harbor, Hawaii.

Eight

The AVG went on a war footing immediately after receiving the news of the Japanese attack on Pearl Harbor. Gas masks, guns, and steel helmets were assigned to ground personnel and at 9:45 A.M. that day Chennault issued orders that were posted on the bulletin board.

> F.A.V.G.
> Point "A," Burma
> 8 December 1941
> 0945 o'clock

FIELD ORDERS)
                :
NUMBER 2.   )

MAPS:

1. (a) 1. JAPAN has declared war on the UNITED STATES and GREAT BRITAIN.

2. This command will be on the alert twenty-four (24) hours daily and be prepared to defy hostile operations of the enemy.

    (a) The 3rd Squadron will constitute the assault echelon.

    (b) The 2nd Squadron will constitute the support echelon.

    (c) The 1st Squadron will constitute the reserve echelon.

3. X. (1) Alert ships will be fully armed and loaded.

       (2) Side-arms will be carried by all members of this command.

> C. L. Chennault[1]

It was followed by a memorandum signed by Harvey Greenlaw for the commanding officer.

Memorandum to: All concerned:

1. No member of this command will leave the Post without permission from the commanding officer.

2. In case of air raid alarms, administrative and operations personnel will gather all important documents and remove them to a place of safety. In case of a normal alarm, clerical personnel will repair to the main road, taking the first transportation to come along. In case of an urgent alarm, personnel will clear building and repair to the jungle, lying down flat, utilizing whatever shelter may be available.
3. Strict watch will be kept for enemy parachute troops at all times.

On December 9, Chennault ordered pilot Erik Shilling to take a photo reconnaissance plane over Japanese-occupied Bangkok. Shilling, a blond, blue-eyed pilot from Washington, D.C., was an excellent flier and a nut about mechanics. He had experimented with his own P-40—each pilot was assigned his own plane—until it could fly fifteen to eighteen miles an hour faster than the rest. As a result, when Chennault was loaned an aerial camera from the RAF, Shilling's plane was the logical choice to carry it. Shilling had cut away a section of the baggage compartment behind the pilot's compartment and mounted the camera there. Because the P-40 was a low-wing fighter, Shilling could not see his target to photograph it. It was necessary to flip the fighter into a vertical bank, then level out again before taking a photo. Shilling was escorted by pilots Ed Rector and Bert Christman, both in fully armed fighters. They flew to Tavoy, an RAF base on the west coast of southern Burma, and there they refueled. Shilling climbed to 26,000 feet and —escorted by the other two planes, which flew at 20,000 feet—flew over Bangkok in cloudless skies at high noon.

Almost thirty Japanese ships were in the harbor, many disgorging troops at the docks. On a field north of the city more than fifty enemy fighters were parked in neat rows. At another field almost as many bombers were lined up the same way. Rector and Christman had to be restrained by Shilling from attacking. Chennault, knowing the impulsive nature of his fighter pilots, had told them: "Get your pictures and get home. Fly high. No fighting." The two circled Shilling as he banked and leveled off to get his pictures, then they flew back to Toungoo.

Chennault was furious when he saw the pictures and realized what an opportunity had been missed. The bombers promised him for so long had never arrived and now that the Japanese had landed in Burma in force, he feared they never would.

"A half dozen bombers could wreck the Japanese Air Force in Southeast Asia," he told the pilots. His cables to Washington urgently requesting anything he could use as a bomber had resulted in nothing. Neither T. V. Soong nor Lauchlin Currie was in a position to supply him with the equipment he so desperately needed. Washington was a madhouse following Pearl Harbor.

Chennault's third field order on December 10 read:

FIELD ORDERS)
                 :
NUMBER 3.   )
MAPS: Rangoon Section
1. a. It is reported that the ENEMY has captured BANGKOK and ground troops are reported proceeding to the BURMA ROAD.
2. No change. [Regarding the disposition of his squadrons.]
3. a. The Second Squadron will send over a reconnaissance flight to designated area taking off at 1130 o'clock.
    b. The First Squadron will furnish patrol for protection of reconnaissance flight.
    c. All other units on the ground will stand by on alert from 1200 o'clock until relieved.

                              By order of the Commanding Officer

On December 11 he received a telegram from Generalissimo Chiang Kai-shek ordering him to keep the AVG at Toungoo for the time being and to cooperate closely with the British. The British were putting considerable pressure on Chiang to help with the defense of Rangoon and wanted him to transfer the AVG under their authority. Chennault resisted to the best of his ability, asking Madame to use all of her influence to prevent it. The idea of operating under the command of Group Captain Manning was unthinkable to Chennault, after all the work and training he'd put in.

Hong Kong was under siege by the Japanese and Chennault was concerned for the safety of Joe Alsop, whom he had ordered to Manila with a note of introduction to General Douglas MacArthur. MacArthur was supposed to have a number of P-40s under his command and Chennault was hopeful that he could help with the spare-part problem. The general dismissed Alsop with the remark that he did not think the AVG was any sort of official outfit. Billy McDonald was still flying for CNAC, and Chennault—had he known Alsop was unable to get a seat on one of their planes because high-placed Chinese were being evacuated—might have cabled McDonald to get him out. As it was, Alsop was trapped in Hong Kong when the city fell to the Japanese on Christmas Day, 1941. He and hundreds of Britons were interned at Stanley Prison. He spent nine months as a war prisoner before being returned to the United States on the *Gripsholm*, a Swedish hospital ship that was used by the Allies to repatriate prisoners of war.

With the outbreak of hostilities, the game plan shifted to the protection of both ends of the Burma Road, now China's only means of getting supplies. Guarding it on the eastern end would be the job of the AVG Squadrons stationed at Kunming, and the southern terminal at Rangoon would be protected by a segment of the AVG and the RAF. Chennault planned to move two squadrons to Kunming as soon as possible. On December 12 he sent the

3rd Squadron under Arvid Olson to Mingaladon Airdrome in Rangoon to do its best to hold off the advancing Japanese. As the rest of the Group watched the 3rd Squadron's shark-painted P-40s roar into the hazy Burma skies from the jungle base, a feeling of excitement swept them all.

Chennault went back to his desk feeling a grim satisfaction that the time for action with his AVG had finally arrived. He knew his hatred of the Japanese was irrational, but he continued to remember the years of bombardment against defenseless cities—the slaughter at Shanghai and Nanking, the flames, smoke, and rubble of what had been Hankow in 1938, and the terrible bombings Chungking had taken for the last few years. His feelings about the Japanese Air Force had become personal, even though he knew that as a military commander he should be dispassionate.

He requested several CNAC DC-3 transports to get the 1st and 2nd Squadron ground personnel, plus some of the rest of the Group, to Kunming. General Chow cabled from Chungking that the planes were busy evacuating Chinese from Hong Kong but that they could be dispatched in several days. As a ruse Chennault set December 17 as the time to leave Toungoo, and, just to make sure the Japanese learned about it from the spies around the base, he posted orders on bulletin boards around the base that the two squadrons would fly to Kunming on the morning of the seventeenth. The Japanese took the bait and all that day reports filtered in through the ground net that Japanese pursuit planes were patrolling the Burma Road—waiting for the AVG. A month earlier the headquarters of the Chinese Fifth Air Force in Kunming had approved the building of dummy P-40s. They constructed the planes of bamboo and canvas to exact specifications and scattered them at Kunming and adjacent airfields at Changi, Tzukung, Yunnanyi, and Yangling, as if other reinforcements had already made the move. That night Tokyo radio triumphantly broadcast that twenty American AVG P-40s had been destroyed on the ground.

In the early evening of December 18 three green transports of CNAC slipped into the jungle base and picked up the equipment and personnel destined for Kunming. Pilots Moon Chen, George Wong, and Frank Higgs were at the controls and began the first of several shuttle trips that night and early the following morning on the approximately six-hundred-mile, four-hour flight. The P-40s were able to make the flight in a little over two hours. Personnel began arriving late at night in Kunming from the first two flights. The transports went back to Toungoo to pick up the rest of the personnel and each made another flight before daylight on the nineteenth. The planes landed by the aid of auto headlights and lamps held by hundreds of coolies who had been working to finish the airstrips.

Chennault had ordered the 1st and 2nd Squadron's of P-40s to leave Toungoo the afternoon of the eighteenth, and by the time the ground personnel arrived that night and early the next morning there were thirty-four P-40s lined up on the field at Kunming. They were fueled and loaded with ammunition by dawn. Chennault, dressed in his Chinese Air Force uniform with the insignia of a colonel, had come up on the first transport and now was making sure the AVG headquarters at the field was hooked up to the Yunnan ground warning net.

After the heat and humidity of the Burma jungles, the clear dry air of the 6,000-foot-high base at Kunming was like a transfusion. The ground crews and pilots could see little from the field but green rice paddies and the bare, reddish outlines of the mountain range across the lake. They sprawled against the base of the adobe-walled operations buildings on the morning of the nineteenth, waiting for the next orders. Chennault sent a patrol of three P-40s along the border of Yunnan with Burma, but there was no enemy contact. He was calm, working at his cluttered desk and checking to make sure all the last-minute details were taken care of. He knew from experience that the Japanese, on learning of their arrival at Kunming, would come.

The next morning, December 20, the phone on his desk jangled. The call was from Wang Hsu-ming, "Tiger" Wang of the Fifth Chinese Air Force in Kunming.

"Ten Japanese bombers have crossed the Yunnan border at Lao-kai, heading northwest," Wang said. Chennault felt his pulse quicken and his breath shorten. He replaced the receiver carefully. It was all going as he had planned.

Calls continued to come in from the ground warning net spread across the thousands of square miles of south China jungle and farmlands as the formation slowly moved deeper into Yunnan. Farmers in conical hats far to the south picked up telephones in remote parts of the province. They simply reported motor noises overhead and in which direction they were headed. Other observers in jungle outposts activated portable radios and called in aircraft engine sounds at high altitude and aiming northwest.

Chennault stood before the situation map on the wall of his office as the calls continued to come in every few minutes. Harvey Greenlaw, Tom Trumble, and P. Y. Shu stood behind him as he plotted the course the planes were flying. By projecting the line, it appeared that they were heading fifty miles east of the base. Chennault knew—since they had crossed the border of Yunnan Province at 9:30 A.M.—that they would reach an attack point near Kunming at approximately 11 A.M. From there they would begin a series of feinting moves to try to confuse the warning net before they began their final dash for the target.

Chennault sent the 2nd Squadron, under the command of Jack Newkirk, to make the interception with a four-plane element. He sent another four-plane element, commanded by Jim Howard, to a defensive patrol over Kunming. Sixteen planes of the 1st Squadron, headed by Robert Sandell, were sent aloft to fly in a standby area slightly west of Kunming, ready to join the battle should it develop. All the planes took off as Chennault fired a red flare at 10:50 A.M.

When the three flights were airborne he and his staff went to the combat operations shelter in a temple on a rise of ground overlooking the field. There John Williams and his communications crew had installed telephone and radio communications to both the warning net and the aircraft.

The weather over Kunming was perfect for flying—high cumulus clouds floating in a clear blue winter sky. The air raid sirens had begun to sound at the field and in the city. When the second red ball of the alert was hoisted to the top of the tower the field was already deserted by coolies and AVG ground personnel. Expecting another rain of bombs, hundreds of thousands of Chinese in the ancient city were running for cover. They could hear the high-pitched drone of engines overhead but had no idea they came from American aircraft. American instructors and Chinese student pilots had taken off in the Fleet trainers and Hawks of the Chinese Air Force Training School and would disperse the planes to smaller fields nearby until the raid was over.

The four interceptor fighters piloted by Jack Newkirk, Ed Rector, Bert Christman, and Gil Bright circled south of the airfield at an altitude of 22,000 feet. All the pilots wore heavy fleece-lined flying suits and thick gloves. Their eyes were covered by goggles, and heavy rubber oxygen masks concealed the bottom half of their faces. Goggles and the Plexiglas cockpit canopy frosted in the extreme cold and even with cockpit heaters the control sticks felt icy.

Suddenly the four interceptors saw the ten green, twin-engine bombers flying toward them in the broken undercast. The red symbols of the rising sun were clearly visible on the wings. The radio in the combat operations temple crackled.

"Shark Fin Blue calling base. Bandits sighted sixty miles east. Attacking."

Chennault's heart raced. God! Finally! He desperately wanted more information, but there was only silence. He quickly ordered the sixteen reserve 2nd Squadron planes to the attack area.

At sight of the Americans, the Japanese bombers jettisoned their bombs and dove for the cover of clouds below them. By the time Newkirk and his wing mates recovered from the shock of seeing a real enemy, the bombers were getting away. They dove after the retreating planes—all firing as they closed—but Newkirk's guns jammed and they lost the bombers in the heavy cloud cover. The other three planes stayed with Newkirk—as they had been taught to do, fighting as an element—but when they pulled into the clear sky Ed Rector was not in the formation.

Meanwhile Chennault guessed, from the position where the interceptors had met the bombers, that the bombers were lost and fumbling their way toward Kunming in cloud cover. He reasoned that they would get rid of the bomb load when attacked and head back toward their base at Hanoi. He radioed squadron leader Sandell, who led the first six planes of the 1st Squadron's reserve formation, to try to intercept the bombers on a course he gave him. Sandell acknowledged the message and again there was silence. Chennault nervously paced the room, glancing from the field to the big map on the wall. The noon sun beat down on the field and Chinese coolies were already coming out of the graveyards around the temple where they had been hiding in the slit trenches—obviously figuring the raid was over and there would be no bombs. Where the hell were the bombers? After all the training and all the careful instructions, were these kids going to fail to find the enemy and fight? He started back toward the radio when it suddenly snapped to life. It was Sandell.

"Shark Fin Red to base. Bandits eighty miles southeast. Attacking."

Chennault let his breath out in a long whistle. He had been right. The bombers were running for home.

Far to the south, the pilots of Sandell's assault squadron of sixteen planes saw the bombers at about 3,000 feet and skimming along above the trees. Forgetting all of Chennault's instructions about two-plane elements, they peeled off and attacked in a long dive, one plane on the tail of the other. Most began firing at three to four hundred yards out, but as they closed to within range their .50- and .30-caliber bullets began to chew up the bombers. The P-40s climbed, turned, and dove through the bomber formation, blazing at each bomber. It was a miracle there were no collisions.

Pieces of engine cowling began to fall from the wings of the bombers and pilots could see shattered glass from the turrets falling behind the planes. Engines smoked and began to catch fire. Bullets from the P-40s' big .50-caliber guns tore through the rear turrets of the grayish-green bombers before the Japanese gunners, with their lighter weapons, could get effective shots at the fighters. The American pilots attacked from all directions and the aluminum skin began to come off the bombers in large chunks as the heavy tracer bullets ripped in. Bits of vertical stabilizers and elevators fluttered back from the speeding bombers and plumes of black smoke began to pour from riddled engines.

Ed Rector, from Jack Newkirk's interceptor flight, had followed the retreating bombers since the first attack and now joined in the attack with Sandell's group. Louis Hoffman dove in behind a bomber and shot out the rear turret with his .50-caliber guns. With the rear turret gone, he calmly poured a withering fire along the entire length of the fuselage until the bomber rolled over and plunged toward the ground. Charlie Bond saw his tracers rake a bomber from one end to the other. Joe Rosbert lost his wing mate, Ed Liebolt, in the clouds and fired a quick burst into the side of a bomber, then broke away down and left. Bob Sandell made a head-on pass at one bomber and saw his tracers eat into the fuselage until a wing fell off and the bomber spun crazily and fell to the ground, where it exploded.

Fritz Wolf attacked the outside bomber on one side of a V formation. Diving below, he came up in a climb. He began firing all his guns at five hundred yards and by a hundred yards saw his bullets tearing into the gas tanks and engine of the starboard wing. The bomber exploded and he had to yank back on the stick to avoid the debris. Turning, he went after an inside bomber. Pulling up behind the tail, he could see the gunner firing at him, but no bullets hit his P-40. At fifty yards he concentrated on a motor and kept firing until the second bomber burst into flame and exploded.

Realizing they were low on gas, the squadron leaders signaled their flights to return to base. Four bombers were seen heading for the distant horizon— several of them smoking badly. Shouts and war whoops filled the radio as they regrouped and headed back for Kunming. Rector, having used up most of his gas on the first engagement and the second attack, ran out of fuel on the way back and crash-landed in a rice paddy east of the field with only minor injuries. He returned to the base a week later, the only casualty.

Chennault, owing to poor radio reception, has not been able to decipher any of the static coming from the planes. His first inkling of the battle was when they returned to the field, the wind whistling in the open muzzles of the machine guns. Several P-40s whipped over into victory rolls as they passed over the runway. He was the first to meet the planes. The pilots were so excited, they could not talk coherently, and they all tried to talk at once. It took Chennault half an hour to get them together in a debriefing room and hear the detailed story of the battle. Chinese spotters reported by radio that four planes had crossed the border on the way back to Hanoi but that several were damaged. Chinese intelligence later reported that only one managed to land safely. Six burning wrecks were scattered from south of Kunming almost to the border of Yunnan.

When the debriefing was over and the pilots had left to celebrate the victory at the bar near their hostel, Chennault excused himself from the office staff, who were still laughing and talking about the battle. He walked out on the turf of the airfield. The sun was still shining brightly and the field was bustling with activity. He headed toward the nearest P-40 and walked behind the wing until he could lean against the gritty metal of the fuselage. There, feeling his throat constrict and his eyes well with tears, he quietly wept with relief and gratitude.

Harvey Greenlaw alerted the pilots in midafternoon that a delegation of grateful Chinese was coming out from town to thank them. The men lined up in front of the alert shack and soon heard a band approaching. Then a long procession of people appeared. Led by the mayor of Kunming came hundreds of people, each carrying something. Little girls with their hair cut in straight bangs and dressed in their finest clothes stepped up and hung strips of purple cloth around the necks of the pilots. Most blushed and all were embarrassed at attention. The girls placed bouquets of flowers in the young men's hands, occasioning more blushing. The mayor made a speech and P. Y. Shu translated. The gist of it was that they were all heroes and saviors of the Chinese people and that the people would forever be in their debt. Both the Chinese and American national anthems were sung and gifts were distributed, mostly native food.

The men were all invited to a dinner that night hosted by General Wang and the other Chinese officers. There were speeches and much food and the Chinese made many toasts. Most of the pilots went back to the hostels quite drunk. After each of the Chinese officers offered his toast he sat down and did not drink again. Only the officer proposing the toast drank with the American fliers. So, out of every five toasts proposed, the Americans would drink five to the one of each of the Chinese officers honoring them.

Chennault, John Williams, and a few others with stronger constitutions went back to Chennault's quarters after the dinner. There had been a lot of drinking and it had been a long day and night, but nobody was ready to call it a day. Too much had happened and it needed to be talked out.

Nine

To the south, in Rangoon, the 3rd Squadron, who had been ordered by Chennault to Mingaladon Airdrome on December 12, saw their first Japanese bombers on December 21, the day after the Kunming victory.

Early in the day a force of twenty-seven enemy bombers was sighted over the Gulf of Martaban by fourteen AVG P-40s and twenty-three RAF Brewster Buffalos. The Japanese, from their base at Bangkok, were headed for Rangoon when they sighted the force of fighters. They dropped their bombs on the RAF staging base at Tavoy and headed quickly back toward Bangkok before the fighters had a chance to attack.

Later that day a Japanese photo observation plane flew over Rangoon at 25,000 feet, taking pictures of the harbor and the airfield. Chennault had told his pilots to expect a bombing raid a day or two after an observation plane flew over, so they were ready on the twenty-third when reports came from the RAF about a force of fifty-four bombers coming in from Thailand. Japanese fighters from Tak had joined up with the bombers over the Gulf of Martaban. The Japanese advance fighter base far up the Ping River was almost halfway to Rangoon and gave the fighters more air time for combat.

Combat crews on the ground at Mingaladon had eaten a cold breakfast of tea, bacon, and bread and were lounging about in the shade after having flown a dawn patrol over the bay. The heat in the late morning had climbed to 115 degrees and most were stripped to shorts.

Arvid Olson broke from the alert shack shouting that the enemy was on the way and men sprinted for the fifteen P-40s baking in the sun. RAF pilots scrambled for their Buffalos at the same time. There was no formal plan of takeoff and planes took to the air as soon as engines were ready. Fifteen minutes later the fifteen P-40s and eighteen Buffalos were circling at 18,000 feet, waiting for the Japanese. The P-40s had split into two flights, one headed by George McMillan and the second by Parker Dupouy. McMillan's flight was the first to spot the Japanese bombers coming in from the east at 16,000 feet. Tiny silver Nakajima I-97 fighters flew above and behind the bomber formation like small dragonflies. As the Japanese spotted the Americans and British above them, they jettisoned their auxiliary belly tanks and prepared for combat.

McMillan waggled his wings and the eight P-40s behind him followed him down in a screaming dive at the formation. The formation leader of the bomber alignment suddenly blew up as Charlie Older flashed down from above, all guns firing. Two other bombers caught fire and blew up as McMillan bored in from a flank. R. T. Smith sent another green bomber tumbling from the sky as his .50-caliber guns set wing tanks on fire. Smith got another bomber on his next pass as two I-97 fighters got on his tail but lost him. Two other bombers fell in flames as Older came in for a head-on attack. The sky was filled with swirling dogfights between the P-40s and the Japanese fighters. Ground crews at Mingaladon could see the sunlight flashing on the silver wings of the enemy fighters in the blue sky overhead. Orange explosions left long curling trails of black smoke as bombers spiraled back to earth.

Surprised at the fury of the attack, the first wave of bombers opened their bomb-bay doors and dropped their loads. They put their noses down and began to dive for speed as they headed back across the huge bay toward home.

The second wave of Japanese bombers met Dupouy's flight, which split up into two sections of three planes each.

Neil Martin, leading one of the three-plane elements, dove for the formation. Concentrated fire from dozens of turrets poured into the planes as they came down and bullets laced Martin's fighter. The plane climbed and hung high in the sky for a moment before winging over and spinning to the surface of the bay below.

Pilot Ken Jernstedt saw a bomber blow up as his tracers ate into the tanks along the wings. Bob Brouk came in low from a flank and saw a bomber wing-over and dive as his bullets cut through the cockpit. Ralph Gunvordahl came up behind a bomber that was trailing the formation and after a long burst to the fuselage saw it turn off with smoke pouring from the engine.

Several Japanese fighters flashed through the formation of bombers on the tail of one P-40 that had just finished a firing run. The P-40 began to spin as the fire cut through the cockpit of Henry Gilbert's plane and it fell in flames to the surface of the water.

Two other Nakajima fighters attacked Gilbert's wingman and the fighter suddenly began to spin toward the ground. The pilot, Paul Greene, bailed out, his parachute blossoming white against the bright blue of the sky. Both Japanese fighters came back time after time to machine-gun the pilot as he hung in the straps, but he swung himself from side to side and finally hung motionless to feign death. The enemy left to take on more P-40s and Greene landed in a rice paddy unhurt.

In spite of heavy casualties to their formation from both the P-40s and Brewster Buffalos, the planes of the second wave of Japanese bombers bore on and let their bombs go over Mingaladon Airfield, blasting barracks, the operations building, and the radio shack. Strings of bombs left huge craters on the field—one going through a hangar and killing a member of English mechanics. Other people died close to the air base as Japanese I-97 fighters swept across the runways, spraying tracers into slit trenches and buildings. Fighter planes whipped down the streets, firing as they went, bullets ricocheting off pavements and buildings.

An American gun crew aboard a freighter anchored in the harbor—the *City of Tulsa*—sent a Japanese fighter spinning and burning into the bay with its deadly turret fire.

Another of the pilots, "Duke" Hedman, shot down two Japanese fighters, then he dived on the bomber formation, knocked a bomber from the sky, and was just as quickly involved with the dogfight again. After setting another fighter on fire, he dove after the diving bomb formation that was heading back across the bay. He finally caught up with them just off the coast and shot down the lead bomber by flying almost in the middle of the formation where it was difficult for the turret gunners to shoot at him without hitting their own planes. Almost out of gas, he had to land at the satellite field at Pegu, north of Mingaladon. Most of the Buffalos had broken off the fight earlier—after losing three of their planes—as they were running low on gas and ammunition.

The fight finally over, the AVG and RAF pilots brought their riddled and battered planes back to the airfield, many landing with shot-up landing gear and inoperable rudders and ailerons. Several crash-landed and others ground-looped on the sod field.

The RAF later reported finding thirty-two wrecks of Japanese planes in the jungles and rice paddies near Rangoon. The Brewster pilots claimed only seven, which left twenty-five Japanese planes shot down by the AVG, althought the AVG did not claim that many. Three AVG planes had been lost and two American pilots had been killed. It had been a long and confusing battle, and nobody was ever sure how many had fallen or just who had shot what plane in the melee. Messages to Chennault at Kunming were being relayed by radio through Toungoo, where pilot Edgar Goyette had been left in charge. The day of the first battle at Rangoon he radioed Chennault.

RANGOON FROM OLSON QUOTE FIFTY-FOUR BOMBERS ACCOMPA-NIED BY FIGHTERS BOMBED MINGALADON TEN-THIRTY TODAY [DE-CEMBER 23] STOP THREE SHARKS DAMAGED TWO MISSING STOP SIX ENEMY SHOT DOWN STOP OPERATIONS BUILDING SUFFERED DIRECT HIT STOP NO WARNING SYSTEM AVAILABLE UNQUOTE.

It was followed by a second wire:

RANGOON FROM OLSON QUOTE SIX PLANES LOST DASH TWO CRASHED ONE MISSING TWO DAMAGED IN AIR ONE IN BOMB CRATER STOP PILOT GILBERT KILLED NO TRACE OF PILOT NEIL MARTIN OR PLANE STOP NO GROUND CREW INJURED STOP CONSTANT PATROL STOP THIRTY-CALIBER AMMUNITION INSUFFICIENT FOR ONE RELOAD FIFTY CALIBER AMPLE ADVISE DISPOSITION OF BODIES AND EFFECTS STOP DAMAGED PLANES REPAIRABLE WITH TIME AND FACILITIES STOP AVAILABILITY OF PLANES TWELVE STOP PILOTS FIFTEEN STOP AWAITING FURTHER ORDERS UNQUOTE.

Chennault immediately sent the following wire:

DECEMBER 25, 1941

TO TOUNGOO

GOYETTE TOUNGOO FOLLOWING FOR OLSON RANGOON QUOTE HOLD ON FEW MORE DAYS DRAW AMMUNITION POINT A AND RESERVE AIR-PLANES IF NEEDED STOP DISPERSE PLANES AND MEN AT NIGHT FOR REST STOP CONGRATULATIONS ON EXCELLENT WORK FIRST COMBAT AND DEEPEST SYMPATHY LOSS OF TWO FINE PILOTS STOP DELIVER BODIES AND EFFECTS TO CAMCO OR AMERICAN CONSUL FOR BURIAL STOP SHILLING FLIGHT LOST EN ROUTE HERE ONE KILLED ONE IN-JURED ALL AIRPLANES LOST TO GROUP STOP REPORT NAMES ALL PI-LOTS ENGAGED IN FIRST COMBAT FOR BONUS STOP WILL MOVE YOU SOON IF POSSIBLE WARMEST XMAS GREETINGS TO ALL UNQUOTE SAME TO YOU AND DETACHMENT STOP DELIVER THIS TO OLSON BY PLANE TODAY IF TELEPHONE LINES CUT.

CHENNAULT[1]

Following the battle at Rangoon, Erik Shilling, Ken Merritt, and Lacy Mandelburg had taken off from Mingaladon Airfield in three Curtiss CW-21 interceptor planes—single-seater Curtiss-Wright planes that had been assembled at Loiwing by CAMCO and delivered to Mingaladon—to ferry them, via Lashio, to Kunming. Not waiting for their P-40 escort, they became lost after being refueled at Lashio about 6 P.M. that day and later all crashed in the mountains between Lashio and Kunming. Shilling's engine quit and, forced to crash-land about fifteen miles south of To Den, he was injured. The other two, unable to get a correct heading to Kunming, circled until dark, then tried to land. Merritt crashed about ten miles north of Tai Jon and he too was injured. Mandelburg tried to land in a valley but when his props touched the surface of a stream he pulled up and crashed into the side of a terraced hill. He was killed instantly.

Chennault would have preferred to stay at his post in Kunming to super-vise the air battles, but he had been summoned to Chungking on December

27 by the Generalissimo for a meeting with British General Sir Archibald
Wavell and his deputy, American General George H. Brett, and Brigadier
General John Magruder of the American Mission. The meeting was con-
cerned with how best to aid the British in the defense of Rangoon. Harvey
Greenlaw took over command in Chennault's absence.

Chennault had come down with a severe case of bronchitis again; he was
running a fever and felt terrible. The meeting with the British and Magruder
did not make him feel any better. The English wanted to have his AVG
transferred under their command and Chennault was adamant that this
should not be done. Neither Magruder nor the Gimo said anything when the
meeting broke up and he returned to Kunming.

Christmas Day dawned hot and clear in Rangoon and the Japanese bombers began to arrive by 11 A.M. Sixty bombers, accompanied by thirty fighters,
began coming over in three waves. McMillan led the first flight of six planes
again and Dupouy the second, also of six planes. McMillan and R. T. Smith
attacked the bombers while the rest of their flight took on the escorting
fighters. After shooting down one bomber, McMillan's plane was hit and his
mates saw him dive away from the battle with smoke trailing from his plane.
After hitting one fighter with a burst from his .50-caliber guns, Duke Hedman was caught by four Nakajima I-97s. The canopy of his fighter was
blown off and he was forced to land at a satellite field.

The rest of McMillan's flight went after the bombers, which had just
released their bombs over Rangoon. Ed Overend saw his tracers cause a wing
to come off one bomber, which spun out of the formation, but he had been
hit by machine-gun fire from one of its turrets and was forced to crash-land
his plane in a rice paddy.

Charlie Older and Tom Haywood, flying as a team, slashed through the
bomber formation and together shot down five of the twin-engined Mitsubishi bombers. Dupouy and Freddy Hodges each shot down a Japanese fighter
and Bill Read shared a kill with an RAF pilot who helped shoot down a
bomber. The RAF put sixteen Buffalos up to join the fray. The battle had
raged over Rangoon and the Gulf of Martaban for an hour and a half. The
Japanese, having lost nearly a third of their force, nursed their battered and
smoking formations back to Thailand.

The AVG lost two planes and no pilots. Both Overend and McMillan were
brought back to the field by friendly natives. The RAF lost nine planes and
six pilots. The British later confirmed that twenty-eight Japanese planes had
gone down, eight of them into the gulf. The AVG claimed thirteen fighters
and four bombers.

The exhausted pilots and ground crews ate Christmas dinner under the
trees on the airfield in sweltering heat. Bill Pawley sent over a truckload of
food and liquor from CAMCO stores in Rangoon. British officers came over
to celebrate with them.

Chennault, after receiving the battle reports, cabled Olson:

DECEMBER 27, 1941

GOYETTE TOUNGOO FOR OLSON QUOTE CONGRATULATIONS AGAIN
UPON RETURN OF TWO MISSING PILOTS FROM YOUR MAGNIFICENT
VICTORY XMAS STOP AM SENDING STRONG REINFORCEMENTS SOON AS
TRANSPORT PLANE AVAILABLE ADVISE MANNING STOP DO YOU WISH
PULL OUT YOUR UNIT FOR REST HERE AFTER ARRIVAL NEW UNIT
STOP IF SO WOULD LIKE TWO OR THREE VOLUNTEERS PILOTS AND
CREW TO REMAIN WITH NEW UNIT FEW DAYS AT LEAST UNQUOTE
BELT 22 THOUSAND ROUNDS 7.92 AMMUNITION THERE AND REQUISI-
TION 75 THOUSAND MORE IF AVAILABLE FROM MAYMYO.

CHENNAULT[2]

Reports about the AVG successes were beginning to trickle out of Rangoon and Kunming. Correspondents from all over the Far East were suddenly making applications to visit both bases. Chennault, down with bronchitis and a terrible cough, was in bed in Kunming. At the meeting in
Chungking Magruder had asked him for a formal report on the AVG combat
and its status. In spite of the knifing cough and fever, Chennault sat down at
his desk and wrote Magruder. He summarized the air battles of December 20
in Kunming, of December 22 and 25 in Rangoon, and totaled the known
enemy losses in these engagements at fourteen bombers and thirteen fighters,
with losses to the AVG of two pilots lost, five planes destroyed and seven
damaged.

He urged Magruder, in light of such combat efficiency, to ask the U.S.
military to send him fifty new or used fighter planes, spare parts, and fifteen
pilots per month as replacements. In addition, he wrote, he urgently needed
thirty-six twin-engine bombers with a minimum range of fifteen hundred
miles and plenty of spare parts. He would need pilots, copilots, navigators,
bombardiers, radio operators, and gunners to man these planes.

The following day Magruder fired off a cable to the War Department in
Washington:

December 27, 1941

To AGWAR Washington
Attention Arnold
Since December 20 AVG has destroyed 13 Jap pursuit and 14 twin
engine bombers, damaging several more, according to report from
Chennault. Immediate reinforcements in personnel and equipment for
AVG mandatory stop time is of essence if shattering defeats give Japs
are to be exploited stop following recommendations submitted which
should be given highest priority in order stated to insure continued
successful operations AVG in this area comma with due consideration
of time and space factors: first, without delay fly to Calcutta 54 airplanes complete with armament from middle east. Second, for these
ships send to Calcutta 25 percent combat spares. Third, send immedi-

ately 15 trained fighter pilots per month by air to Calcutta for reserves and replacements. Fourth, at earliest date provide two squadrons medium bombers for this theater of operations.

Magruder[3]

Chennault felt Magruder was doing his best to aid the AVG, but he still had some suspicions that the War Department—and Generals Marshall and Arnold in particular—wanted more control over the AVG. His suspicions were strengthened a few days later by a message from Madame Chiang.

Radio (December 30, 16.5)
Received at 17.30

From Chungking
To Col. Chennault
    Can you come immediately to participate in discussion of induction of AVG into USA Air Force. Please reply.

Madame[4]

Something, indeed, was up. He would stall for time; in any case his illness would keep him from flying to Chungking for a few days. He cabled back:

December 30, 1941

(2310)
To: Gen. C. J. Chow, Chungking
Following for Madame Chiang Kai-shek quote am confined to bed with severe bronchial attack stop because of many problems involved do not believe AVG should be inducted into US Air Corps stop AVG in present status is more effective and pilots unanimous in perferring to remain under my leadership and Generalissimo's control stop do you desire me come Chungking when able stop happy new year from AVG unquote regards.

Chennault[5]

Ten

Chennault sent the 2nd Squadron, with twelve planes under the command of Jack Newkirk, down to Mingaladon Airfield in Rangoon to relieve the exhausted pilots of the Hell's Angels on New Year's Day.

Newkirk was still angry at himself for not shooting down the Japanese bombers he had intercepted over Kunming on December 20 and was spoiling for action.

On the morning of January 3 he, David ("Tex") Hill, and Jim Howard took off to strafe the forward fighter base at Tak, on the western border of Thailand. Combat reports of that day from Newkirk read:

"Approached enemy base from south east diving at 250 miles per hour out of the sun. I saw two enemy aircraft circling the field at 2,000 feet and attacked the nearest plane, a model 'O' from astern. After two twists it turned to the left streaming smoke, rolled over and crashed into the jungle. Vice Squadron Leader J. H. Howard at this time strafed the field and I saw a large fire as the result. When Howard turned to make another run, an I-96 attacked me. He must have lost sight of me as I did a steep turn under him and came out on his tail at 500 yards. I fired several bursts and closed up to 200 yards. The enemy aircraft then immelmanned in the most quick and surprising manner. Both of us were firing head on at each other and he pulled up over me. Several particles fell from his plane and he stalled and spun into the jungle. He did not burst in flames at that time. Tex Hill attacked a plane which was chasing Howard. He fired several bursts and the enemy aircraft fell off on the left wing out of control. I then saw four enemy aircraft climbing into the sun and as we were heading south they had the advantage. The field was in flames in several places and we scrambled for home."[1]

The Japanese, smarting from the ground attack, came back with a vengeance the following day. They sent a force of twenty-seven Type 96 fighters, without bombers, to Rangoon and the AVG picked up the warning a bit late. Newkirk sent aloft six P-40s—piloted by Bert Christman, Gil Bright, Frank Swartz, Hank Geselbracht, George Paxton, and Ken Merritt. He sent another eight fighters up to fly cover for the first six, but the Japanese caught the first flight circling down through the clouds in an effort to locate the enemy. Outnumbered five to one, the AVG took a beating.

"I tried to evade the enemy by diving and turning," Bert Christman recalled. "The wings, fuselage, tanks, and cockpit of my plane were riddled. The engine stopped after five minutes of flying. Smoke came into the cockpit and the controls were damaged. I abandoned the plane and it crashed and burned. The duration of the attack lasted ten seconds."

Swartz got in a couple of bursts that probably damaged a Japanese fighter as it was following another P-40 down. Bright rolled and dived away from the slashing attack from above but got his plane shot up and was forced to land.

Paxton's cockpit was riddled by the first attack and the oil lines were hit. He rolled away and spun down in a long dive and landed back at the field. On landing he ground-looped and washed out the undercarriage and a right wing. Merritt shot down a fighter that was attacking another P-40. Paxton was found to be wounded, with two bullets in his right side and another lodged in his back; but for the armor plate, he would have been killed.

The Japanese had knocked out three AVG planes in one fight. It was a demoralizing day for the Americans. The ground-to-air radios to the planes had failed again and the top cover squadron was unable to help out the six fighters being attacked. Later on crew chief Alex ("Mickey") Mihalko devised a radio mounted on an Army Jeep in which he raced back and forth over the field warning the pilots what he could see of attacks. Another mechanic threw a wrench at an attacking Japanese fighter.

On January 7 four planes flew a mission to strafe the airfield at Mae Sot in Thailand. The planes were piloted by Charlie Mott, Percy Bartelt, Bob Moss, and Gil Bright. The flight dove out of the sun on six Japanese fighters parked in a line on the field.

"I made three passes down the main line of the parked enemy aircraft," Bob Moss said in his report later. "Mott made two passes and went down. The smoke and fire from the burning aircraft was so bad I turned perpendicular to the line and made passes on the enemy aircraft which were not ablaze." Mott was declared missing in action. The Japanese planes were left burning. Mott had crash-landed and was captured. His squadron mates heard him broadcast over a Bangkok radio station a week later. He said he was unhurt and was being treated well in prison.

Ken Merritt was killed in a freak accident that night when another pilot, Pete Wright, landed in the dark after trying to make contact with Japanese bombers. A hydraulic line in his cockpit ruptured as he landed, spraying fluid in his face. The runway had been illuminated by car headlights and to avoid hitting the cars Wright swung his plane off and struck an unlighted car in which Merritt was sleeping after a day on patrol. Merritt was killed instantly.

The next five days were a constant battle, with waves of Japanese bombers and fighters attacking Rangoon. The outnumbered AVG and RAF pilots flew day and night, trying to stem the Japanese tide. The Japanese tried bombing by the light of the moon, only to be intercepted by Brewster and Hurricane fighters manned by pilots who had learned their trade fighting the Germans over London.

Rangoon began to look like London, with fires raging unchecked in all parts of the city. The fires spread through the dry countryside as burning aircraft and bombs set dry rice and cane fields alight. The AVG pulled its P-40s under mango and banyan trees alongside the runways while the Chinese mechanics made dummy planes on the field to decoy the Japanese fighters. The Japanese, knowing their only danger was from the American and British fighter pilots, kept up a steady stream of small night bombardments to prevent the pilots from getting any sleep.

Besides trying to intercept bombers both night and day, the AVG continued to fly missions over the enemy fields in Thailand. On January 8, Newkirk, Tex Hill, and Jim Howard hit Tak Airfield again while the Japanese were putting on a show for Thai officials. Hill got one fighter that was coming at Newkirk, and Newkirk blew up a Japanese fighter that was landing in front of the crowd in the grandstand.

Word of pressure from the American Mission in Chungking to make the AVG a part of the U.S. Army Air Corps had been leaking to Chennault from all directions. Lauchlin Currie and T. V. Soong in Washington had passed the word along, and Magruder—unofficially—had told Chennault it was inevitable. As a result, Chennault had given a lot of thought to his status. It was clear he would need more clout than what could be exerted by an honorary colonel in the Chinese Air Force. On January 20 he wrote a letter to General Magruder, summarizing the accomplishments of the AVG and discussing its future. After saying he thought induction of the AVG into the Air Corps would "result in destroying the combat effectiveness of the Group for a long period of time, possibly four to six months," he came up with a suggestion:

"Personally, it is my desire to be of the greatest service in inflicting a rapid and decisive defeat upon the enemy. To accomplish this purpose, I am willing to serve in any capacity desired. Being thoroughly acquainted with condtions [sic] in China, as well as with Japanese tactics and their general situation, I believe that the best possible arrangement would be to have me appointed a General Officer in the U. S. Air Corps, and Air Officer Commanding, in China. In this position I could control both the AVG and any regular Air Corps units sent to China in the future. I could continue to supervise flying training in China and exercise operational control over available Chinese Air Units. I could supervise the transitional and unit training of Chinese Units with Lend-Lease equipment. Because of my peculiar position in China, I do not believe that any other officer coming out here as a stranger could possibly do these things as well as I can."

Knowing that Magruder was on his side and feeling sure he would suggest this idea to General Arnold, Chennault also attempted to stack the deck on another side. Counting on Madame Chiang to suggest the same to Currie and T. V. Soong in Washington, he wrote her the same day and enclosed an "unofficial" copy of his letter to Magruder. In his letter to her he said:

Dear Madame,

Inclosed herewith is a copy of the letter which I have just sent to General Magruder. In this letter, I have tried to sum up in the clearest terms, the situation regarding the present status of the AVG and its probable status if inducted into the U.S. Air Corps. Abandoning all modesty, I have also tried to indicate the position in which I believe I could be of the greatest service to the Allied cause. This copy of Magruder's letter is sent to you for your private information only, of course.

Chennault[2]

By mid-January the British were exerting all the pressure they could on both Washington and Chungking to have the AVG transferred under the command of Air Vice Marshal D. F. Stevenson for the defense of Burma.

Fearing he would lose control of his forces and that his men would be trapped in Rangoon, Chennault cabled Newkirk via Commander Dewolfe at Rangoon and Goyette at Toungoo:

JANUARY 11, 1942 (1531)
CURRENT NO. 66-KT-27

GOYETTE

TOUNGOO

FOLLOWING FOR DEWOLFE QUOTE SECRET STOP CONTINUING LOSS OF EQUIPMENT MAKES IT NECESSARY TO WITHDRAW ALL UNITS AVG FROM RANGOON ON OR BEFORE JANUARY 18 STOP PLEASE REPORT ON POSSIBLE POLITICAL EFFECTS AND ADVISE NEWKIRK TAKE STEPS PREPARE FOR WITHDRAWAL ON DATE MENTIONED UNQUOTE PREPARE FOR WITHDRAWAL AVG DETACHMENT FROM TOUNGOO ABOUT JANUARY 20 STOP ADVISE WHETHER YOU CAN EVACUATE ALL AVG PROPERTY BY THAT DATE SECRET END.

CHENNAULT

Apparently there were few secrets in Rangoon, as the British got wind of the message. Stevenson cabled Chennault on the twenty-fourth that he had seen a cable from Chennault to Newkirk telling him to prepare for withdrawal. He said he understood the AVG was being inducted into the Army Air Forces and would be placed under Magruder and that he had wired Magruder not to withdraw the AVG from Rangoon.[3]

Realizing he was far outranked and in danger of losing the fight, Chennault resorted to Madame. On January 26 he cabled her, enclosing the cable from Stevenson and saying that it was obvious the British would demand the use of the AVG as soon as it was part of the U.S. Army and would use it in an area they had not fully prepared themselves to defend. He added that a large number of AVG personnel would terminate their contracts with CAMCO if forced into the Army and there would no longer be any AVG if this happened. He said he thought that, while this would not be any great loss to the British, it would certainly be a loss to the Chinese.

Madame must have exerted considerable pressure on the Generalissimo because he finally sent Chennault an order to withdraw all units of the AVG from Burma by January 31. Actually, she had not needed to prod that much, he learned later. The Chinese were still smarting about the British decision to appease the Japanese and close the Burma Road. Wavell, his mind occupied with the threat to Burma, had made it rather obvious to the Chinese that he was only interested in what they could supply him in the way of Chinese divisions and the AVG planes.

Getting no help from the States on more fighter planes and bombers, and realizing that the Japanese buildup in Southeast Asia would soon engulf all of Burma and the Malay Peninsula, Chennault turned to Chungking for bombers. The Chinese had been getting a few obsolete Russian SB-3 bombers across Turkestan by rail and truck. The Chinese Air Force, under General Mow, agreed to raid the huge supply dumps and airfields at Hanoi and Chennault agreed to send the AVG as escort from Kunming.

On January 22 the eighteen bombers, manned by Chinese crews, lumbered off the dirt runway at Changi, north of Kunming, with full bomb loads. The 1st Squadron, commanded by Sandy Sandell, furnished ten P-40s for the mission. An additional flight of four planes commanded by Gregory Boyington joined the squadron at Mengtzu. All ships were in the air and accompanying the bombers toward Hanoi at 11:20 A.M. While Chinese intelligence later claimed many direct hits on the airfield at Hanoi, the flight report of Squadron Leader Sandell told a different story:

"There were 18 bombers in this formation flying in two squadrons of nine each respectively. The bombers headed on a course of 135 degrees failing to make any correction for wind. I dove down to the leader of the formation and indicated the direction of flight to be 150 degrees because a very strong wind was blowing from the southwest. After a few minutes the bombers returned to 135 degrees. The second squadron of the bomber formation started to stop soon after the pursuit joined the formation and continued to remain about one mile behind the first bomb squadron for almost an hour making it very difficult to escort them.

"After flying for 1:35 hours on a haphazard course varying from 150 to 120 degrees, over a solid overcast without finding a single hole in the clouds, the bombing formation turned to a course of 240 degrees and flew this course for several minutes, then they dropped their bombs through the clouds. I estimated the position to be about 20 miles east of Haiphong because I saw one hole in the clouds that was near the Gulf of Tonkin. This hole was over the mouth of a wide river or a very marshy back bay region. This hole was about five to ten miles west of the position where the bombs dropped. As the bombs were dropping, I saw the first explosion of black smoke very close below to the last element of the second squadron. I wondered whether it was bombs exploding or anti-aircraft fire. Immediately after this first explosion, I saw about 20 other similar bursts of smoke varying in height from 50 to 2000 feet below the bomber formation.

"At this time, the bomber group turned to a course of about 340 degrees and headed for home. The leader increased his indicated air speed from 140 miles per hour to about 180, thus scattering his group. I assembled my squadron and flew a course of 285 degrees to Mengtzu. This return flight was over a solid overcast. We landed at Mengtzu after an elapsed flying time of 3:05 hours. We refueled and took off for Kunming landing there at 1610. Probably Hanoi was under broken clouds but we passed about 50 miles northeast of this area so couldn't tell."[4]

Meanwhile in Rangoon the situation was becoming acute. The Japanese were pushing up the Tenasserim coast, approaching the outskirts of Moulmein just across the mouth of the Gulf of Martaban from Rangoon. The 2nd and 3rd Pursuit Squadrons were fighting night and day to hold back the waves of Japanese aircraft. While the matter of a $500 bonus for each confirmed Japanese plane had not been written into the CAMCO contracts, there was a gentleman's agreement with the company. Chennault had verbally told each pilot he would receive the pay and now the pilots were enthusiastically adding up their scores from the many air battles. By the end of the month Chennault wrote CAMCO in New York, listing the first claims, and gave a copy to each pilot. The money was to be deposited to their Stateside bank accounts.

On the afternoon of January 23, Japanese Type I-97 fighters attacked a flight of P-40s over Rangoon and the battle raged for several minutes in the bright sky. Bert Christman had his engine shot out and was trying to bail out of the smoking fighter when a burst from one of the Japanese planes caught him in the chest and head. His parachute, trailing the dead pilot, failed to open before the body struck ground. Ed Rector, firing all his guns at once, followed the Japanese fighter down until the pilot bailed out at three hundred feet. His chute, too, failed to open.

In Kunming, Chennault received the news of Christman's death stoically. He was running low on flyable P-40s and he needed every experienced pilot he had. As if that were not enough, Louis Hoffman was shot down and his body found in the cockpit of his riddled plane on January 26. When Tommy Cole was killed on a strafing mission to Thailand, Chennault had had enough. He was heartsick at the loss of pilots.

Disgusted with the results of the Chinese bombing raid and equally fed up with the lack of response from the United States on his requests for additional planes, Chennault sent a message to Currie and T. V. Soong via Madame.

GENERAL C. J. CHOW
CHUNGKING
SECRET FOR H. E. MADAME CHIANG KAI-SHEK STOP PLEASE TRANSMIT FOLLOWING TO H. E. DR. T. V. SOONG AND DR. CURRIE QUOTE CAN BEGIN ATTACKS ON JAPAN'S INDUSTRIES AT ONCE IF YOU CAN SEND REGULAR OR VOLUNTEER BOMBARDMENT GROUP EQUIPPED WITH LOCKHEED HUDSONS AS SPECIFIED BY ME IN JUNE 1941 AND AMERICAN KEY PERSONNEL TO OPERATE UNDER MY COMMAND AND CONTROL OF THE GENERALISSIMO ONLY UNQUOTE.

CHENNAULT

There was no answer and he was preparing to send another wire when he received one from Madame that changed the whole picture. As he read, a feeling of elation swept over him.

CURRENT NO. 223
DATED: FEBRUARY 3, 1942 (15.00)
REC'D: FEBRUARY 3, 1942 (16.10)
FROM PXM
TO: GEN. CHENNAULT
STRICTLY CONFIDENTIAL UPON INDUCTION AVG INTO U. S. ARMY WITH YOU AS CHIEF AIR OFFICER IN CHINA UNDER COMMAND GENERALISSIMO AND WITH RANK BRIGADIER GENERAL AND IN HELPING TRAIN CHINESE FOR CHINESE AIR FORCE WHAT STAFF OFFICERS AND OTHER ASSISTANTS DO YOU NEED FROM AMERICA STOP URGENT YOU REPLY IMMEDIATELY.

MADAME

Eleven

By the end of January 1942, Chennault—from an obscure, retired Air Corps captain—became front-page news on every continent. Correspondents poured in from America and Europe across India and infiltrated the bases at Rangoon, Toungoo, and across the mountains into Kunming.

The initial air battle of Kunming on December 20 had brought the AVG to the attention of the world press, but the succeeding battles over Rangoon had caught the imagination of the whole world.

In the thirty-two days the 2nd Squadron had been fighting in the skies over Rangoon, Newkirk and his pilots had strafed hundreds of Japanese troops on the ground, had shot down or burned more than a hundred and fifty enemy planes—while losing more than half their original eighteen P-40s. Three of the AVG pilots had been killed and one was a prisoner.

The British, seldom complimentary about American fighting in the Far East, wrote Chennault to express their admiration for the fighting qualities of the AVG pilots. Winston Churchill cabled the governor of Burma:

"The magnificent victories these Americans have won in the air over the paddy fields of Burma are comparable in character, if not in scope, with those won by the Royal Air Force over the orchards and hop fields of Kent in the Battle of Britain."

Stories of the AVG exploits appeared under the bylines of Leland Stowe in the Chicago *Daily News;* Dan de Luce of the Associated Press; Jack Belden of *Time-Life;* Darrell Berrigan of United Press and Harrison Forman of the New York *Times.*

The phenomenal successes of these unknown fighter pilots came at a time when the war picture was darkest for the American people. The United States was at war with Germany, Japan, and Italy. The Germans were launching a new offensive under Field Marshal Erwin Rommel in North Africa. The British Eighth Army was about to evacuate Derna. The Japa-

nese were invading the Dutch East Indies and Japanese bombers were striking at Malayan airfields from Thailand, Singapore was in danger of falling,
and America—with the Pacific fleet badly damaged at Pearl Harbor—was
looking at a long island-hopping war.

And suddenly—in the midst of all the dreary news of worldwide defeat—
the spectacular victories of a handful of obscure American soldier-of-fortune
fighter pilots burst upon the front pages of newspapers and on the newsreels
of local movie theaters. Chennault's name became a household word, as did
the "Flying Tigers."

The Chinese newspapers had started to refer to the AVG as Flying Tigers
after the December 20 victories over Kunming, and the term caught on with
the American press. Since the birth of the Chinese Republic in 1912 the tiger
had been used in place of the dragon as the Chinese national symbol. "Flying
Tigers" was a natural for the press.

"How the term Flying Tigers was derived from the shark-nosed P-40s I
will never know," Chennault wrote later. "At any rate we were somewhat
surprised to find ourselves billed under the name."

The name was emblazoned across hundreds of front pages. Chennault was
overwhelmed with requests for interviews from both European and American correspondents. He did what he could to accommodate them and still
run the AVG.

Meanwhile, in the south, Rangoon was a dying city. This modern city of
nearly a half million people had become a charred hulk. Its inhabitants were
fleeing to India and up the Burma Road to China. Daily bombing had reduced it to a burning shambles. Wealthy Britons had begun to leave the city
and a few had given the keys to their palatial homes to AVG people with
directions to burn down the houses when they left. Shopkeepers were abandoning their places of business in the face of native looters.

The 1st Squadron, under Bob Sandell, moved down to relieve Newkirk's
battered fliers on January 28, and was fighting a desperate battle against
daily bombing raids. Knowing it was simply a matter of time before they had
to evacuate, Chennault ordered the AVG there to begin forming convoys to
move supplies to Kunming. The docks at Rangoon were piled high with the
accumulation of months of unloaded Lend-Lease supplies for China. Ships
were no longer coming into the port and the ships already there were laden
with supplies but there was no one to unload them. Rows of GM trucks,
Army jeeps, and staff cars—all in crates—lined the docks. Block-long rows
of crates containing rifles, machine guns, antiaircraft guns, and grenades rose
into the air. Cases containing canned goods of all kinds were mixed with
cases of whiskey, sherry, and gin. Crates of Brewster Buffalo fighters and
parts for Hurricanes and the Lockheed Hudsons, meant for the RAF, were
everywhere. Native coolies refusing to unload the ships, it fell to CAMCO
Rangoon staff, some Chinese officials, and some Rangoon police to pitch in

and help. Chennault directed Paul Frillman to head up a convoy and the chaplain gathered all the AVG staff he could muster—clerks, mechanics, armorers, and some of the medical staff—to help him pile supplies into trucks for the long trip north. Open fighting had broken out between police and looters in parts of the city and the AVG personnel traveled with rifles, pistols, and submachine guns from the docks to their quarters. The trucks were filled with everything and anything that might be of use to the AVG at Kunming.

Chennault asked Madame to contact the Chinese customs officials at the Chinese border and tell them to let trucks with the AVG marking on them through without paying duty. This led to a lot of black marketeering on the part of some AVG men who had been sent down from Kunming to drive the trucks as well as some of the pilots and ground crews who had earlier re-signed from the Group. They drove the trucks to Kunming and sold the war supplies at fantastic profits—unbeknown to Chennault. The reputation of the AVG was to be tarnished later by reports that there had been widespread war profiteering on the part of the entire Group. When Chennault heard reports of the black marketeering he called a meeting of the Group and threatened those involved with dishonorable discharges and fines, insisting they give the money back. Most did, but several set up businesses in Kunming and made fortunes in the black-market supplies. They had agents on both sides of the Burma Road and one enterprising man set up gasoline stations, at which he reportedly charged nearly a dollar a gallon, as opposed to normal costs of twelve to fifteen cents.

The distinction between stealing and "liberating" became extremely vague in Rangoon.

By mid-February the law of the jungle took over in Rangoon. Native looters were out of hand—shooting at foreigners on the streets and breaking into the Hindu shops. The fleeing authorities emptied the jails and turned animals loose from the zoos. Criminals joined the natives in knifings and lootings on the nighttime streets. Hospitals were filled with the victims of incessant bombings and those unable to reach a hospital died in the streets. Dogs, ravens, and vultures fed on the dead in the gutters and a heavy pall of black smoke hung over the city.

Frillman and his crew fought their way through some streets in order to get to the dock area. One day he came upon an automobile agency with the doors wide open and the owners gone. He and a mechanic helped themselves to two new American-made Buicks. The mechanic wrapped his around a tree a few blocks away, but Frillman loaded his to the roof and drove it to Kunming along with the convoy, which left Rangoon on February 16.

On almost every truck in the convoy sat an Anglo-Indian girl beside its American driver. The AVG men said they could not stand the thought of these girls being left behind in the falling city. Most of the girls wore attractive print dresses and modern American movie-star sunglasses as they perched high in the olive-drab trucks. It was a motley-looking group that began the long, arduous task of grinding up the winding and dusty Burma Road on its snakelike route to China.

One of the most amusing accounts of that voyage was given by Frillman in his book, *China: The Remembered Life,* published in 1968. In it he tells of encountering General Stilwell, who had just arrived in the Far East, at his command post along the Burma Road at Lashio:

"We found his headquarters in a British Army compound, a group of comfortable bungalows in park-like grounds. The British soldiers guarding the gate grinned and waved us past, so we went blundering on with a great grinding of gears and honking of horns. As luck would have it we stopped right in front of Stilwell's own bungalow, just as he was coming out to see who was making the noise.

"His days in the dust and mud of Burma were still ahead, and he looked as if he had stepped out of a military tailor's shop in Washington, with dress uniform crisply pressed and decorations all in place. We could not have looked worse or less military. Most of the men had several days' growth of beard and we were all filthy, dressed in patchings of civilian and army clothes. The Anglo-Indian girls, quite a bit the worse for wear, could hardly be passed off as WAC's or WAVE's. They were vigorously shaking the dust out of their hair and beating it off their finery before settling down with their lipsticks and compacts.

"I got out of my Buick, shoving the cats back into it behind me. Perhaps I have forgotten to mention that I was taking two Siamese cats to Kunming for one of the RAF officers who always cooperated with us at Rangoon. The female cat was in heat, as they immediately began proving.

"In the next few minutes I learned how Stilwell earned his nickname, 'Vinegar Joe.' I was glad he didn't recognize a former young Hankow missionary as chief of what he saw as a gang of bums, but he didn't need the extra ammunition. Before I finished trying to tell him who and how many we were, and what billets we hoped to find, he was launched. I'm afraid he most resented our being a disgrace to the U. S. Army, which we weren't in. None of us realized he might be dressed up because he was expecting the strait-laced Generalissimo and Madame for tea. Without us he still had plenty of problems with them.

"The drivers gathered behind me, muttering about desk pilots who didn't understand a real war. I kept mumbling excuses, then a station wagon came swerving up the drive and skidded to a halt beside us. It was driven by an ex-AVG black marketeer called Dutch, and in his load were his fat and rather old Anglo-Indian girl, her dark and spidery mother, a varicolored batch of her children, and a full cargo of contraband gin. Dutch and the women must have been drinking all day, for he could hardly keep his eyes open and they were waving empty bottles at us weeping all the while. This skirmish was lost by the AVG.

" 'See what I mean?' said Stilwell sarcastically, going back into his bungalow and slamming the screen door with a crack like a pistol shot. We drove on up the road to China and camped for the night on a barren mountain ridge."

Nearly two weeks later the battered convoy of exhausted AVG ground personnel arrived in Kunming, while the AVG was flying its last sorties against the Japanese. Chennault had suffered more combat losses and the AVG was beginning to feel the strain of constant battle. Bert Christman had been shot down over Rangoon on January 23; Louis Hoffman was also lost over Rangoon, on the twenty-sixth, and Bob Sandell was killed in a flying accident on February 7 when he took a damaged P-40 up to test it out. The tail had been sheared off by a dying Japanese fighter pilot who had tried to ram Sandy on the ground. Line chief Harry Fox replaced the tail assembly but warned Sandell to be careful while testing it. Unable to resist the urge to slow-roll the craft, Sandell was killed when the tail came off at 1,000 feet and the fuselage spun to earth. His place as squadron leader was taken by Bob Neale.

When Singapore fell in mid-February the Japanese transferred more aircraft north to bases in Thailand and threw more bombers and fighters into the attacks on Rangoon. New Navy Zeros began to appear in greater numbers. The Zero was the latest fighter in the Japanese arsenal and could outclimb the P-40 by 2,000 feet per minute. It could turn quicker than any other fighter built. New Mitsubishi bombers with bullet-shaped fuselages and tapered wings also began to show up in the formations over Rangoon. Faster than the older models, they had remote-controlled turrets and several 20-mm. cannon in the top turrets in place of the earlier .30-caliber machine guns. They had more protective armor plate for the crew as well.

The 1st Pursuit Squadron's engines were worn out and no replacements were available. Chennault advised Neale to cease escorting the Blenheim bombers of the RAF on long missions and to save the engines for the shorter interception flights against enemy bombers. On February 25 nine P-40s joined the RAF Hurricanes against a flight of Japanese bombers. They shot down thirteen enemy planes. Neale and Mac McGarry got two planes each while Charlie Bond, George Burgard, Bob Little, and "Snuffy" Smith shot down three planes each. Bob Prescott was credited with two planes and Dick Rossi and John Blackburn each shot down one. The Japanese commanders, furious at the losses, sent more planes back each day.

The AVG was operating out of both Rangoon and Magwe—an auxiliary field just to the north. Conditions at Magwe were not the best, as Flight Leader Fritz Wolf reported on February 24:

"I left Rangoon about 1400 o'clock on the 23rd of February, 1942. Landed at Magwe at approximately 1530 that same day. We were nearly out of gas. On landing we were told that the Japanese planes were overhead so we took off immediately. After circling at a high altitude above the field for a time and seeing nothing we came down and landed. There was very little gas left in the planes and we tried to get our planes refueled but we were told by various RAF people on the field, whom we contacted in this effort, to get to other people to see about refueling.

"We tried in vain to find someone responsible on the field but were unable to do so. This morning we went down early to the field to get gassed up so we could leave for Kunming, and it was not until 0830 that any RAF personnel showed up at the field. Then it took us another hour and a half before we could get any fuel. There were both 80 and 100 octane gas on the field but no one seemed to know which was which. The planes at Rangoon and Magwe were in an almost unflyable condition. The tires were hard and baked, and blew out on us continually. They were very much chewed up. We were short on batteries, the battery plates thin, when we recharged them at Rangoon, but they would wear out rapidly and need recharging in a short time. There was no Prestone available down there at all. And there was no oxygen whatsoever. The British in Rangoon destroyed the battery charging depot and the oxygen supply depot without any advance warning, so that we were unable to stock up. We were completely out of auxiliary gear shifts, and they were wearing out in the planes every day. Fresh foodstuffs of any description were completely lacking in Rangoon. We were completely without boys to take care of cooking and our messes. We were living on canned goods entirely. Water was difficult to obtain, most of the water supply in town had been cut off.

"The field at Magwe was very difficult to operate from. The RAF were using two E-2s, four Hudsons and several Blenheims to evacuate RAF Personnel from Magwe to India. They were continuously landing and taking off. The only warning system that they had at Magwe was a Blenheim circling around overhead about 80 miles from Magwe. The dust at Magwe and Rangoon fouled up the ship's engine considerably. It clogged up the carburetion system to such an extent that it was dangerous to increase the manifold pressure of the Sharks because the engines quit cold.

"The entire systems were cleaned up on the ground but in a day's time it was back in the same condition. This tendency of the engines to quit made it impossible to dogfight or strafe, especially at low altitudes, as the engine was liable to quit without warning. Out of eight planes which were started off on an air raid alarm two days earlier, only five were able to leave the ground. When we tried to contact the ACC at Magwe to see about getting some gas, he told us he was too busy with evacuation problems to take care of us. He said for us to see if we could find the Duty Officer.

"Conditions in Rangoon were getting dangerous. The authorities had released the criminals from the prisons, the lepers and insane in Rangoon, and had turned them loose to fend for themselves. The natives had broken into the liquor stocks which were now unguarded. There were knifings and kill-ings continuously. Three British were killed near the docks a few nights earlier by natives. The stores were all closed."

On February 26, Dick Rossi and Ed Liebolt were on patrol south of Rangoon when Rossi saw Liebolt suddenly bail out. The plane spun and crashed far below. Rossi followed Liebolt and watched him land in a rice paddy. Thinking he would find his way back to the field, the squadron did not give the matter much thought, as bailing out was a common occurrence.

During the hectic last battle of that day and the next, the 1st Squadron shot down eighteen fighters in a series of dogfights that raged all around the stricken city. George Burgard shot down three more to boost his total to seven planes, Mac McGarry got two more, Joe Rosbert got two, Bob Little got three as did Bob Neale. Dick Rossi was credited with three planes, and Snuffy Smith and Charlie Bond shot down one each. During the final big battles the 1st Squadron shot down forty-three Japanese planes in two days —a percentage of kills unheard of in aerial warfare.

Ed Liebolt had failed to show up and the other pilots were forced to believe he had been killed or captured, as the Japanese were close to the city. He was later listed as missing due to an accident while flying.

Chennault ordered all planes back to Magwe. The British took all the radio detectors out of Mingaladon on the twenty-seventh, leaving the AVG with no warning system. It was time for the AVG pilots to evacuate. The ground crews had left on the last convoys in mid-February, taking the Prome Road to Magwe and from there on to Kunming. On the twenty-eighth, Neale and Smith took off, leaving a few P-40s that could not be repaired in time on the ground. As they circled the burning city bombs began to fall on the southern outskirts from approaching Japanese bombers. Rangoon fell on March 4.

While the 1st Squadron was defending the falling city of Rangoon to the south, life in Kunming was far pleasanter for the 2nd and 3rd Squadrons.

Pilots spent their time in the alert shack playing acey-deucy dice games and poker. Their quarters in the hostels at Kunming University were sumptuous compared with quarters at Toungoo and Rangoon. Off duty they slept, went to Kunming, or went hunting in the marshes near the lake. The AVG hostel bar was open from four to six for soft drinks and from six to midnight for hard liquor. Harvey Greenlaw had posted the regulations on the bar and personnel were able to buy drinks by the shot but not by the bottle. A bottle of American or British whiskey was selling for $40 U.S. so only the most dedicated drinkers bought their liquor by the bottle—on the black market. A radio in the bar could get broadcasts from Shanghai, Saigon, and Bangkok— with American jazz—but the pilots had to listen to Japanese propaganda to get the music. Radio station KGEI in San Francisco was able to reach China with directional signals and the men picked up news from that station, although there was a lot of static.

Chennault was having problems with his upcoming rank of brigadier general and his authority. General Marshall and General Arnold, irked at the civilian pressure T. V. Soong had been putting on Currie—and eventually President Roosevelt—to promote Chennault to a general officer, had decided to limit his authority. Following the encouraging cable from Madame Chiang on February 3 had come one from Currie the next day.

Incoming Radiogram

Current No. 237.
Dated: Feb. 4, 1942 (19.05)
Rec'd: Feb. 4, 1942 (22.05)

From: Chungking
To: Gen. Chennault
Gen. Chennault Washington DC SEGAC Chungking. for CROCO. Believe it to be in China's interest for you to accept command of (a) portion of Group wishes remain volunteer (b) regular army pursuit (c) regular medium bombers (d) Chinese groups. [Col. Harry A.] Halversen would command heavy bombers. [Clayton] Bissell over all although attitude toward you in army is excellent. Bissell would be in much better position secure army cooperation for really large scale effort. Trust you understand my motive in suggesting sacrifice on your part.

Currrie

It was Bissell—his old nemesis from Air Corps Tactical School days—who had advocated dropping the ball and chain device from fighters on bombers. Chennault was outraged at the suggestion that Bissell be put over him, especially in the light of Madame's cable about his being named "Chief Air Officer in China." Angrily he wired back:

RANGOON
FROM MR. R. C. CHEN NUMBER EIGHT STOP PLEASE FORWARD FOLLOWING TO DR. CURRIE THROUGH H. E. DR. T. V. SOONG QUOTE PERSONALLY AM WILLING MAKE ANY SACRIFICE FOR SAKE OF CHINA AND ALLIED CAUSE BUT CANNOT UNDERSTAND HOW EITHER WILL BE BENEFITED BY SUPERSEDING ME AS SENIOR AIR OFFICER CHINA STOP PARTICULARLY WHEN OFFICER SELECTED COMMA BISSELL COMMA WAS JUNIOR TO ME UNTIL MY RETIREMENT STOP IN ADDITION HE HAS NO KNOWLEDGE OF CONDITIONS IN CHINA SUCH AS I HAVE GAINED IN ALMOST FIVE YEARS AND HE AND I HAVE ALWAYS DISAGREED UPON PURSUIT TACTICS AND EMPLOYMENT STOP IF METHODS USED IN TRAINING AND EMPLOYING AVG REQUIRE IMPROVING COMMA SUGGEST SELECTION OF OFFICER WITH WHOM I CAN WORK HARMONIOUSLY SUCH AS M. F. HARMON COMMA G. C. BRANT OR LAWRENCE HICKEY STOP AM MOST DISCOURAGED BY ATTITUDE WAR DEPART-

MENT AND QUITE WILLING RESUME PRIVATE LIFE AS HEALTH CON-
TINUES POOR UNQUOTE REGARDS.

CHENNAULT

It took nearly two weeks for the answer to come back. Chennault had
worked himself from a rage back to quiet resentment by the time it arrived
on February 13.

Communications Office
First American Volunteer Group
Rangoon.

Dear Sir,
   You are kindly requested to transmit the following message to Brigadier General Chennault in your private code:
   Number fifteen following message from minister Soong dated February tenth quote following is for Brigadier General Chennault from Dr.
Currie message begins Arnold is of opinion that you are A-1 as combat
man and has fullest praise for AVG but he wants member of his own
staff to head larger show stop and paragraph Harmon unavailable because at present chief of air staff while Hickey is not a staff man leaving
only Bissell stop and paragraph Harmon says Bissell has now changed
to your views on tactics and Stilwell adds you will have free hand regarding tactics stop and paragraph Bissell can pull stuff from Army this
being essential for large efforts stop we feel proposed set up deserves fair
trial because China's interest demand good tactics as well as good material support stop and paragraph we hope you will cooperate and participate stop your promotion to Brigadier General will shortly be made
message end unquote.

Yours truly,
For China Defense Supplies, Inc.
P. S. KAO (For T. V. Soong)
Secretary

Chennault—a veteran of twenty years of Air Corps politics—knew when
he had been outplayed. He cabled T. V. Soong the next day.

   FOLLOWING THE H. E. MINISTER SOONG QUOTE PLEASE BE ASSURED
THAT I WILL CONTINUE TO SERVE IN ANY CAPACITY AND ORGANIZA-
TION CONSIDERED MOST SUITABLE FOR EFFECTIVE ACTION STOP AD-
VISE DOCTOR CURRIE STOP HIGHEST REGARDS UNQUOTE.

CHENNAULT

BRIGADIER-GENERAL C. L. CHENNAULT,
FIRST AMERICAN VOLUNTEER GROUP,
KUNMING.

On February 23 he received the following:

Dear Sir,

I beg to forward to you the cable dated February 17 from His Excellency Minister T. V. Soong, reading as follows:

"Your very fine spirit of co-operation expressed in your telegram of February 15 will meet with deserved appreciation in all quarters."

T. V. Soong

In his Kunming office, Chennault turned the telegram over in his hands and smiled grimly. The fortunes of war.

But his troubles were not over. Unbeknownst to him, Chiang Kai-shek and his chief of staff, General Ho Ying-chin, had been insisting since Pearl Harbor that the American Air Corps come to the protection of China. The demands had come through T. V. Soong and had been insistent. The President had passed them along to Chief of Staff George Marshall, who had called together his unified command—which included the British in the Far East. Chiang was angry at the British for grabbing the cargo of the *City of Tulsa* freighter in Rangoon Harbor for themselves when its supplies of .30- and .50-caliber machine guns had been destined for China. Chiang, in an effort to cooperate in the defense of Burma, had offered to send 100,000 Chinese troops to Burma, but General Wavell refused the help—causing a loss of face to China. Marshall, trying to satisfy Chiang, was attempting to find the right high-ranking American officer to go to China. The name of Lieutenant General Hugh Drum had come up but Drum finally said he didn't want the assignment. Marshall had begun to think of his old friend and China hand, Joseph Stilwell—who just happened to be in Washington at the time. The Joint Chiefs of Staff had asked Stilwell and a number of other top generals to submit plans for the possible invasion of North Africa in the near future. The code name for the operation was Gymnast. Stilwell had been preparing to head the operation. Realizing that Stilwell had considerable China experience as an infantry officer, spoke Chinese, and might be the man, Marshall talked it over with Secretary of War Harry Stimson. Stimson also thought it a good idea and had a long talk with Stilwell about it. Stilwell, much preferring a combat post, wrote in his diary of January 1, 1942:

"George [Marshall] looking for a high-ranking man to go [to China]. Drum? Pompous, stubborn, new to them, high rank. Me? No, thank you. They remember me as a small-fry colonel that they kicked around. They saw me on foot in the mud, consorting with coolies, riding soldier trains. Drum will be ponderous and will take time through interpreters; he will decide slowly and insist on his dignity. Drum by all means."[1]

A few days after his talk with Stimson, Marshall asked Stilwell to assume responsibility for the mainland China front against the Japanese. Chiang had assumed the title of Supreme Commander, China Theater, and had asked for an American officer who could serve as chief of his Allied staff. Marshall wanted Stilwell to serve in a combat capacity as much as Stilwell wanted to, but he also knew this China post would be good careerwise for his old friend. Stilwell said he would only consider it if he were in command. Marshall gave Stilwell twenty-four hours to think of a better candidate for the job, otherwise he would have to send Stilwell. The two sent a note to T. V. Soong asking if Chiang would give full command power over Chinese troops to the American officer selected. Chiang answered that he would. On January 23 they all agreed Stilwell was the man for the job and he began collecting his staff.

As early as January 25, Stilwell knew the AVG was to be inducted into the U. S. Army Air Corps. In his diary he wrote: "The AVG is to be the U. S. 23rd Pursuit Group: it will be kept at full strength. Replacements are on the way, by boat. If we can hold on to Rangoon, and develop the bases in China, the bombers can be delivered, and along about summertime the Japs will begin to get it on the nose at home. What a pleasure that would be."[2]

While discussing with the Generalissimo the absorption of the AVG into the Air Corps, Marshall had promised Chiang that Chennault would be the ranking air commander in China. That was where Madame had heard it and that was why she so notified Chennault. But T. V. Soong—when approving the changes in a strategic air plan for the theater and knowing the structure of command would require that the 23rd Pursuit Group be included in the projected air force for China-based operations—forgot to tell Chiang that Bissell would be senior air officer. As a result, Chennault would be second in command to an overall air commander stationed in India and on Stilwell's staff. When Chennault raised hell about his promised position being downgraded Stilwell was sent for. Secretary Stimson got into the act and General Arnold—who remembered Chennault as a maverick from the old days—got angry. Urged by Stilwell, as ranking commander of all United States forces in the China theater, to rank Bissell over Chennault, Arnold did so. He set Chennault's date of rank as brigadier general one day after Bissell's—effectively making him a junior officer. It was an old military trick and one that worked well, as Chennault knew.[3]

So Chennault—before he had taken command of the 23rd Pursuit Group in China—had already made three high-ranking enemies: Marshall, Arnold, and Stilwell. Stilwell, writing in his diary on February 9 said:

"It seems that George Marshall promised Chiang Kai-shek that Chennault could be the ranking air commander. Soong made an unauthorized statement to me, and then reneged on telling Chiang Kai-shek he had done so. Then Currie stuck in his wire, urging Chennault to play ball. When Chennault unexpectedly refused to play, Bissell bossed him. So we were put in the position of Chinese telling the War Department who could and could not be on my staff. Currie made a date with Arnold to talk it over and sprang this announcement from Chennault, urging that a man other than Bissell go. Arnold hit the ceiling. I spoke for Bissell, and insisted that he rank Chennault. Arnold so ordered. Currie pulled in his horns. I told him my opinion of Chennault had dropped a lot since hearing that. It was arranged for Currie to send Chennault another wire telling him to get in the game and play ball or else. They are acting like a couple of kids, and they'll both have to behave."[4] Thus was begun what would turn out to be a long-lasting, disruptive feud between two strong leaders.

Stilwell—his staff chosen for the Far East—left the States on February 13 from Miami bound for Africa, India, and the CBI, now officially called the China-Burma-India theater.

Hearing rumors about Stilwell and his new command, Chennault asked General Magruder where Stilwell was and what his itinerary was. Magruder answered on February 15 that he had no idea where Stilwell was but that he was definitely on his way to China by air. Chennault, aware that his military future was at stake, shrugged off the answer and went back to his problems with the AVG and its upcoming induction into the Army Air Corps.

Twelve

As if Chennault did not have enough trouble with the Japanese and his command problems, William Pawley issued orders to his American staff at the repair facility at Loiwing not to undertake any more repairs of AVG P-40s as of January 1. The AVG had been sending damaged planes from the Rangoon and Toungoo area to Loiwing for repair. The facility there had been busy with the assembly of Curtiss-Wright Model 21 interceptors Pawley had sold to the Chinese and he evidently felt he had enough to do without repairing the AVG planes.

The original contracts between CAMCO and the Chinese government stipulated that CAMCO was to supply Chennault, as commander of the Group, with technical personnel, tools, and material for the repair of damaged P-40s. A later agreement between Pawley, Chennault, and General Chow, head of the Chinese Aeronautical Commission, stated in September 1941 that all repair work on damaged P-40s west of the Salween River in Burma be done by CAMCO at Loiwing while all damage to P-40s east of that river be done by Chinese repair shops in Kunming. CAMCO had sent some mechanics to Toungoo in the early days of fall to help repair the damaged fighters, but it was decided to ship the more severely damaged craft by rail to Lashio and then by truck to Loiwing. This was done, but as the planes began to pile up there, very little work was done on them.

Disgusted with Pawley's attitude and considering him unpatriotic in letting down the AVG, Chennault took the matter up with Madame and the Generalissimo in Chungking. Chiang ordered the Chinese manager of the Loiwing plant, Colonel Chen, to continue repairing the AVG fighters. Chen, knowing where his allegiance lay, ordered his Chinese staff to do so. The Chinese government immediately acquired the interests Pawley had in CAMCO and Pawley left for India, where he began assembling another aircraft plant. It was the culmination of a long battle between Chennault and

Pawley that had originated back in the days of Shanghai and Hankow. There had been hard feelings between the two for years. In 1982, when A. L. Patterson, the legendary aeronautical consultant and old China hand, was eighty-two years old and still living in Hong Kong, he wrote of the conflict:

"Few people knew that Chennault was the co-designer with Severksy of the P-35. He was up against Hap Arnold who was a Curtiss advocate and that is where he and Hap fell out. Chennault had a different and more modern idea of fighter tactics than Hap which finally led to his resignation. I had been an old friend of Chennault's from the time he led the 'Three Musketeers' [sic] precision Curtiss Hawks at the first International Air Show at Mines Field in 1927. So when Chennault resigned and came to China he suggested I secure the Severksy representation which I did. I got the order for the 50 P-35s with funds etc. But Bill Pawley pulled such unbelievable stunts to kill it, that H. H. Kung finally cancelled the order and gave me additional North American NA-16 aircraft.

"However, the order for the P-35 to Seversky Aircraft did result in the company getting financed and changing the name to Republic Aircraft Corporation. It almost broke Chennault's heart.

"The story of what Pawley did would take a book to tell."[1]

Pawley, however, before leaving for India, got in his last licks[2] at Chennault in a letter from Loiwing. He denied there had been any shirking of responsibility on his part, saying he had more than fulfilled his duties as stipulated in his CAMCO contract with the Chinese and accused Chennault of repeatedly trying to discredit him in order to deprive him of any share of credit in forming the AVG. He told Chennault that he had neglected his AVG pilots during the battles of Rangoon by staying up in Kunming away from all the fighting—which really irked Chennault and made any reconciliation between the two men almost an impossibility.

The AVG of Kunming was treated to the relief of a wedding in the middle of March. "Daffy" Davis, who had been acting as an operations officer at both Kunming and Loiwing, heard from his fiancée, Doreen Lonberg, who had escaped from Hong Kong. Davis had given her up for lost and assumed she would be a prisoner of war for the duration. An Englishwoman who had been married to a Dane, Doreen had evidently been able to convince the Japanese she was a neutral. Speaking both Japanese and Chinese fluently, she had shown her Danish passport to a Japanese officer and he had allowed her and her houseboy to leave on a boat headed for Hainan Island and Haiphong. She got off at a port on the south China coast and they caught truck rides north until they reached Kweilin. From there she phoned Davis at Kunming.

They were married in an auditorium on St. Patrick's Day, with Chennault giving the bride away. Because the bride had been forced to leave Hong Kong without much in the way of personal belongings, Olga Greenlaw lent her the necessary clothes and makeup. Chaplain Paul Frillman performed the ceremony and everyone adjourned to Chennault's quarters for a celebration. An extremely capable typist, Doreen later joined the office staff of the AVG.

After the fall of Rangoon the AVG faced its darkest days. It had been pulled back to the small British base of Magwe, about two hundred and fifty miles up the Irrawaddy River from Rangoon. It was a hastily built dirt strip in the jungle and it had neither dispersal nor revetment facilities. Its warning system was faulty and faced only one way—toward Rangoon. Emergency telephone lines had been strung down the river valleys but there was no effective warning system. The sight of Japanese bombers over the field was usually the first warning the AVG had. By mid-March the Japanese began to send bombers, accompanied by the new fighters, over in waves. On March 21 the Japanese caught the British unaware and burned dozens of Blenheim bombers that were being refueled at the time. Only a few RAF and AVG fighters got into the air in time to shoot down a few enemy fighters. Parker Dupouy was injured when he and his flight jumped the first wave of bombers just returning from Magwe—with their bombs already dropped. He landed out of ammunition and was hit by 20-mm. cannon fire. The rest of his flight escaped injury but were shot up by Type 97 fighters.

Zeros strafed the field constantly, setting fire to hangars and Hudson bombers and killing ground personnel. AVG ground crews returned their fire with pistols, rifles, and submachine guns taken from the supplies on the Rangoon docks. One Zero fell back to the ground after a strafing run, the pilot dead from a .45-caliber wound to the head. Ground crewmen Joe Sweeney, Keith Cristtensen, and Manning Wakefield, all firing at the plane, never knew who had hit the pilot.

Frank Swartz was wounded by bomb fragments as he raced for the cockpit of his P-40. The same bomb sent splinters into crew chief John Fauth and mechanic Bill Seiple. They were picked up by Dr. Lewis Richards in a jeep and raced to a hospital filled with RAF wounded. Fauth later died of his wounds, but Seiple recovered. Swartz was flown to a British hospital in Calcutta but later he, too, died of his wounds.

The pilots alternated between attacking bomber flights and strafing the enemy on the ground. On March 18, Ken Jernstedt was wounded by Zero bullets as he landed among burning Blenheims and Hudsons, but not before chalking up considerable damage:

"While on a reconnaissance hop in the Moulmein area," he reported, "Pilot W. N. Reed and I saw at least 30 planes on a field ten miles south of Moulmein. It was 7.35 o'clock. Planes were parked rather close together on either side of this one runway. We each made six passes. On my first pass, I set a fighter on fire and scattered some lead up the line of planes. On my second pass, a transport plane folded up on the ground after receiving the main part of my fire. On my third pass I hit several planes but nothing happened to them except that pieces flew from some. My next pass resulted in one bomber being set afire and other planes being hit. On my fifth pass a fighter crumbled to the ground with parts flying from the engine. During my last pass on this field I set another fighter on fire and sprayed up the line. When we left this field I saw at least five large fires. We then proceeded towards Moulmein and saw the main airport with at least 30 more planes on it, mostly bombers. I passed over the hangar on my approach and tried to hit it with an incendiary bomb, but I missed the hangar and hit an Army 97 bomber parked in front of the hangar. This ship was soon ablaze. Reed made one more pass. A.A. guns shot at us here, the shells bursting as low as 200 feet. Each of us had a lone bullet hole in our planes, but where we picked them up I don't know. After Reed had made his last pass I saw two planes taking off. I turned and headed west. We left this field with five planes ablaze. I claimed: One transport, two bombers, four fighters. It would be hard to estimate the amount of damage done to other aircraft but I feel that it was considerable."[3]

Reed claimed one transport plane, five fighters, and two bombers.

The AVG was out of serviceable planes, oxygen, and tires, and ammunition was almost expended. In Kunming, Chennault, getting up from a sickbed where he had been down for days with a bad case of bronchitis, radioed Dupouy, the flight leader of the 3rd Pursuit:

> SECRET URGENT STOP BEGIN MOVEMENT SQUADRON TO LOIWING WITHOUT DELAY STOP LEAVE SERIOUSLY WOUNDED IN HOSPITAL WITH RICHARDS AND ONE CAR STOP DO YOU NEED ASSISTANCE LASHIO OR LOIWING QUESTION MOVE RADIO STATION LAST STOP ADVISE ME OF DEVELOPMENTS CHENNAULT.

The AVG planes left Magwe and moved to Loiwing, where Chennault had set up a headquarters to attack the Japanese Air Force fields in northern Burma and Thailand. Compared with Magwe and Toungoo, the base was sumptuous. Pawley had set up a regular American oasis in the jungle—a long asphalt strip, neat wooden bungalows for the staff, a dining room, mess hall, and even a clubhouse with a jukebox and chintz curtains at the windows. The aircraft assembly plant—all concrete and steel—was probably the most modern in the Orient. The clubhouse sat at the edge of the river with a marvelous picture-window view of the Yunnan Mountains. It would have been luxury except for the Japanese.

On Tuesday, March 24, Jack Newkirk was killed. Frank Lawlor was flying near him at the time and filed the following report:

"I took off from Namsang airport and made rendezvous with three other pilots. When the formation had reached an altitude of 6,000 feet we headed on course of 150 degrees. At 0710 we sighted Chiengmai below us. At this time of morning the light was poor and visibility was satisfactory only when looking straight down. Our objective was to strafe the airfields at Chiengmai and Lamphun. Due to the poor visibility and the fact that we approached Chiengmai along the east when the airfield was located to the west we did not find the field and after strafing the railway depot we continued south to Lamphun. Along the railway that turned between Chiengmai and Lamphun were a row of 15 warehouses. All four pilots strafed these and several were seen by me to be on fire. Since these buildings were very close to each other I believe the whole block eventually burned up. We approached Lamphun making a wide circle. We flew over two small satellite fields but no airplanes. A third and larger field also had no planes but the area surrounding the field had several barracks. These were strafed and I noticed one that was smoking. No enemy return fire was noticed during the period up through this attack. Immediately after leaving the area of the barracks Squadron Leader Newkirk headed back up the road to Chiengmai. He went into a dive to strafe what appeared to be an armored car and I saw his plane crash and burn. Since by this time visibility had improved considerably and there appeared to be no unusual circumstances, it was evident that Newkirk had been hit by enemy fire, possibly from the armored car. Continuing on to Chiengmai I took over the lead as directed by Newkirk in case of any accident to himself. Over Chiengmai, we encountered very heavy enemy anti-aircraft [fire] undoubtedly the aftermath of an attack by Squadron Leader Neale and a flight of five. The field could now be seen and several large fires were burning on it. We continued on north to escape anti-aircraft which became extremely heavy. When clear of the danger area I turned on course for Heho and the remaining three planes landed there at 0835."[4]

Flight Leader Charlie Bond, returning from another strafing mission with four planes, noticed one of the planes falling behind. He circled to see what the trouble was and noticed that wingman Mac McGarry was having trouble —black smoke was pouring from an engine. McGarry was unable to stay with the formation and finally bailed out at 1,000 feet. He landed safely and Bond circled him, dropping maps, then flew on and landed at Mamsang at 8:25 A.M. The RAF and the Chinese in the area were notified of McGarry's whereabouts but he was not found. Later it was learned he had been arrested by a Thai policeman and spent the next three years in a tiny town jail. The Thais did not turn him over to the Japanese and he was rescued by the American OSS in 1945. Both Newkirk and McGarry were leading AVG aces, with ten victories each. Later that night Tex Hill was named squadron leader to replace Newkirk.

Squadron Leader Olson and his 3rd Pursuit Squadron moved into the base on March 26. Two more planes, with Greg Boyington in charge, went down to Loiwing two days later to reinforce the 3rd Squadron. A day later, the twenty-ninth, Charlie Older and P. J. Greene intercepted a Japanese observation plane heading up from the south and both pilots dove on the plane,

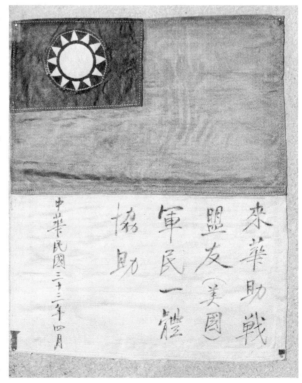

12 and 13. Flags worn on the jackets of AVG and Fourteenth Air Force flight crews. They were called "blood chits" and said—in Chinese and Burmese—that the wearer was an American and to get him safely back to friendly lines.

14. Chennault behind his desk at the Fourteenth Air Force headquarters in Kunming. (Courtesy of Malcom Rosholt)

15. Chennault chats with fighter pilots of the 26th Fighter Squadron, 51st Fighter Group. (A P-51 is in the background.) (U.S. Air Corps Photo)

16. Chennault with Lieutenant General Henry H. "Hap" Arnold, Commanding General of the Army Air Force, during Arnold's inspection trip to China in 1943. In the background are the shark-nosed P-40s of the China Air Task Force. (U.S. Air Corps Photo)

17. Chennault at the bat in one of the Fourteenth Air Force baseball games at Kunming. (Fourteenth Air Force Association)

18. An Air Transport Command C-46 that undershot a runway while bringing supplies over the Hump from Assam to Kunming. (Fourteenth Air Force Association)

19. A B-25 medium bomber of the 491st Bomb Squadron after a crash landing. (Fourteenth Air Force Association)

20. The bitter aftermath of a raid—a B-24 that crash landed after being shot up by Japanese fighters. (Fourteenth Air Force Association)

21. A B-24 Liberator of the 425th Bomb Squadron, 308th Bomb Group, pulling away from the target after a successful bombing mission to the railroad yards at Vinh, Indochina. (Fourteenth Air Force Association)

22. Major General Chennault in Kunming, 1944. (Photo by Sydney Greenberg)

23. Colonel Fred C. Milner, Adjutant General of the Fourteenth Air Force, awards Chennault an oak-leaf cluster to the Air Medal. (U.S. Air Force Photo)

24. Lieutenant General Joseph Stilwell returns a salute from Brigadier General Buzz Glenn, Chief of Staff of the Fourteenth Air Force, as Chennault looks on, Kunming, 1944. (U.S. Air Force Photo)

which was cruising at 27,000 feet. The plane burst into flames and crashed into the jungle below.

Chennault finally got the replacement planes for which he had been pleading. The first P-40Es—Kittyhawks—had been detached from a shipment of fighter planes heading for the RAF in Libya. The new version of the old Tomahawk had more speed, range, and firepower than the older model. It had better radios and—what was far more important to Chennault—auxiliary bomb racks that could carry six 35-pound fragmentation bombs or one 250-pound general-purpose bomb. Chennault sent six pilots from Kunming on the long trip to Africa to pick up the new planes. Charlie Olson, George McMillan, R.T. ("Tadpole") Smith, Paul Greene, Tom Haywood, and Link Laughlin climbed aboard a CNAC airliner and headed west. They finally reached Takoradi on the Gold Coast of Africa, but they had to wait until the white stars of the Chinese Air Force were painted on the wings of the shiny new planes. Even then it was fifty-two flying hours for the fighter pilots before they skimmed across the Himalayas and delivered the planes in late March. Two of them were immediately flown down to Loiwing by Olson and Little to reinforce the squadron there. The rest were assigned to Kunming.

The Japanese ground armies were relentlessly pushing up from Prome and Toungoo and their planes were blasting Lashio and Mandalay daily. The AVG was assigned the hazardous job of strafing Japanese ground forces—a dangerous task for the P-40. Much slower than the Japanese fighters, it was a sitting duck close to the ground, where it could not outdive the enemy planes. Long-range Zeros were beginning to strafe the field at Loiwing and were wreaking havoc with the repair shops. On April 8 a flight of Zeros was jumped from above while it was attacking ground installations. Squadron Leader Olson led his mates in a dive and four enemy planes were shot down on the first pass. Both Olson and John Donovan got a plane each. Pilots E. F. Overend, C. G. Groh, and Bob Little each shot down one more and Fred Hodges followed one so closely that it crashed into a hillside. Tadpole Smith and Fritz Wolf each shot down two Zeros to make a grand total for the day of ten enemy planes destroyed.

The Japanese came back with a vengeance two days later, catching the AVG at dawn. They strafed the field at will as the pilots and ground personnel huddled in slit trenches. When they left they had destroyed a number of P-40s, including the two new P-40E Kittyhawks.

The AVG was getting tired. A message from Washington—brought down from Kunming by Chennault—helped the morale a bit.

COLONEL CHENNAULT

AVG, KUNMING

SECRETARY OF WAR SENDS THE FOLLOWING MESSAGE: WAR DEPARTMENT JOINS WITH AMERICAN PEOPLE IN ADMIRATION FOR THE GALLANT AND FIGHTING RECORD OF AVG UNDER YOUR LEADERSHIP STOP

YOUR MEN AND YOU ARE MOST HIGHLY COMMENDED STOP END OF
COLONEL STIMSON'S MESSAGE.

MAGRUDER[5]

The death of Newkirk and the capture of McGarry caused a drop in
morale. The Japanese were moving rapidly up the Irrawaddy, Sittang, and
Salween river valleys, intending to capture the British strongholds at
Yenangyaung, north of Magwe on the Irrawaddy; Mandalay on the Sittang;
and eventually Lashio, Loiwing, and the Burma Road by following the Salween all the way to northern Burma. The Chinese Fifth and Sixth Armies
had finally been released to fight on the border between Burma and China.
Chennault had hoped to knock out the advance fighter bases at Chiengmai
and Lamphun in northern Thailand when he moved the AVG to Loiwing,
but the Japanese were pouring fighters and bombers into their new bases in
both Burma and Thailand. The Japanese were using heavy artillery and
tanks in the valleys, and strafing them became more and more hazardous for
the fighter pilots.

In India, Air Vice Marshal Stevenson was doing his best to hold on with
the RAF. He wanted to develop a retaliatory air force, as evidenced by a
MOST SECRET letter to Chennault in which he outlined his plan to form a
number of fighter and bomber squadrons which he could deploy into Burma
in an effort to slow the Japanese advance. He reaffirmed his close cooperation
with the AVG and said that together they might be able to stem the invasion
if they could hold Upper Burma until the monsoons started that spring. He
ended by saying that he was impressed with the performance of several of the
AVG members during the battles for Rangoon and was putting both Bob
Neale and Charlie Bond in for Distinguished Flying Crosses and line chief
Harry Fox in for an Order of the British Empire medal for gallantry under
fire. (It was Fox, incensed at the constant strafing by Japanese fighter planes
at Mingaladon Airfield, who had thrown a wrench at a strafing enemy
fighter.)[6]

In Chennault's answer to Stevenson he talked about his plans for northern
Burma. He suggested setting up a warning net with a minimum radius of
seventy-five miles south of Lashio, Mandalay, and Magwe; he thought it
could be done during the monsoon season and would make both Chennault
and the RAF better prepared for the Japanese advance by October when the
rains ceased.[7]

Neither Chennault nor Stevenson knew the size or the strength of the
invading Japanese armies. In little more than a month Lashio, Mandalay,
Magwe, and Loiwing would have fallen.

The forests of Burma had been set afire just prior to the monsoon. A pall
of heavy smoke hung over northern Burma, making it exceedingly difficult
for the AVG fighter planes to see the ground. It was necessary to fly on
instruments below 10,000 feet and it was impossible to maintain formations.

The Japanese were sending a steady stream of fighter patrols over the area and an AVG plane that was caught below them had almost no chance to get away. Japanese ground forces were able to throw up a concentrated curtain of small arms fire against the AVG as it swept over on strafing runs. Orders for such flights kept coming down from Chennault—who was getting them from Stilwell and Bissell. The Chinese high command felt it was a great morale booster for the soldiers of the Fifth and Sixth Armies to see their own fighter planes overhead. The Generalissimo requested Chennault to send formations of AVG fighters over the troops at little more than treetop level, so that they could see the white stars of the Chinese Air Force on the wings.

Like many old-line infantry officers, Stilwell thought the role of the fighter plane was one of observation. He continually asked for visual reconnaissance of Japanese front-line positions, where the ground fire was intense. The combination of these low-level missions and the requests from the British to escort the heavy, lumbering Blenheim bombers far into heavily defended enemy territory finally got to the exhausted pilots.

In mid-April the pilots at Loiwing decided to hold a meeting to protest the low-level missions. They claimed they had signed up to fight and didn't mind defending airfields or flying other high-altitude missions where they had a chance against enemy fighters, but they felt they were being sacrificed on these strafing runs. A petition of resignation was drawn up. Chennault attended the meeting and one by one the pilots spoke their minds. His face set in anger, Chennault heard them out but then carefully reminded them that their action—in the face of the enemy—could be considered desertion. There was silence in the room while he talked. He told them that under the Articles of War the punishment for desertion was death. (He did not add that they were all civilians and did not fall under the same rules as the military.) When he left the room Tex Hill rose to his feet and said he wanted them all to know that he was not in favor of the resignations. He had not signed the protest, nor had four other pilots—Ed Rector, Bob Hedman, Frank Schiel, and R. J. Raines. Hill told them it was true they had all started out as mercenaries, but since Pearl Harbor they had all been at war and it was a matter of fighting the Japanese any way they could.

In a few days the "revolt" was over. The pilots at Kunming were not involved in the petition and Bob Neale volunteered his squadron to fly the strafing missions if the rest refused. In the end twenty-three pilots left their resignations on the petition, but Chennault never took any action to accept them. The whole thing died down slowly and they were back to flying by April 28. A few pilots actually did resign—among them Boyington—but all for reasons other than the strafing missions. Although Boyington had been a hard-drinking brawler and a source of trouble to Chennault since Toungoo days, he was an excellent fighter pilot. He resented his dishonorable discharge from the AVG and never spoke kindly of Chennault afterward, but in

April, along with other citations for his men, Chennault sent the following to General Chow in Chungking:

April 27, 1942

Citation

On February 6, 1942, in company with other members of his squadron, Vice Squadron Leader G. Boyington, AVG, engaged in combat with a number of Japanese pursuit planes near the city of Rangoon, Burma. In the combat which ensued, he personally shot down two enemy fighters in the air. On March 24, 1942, in company with five other pilots of the AVG he attacked the airdrome at Chiengmai, Thailand. As a result of this flight's attack, fifteen enemy planes were burned, and the credit for the attacked was shared equally, giving Vice Squadron Leader Boyington credit for destroying two and one half enemy aircraft. This pilot has destroyed a total of four and one half enemy planes; two of which were destroyed in aerial combat, and two and one half burned on the ground. He is commended on his performance and achievement in combat.

C. L. Chennault
Commanding, AVG[8]

Later in the war Boyington was to become a much-decorated Marine fighter ace.

A number of pilots did not want to be inducted into the U. S. Army Air Forces and rumors had it they would have no choice. Some went back to the States because they preferred to be taken back into the Navy or Marines. A number of other pilots were let go for reasons ranging from bad attitude and insubordination to excessive drinking. Factors contributing to the low morale about induction included a cable received at Kunming—which spread about the base.

Chennault
AVG Headquarters, Kunming
Information received that 70 ground personnel formerly employed by CAMCO being inducted into U.S. Army in Australia in accordance with instructions from War Department.

Magruder

Chennault, also worried about what the War Department was up to, cabled Madame that he was sure at least 90 percent of AVG personnel would terminate their CAMCO contracts rather than accept induction into the Army Air Forces. He said one of the reasons was that the men wanted leaves before joining the military and the War Department showed no signs of agreeing. He suggested that more of them might consider joining up if he could get a guarantee from the military that they could all be kept together in the new 23rd Pursuit Group which was being proposed for China. He sent a copy of this cable to Magruder.[9] In a separate message he appealed to the Generalissimo to cease using the P-40s as low-level reconnaissance planes for the Chinese Army because of the danger involved from low-altitude ground fire and bad weather. Chiang consented and cabled back—through Madame —that the AVG planes would be used only for fighting against Japanese aircraft.[10]

On April 20, Chennault received word from Madame Chiang that President Roosevelt had recommended to the Senate that he be promoted to brigadier general. Later that day he learned that his permanent rank had been effective as of April 18 and he immediately wrote General Chow to ask that his pay and allowances from the Chinese government cease immediately. He also told Chow that from now on he was prohibited from accepting any gifts from the Chinese government or its people.

One of Chennault's biggest problems was trying to obtain bombers. His repeated requests for them had been largely ignored and he now discovered that several B-25 Mitchell medium bombers had been assigned to the Tenth Air Force in India. He cabled General Lewis H. Brereton, commanding officer of the Tenth in New Delhi, asking that they be reassigned to him for use in Kunming against Japanese bases in China, Indochina, and Thailand.

While he was waiting for a reply from Brereton a message came in from General Marshall marked SECRET. It was from President Roosevelt and read:

From President for AVG

The conspicuous gallantry and daring of the AVG officers combined with their extraordinary efficiency is a source of tremendous pride throughout America. The shortages and difficulties under which they have labored are keenly appreciated.

Large numbers of new airplanes are on the way to bring the 23rd Pursuit Group to full strength and to maintain that strength for the coming periods of critical combat. Reinforcements for AVG in ground and in flying personnel are enroute and more will follow. A tremendous effort is being made to get this material into the hands of our men. Losses of planes by unfortunate sinkings west of Australia and in the Indian Ocean delayed reinforcements at a critical moment but planes are now going forward rapidly.

As quickly as replacement personnel have absorbed your experience and tradition, leaves of absence should be granted to AVG veterans for rest and recuperation. When replacements are adequately trained, it is planned that selected AVG veterans will be recalled to the States or other theaters of operation to impart their combat experience and training to personnel in newly formed units. The President is greatly concerned during the critical phase of the operation now impending. He has taken great pride in the world acclaim given its pilots and places great hope in its future fighting as rapidly as it is reequipped.

                                                                Marshall

Chennault smiled to himself. It was wonderful what international publicity would do. He also found a long letter from General Clayton Bissell, who was already deep in plans for the time when the AVG would be inducted into the U. S. Army Air Forces—as if they did not have enough problems fighting the Japanese in the skies to the south. Bissell said July 4, 1942, had been set as the date for the final dissolution of the AVG. All outstanding contracts would be liquidated on that date—either on the basis of lump-sum payments or the difference between the salaries called for in the contracts and pay to be received from the United States in the rank or grade of inducted AVG personnel. In addition there was to be a $500 travel allowance. Agreement had been reached between the United States Government and Chiang Kai-shek, and Bissell added that General Stilwell had been given broad powers to recognize previous meritorious service by suitable and appropriate grade in the United States Army. Chennault was to make recommendations about such promotions. Ex-Navy and Marine personnel could elect to join the Army if they wished or could join the Navy or Marine Corps. He added that AVG personnel who were United States citizens and who declined induction into the armed forces would be subject to Selective Service upon return to the United States and that former reserve officers now in the AVG would be reinstated and called to active duty upon arrival in the United States.

He wound up by saying he had authorized the transfer from India of the 51st Pursuit Group, consisting of seventeen officers and two hundred and fifteen enlisted men—minus planes—to Chennault's command in Kunming and wanted him to confirm that he could house and feed the men.

Another letter in the mail was from the CAMCO representative in Calcutta, reporting that fighting had broken out in Lashio—apparently between Japanese sympathizers and Burmese nationalists—and that the British military had destroyed the RAF radio station and the CNAC operations office and radio there. CNAC personnel were reportedly being evacuated to Kunming. Things were deteriorating rapidly in northern Burma.[11]

At Loiwing the few pilots still there were staging a holding action against the rapidly advancing Japanese. On Monday, April 20, Ed Rector reported:

"At 0645 on 20 April, Hill, Hedman, Raines and myself took off from Lashio for aerial patrol over Pyinmana. We arrived over the target an hour later and began circling at 8,000 feet. Shortly after we received a barrage of AA fire and turned north and continued our patrol. Raines saw an enemy ship below us and to the south circling a small town. His message was so garbled however we could not read him. We had circled for 20 minutes at 9,000 feet when I observed an enemy ship approaching from the south and 2,000 feet above us. I informed Hill by radio, then turned toward the plane and started climbing. The plane turned west on sighting us and poured on all gas to escape. I chased as he turned south. I gave him three bursts in the turn, one more long one as he straightened out eastward and started in a dive toward the ground. Hedman meanwhile had made a pass at him, and gave him a final burst setting him on fire. As [sic] he rolled over on his back and went in. The two of us then proceeded to Loi-wing."[12]

The following day operations officer Harvey Greenlaw wrote in his daily report:

"At 0730 ten Model '0' Fighters attack [sic] Namsang Airdrome. At that three P-40 airplanes were on the field. Flight Leader Brouk, Third Pursuit Squadron was just making a landing. The Japanese came in from the East at about 10,000 feet. As they approached the field they dropped to about 5,000 feet, and three of them peeled off to strafe Brouk who was landing. He was caught by surprise and hit by the first burst. With his airplane still rolling he jumped from the cockpit and dived head first into a trench. His airplane rolled a short distance and stopped. The Japs made about four passes each until the plane began to burn. It was completely burned, and Brouk was shot three times in the legs.

"At about 0930 four P-40s contacted 18 I-97 Fighters over the Front at Pyinmana. No certains were claimed. The ground situation has been moving very fast. The Japs have continued their advance against the partially collapsed British and Chinese Forces. The Japs are now between Kyidaunggan and Pyokwa about 15 miles north of Pyinmana. On the Loikaw Front they are near Hopeng, and near Taungdwingyi, Natmauk, Kyaukpadaung in the Yenangyaung area. Stilwell will send daily reports on the situation. The AVG personnel stationed at Namsang have been ordered to evacuate. They left for Loi-wing at 1800. Under the present situation Namsang and Heho can no longer be used."[13]

Stilwell had by now been appointed chief of staff of the Chinese Fifth and Sixth Armies fighting in northern Burma and had his hands full. The Japanese armored forces were almost at Hsipaw—between Mandalay and Lashio —and were moving fast. Stilwell, constantly fighting with the Chinese commanders, in whom he had little faith, was by now becoming frustrated. The Chinese generals, disliking Stilwell's heavy-handed manner of command and his sarcastic attitude, had been taking their orders directly from Chiang Kai-shek. Stilwell, as field commander, was on the march near Lashio with his staff and some British who were attached to his command.

At Loiwing on April 24, Tex Hill wrote in his diary report:

"Took off six P-40s from Loi-wing 10:00 to bomb and strafe enemy convoy. Five Tomahawks went along for top cover. Arrived over Loilem about 1110 sighted a convoy of about 30 trucks bottle necked one and one-half miles on road running NE of our city. I could see bombs landing in a nice string about fifty feet apart, some on the convoy and some to the right of road which was ideal for the people who had left the trucks to take cover in the field. I came down the line of trucks strafing after the last man had bombed. The trucks were probably carrying gas as they burned readily. I counted eight burning. As I pulled up I saw a Jap recco off to my left—I pursued him immediately. Two other planes were also chasing him. We overtook him immediately and shot him down. His rear gunner returned fire. I saw the plane crash on the ground, I saw another Jap plane crash on the ground in the same area. I had shot up all my ammunition so proceeded to Loi-wing via Hsipaw road making reconnaissance. I saw nothing—arrived Loi-wing 1230."[14]

The following day Ed Rector reported:

"Hill, Wright, Petach, Ricketts, Raines and myself took off from Loi-wing at 0950 and proceeded south to Namsang arriving one hour later. Over Loilem we saw a convoy of 25 trucks just leaving the town heading northward. We went into a string and dropped bombs on the trucks, ahead, behind and on both sides. We then circled and strafed the line, pulling up for another run. I saw a Jap recco ship heading west with Hill, Wright and Petach in hot pursuit. As they started firing the Jap nosed down turned 180 degrees and flew up a slight valley. I fired a head-on as he headed towards me, then turned sharply to keep from hitting him. He made another turn in the valley and crashed into a hill as one P-40 made a final run on him. Petach, Wright and myself returned and continued strafing the trucks making about four runs each. I expended all ammunition and Petach and I started back to base. Petach continued making attacks up the road on scattered convoys. We followed the road to Laihka observing trucks pulling artillery and loaded with men and small groups of trucks all along the route. The town of Laihka was partially burned and just south of the town was another convoy of 30 trucks parked along the road. We left the road at this point and proceeded to Loi-wing."[15]

By the twenty-eighth, it was almost over. The Japanese were overrunning almost all the roads. Tex Hill flew on that day:

"I took off from Loi-wing with five P-40Es at 0930 as top cover for a flight of ten P-40 and P-40Es mixed, to make a sweep to Laihka and back to Loi-wing. The Third Squadron was flying at 10,000 stepped up to 12,000 feet. My flight was at 15,000. At about 1015 I sighted 27 enemy 20 miles out of Hsipaw which I estimated at first to be 30 fighters. I did not have direct communication with the leader of the flight of ten planes but made my report to him through one member of his flight. In the meantime I turned my flight on an interception course of the enemy. As I drew closer I could see there was a formation of 27 bombers in three nine plane flights echeloned. Behind them at the same altitude of 15,000 feet were a string of model '0,' I counted 12–15 of same. When we drew near the fighters tried to get into some semblance of a formation but I couldn't tell exactly what type. Four of us made the initial contact with eight '0s' that we [sic] (re) in the immediate vicinity. My fifth man had wandered off somewhere. We were flying a good two ship [formation] when we hit them they were apparently trying to work in threes. I fired four short bursts at my first opponent before I got him. In the fourth burst he started off in a shallow dive smoking and never did change his altitude until he crashed into the jungle. From then on the fight was a rat race with '0s' and P-40s on each other's tails. I got my second '0' on a head on approach with him having a slight altitude advantage. My first burst went low. The range was closing so fast that I had to haul back on the stick violently in order to get a bead on him."

Chennault, back at Loiwing to see to the evacuation of the base, if necessary, cabled General Peter Mow of the Chinese Air Force in Kunming for aid in the form of Chinese bombers—however obsolete. Mow cabled back that he would do what he could with the old Russian bombers. Mow was doing all he could to try and stem the Japanese advance.

In the midst of the confusion at Loiwing a cable arrived from the Generalissimo:

For the AVG

I am proud to be the commander in chief of such men as the members of the AVG, during the past five years. Despite the inferior equipment and strain attendant upon prolonged warfare, the fighting morale of the Chinese Army has risen to greater heights with the passage of time. You, the AVG, are a worthy part of China's Army and you have added brilliance and glory to it by your resolute spirit and indomitable will in combating superior numbers of enemy planes at every encounter. April 25 when you shot down four observation planes, destroyed 30 trucks and damaged over 100 more is indeed a red-letter day, for by your own efforts you prevented the enemy from consolidating at Lashio and thus at a most critical juncture you were instrumental in causing what may prove to be the turning of the tide in the battle of Burma. The entire Chinese nation has taken you to heart and hails you as true comrades in arms. I feel certain that you will fight to a finish to victory with the same ardent enthusiasm and tenacious will to win that have characterized your performance in the past. The recognition of merit which the American government has recently given to General Chennault is a tribute to you as well and should spur every man of you to even greater devotion to duty. Let your present objective be the annihilation of the Japanese Air Force so that in the near future the AVG will control Burma skies as the Chinese land forces will control that portion of Burma soil entrusted to them to defend.

Generalissimo Chiang Kai-shek

Chennault posted the telegram on the bulletin board in the ready room. He returned to his desk. First of all he had to hold this place—before he could "annihilate the Japanese Air Force."

Thirteen

General Clayton Bissell had been sent to China by George Marshall to handle the China end of the top-secret air raid on Japan, in which B-25 bombers—commanded by General Jimmy Doolittle—took off from the U.S. aircraft carrier *Hornet* at sea on April 18 and bombed the home island of Japan. While inflicting relatively little damage on the Japanese, the flight was a great boost to American morale at home—the first bombing mission against Japan itself. Forced to take off from the carrier earlier than they had planned, the flight of B-25s bombed Japan and was forced to fly on over China in darkness and bad weather. As a result, many of the planes crashed and other raiders bailed out in darkness. Doolittle himself bailed out near Japanese lines and narrowly escaped capture. One crew landed in Poyang Lake near Nanchang in Japanese-occupied territory and were captured and later executed in Shanghai—an event that enraged Chennault.

The secretive Bissell had neglected to inform Chennault that the raid was to take place. The extensive east China warning net that Chennault and the Chinese had worked so long to develop could have been utilized by the AVG to talk the Doolittle crews down to friendly fields—had it known. The first Chennault heard was when he received a message from Bissell on May 2:

General Chennault
Kunming
General Marshall wishes to maintain a veil of mystery regarding the sources, routes, identity of aircraft, objectives and results of any bombings of Japan by American aircraft. It is desired urgently that all knowledge of or connection with such missions be denied. No publicity (repeat no) is to be released regarding this.

Bissell[1]

Chennault was later to write: "The Doolittle raid is another good example of the singularly one-sided view of the Chinese war effort that affected many Americans in China. As a result of the Doolittle raid, the Japanese sent an expeditionary force of a hundred thousand men, supported by a sizable air force, to seize the airfields that were to have been used by the Doolittle mission and Force Aquila, a group of B-17s and B-24s that were scheduled to bomb Japan from East China fields shortly after the Doolittle raid.

"In a three-month campaign, the Japanese drove their bloody spear two hundred miles through the heart of East China, devastating 20,000 square miles, ploughing up landing fields, and exterminating everybody remotely suspected of aiding the Doolittle raiders. Entire villages through which the raiders had passed were slaughtered to the last child and burned to the ground."[2]

In northern Burma the Japanese trap was about to close on the Americans, British, and Chinese. The Japanese ground armies captured Lashio on April 29, cutting the Burma Road. On the west they cut the British retreat to India by taking Monywa on the Chindwin River. Stilwell, on the road near Myitkyina with General Harold Alexander, commander of British forces in Burma, and his chief of staff, Major General T. J. Winterton, had planned to set up his headquarters at Myitkyina when he learned the Japanese were en route to that town. In his diary of April 30, Stilwell wrote:

"They will blow the bridge [the Ava railway bridge south of Mandalay] tonight. Last night word came that Lashio was taken. (Chiang Kai-shek sent a radio that we were to hold Mandalay!! This a.m. he sent another that we need not hold Mandalay.) Alex and Winterton in. Alex's wind is up. Now it looks as if the Japs would rush to Bhamo. Radioed for plane to go back to Lashio front. [General] Lo wanted to go by railroad for some reason. His gang will, but he and I will take the plane. Our crowd direct to Myitkyina. Asked the War Department where to go—India or China. (Alex has 36,000 men to take out! Where the hell have they all been?) Imminent danger of disintegration and collapse. . . ."[3]

Stilwell was never to reach Myitkyina. On May 1 he found the "Lo" he referred to in his diary—Chinese General Lo Cho-ying—had commandeered a train at gunpoint and had wrecked it twenty-five miles away. Stilwell's comment in his diary the next day was typical. "Lo's train collided last night with another. Unfortunately he was not killed."[4]

On the thirtieth, Stilwell radioed Chennault:

"Has my plane arrived yet from Chungking en route Shwebo? Can Loiwing field be used for a few more days. I want return there soon. Can you make available for my temporary use two passenger cars for use on road Loiwing, Lashio."[5]

Chennault radioed back: "Chinese have evacuated Loi-wing and AVG leaving today. Suggest you use Mengshih en route to Lashio. Moving to Kunming station BG.8 this date."[6]

Stilwell cabled back: "Chennault, am staying on this front."[7]

Colonels Caleb Haynes and Robert Scott flew a DC-3 from Chungking to Shwebo on May 1 to evacuate Stilwell, on orders from Hap Arnold. The commanding officer of all Chinese and American forces in the Far East decided to stay but ordered his staff officers—plus some women—to fly out. With a small group of a hundred and fourteen people—Americans, British, Chinese, Indians, Malays, and some Burmese nurses—he began his twenty-day walk across northern Burmese jungles to India. The Chinese units in Burma were left to fend for themselves against the mobilized invader. General Sun Li-jen got the 38th Division out safely through northern Burma to India on May 30. The 200th Division of the Fifth Army—along with parts of the Sixth Army—battled its way to south China. Two more divisions of the Fifth Army were caught by the monsoons in northwest Burma and, after air drops (of food and medicine) by the RAF and American Air Forces, remnants finally reached India and China in July.

The American press—under the mistaken notion that Stilwell was still in charge of the fighting in northern Burma—wrote glowing stories for newspapers in the States about his brilliant defeats of the Japanese in the jungle fighting.

While Stilwell was making his stubborn walk through the jungles, an armored force of Japanese tanks and artillery was invading China up the Burma Road—taking Wanting on May 8. The Chinese 29th Division had fallen back before the onslaught of the rapidly moving Japanese, whose armor soon reached the steep gorge of the Salween River. After crossing the Salween gorge, all the Japanese would have to do would be to drive into China and take Kunming and Chungking. The war would be over.

In Kunming, Chennault directed the evacuation of Loiwing, where the AVG had to abandon twenty-two damaged P-40s that could no longer be repaired in CAMCO's abandoned shops. He moved the remaining planes to Kunming—with an element of five P-40s sent to Paoshan, a city on the Burma Road just east of the Salween gorge. Paoshan was the last large city between the Japanese and Kunming—if they succeeded in breaching the Salween.

Chennault's carefully built Yunnan warning net was falling to pieces in the face of the Japanese advance. Some of the mobile warning units in northern Burma had been put out of action by the rapidly advancing Japanese forces and some Yunnan Chinese units had not been paid by the government in months. Others had been bribed by Japanese agents to stay off the air.

The Japanese Air Force—softening the way ahead for the advancing armored forces approaching the Salween gorge—attacked Paoshan on May 4 with fifty bombers. Because of the lack of warning stations, the AVG was caught unawares. The ancient city was filled with refugees fleeing ahead of the advancing Japanese and trying to reach China. The bombs devastated the city, killing thousands and setting the walled city on fire. Old adobe buildings crumbled before the rain of bombs and the streets were littered with the dead and dying. One AVG pilot, Ben Foshee, was cut down by the bombs as he ran for his P-40 at the small dirt strip five miles from the city. He died later in the day of his wounds.

Charlie Bond reached his plane and took off in the midst of the bombing. He reported:

"I took off from Paoshan at about 11 A.M. and climbed to 18,000 feet to attack the bombers. There were two waves, 25 each, no escorting fighters. They came in from a direction of about 50 degrees. I caught the second wave about half way to the border of Burma and China about 30 minutes after take off. I concentrated all attacks on the flank ship. His left engine blew up on about the fourth pass, caught fire and went down through the overcast. I expended the rest of my ammunition in a similar maneuver on the other flank bomber with no results but I know some of the bullets must have hit this ship. Out of ammunition I returned to the field at Paoshan, China. I buzzed the field and did a slow roll, circled the city at about 1,000 feet and then prepared to lower my wheels for landing. Suddenly I heard bullets hitting my armor plate from behind and looked back to see three '0' fighters on my tail. My ship caught fire and I bailed out. I received burns about the face, neck and shoulders and both hands. My plane crashed and burned."[8]

The following day Chennault sent a flight of nine P-40s down to the auxiliary field at Yunnanyi to wait for further word of incoming Japanese planes. No longer able to trust the warning net, he could only hope the ground stations near Paoshan would give him some slight warning. Just before noon AVG radioman Ralph Sasser—on the ground at Paoshan—radioed Chennault in Kunming: "They're strafing the field—bombers too." Chennault sent the flight of P-40s over Paoshan with orders to patrol at 23,000 feet and await orders. In the operations report for that day, pilot Frank Schiel wrote:

"At 1115 we received radio information that bombers were headed toward Paoshan. At 1135 we took off for Paoshan. Shortly after take off Flight Leader Lawlor took the lead as Flight Leader Rector had to return to Yunnanyi to tighten a loose gas cap. At 1205 our seven planes arrived over Paoshan and took up a patrol at 23,000 feet. At 1240 we were notified by BC-5 that 16 enemy planes were circling the city. Through the calm, accurate directions of the BC-5 crew we were able to quickly find the enemy. They consisted of 16 I-97 fighters circling at an altitude of about 18,000 feet. Flight Leader Lawlor led the flight into attacking position and started the first run. Lawlor got a flamer on his first run. After the first pass the fight broke up into individual fights; that is, one P-40 against each individual group of Japs. The Japs broke up into groups of three to five. At about 1250, 36 Type I-97 bombers approached from the southwest at an altitude of 20,000 feet. They were escorted by about 10 Model '0s' at 21,000 feet. I continued my engagement with the I-97s. On my first rear attack I got in a good burst. When I looked back the plane was burning in a spin. I made a total of four or five more attacks. On two of them I got good bursts in on a front quarter approach, from close range. I could see the tracers enter the planes. Both rolled over and disappeared. At 1230 I started back to Paoshan from the location of the Fifth which had drifted about 10 miles southwest of Paoshan. At Paoshan BC-5 notified me that the Chinese were firing all their anti-aircraft at P-40s. My transmitter was out, along with the propeller and the airspeed, so I was unable to get any information about the field. At 1328 I took up a course for Yunnanyi, and adjusted the engine for slow cruising."[9]

Frank Lawlor—in the same battle—reported:

"I was leading six planes on patrol over Paoshan. At 1200 a formation of 20 I-97s were sighted about 6,000 feet below us at 17,000 feet. The formation made an attack in string from above rear. I saw the plane I shot burst into flames and pieces of it that were shot off filled the air with debris. After first attack, the speed gathered in the dive down enabled me to pull back up into an advantageous position for another attack. I dove down on another I-97 and shot it down. Parts of the plane passed through my propeller and damaged my undercarriage."[10]

Before the battle was over the AVG had shot down eight of the attacking fighter aircraft and the bombers turned and headed for home without dropping their bombs. But Foshee was dead and Bond too badly burned to fly.

The Japanese reached the west bank of the Salween gorge the same day. There were thousands of refugees and Chinese soldiers on the twisting road just ahead of the advancing Japanese columns. The pilots of the P-40s reported to Chennault that the column of armor was moving up the center of the highway between lines of unarmed and helpless refugees and soldiers, plodding toward the Chinese border. There was no way the P-40s could get at the Japanese without killing refugees and soldiers. Chennault called on Madame:

FOR H. E. MADAME CHIANG KAI-SHEK STOP AVG SHOT DOWN EIGHT JAP FIGHTERS NEAR PAOSHAN YESTERDAY STOP JAPS BOMBED CITY AND AIRDROME STOP ONE AVG PILOT MISSING STOP ALL COMMUNICATIONS WITH PAOSHAN CUT STOP LAST REPORTS STATE JAPS ON WEST BANK SALWEEN RIVER 1500 HOURS 4 MAY AND BRIDGE DESTROYED STOP JAPS MEETING NO OPPOSITION ANYWHERE AS SOLDIERS CIVILIANS PANIC STRICKEN AND FLEEING EAST ALONG ROAD STOP CONSIDER SITUATION DESPERATE AND JAPS MAY DRIVE TRUCKS INTO KUNMING UNLESS ROAD AND BRIDGES ARE DESTROYED AND DETERMINED OPPOSITION IS DEVELOPED STOP DUE TO FACT MANY CHINESE TRUCKS STILL WEST OF SALWEEN PRESUMABLY IN HANDS OF ENEMY REQUEST AUTHORITY H. E. THE GENERALISSIMO TO ATTACK TARGETS IN BETWEEN SALWEEN AND LUNGLING CITY.[11]

Knowing it would mean the deaths of hundreds, perhaps thousands of her people, Madame replied on May 7:

GENERAL CHENNAULT YOUR TELEGRAM MAY 6 RECEIVED STOP GENERALISSIMO INSTRUCTS YOU SEND ALL AVAILABLE AVG ATTACK TRUCKS BOATS ETC BETWEEN SALWEEN AND LUNGLING CITY.[12]

The cable was followed by a phone call from the Generalissimo to General Wang Hsu-ming with a message for Chennault:

"1) According to the recent intelligence, on the west side of Hweitongchao [Salween Bridge] near the ford, there were activities of the Japanese artillery which was reinforced yesterday, threatening our ground forces a great deal. It is imperative that AVG planes be dispatched to observe the position of the artillery and destroy it directly.

2) It is imperative that AVG planes be dispatched to dive bomb and strafe the Japanese trucks along the highway from the west side of Hweitongchao [Salween Bridge] to Lungling, so that our troops can get enough time to be reinforced."[13]

The situation was desperate: Chennault needed every available airplane— both his fighters and the bombers of the Chinese Air Force. They were the same old Russian bombers with which he had bombed Hanoi. He cabled General P. T. Mow to send even the Hawk IIIs used in training at Kunming for bombing.[14]

On the afternoon of May 8 four planes led by Tex Hill flew an observation mission over the gorge and strafed the columns. Chennault cabled Madame:

MADAME CHIANG KAI-SHEK STOP AVG BOMBED WEST SALWEEN AND SECOND MISSION SUPPORTED CHINESE BOMBERS IN ATTACK ON TRUCKS NEAR LUNGLING STOP NO ENEMY AIR ACTIVITY BUT NOTED MOVEMENT LARGE NUMBER EMPTY TRUCKS TOWARD LUNGLING STOP WILL ATTACK TRUCK COLUMNS HEAVILY THIS AFTERNOON STOP HAVE NOT LOCATED ARTILLERY POSITIONS END. CHENNAULT.[15]

The P-40s were equipped with bomb racks and two of the AVG armorers —Roy Hoffman and Charlie Baisden—had improvised a belly rack capable of carrying a 570-pound Russian bomb, of which the Chinese had bought quantities. A number of the AVG pilots had had dive-bombing training in the Navy. They were Tex Hill, Ed Rector, Tom Jones, Frank Lawlor, Lewis Bishop, Link Laughlin, Frank Schiel, and Bob Little. All volunteered to bomb the armored column on the west bank of the Salween River.[16] Tex Hill led a flight of three dive-bomber pilots—Jones, Rector, and Lawlor—while top cover was flown by a flight of P-40s consisting of Arvid Olson, R. T. Smith, Erik Shilling, and Tom Haywood.

The P-40s arrived at the gorge to find a Japanese engineering battalion attempting to repair the bridge across the huge river. The P-40s—loaded with the heavy demolition bombs—dove on the massed columns of Japanese armor and artillery vehicles that wound down the tortuous road from the top to the jumbled rock at the river. The huge bombs blew out sections of the road, causing landslides that wiped out other areas on the way down. The enemy fire was intense as the P-40s dove and twisted up through the steep gorge, climbing high into the sky after each bombing run. When the heavy demolition bombs were expended, the fighters made repeated attacks with smaller fragmentation bombs against the massed vehicles. When the bombs were gone they continued to strafe the enemy with machine guns all along the road as far back as the border of Burma.

Lewis Bishop told of his flight:

"Circled low over objective and located trucks on open and straight stretch, lined up close together. Made first pass from W to E and at an angle of about 50 degrees, speed 300 miles per hour. Dived to within 100 feet of trucks releasing bombs in string. Continued on down gorge gaining altitude and turned back. Noticed results of attack as four bombs burst amidst line of trucks other two slightly beyond but close enough to do destruction by fragmentation. Made three strafing passes from same direction and after first attack noticed small fire upon looking back. On third and fourth attacks drew fire from anti-aircraft gun stationed near road. By the time I completed my last strafing attack, I noticed one extemely large fire and two smaller fires amid trucks. Believed to have destroyed about 50 trucks during the course of attacks made by the four planes. Estimate 200 casualties among personnel on ground. There was not any interference by enemy aircraft. All planes returned safely to base together after raid."[17]

The same day a dozen Russian SB-3s bombed from high altitude and the Hawk IIIs from Kunming training school dive-bombed the gorge and the truck convoy with fragmentation. Other P-40s from Paoshan screamed over the packed roads with .50-caliber machine guns blazing—setting fire to vehicles and scattering Japanese troops into the ditches. The Japanese tanks which had been sent up to escort the motorized infantry were also caught on the road and bombed. Although the heavy tank guns were unable to fire effectively at the rapidly moving fighters, the machine guns on the motorized infantry trucks were deadly. On the ninth Chennault radioed Madame:

FOR H. E. MADAME CHIANG KAI-SHEK STOP AVG ATTACKED JAP ARTILLERY TRUCK COLUMN ABOUT 5–10 KILOMETERS WEST SALWEEN BRIDGE SITE WITH BOMBS AND .50 CALIBER GUNS AT 1640 YESTERDAY STOP MANY TRUCKS WERE BURNED AND A GREAT MANY MORE RIDDLED BY BULLETS STOP ALL OUR PLANES RETURNED BUT ONE DAMAGED BY GROUND FIRE STOP NO JAP PLANES SEEN STOP LOW CLOUDS PREVENT AIR ACTION THIS MORNING STOP PLEASE ADVISE ANY CHANGE GROUND SITUATION END CHENNAULT.[18]

The attacks continued on the tenth. Frank Schiel wrote:

"The flight was given instructions to strafe only west of Mengshih. Approximately 1000 trucks were seen lined up on the east side of the Salween Gorge, but no activity. Both bridges were out. West of the Salween a large number of trucks were seen moving west towards Mengshih. From there to a point about 20 miles south scattered trucks were seen moving West. From Wanting to Chefang a large number of trucks and some armored cars were seen moving east. At about 0945 Bolster and I strafed about 10 trucks of the column moving east. Two or three were set on fire indicating that they were carrying gasoline. A few minutes later we saw the head of the column on a straight stretch of road. They were evidently waiting for the support column. Bolster and I each made two passes, raking the whole line and setting some of them on fire. The only personnel that seemd to be present were the drivers. After strafing a few individual trucks east of the main column, we proceeded to Yunnanyi landing at 1030. We landed at Kunming at 1210."

James H. Howard, vice squadron leader, Second Pursuit Squadron, had this report:

"A report was given us that an enemy column was moving south at Meng Shih. However, we proceeded all the way to Wanting before we encountered enemy trucks. Schiel and I hit the stragglers, and Jones went 15 miles further and happened upon about 50 trucks which he attacked. My bombs hit a group of trucks and low buildings which looked like barracks."[19]

Marshall must have been worried about his friend Stilwell's fate. On May 10 he cabled through Magruder:

General Chennault and Colonel MacMorland
Kunming
K-37 Tenth
Following is paraphrase of message from Chief of Staff repeated for your information and guidance: "In absence of General Stilwell you will acquaint other officers of the following and they will govern themselves accordingly: the War Department policy of the *greatest* practical aid to China remains unchanged. In view of the recent setbacks in Burma it is particularly important that officers of the American Army in China observe an attitude of optimism and calm regarding the Chinese future. Neither in conversation nor plans should there be implied any suggestion of U.S. abandonment of China or any thought of hopelessness in the situation. While the War Department does not intend to limit the logical distribution of personnel it is important that the shifting of officers be so regulated that it cannot possibly be construed as an evacuation by Americans."

Magruder

By the end of the day on May 11, the Japanese advance had been stopped. The only trucks reported by the P-40s were a few straggling south toward the Burma border. Chennault cabled Madame on the twelfth:

AVG FLIGHT BOMBED AND MACHINE-GUNNED 75 TO 100 JAP TRUCKS HEADED SOUTH YESTERDAY STOP REAR OF COLUMN JUST ENTERING WANTING CITY WHILE HEAD WAS SOUTH OF CITY STOP MORE THAN 20 TRUCKS BURNED MANY MORE DAMAGED STOP RETURN FIRE RE-CEIVED FROM LIGHT TANKS IN COLUMN STOP RECONNAISSANCE ALONG ROAD BACK TO SALWEEN DISCOVERED ONLY SINGLE TRUCKS AT LONG INTERVALS STOP BELIEVE NO JAP UNIT LARGE AS BATTAL-ION NOW NORTH OF WANTING STOP RECONNAISSANCE THIS MORNING ALONG WEST BANK OF SALWEEN DISCOVERED NO SIGN OF JAPS.

CHENNAULT[20]

Charred pontoons on the west bank of the Salween River marked the high tide of the Japanese invasion of West China. Landslides had all but wiped out the Burma Road on the west side of the Salween gorge. The Chinese armies dug in on the east bank and stayed there. Japanese infantry and artillery took up positions on the west bank, where they remained until they were slowly driven out in 1944.

In India, General Stilwell and his band of weary, footsore stragglers finally reached Imphal after the long march across mountains and river valleys. They had walked to the Uyu River and there built rafts and floated down to the Chindwin River. From there they climbed over the mountains to Imphal.

The Associated Press, in a story filed from New Delhi on May 25, report-ing on the successful walk of 140 miles, quoted Stilwell as saying Burma could—and must—be retaken from the Japanese.

". . . He said he regarded Burma as a vitally important area for re-entry into China, now blocked from the Burma Road supply route."

"I claim we got a hell of a beating," he said. "We got run out of Burma and it is humiliating as hell. I think we ought to find out what caused it, go back and retake it."[21]

Fourteen

Following the bombings and strafing of the Japanese at the Salween gorge, Chennault switched to bombing the airfields at Hanoi—where the Japanese were concentrating a number of aircraft.

The Chinese continued to ask for AVG aid in reconnaissance—a task totally unsuited to the P-40. There were times when Chennault wondered if the Chinese had any more idea what a fighter aircraft was designed for than did Stilwell and the rest of the ground officers. Madame wired him on May 12, 1942:

GENERAL CHENNAULT: BEGINNING MONDAY PLEASE SEND AVG TO FLY BETWEEN MYITKYINA AND BHAMO ALSO BETWEEN INDAW AND SIMBO TO PROTECT OUR GROUND FORCES NEAR SIMBO IN CROSSING THE IRRAWADDY FROM WEST TO EAST SO THAT ENEMY PLANES CANNOT ATTACK OUR TROOPS STOP IF POSSIBLE PLEASE SEND FROM THREE TO SIX PLANES ON EACH MISSION AND SEND THREE MISSIONS PER DAY AT VARIOUS HOURS STOP GENERALISSIMO WOULD LIKE TO HAVE THIS PROGRAM CARRIED OUT FOR FIVE DAYS.

And later that same day she cabled again:

GENERAL CHENNAULT: PLEASE SEND PLANE TO SEE WHETHER ANY JAP AT MYITKYINA AND BHAMO BECAUSE JAP CLAIM THEY HAVE OCCUPIED THOSE CENTERS STOP ALSO SEND PLANE TO SIMBO WHICH IS BETWEEN MYITKYINA AND BHAMO TO SEE WHETHER ANY OF OUR TROOPS HAVE ARRIVED THERE STOP ASK PILOT OBSERVE ANY MOVEMENT EITHER OF ENEMY TROOPS OR OURS ALL ALONG THESE CENTERS AND ROADS STOP TELL AVG AM APPRECIATING THEIR EXCELLENT WORK STOP PERSONAL REGARDS.[1]

Carefully resisting an urge to send a brusque refusal, Chennault sat down and carefully composed a letter in reply:

May 14, 1942

H. E. Madame Chiang Kai-shek
Headquarters of the Generalissimo
Chungking, Szechuen [Szechwan], China

Dear Madame:

After making a careful survey of the situation and all the factors involved, I regret to inform you that it will not be possible for the Group to conduct the missions as directed in your radio, current No. 927, dated May 12 for the following reasons:

1. The distances involved are too great. The distance from Kunming to Myitkyina to Simbo and return to Kunming is 785 miles. The distance from Kunming to Indaw to Simbo and return to Kunming is 897 miles. Both of these figures exceed the range of the P-40 airplane. If Yunnanyi could be used as a base, the distances involved would be reduced to 500 and 607 miles respectively. In the first case, a P-40 could remain over the front for approximately 20 minutes, and in the second case it could barely make the round trip.

2. Flying conditions in the entire area from Kunming to Indaw are rapidly deteriorating. Low clouds and rain are encountered in this area throughout the day. For this reason it is not believed that the army in the Simbo area will require fighter protection since the Japanese Air Force cannot operate consistently because of clouds and rain. Troops moving at night and during the cloudy periods of the day will not be seen or attacked by Japanese air units.

3. While patrols can barely be conducted from Yunnanyi, it is not practicable to use Yunnanyi as our base. The entire group will be required to conduct the mission as directed, and Yunnanyi does not have accommodations for more than one squadron. The aircraft warning service at Yunnanyi is very unreliable. It operates on the principle of safety first, and there is no attempt apparently to evaluate information. An air unit based there would be compelled to fly on alert missions all day long, or sit on the ground under risk of being bombed unexpectedly.

4. Paoshan cannot be used as a base, although it is within effective range of the area designated. The air raid warning system around Paoshan broke down before that city was bombed, and my squadron there was caught on the ground. Since the bombing of Paoshan there is no pretense of maintaining an air warning system which could be relied upon.

5. AVG airplanes and equipment require considerable overhauling, and the airplanes are not in condition to conduct such long missions.

Due to the fact that the weather in this region is day by day becoming more unsuitable for flying, it is respectfully suggested that the original plan to move to Chungking be carried out as soon as preparations are completed there. In the meantime our equipment can be overhauled, and a large number of new planes can be brought over from India by our pilots.

I have begun the movement of Command Post radio stations and certain items of equipment by truck convoys to new airdromes in the central area already. Within a week or ten days, the Group can begin to operate effectively in that area. If the action of ground forces in designated sections can be coordinated with our air action, I am confident that very satisfactory results will be obtained.

Awaiting your further instructions, and with assurances of our desire to be of the greatest assistance, I am,

> Most sincerely,
> C. L. Chennault
> Brigadier General (Temp), USA
> Commanding, AVG[2]

The battered P-40s were not only unsuited to low-level reconnaissance flights for the Chinese Army, they were becoming almost too war-weary for combat flights. Maintenance was still the most difficult problem—next to aircraft replacement. The pilots too were becoming exhausted with the constant flying.

Another pilot was lost on the May 12 during a raid on the airfield at Hanoi. Six P-40s had taken off for the flight from Kunming with orders to strafe as many planes as they could find on the ground. At least sixty were spotted. One transport plane and fifteen fighters were destroyed. Pilot John T. Donovan's plane was hit and he was seen by wingmates to bail out over the airfield.

On the seventeenth, eight P-40s were ordered to bomb and strafe the Hanoi-Lao-kai complex and were to attack the railway freight yards at Lao-kai. The operations report of that day contains a report by wingman Peter Wright:

"We took off and flew down the railroad to the spot where we were to bomb a train. The train was not there so we turned north and proceeded to Laokay [sic] which was our alternate objective. We dove down on the rail-road freight yard from south to north. I was number two to dive and directly behind Bishop who was leading. As I was releasing my bombs at about 500 feet, I saw Bishop pull up with about four feet of flame coming out of his tail. He pulled up to the left and rolled on his back and bailed out. His chute opened immediately and his plane crashed into a mountain setting it on fire. Bishop landed in that part of the town of Laokay, Indochina that is on the west side of the river. He landed in the town proper and was alive as he disappeared into the trees. In the meantime, I had noticed that his bombs, mine and the plane behind me, flown by Howard, had all gotten direct hits on the three lines of freight cars in the freight yard in the town of Laokay. I joined up on Howard and proceeded to Mengtze where he landed and I proceeded directly to Kunming."[3]

Lewis Bishop, who had five Japanese planes to his credit when he took off that day, was taken prisoner. He was interned by the Japanese in Indochina for several years but finally escaped by jumping from a moving train in north China while being transferred from Shanghai to Manchuria. He returned to serve with Chennault in the Fourteenth Air Force in 1945.

Tom Jones—a pilot who had distinguished himself on several recent raids in the Hanoi area—was accidentally killed at Kunming while practicing dive-bombing tactics. He failed to pull out in time from a practice dive.

The AVG lost another one of its veteran pilots on May 22. Bob Little had ten and a half Japanese planes to his credit when he flew a bombing mission against a Japanese artillery position west of the Salween River.

The report of wingman R. H. Smith is detailed:

"Four P-40Es for bombing and four P-40s for top cover went to target areas, approximately where Burma Road crosses Salween River, south of Paoshan. We could not find the target, which was a group of tents, for several minutes due to bad visibility. After making several circles, Little peeled off and following him I saw he was diving on the target. At about 1,000 feet, before Little had leveled off, I heard an explosion. Glancing at his plane I saw a burst of flame and black smoke midway of his left wing. He immediately went into a tight spin, I then noticed half his left wing was missing. He made no attempt to jump, or pull out, and was on fire when he hit the ground, when his plane exploded. I was now level at about 600 feet so I dropped my bombs and then climbed in sharp turns. I overshot my target-hitting, dropping bombs about the hillside. I observed no bursts of anti-craft fire, not [sic] any tracer from the ground. Circling for several minutes we rejoined and came home."[4]

"Bob flew more missions over enemy territory than anybody else in the outfit," said his squadron leader, Bob Neale. Little was posthumously awarded both the American and British Distinguised Flying Crosses.

The rest of May was taken up with patrols and bombing and strafing attacks from the base in Kunming. The bomber replacements promised the AVG for so many months still had not shown up—nor had replacement pilots. The first classes of Chinese student pilots had been sent to the States for training, freeing a number of flying instructors at both Kunming and Yunnanyi to join the AVG. Two resigned and returned to the States, but John Blackburn, Harry Bolster, Arnold Shamblin, Lester Hall, Ed Loane, Van Shapard, Jr., and Allen Wright joined. Blackburn was later killed when his P-40 crashed into Tienchich Lake.

General Bissell, acting on orders from the War Department, was furiously trying to work out the details of getting the AVG inducted into the Army Air

Forces. He had finally succeeded in getting both T. V. Soong and the Generalissimo to agree to the move.

Chennault had been asked for his proposals for a dissolution of the AVG by July 4 and he wrote Bissell on May 12, attempting to clarify his earlier memo. He reiterated his opinion that every AVG member should be given a $500 travel allowance to the United States. He added that he had thought out carefully the promotions for those AVG personnel—both Army and Navy men—who wished to stay in China and serve with the 23rd Pursuit Group. He asked for clarification of pay scales for enlisted men who were on flying status and told Bissell that, owing to the much higher cost of food and labor in China, the cost of rations would be higher for American military personnel. He asked for additional administrative help for the proposed new group—knowing his administrative ability was not his strongest suit.[5]

Bissell apparently forwarded his letter to Washington because, on May 26, Chennault received a long letter from General Chow in Chungking saying the Generalissimo had approved the termination of the AVG and had worked out the terms of the AVG contracts. Most of the contracts would be honored and personnel would be paid the full balance owed them and would receive the travel allowance for home. Chennault was satisfied with the arrangements as they had been worked out.[6]

A few days later, on May 15, 1942, Chennault received a letter from Lauchlin Currie that surprised him because of its informality.

Dear General:

I have not heard from you since January 12, but I have heard a great deal about you and the group. As you know, both you and the group are famous in America. Hardly a day passes but what there is some story of the AVG. The Army has been very decent about it all and its public relations branch has released a lot of material, all of it favorable. Nothing that I have ever done has given me as much satisfaction as the little I have been able to do in helping you. I greatly value your remark that I am truly a member of your group.

I have felt very badly over your failure to secure adequate support from here. It was particularly tragic and I think quite unnecessary that you should have had to go through that low and critical period about the time of the bombing of Mandalay with hardly any planes. . . .

The Lockheed-Hudson story is a particularly sad one, not only in the interminable delays in delivering the planes, but also in the fact that it tied up 32 of your proposed pilot replacements. I was, needless to say, opposed from the beginning to the idea of putting your pursuit replacements onto these bombers, but since we have been at war I am afraid I have not had very much influence with the air force. . . .

I am sorry that it was not possible to continue the AVG. The difficul-

ties at this end appeared insuperable and without induction you faced a
rapid end through attrition.

There are certain parts of the story which I prefer not to write and
must wait until we have a chance for a good long talk. In the meantime,
rest assured of my unswerving friendship and admiration.

Sincerely,

Lauchlin Currie[7]

Chennault—realizing he still had a long way to go to discourage the Japanese from hitting airfields in China—decided to surprise the enemy with a bit
of sleight of hand. He knew that the big concentrations of Japanese aircraft
in the strongholds of Hankow in north central China and Canton in the
south had not been bloodied by combat as yet. He also knew they had
repeatedly bombed Chinese cities and airfields in both Kwangsi and Hunan
provinces for several years. The big Japanese Air Force base at Canton's
White Cloud Airport was an advanced bombardier training base and its
students had regularly used Kweilin as a target. Chennault and the Chinese
had for years been building advanced airfields in east China in preparation
for the day when they could bomb Japanese supply lines and bases along the
coast. Chinese coolies had constructed a 6,000-foot crushed rock airstrip at
Kweilin, making it a base fit for everything from fighter aircraft to medium
and heavy bombers.

The commander of the AVG had earned a reputation among the men for
having an uncanny ability to anticipate Japanese Air Force moves before the
enemy made them. His many years of watching Japanese air tactics gave him
an advantage not enjoyed by American airmen new to China. This time he
figured the Japanese would not expect him to move fighters east to intercept
their bombers. He correctly thought the Japanese would expect him to keep
his full strength of three fighter squadrons near Kunming and Chungking to
protect the wartime capital.

On the morning of June 11, Chennault ordered two squadrons of the
AVG, sixteen planes, to fly the four hundred and fifty miles east to Kweilin
and took his headquarters along. He left only six or seven P-40s at Kunming
and Chungking to protect those two fields against Japanese air attacks from
either Burma or Indochina—a big risk. Kweilin had been raided the day
before by nine twin-engine bombers and the people of the city had gone into
the large caves that had been carved into the sides of the peculiar ice-cream-
cone-shaped hills surrounding the city and airfields. They had been bombed
regularly for several years and were used to seeing their homes burned and
flattened.

Just after dawn on the twelfth an air raid alert sounded at Kweilin and the
populace began its regular evacuation. This time the AVG was waiting. The
warning net was operating efficiently and the Chinese spotters had reported
the Japanese bombers' takeoff from Canton and their flight toward Kweilin.

Bob Neale was in command of a flight of three P-40s which circled over the assault flight below—led by Charlie Bond. George Burgard and Joe Rosbert circled high above at 18,000 feet as top cover.

Nine Mitsubishi twin-engine bombers came in from the southwest at 15,000 feet escorted by a flight of silver Nakajima I-97 fighters and a handful of new twin-engine Ki.45 fighters. The AVG pilots dove on the bombers, scattering them from the target and causing them to head for home. Dick Rossi shot down one bomber while John Dean and Bob Prescott set fire to two others. Charlie Bond set fire to another as the fighters of Bob Neale's flight took on the Japanese fighters. Neale later reported:

"My first run was unsuccessful due to a full deflection shot. My second run was headon with an I-97 fighter which started to smoke. Did not see it crash. Proceeded in a southwest direction and another pass at a fighter which also started to smoke. I did not see it crash. After this pass a twin-engine fighter got on my tail and chased me five to 10 miles west before I could get enough distance on him to make headon run. I did not see any effect from my fire on this run. . . . Proceeded south after losing fighter and engaged an I-97 proceeding in a southwest direction. It was damaged but was not seen to crash or burst into flames."[8]

Unaware that he was fighting a new twin-engine fighter plane, George Burgard reported later:

"I started cruising south at 13,000 feet at 150 degrees. Masters joined me and about 75 kilos southeast we overtook a Jap two-engined bomber and a Jap fighter above him. I shot at the I-97 and then as he turned in to me I went on by the bomber. The bomber was light, fast and exceptionally maneuverable. He dove sharply for the ground and made sharp turn. I overshot him the first time and had to climb back above for another run. The I-97 fighter apparently caught us then for he put a burst through my left aileron and dove away. I made a sharp diving turn and poured three long bursts at the fighter on a deflection shot. The fighter skidded badly and fell off on a wing. I pulled up and saw he had run into the side of a sharp peak and blew up. I got back some altitude and picked up the bomber hedge-hopping through the sharp hills. Each time I got at him from the rear he would slip in and out of the peaks. My .50s were inoperative at the time. After about five or six runs I caught him in a valley and got right in behind him but he turned almost 90 degrees and began making 360 degree vertical turns around a sharp cone. My speed was too great to stay behind him and when I pulled up to kill speed he headed south again. We were never more than 150 feet from the ground. On a pass from above my right .50 started working and in a brief interval his left engine caught fire. He attempted to maintain his altitude but I throttled back and continued to shoot until he dragged his wing on a small knob and mushed in. The fuselage was broken in the middle by the impact and the right wing was still burning when I circled the crash. The approximate location was 20 kilos south or south-southeast of Tsang Wi."[9]

By the time the battle was over the P-40s had shot down eleven out of eighteen Japanese planes in one of the last great air battles for the AVG. The people of Kweilin—amazed that no bombs had fallen on their city—treated the AVG to a banquet complete with congratulatory speeches.

Chennault was so pleased with the day's score and his revenge against the Japanese at Canton that he cabled the Tenth Air Force headquarters in India:

FOR BISSELL: BELIEVE WE GOT 9 OUT OF 28 JAPS TODAY BUT CONFIR-
MATION LACKING STOP KWEILIN AREA MOST SUITABLE FOR PURSUIT
OPERATIONS BUT NEED PURSUIT PLANES AND PILOTS STOP.[10]

Hoping to inflict more damage on the airfields at Canton and Hankow with bombs from the P-40Es, he wired Skip Adair, operations officer at Kunming;

Adair: send six Sharks with belly tanks today weather permitting. We claim eight or nine in morning combat. Wright slightly injured and two Sharks lost. Send four crew chiefs and two armorers via USA transport or CNAC.[11]

Awaiting the arrival of the replacement planes, Chennault moved part of the 2nd Squadron to an advanced base at Hengyang from which he could easily reach Hankow. The rest of the P-40s and his headquarters returned to guard Chungking, now that the winter fogs were lifting from the beleaguered city.

In almost the last combat while still active, the AVG flew out of Hengyang to bomb and strafe airfields and boats on the Yangtze River near Hankow. Charles Sawyer reported on June 22:

"I took off at 1300 joined Squadron Leader and Capt. [Albert] Baumler, climbed to 20,000 and circled in the vicinity of the aerodrome. We spotted 14 I-97s 8,000 feet below us and attacked. My first attack was a headon run, after one good burst a large stream of smoke started coming out his motor. I passed under him in a dive and didn't see what happened. Later I made a rear quarter attack on one and again smoke poured out of his engine, how-ever, I dove away and didn't see him crash. I made several attacks later with no visible results. Finally, I got in position to make a direct stern attack; I came upon him slightly below and directly from the rear. I opened fire at approximately 500 yards and closed into about 250 yards with pieces flying off and smoke coming out. He turned 90 degrees to the left and I got in a good burst at close range and he seemed to explode and disintegrate."[12]

Chennault cabled Madame:

FOR H. E. MADAME CHIANG KAI-SHEK STOP YESTERDAY AVG DIS-
ABLED JAP GUNBOAT AND DESTROYED THREE SMALL BOATS ON RIVER
SOUTH HANKOW STOP IN FIGHT 21 JAP FIGHTERS WE SHOT DOWN ONE

CERTAIN AND FIVE PROBABLE STOP ONE OF OUR PLANES DAMAGED
ON FIELD AT HENGYANG BUT REPAIRABLE STOP NO OTHER LOSSES OR
DAMAGE END WEATHER VILE TODAY STOP YOU MAY RELEASE ABOVE
REPORT.[13]

It was ironic that the AVG began to enjoy its sweetest victories as the
organization drew to a close. On June 20 a joint Army-Navy induction board
began to visit the bases in China to talk with the AVG personnel. It had been
made clear by both General Stilwell and General Bissell that the AVG would
be shut off from supplies unless it chose induction. Stilwell had promised to
replace the AVG with a complete fighter group in China. He also promised
the Generalissimo that Chennault would be kept on as senior officer in China
for the duration. Neither promise was kept. On the day the AVG was demo-
bilized, only a handful of Air Force pilots and fifteen ground crewmen were
ready to make up the new 23rd Fighter Group.

Most of the members of the AVG were unenthusiastic about induction into
the Army Air Forces. The majority of the pilots were reservists and preferred
to join up under their own terms—preferably after a leave back in the States.
Most had lived for a year with the War Department promises to send them
replacement parts, planes, and pilots and they were cynical about these new
promises made by the military. The Navy officers who interviewed ex-Navy
pilots did not fare well either. Charlie Bond was at Kweilin when the induction board arrived. On June 22 he wrote:

"The US Army Induction Board came to see us in Kweilin. Col. Haynes
brought them in a DC-3, and with them was General Chennault. There also
was a member of the U. S. Navy, and his talk was slanted toward the former
Navy pilots. He was too abrasive and arrogant. We all listened to an Army
colonel about induction and our alternatives. Later Bob Neale and I got
together and agreed that it was about time to make up our minds; it wasn't
easy. We decided to go home. My conscience is bothering me for not staying,
but I'm going to Washington, D.C. to try personally to get a regular commission." (Bond had been refused a regular commission in the Air Forces because he was a few months over age.)

Chennault—though he felt the most important thing was to fight the Japanese—nevertheless did not blame the pilots for leaving. He had fought induction as long as he could but had given in when he saw it was useless.

In a diary entry Charlie Bond wrote: "My respect for The Old Man soared
higher than ever tonight. George Burgard told me that in a discussion with
Chennault the General told him he didn't blame any of us for not staying.
That made me feel much better. Maybe I can sleep now." Bond had more
than eight Japanese planes to his credit.

The members of the induction board were far from tactful. Many told the
interviewees that they would be met at the dock by the Draft Board if they
did not agree to induction in China. In spite of such treatment, most of the

AVG pilots might have joined up if they had been allowed to fight as a unit and if they had been given a short leave first. Most had been fighting together under the most trying combat conditions for almost a year. The Board said no to both suggestions. Some were offered considerable rank. Bob Neale was offered the silver leaves of a lieutenant colonel but he refused.

In the end, five members of the administrative staff joined the Air Forces: Skip Adair, Tom Gentry, Roy Hoffman, Sam Prevo, and John Williams. Five pilots—Tex Hill, John Bright, Ed Rector, Charlie Sawyer, and Frank Schiel—also signed up. Twenty-nine members of the ground personnel also enlisted, all to serve with Chennault. A total of 237 AVG personnel elected to return to the United States.

Stilwell, trying to find as much wrong as he could with Chennault's operation in China, wrote a letter on June 23 to General Marshall marked "For the eyes of Gen. Marshall only."

"Report came in yesterday that a house of prostitution is being set up in Kunming for use of air corps personnel, that an air corps officer is in Kweilin selecting inmates, that 13 women were brought to Kunming today in one of our transport planes. Chennault is here. I questioned him, and he disclaimed any knowledge of officers being implicated although he admitted that he knew certain Chinese were organizing such an enterprise. He tried to get a similar set-up for the AVG. I have ordered our inspector over from Chabua to make immediate thorough investigation. I am afraid Chennault does not realize the difference between the AVG and the U. S. Army! Unfortunately this matter is reported to be common knowledge in Kunming. There is also some talk that Chennault knows all about it. The newspaper men have gotten hold of it, too. It is a bad mess, which I am sorry to have to report. Will keep you informed as I get further data."[14]

Chennault, busy with the fighting and having been through Burma and China with his men since the fall of 1941, shrugged off Stilwell and went back to work.

Correspondent Theodore White, who was with Chennault at the time on a field story about him for *Time* (which turned out to be a cover story in the December 6, 1943, issue) asked about it.

"That whorehouse of mine," Chennault said. "That's worrying me. The boys have got to get it and they might as well get it clean as get it dirty."

It was just another arrow in the quiver for Stilwell and Marshall.

Crews of the Army Air Forces began to arrive by boat at Calcutta and a number of them were ferried over the Hump by the Air Transport Command and CNAC, destined for China service. A squadron of B-25s arrived in Kunming, and Chennault immediately moved it to Kweilin and Hengyang to bomb Canton and Hankow. The Japanese, through their intelligence network in Kunming and Chungking, knew all about plans to dissolve the AVG. As a result they began hitting at Hengyang and Kweilin in an effort to knock out the last of the P-40s. Chennault, realizing he would be caught short before replacements came, asked for volunteers to stay an extra two weeks after July 4. Most of the men refused, but eighteen pilots and thirty ground personnel volunteered. These were the men who were manning the forward bases in the first part of July. Among the pilots who stayed the extra time was Bob Neale, who commanded the AVG squadron.

On July 3, Chennault received the official order to dissolve the AVG.

> Chungking, Szechuen [Szechwan]
> July 3, 1942
>
> To: General C. L. Chennault
> Commanding General
> American Volunteer Group
>
> You are directed to demobilize the American Volunteer Group and to discharge the personnel of that Group in accordance with plans which I have approved.
>
> By Command of
> Generalissimo Chiang Kai-shek[15]

The claims for enemy planes had been rapidly piling up and, while Chennault had been submitting individual claims since the first battles in December and January, he submitted his final corrected list in July to CAMCO (See Appendix.).[16]

On the day the AVG was dissolved, he wrote to T. V. Soong, expressing his deep appreciation for the help he had provided the AVG since its inception and saying his leading the AVG had been "the most interesting experience of my life." He expressed his thanks to the Chinese people for their unselfish help in aiding the AVG and in particular to the Generalissimo, Madame Chiang, and the Chinese Aeronautical Commission.

"I hope that you find satisfaction," he wrote, "in knowing that the 'experiment' which you backed so courageously despite the advice of experts, has proved so successful. I am extremely gratified that I had the opportunity to take part in it and to serve under your direction. You may be assured that I shall continue to exert my utmost efforts to accomplish the final and complete defeat of the common enemy," he concluded.[17]

Chennault dispatched George Paxton, one of the pilots, who had been named finance officer, to CAMCO headquarters in New York with all the financial records of the AVG.

On July 3 he answered the May 15 letter of Lauchlin Currie, which had reached him only a short time before. He lamented the end of the AVG, saying he did not believe the War Department had any intention of replacing it with a first-class pursuit force. However, he said, the personal satisfaction he derived from doing a good job with the AVG had been worth it and he had made many friends upon whom he could depend under any conditions. He said he hoped he could continue to work with Currie even though the

AVG was finished and hoped they could meet when he returned to the United States.

As Chennault was finishing up the loose ends of the dissolution of the AVG, far to the east the handful of AVG pilots who had volunteered to stay on duty for the extra weeks were encountering Japanese bombers attacking Hengyang from airports in Hankow. On July 4, the day of demobilization, Ed Rector reported:

"At 0530 12 bombers were reported enroute from Nanchang to Hengyang. Our six planes took off and climbed to 18,000 feet and patrolled 90 degrees to the course of the approaching planes. The B-25s meanwhile took off on their mission to Canton and Neale and one other plane took off from Lingling to aid us. The 12 bombers turned out to be I-97 fighters, and we sighted them west of the field at 13,000 feet as they dived on Neale's approaching flight. We immediately attacked and had enemy planes outlined against a white cloud layer at 7,000 feet. I fired a four second burst at an I-97 in a slight diving turn, and he burst into flames and bits of debris flew from his plane as he dived through the cloud layer. I climbed up to the outside and made several more passes, but only full and quarter deflection shots were obtained. One I-97 forced me to dive out, but in doing so I got in a head-on burst at two fighters in close formation coming up at me. I got a fleeting glimpse of a wingman's engine letting out a large burst of smoke as I passed over them. Lost sight of them in the early morning haze, and failing to intercept them as far north as Changsha I returned to base."

Chennault took as many of the pilots and ground crews as he could to Chungking for the ceremonies ending the seven months of the AVG. Generalissimo and Madame Chiang had invited the members of the Group to a barbecue dinner. As honorary commander of the AVG, Madame gave the party at the home of China's aged President, Lin Sen. Attending the ceremonies were her sisters Mesdames Sun Yat-sen and H. H. Kung. A large oil painting of the Generalissimo, Madame, and General Chennault was unveiled. General J. L. Huang, director of the War Area Service Corps, which had been responsible for the feeding and billeting of the AVG in China, was master of ceremonies. Toasts and speeches were given and the Generalissimo told the group:

"General Chennault and his company of air knights will always be remembered by the Chinese people as comrades-in-arms and as the friendly representatives of a friendly people."

At midnight the American Volunteer Group became a part of the U.S. Army Air Forces.

The AVG—whom most military experts in the States had said would not last three weeks in combat—had fought in the skies over Burma, Indochina, Thailand, and China for seven months, destroying 297 confirmed Japanese aircraft and probably shooting down 150 more. Four pilots had been killed in air combat, six by antiaircraft fire, three by enemy bombs on the ground, and three were taken prisoner. Ten others had been killed in aircraft accidents. The AVG had lost twelve P-40s in combat and sixty-one on the ground. It was an air combat record—percentagewise—never equaled.

As compiled by Robert Hotz in his book *With General Chennault,* the list of top confirmed air victories by the AVG read: R. H. Neale 15½; D. L. Hill 12¼; W. N. Reed 10½; W. D. McGarry 10¼; K. A. Jernstedt 10½; R. L. Little (killed in action) 10½; G. T. Burgard 10¾; J. V. Newkirk (killed in action) 10½; C. H. Older 10¼; C. R. Bond 8¾; R. T. Smith 8⅔; F. Lawlor 8½; F. Schiel 7; E. Rector 6½; J. R. Rossi 6¼; J. H. Howard 6⅓; J. G. Bright 6 . . . and so on down the line.

Pilot deaths in the AVG, unfortunately, did not end with July 4. Two of the pilots who had volunteered to stay on for the extra two weeks, John Petach and Arnold Shamblin, were killed in a bombing and strafing attack on Japanese installations north of Hengyang on July 10. Air Force Captain Baumler was on the same flight:

"Mr. Petach changed formation from two ship element to string over city of Chang Kiu, no anti-aircraft in vicinity. We started dive from 6,500 feet in formation. Mr. Petach had just reached terminus of his dive at about 2,300 feet when his airplane burst into flames around the cockpit and main fuel tanks. His airplane went into a violent tumbling spin completely out of control and a portion of left wing separated from airplane. His airplane crashed in flames on river edge at northeast side of wall around city. The pilot remained in plane and it is my opinion that his plane received several direct hits from 20mm anti-aircraft immediately after he had released his bombs. I released my bombs at about 2,800 feet and after observing Petach's plane strike the ground I continued in a shallow twisting dive up the river which was original rendezvous after dive bombing attack. Then I noticed that Mr. Shamblin, my wingman, was not in formation on my wing. I circled back at 1,500 feet toward town and observed that all bombs dropped had dropped in the city on target. Several fires were observed. Still no hostile aircraft, no sight of parachute or Shamblin's plane. Flew southwest toward Hengyang and going above overcast—still no evidence of aerial combat, and no sign of Shamblin. Returned to Hengyang and landed at 1315."

Petach had, a few months earlier, been married to redheaded Emma Foster, one of the AVG nurses who had also volunteered to stay on with other ground personnel. She was pregnant and returned to her home in the States where a daughter, Joan, was born the following February.

A United Press dispatch from Chungking dated July 4 quoted Chennault on his feeling about the dissolution of the AVG:

"They deserve to go home. But I regret their disbandment. It was the greatest opportunity an Air Force commander ever had to get together and train under complete freedom of action a group of fighting men. I'll never have a similar experience."

PART II

Fifteen

In the spring of 1942 the Japanese had effectively sealed off China from the ground and from the sea. They had taken all the coastal ports from Shanghai in the north down to Foochow and Amoy in Fukien Province and Swatow and Hong Kong in Kwangtung Province. Swinging around the south, they had occupied French Indochina—the southern door to China—and then had moved up through Burma to seal off China from the west. There was now no way to get into China except by air from India. The loss of Myitkyina in northern Burma robbed the Allies of their only intermediate air stop from India to China along the southern route across the Himalayas. Allied aircraft had to take an even more northern route from the Assam Valley in India across the high Himalayas to Kunming, at altitudes approaching 20,000 feet. The wear and tear on airplanes and crews from such high-altitude flying was considerable. Flying such routes required more aviation gas and more time. Crews had to go on oxygen and the danger of icing conditions was far greater.

The loss of Burma forced the Allies to open more western ports in India, causing transportation routes across India to become snarled with traffic and air routes to become congested. Supply lines to China stretched far around or across Africa to the United States and Europe. These same American supply lines to China—the longest of any the United States had in the war—were also subject to the demands of our British allies, who were fighting in North Africa and the Near East. Much of the matériel intended for the British in India and for Chennault in China was diverted before it ever arrived in the Far East.

Such was the picture when General Stilwell was appointed commander of the China-Burma-India Theater of Operations in February. All three countries had been grouped together for the purpose of the U.S. strategy. Stilwell had no U.S. forces to command when he arrived except for a small group of personnel recently activated under the U. S. Tenth Air Force. The CBI was, and would remain throughout most of the war, an Air Force theater because of the nature of the geography and the Japanese encirclement. It could be argued that both Secretary of War Stimson and General Marshall erred when they named a ground officer to such a command—since in hindsight an air officer would have been the more logical choice.

Stilwell's headquarters—because he was chief of staff to Generalissimo Chiang Kai-shek, who had been named by the Allies as Supreme Commander of Allied Forces in China—was in Chungking. However, the Tenth Air Force, his only U.S. force, was headquartered in New Delhi, India, and had been operating there since committed to the defense of the air route from India to China.

Following Stilwell's unsuccessful defense of Burma, where he had been in command of the Chinese Fifth and Sixth Armies, he had hoped to train new Chinese group troops in India. In addition to his military duties, he had been instructed by President Roosevelt to take charge of all Lend-Lease matériel in China prior to its delivery to the Chinese. This enabled him to wield considerable power in negotiations. But in the spring of 1942 the only CBI troops under his command were 3,000 officers and men of the Tenth Air Force—mostly in India—and ninety-four ground personnel.[1]

It had been anticipated that the AVG, when it was deactivated in July 1942, would be absorbed into the AAF as the 23rd Fighter Group, which was to be the nucleus of a task force in China. But when it was realized that most of the AVG had no intention of being inducted into the Air Forces, it became necessary to wait until the 23rd Group could be sufficiently built up as a replacement. When it became obvious, because of paperwork and supply problems, that the replacements were not coming through rapidly enough, plans were made to deploy some of the Tenth Air Force units in India to serve under Chennault in China. But they would still be assigned to the Tenth Air Force. The situation can best be described in Chennault's own words:

"The China Air Task Force was patched together in the midst of combat from whatever happened to be available in China during the gloomy summer of 1942. There was precious little. As the stepchild of the Tenth Army Air Force in distant Delhi, the C.A.T.F. had to fight, scream and scrape for every man, sparkplug, and gallon of gas."

Stilwell had solemnly promised the Generalissimo that he would replace the AVG with a full-strength fighter group of four squadrons and a hundred planes. On the delivery date set for them—July 4, 1942—the Generalissimo found himself exchanging the veteran AVG for three newly activated squadrons of the 23rd Fighter Group that existed largely on paper. Actually the Army supplied only a dozen green pilots and twenty clerks and mechanics. Everything else in the 23rd Group was AVG equipment bought and paid for by the Chinese. The Army provided no fighter planes, no trucks or jeeps, no radios, no administrative or maintenance equipment, not even an extra pair of uniform pants or an experienced group commander. Bob Neale, senior AVG squadron leader, commanded the 23rd Group and led it in combat until July 19, when he was succeeded by Colonel Robert L. Scott, Jr. Army ground equipment for the 23rd Group did not reach India until one year later, in the summer of 1943. It arrived in China the next fall.

The fourth squadron for the group was acquired by subterfuge. The 16th Fighter Squadron of the Tenth Air Force, 51st Fighter Group, was bogged down in the monsoon weather of India's Assam Valley where fighter operations were impossible during the summer. "By inviting a single flight at a time to China for 'experience' I lured the entire squadron to Peishiyi during June and July and never returned them. . . . The 16th stayed on in China until the end of the war and fought through all the hottest actions along with the 74th, 75th and 76th squadrons of the 23rd Group,"[2] Chennault later wrote.

Major General Lewis Brereton was in command of the Tenth Air Force in the spring of 1942 when he suddenly received orders to move to the Near East—with all his heavy bombers, transport planes, and as many ground personnel as he could spare—to help the British. General Rommel was threatening to break through the British lines to Suez. Brereton got together his force as fast as he could and departed in June, leaving the Tenth Air Force in India with a skeleton staff. This, as much as anything else, contributed to the shortage of planes and pilots that were supposed to go to China to relieve the AVG on July 4.

Brereton's former chief of staff, Brigadier General Earl L. Naiden, was left in charge. Trying to get supplies to China by air without sufficient men or equipment, he was faced with an almost insurmountable task. He had two bomber squadrons—the 436th, a heavy bombardment squadron, and the 22nd, which was composed of medium bombers. These were, however, scattered halfway across India. One section was in Karachi on the far western border and the rest in Calcutta in extreme southeast India. Of the 51st Fighter Group, the 16th Squadron had been sent to China, so he had only a few fighter planes with which to escort transport planes on the air route to China.

Naiden's biggest problem from a tactical standpoint was the protection of the transports flying from fields in Assam to Kunming. Fortunately for him, the monsoon weather was so bad that the Japanese were not flying north from their bases in northern Thailand and Burma. But he knew that as soon as the weather cleared in October he would have his hands full with the Japanese fighters and bombers. He had been promised by General Arnold that he would have two squadrons of the 51st Fighter Group ready to fly from Assam bases by the end of the summer, but that was a long way off.

In the meantime, he was responsible for the supply of the squadrons that were being assigned to China. Brereton had taken twelve transports with him to the Near East and the planes Naiden had were beginning to fall apart from constant use. He could not get replacement parts for the C-47s (the military version of the DC-3) and he began to experience the same feelings of frustration that Chennault had been living with for almost a year in Burma and China. He even resorted to using engines for the P-43s—interceptors that were destined for China—as replacement engines for S-47s, but there were not enough of these to keep him flying supplies.

After the loss of Myitkyina, he could no longer fly supplies to Kunming via the low-altitude southern route. With the heavy downpours of the monsoon season, airfields in the Assam Valley and in China became lakes in some cases and mudholes in others. The weather over the Hump, as the route came to be called, was terrible most of the time and icing conditions at 20,000 feet were constant. As a result, the runs from such fields as Dinjan and Chabua to Yunnan became some of the most hazardous in the Far East. His air crews were overworked and many cracked under the strain of constant flying. Living conditions in the hot and humid bases of Assam were primitive at best and the boredom was almost unbearable. There was a shortage of mail and rations; hospital care and quarters were substandard. Morale of the 1st Ferrying Group was very low in the spring and summer.

The China National Aviation Corporation had been flying the Himalaya route for years and knew the region well. Many of the pilots were longtime Chinese employees, and a number of AVG pilots had gone to work for the company rather than enlist in the Air Forces. CNAC had been carrying both air cargo and passengers. In light of Air Force failure to develop a set cargo system, Washington had been considering a plan whereby the company would take over full control of the flights from India to China. Stilwell opposed the plan because he did not consider it fair to have military pilots flying alongside civilians who were being paid far more money. He also had the old military view that it was unwise to have the military under civilian control in a combat area. Wanting to keep the operation under his control, he recommended that he be allowed to make arrangements with the Chinese to have all CNAC planes leased to the U.S. Air Force. To make sure this took place, he suggested that, if the Chinese refused, no more transport planes would be allocated to them. The Chinese then had no choice, and Chiang agreed in principle to the leasing proposal.

The pilots flying battered DC-3s which had seen service over much of China for years had no easy job. The weather was a constant worry throughout much of the year and many crews were lost over the Himalayas; only a few managed to get out.

Joe Rosbert, a former AVG ace, had joined CNAC rather than be inducted into the Army Air Force in Kunming. He flew from the bases in the Assam Valley of India for months, bringing supplies to Kunming for Chennault.

He and his copilot, Ridge Hammill, along with a Chinese radio operator, took off in April 1943 from Dinjan on a flight to Kunming. At 16,000 feet over the Hump, the plane began to ice up; the two pilots fought it as long as they could. At last the plane—barely maintaining flying speed—bounced off one ridge at 14,000 feet and slammed into another. The radio operator, P. T. Wong, was killed on impact and the two Americans were badly injured. Rosbert had a broken ankle and other cuts and bruises while Hammill had a sprained ankle and severe cuts on his head. In spite of their wounds the two men made splints from bamboo wrapped with nylon from parachutes and walked down the mountain in thigh-deep snow. They were finally discovered my Mishmi natives and given food and shelter. The natives—sometimes leading the Americans and occasionally carrying them over steep mountain passes—finally brought them out of the mountains near their home base. The trip took forty-six days and covered a hundred and fifty miles.

Stilwell, watching the difficulties of air transport in the region, reasoned that Naiden should have more time to devote to the problem. He contacted his friend Marshall, who ordered General Arnold to relieve Naiden of command of the Tenth Air Force and assign him full time to air cargo. Naiden subsequently became ill and was returned to the States for hospitalization. Stilwell recommended his staff air adviser, General Clayton Bissell, to be commanding general of the Tenth Air Force. Bissell assumed command on August 18, 1942, and immediately asked Washington to replace the officers and men General Brereton had taken to the Middle East. His first act was to assign Colonel Caleb Haynes to command a task force in India comparable to the China Air Task Force presently being set up; it was to be called the India Air Task Force (IATF). Chennault would command the China Air Task Force (CATF). The X Service Command in India would be in charge of Colonel Robert C. Oliver; the India-China Ferry Command would be headed by Colonel Robert Tate; and the Karachi American Air Base Command would be under Brigadier General Francis M. Brady.

While Bissell was technically above Chennault as overall commander of the Tenth Air Force, his job was by no means simple or one that promised to bring him much joy. The weather, difficulty of getting spare parts, supplies, and maintenance facilities, plus the loss of the Burmese bases and most of his transport planes to the Near East—all combined to give him problems. He was to be responsible for keeping open the China supply lines and delivering the tonnage that was needed—something that he never succeeded in doing. He did the best he could, although that was not the way Chennault saw it on his end. Bissell immediately transferred service troops to Assam, gave the highest priority to transport aircraft, put all the planes available on the Dinjan–Chabua–Kunming route, and ordered stepped-up construction of airfields. Just when it looked as though he was making headway, Washington notified Stilwell that the responsibility for all cargo flights over the Hump to China would fall under the Air Transport Command rather than the Tenth Air Force. This left Bissell with the protection of the route, if not the operation. His next task was to try to improve the Assam warning net to ensure notice of Japanese bomber raids and incoming fighters when the monsoon lifted. Brereton had set up some rudimentary warning bases on the hills east of the Assam Valley, but they had to be supplied by air and were not very effective. Although Bissell tried to implement these, the Japanese planes still got through.

Adding to Bissell's problems in India was Gandhi's "Quit India" policy, which was aimed at the British. His agitation for political autonomy—plus propaganda tossed in by the Germans and the Japanese—had caused considerable civil strife in the midst of the war. The British, fed up, threw him in jail in August, which led Nehru and other Indian Congress Party leaders to organize riots in the major cities. Transportation and communication lines were sabotaged in the name of independence. Bissell had to increase security around all United States installations and restrict his personnel to the bases.

Meanwhile in China the newly activated China Air Task Force had come under the command of Chennault. Like the AVG, it was wholly dependent upon air supply from India for planes, personnel, spare parts, bombs, ammunition, guns, and—most important—gasoline. And because of manpower shortages it was defended on the ground by poorly equipped Chinese Army units. However, Chennault was convinced there would be no Japanese ground offensive against the Kunming-Chungking area. He reasoned that it would not be worth the effort to divert such a substantial ground force from other combat theaters just to take the wartime capital. He knew he could harass Japanese shipping lines off the China coast and could protect airfields in China with his fighters as long as he kept up his warning nets, as he had done with the AVG. He knew that the supply lines the Japanese maintained to Indochina and Burma were of the utmost importance to the enemy and he intended to cut them whenever he could. His CATF would be dependent upon the Chinese for quarters and food, but then his AVG had been too and it had worked well. On July 29 he had sent a secret letter to the then commanding general of the Tenth Air Force, General Naiden:

> Subject: Acknowledgement of directive for objective, China Air Task Force.
>
> To: Commanding General, 10th U. S. Air Force.
>
> 1. Receipt of your radio dated July 24 in which you state that Myitkyina is the first objective of the CATF, is acknowledged.
>
> 2. It is essential that I receive from you by radio as soon as possible all authenticated intelligence regarding Japanese activities at Myitkyina; and I so request. Frankly, Myitkyina seems to be a typical Japanese dummy threat in an effort to focus our attention on it while more important preparation goes on elsewhere. Of course there exists the possibility of Myitkyina being used by the Japanese at some time, and I urge the full use of both aerial and secret intelligence by you to ascertain when it may be so used. However, during my years of air command in

the Far East, I have always found it unpracticable to try to prevent the enemy from using an airfield by expedient bombing while yet unoccupied. Certainly the Japanese attempted to prevent the CATF from occupying the Hengyang-Kweilin area by daily bombardment while these airfields were not used by me. The uselessness of their tactics was shown by the fact that I was not hindered or delayed by one day when I decided to move both fighter and bombardment aircraft onto these fields.

3. My experience insofar as China is concerned has also proved to me that the best way to endeavor to keep our Ferry Route open is to follow out a careful plan which will contemplate the destruction of enemy aircraft on the ground and the engagement of his aircraft in destructive combat when flying within our territory.

4. With the above views in mind, it is my opinion that the real threat to the India–China Ferry Route lies in the enemy air bases south of the route, particularly those bases which the Japanese already occupy with aircraft and, on which, I believe they have been constantly working in preparation for direct attack on our air route as soon as the monsoon breaks, or perhaps, even sooner. I refer specifically to the Japanese air bases at Mengshih, Loiwing, Lashio, Shwebo, Mandalay, Magwe, Toungoo and Rangoon. As you know, these range from 150 miles to 600 miles from the India–China Ferry Route. It is possible for the Japanese from these bases, to operate bombers capable of striking at either the eastern terminus of our ferry route to Kunming or the western control station at Dinjan. It is also possible for the enemy, from these bases (or using them as staging bases) to use long range fighters which can attack our transports in flight. Bases from which the enemy may quickly move by staging routes, that should be also considered, are those at Chiengmai and Lambhun.

5. In order to meet this situation and also to accomplish the strategic missions assigned to me by the Generalissimo through the Commanding General, American Army Forces, CB&I, I urge the following steps:

a. The organization and operation of an effective aerial reporting net in the Dinjan area—this net to be of sufficient extent to give adequate warning of the approach of hostile aircraft both by day and by night.

b. The augmentation of intelligence by you which will give us daily information of Japanese aircraft and installations on the bases named in paragraph 4 above, so that we may be adequately warned and prepared for any air movement by the enemy.

c. The constant and regular reinforcement of the CATF by such numbers of most modern aircraft, personnel, and supplies, that will permit me to destroy the enemy at his bases, and prevent him from interdicting the Ferry Route.

I am confident if reinforced by both fighters and bombers to the extent already requested by me, and if the above suggestions are followed out, I not only can keep the India–China Ferry Route open, but can drive the Japanese Air Force out of China. I would appreciate if you will let me know what steps you have taken to give me a constant flow of aircraft of the most modern types, personnel and supplies.

6. If some action is not taken along the lines suggested in this letter, it is my duty to warn you that I must soon face the necessity of fighting greatly superior numbers with ill-equipped forces. I wish to reaffirm it is my firm conviction that if the CATF is made one of strength, I will not only drive the Japanese Air Force out of China, but I will be able to cut his lines of communication from Japan to Malaya and in the future bomb Japan itself.

> C. L. Chennault
> Brigadier General, U.S.A.
> Commanding[3]

It may have seemed to the rest of the Air Force and particularly to Washington that Chennault's claims were too optimistic but he had several factors in his favor: his squadrons were equipped with P-40s with which Chinese mechanics had become familiar over the preceding years; maintenance on these could be done well in Kunming; and his well-proven air warning system was still in use, providing him with advance warning of the Japanese and also a net with which to bring back to the bases American pilots who had bailed out or crashed. In addition he had built a linking system of east China airfields connected by communications lines that would allow him to hit Japanese bases at will. By switching his bomber and fighter squadrons from base to base, he could hit the enemy and yet not be there when they struck back. And he knew his enemy as no other American in that part of the world did, having observed the Japanese since 1937.

General Naiden had designated Colonel Robert Scott as commanding officer of the 23rd Fighter Group. Scott, a full colonel and West Point graduate, had many hours in fighter planes, although for several months he had been flying C-47s over the Hump on supply runs to China. He had wanted to be a part of the AVG and had flown a few combat missions with them in the last days before they were deactivated, and he had moved in with Chennault and Colonel Tom Gentry.

Chennault's house, which was close to the airfield, was an adobe structure with a tile roof and was shaded by eucalyptus and pepper trees. It had been part of a school and one mud wall was still standing to form a patio approach to the front door. Inside, Chennault had spread rugs over the dirt floor and on one wall was a picture of the Generalissimo. The walls were pockmarked with holes from bomb fragments. The three men were cared for by four Chinese servants—a cook named Wang and a chauffeur with the same name, a houseboy called "Houseboat," and "Gunboat," a mess boy who had served on the U.S. gunboat *Panay* before it was sunk by the Japanese in 1937. In addition Chennault had a young male dachshund named "Joe Dash," which carried on a constant war with the rats that infested all Chinese dwellings. Chennault doted on the dog and taught it many tricks, as well as how to retrieve ducks, geese, cranes, and doves.

Two additions were made to his staff in July. Lieutenant Colonel Henry Strickland was sent from New Delhi to be his adjutant general and Colonel Merian Cooper became chief of staff. Cooper had been a Polish Air Force fighter ace following World War I and had come to China as part of the Doolittle raid (as had Robert Scott). He had made documentary films in Africa and Asia and had been a Hollywood director. He also moved in with the rest at Chennault's quarters. A master tactician, he became invaluable to Chennault and the CATF.

Colonel Clinton D. Vincent had been sent over by Bissell to be Chennault's chief of staff, but he was more interested in combat flying, so Chennault sent him to learn more about the Japanese fighter tactics at Kweilin and Hengyang. Colonel Bruce Holloway, a slow-speaking pilot from Tennessee, was sent over to be operations officer. Caleb Haynes managed to get himself transferred from India and operated out of China as commander of the heavy bombers, although he was still attached to the Tenth Air Force.

But in the summer of 1942 the CATF was hardly a potent striking force. It had seven B-25 bombers of the 11th Bomb Squadron and forty P-40s to fly against an estimated four hundred Japanese planes based in east China, Indochina, and Burma. Chennault made Colonel Tex Hill leader of the 75th Fighter Squadron and Colonel Ed Rector leader of the 76th, so he had two combat-wise veterans to lead those two squadrons.

By August—in spite of the lack of replacements—he was at least ready to hold his own against the Japanese when the monsoons lifted.

Sixteen

While Bissell and the new Air Transport Command were struggling to iron out the difficulties involved with getting supplies over the Hump into China, the CATF was living off the land. Before the arrival of U.S. forces the Chinese had carefully stored gas, bombs, and ammunition at airfields scattered all over China. This 100-octane gas and ammunition had been purchased early in the war—long before the Lend-Lease supplies began to trickle in—and was from French, Russian, and even Japanese sources. The ammunition was in every conceivable caliber and fitted a variety of guns. The CATF flew its missions using these depots of stored equipment—dropping the foreign- and Chinese-made bombs on Japanese installations in east and south China and in Indochina. The Chinese made belly tanks for the P-40s out of bamboo and fish glue so the fighters could fly longer missions.

Chennault and his men ate off the land as well, since no food supplies came in from India. For meat, they ate locally raised pigs and chickens and butchered water buffaloes. All the vegetables were grown in Yunnan and the CATF personnel got used to drinking tea instead of coffee. American whiskey on the black market was running $60 to $70 U.S., so most of the men drank local beer or Miss Kweilin Grape Wine and the gagging local brandy. Somewhat better was the British or Indian Haywoods rum and gin, which was regularly smuggled over the Hump in CNAC and Air Corps planes.

The chain of command of the new CATF was unbelievably complicated. Stilwell had headquarters in both Chungking and New Delhi—two thousand miles apart. Bissell was stationed in New Delhi and Chennault was forced to clear most administrative problems with him. In order to communicate with General Chow or General Peter Mow of the Chinese Air Force, Chennault had to write to New Delhi and the letter or memo had to be forwarded back to Chungking from there. The brass at Tenth Air Force headquarters was far more concerned with the impending Japanese attack on India—when the monsoon ended in October—than it was with Chennault's problems in China.

Chennault sent the 75th Fighter Squadron to Hengyang and the 76th to Kweilin. To protect against any possible raids on Kunming or Paoshan from northern Burma, he dispatched the 16th Fighter Squadron under Major George Hazlett, to Yunnanyi, and the 74th Fighter Squadron, under Major Frank Schiel, was left to defend Kunming. The 11th Bomb Squadron of B-25s was at Kweilin and Hengyang temporarily but was shuttled back and forth between there and Kunming when Chennault wanted to bomb Indochina, Burma, or Thailand. But for most of the summer their best targets were Hong Kong, Canton, and Hankow, which they could reach with escort from Hengyang and Kweilin.

All through July the Americans attacked targets of opportunity and the Japanese counterattacked. On July 20 the medium bombers of the 11th Bomb Squadron plastered a cotton yarn factory at Kiukiang, but ten days later the Japanese sent wave after wave of bombers and fighters over Hengyang in a massive effort to immobilize the advanced air base. The P-40s shot down seventeen of the estimated one hundred and twenty enemy planes that attacked—four of them at night.

By the end of July the claims Chennault had made about destroying the Japanese Air Force did not seem so implausible as earlier. Even the brass in New Delhi began to take notice as the tally rose to twenty-four fighters and twelve bombers destroyed at a cost of five P-40s, one B-25, and no pilot loss.

Chennault's father died in early July. He received a letter from Chungking from H. H. Kung:

> Huang Shan, South Bank
> August 12, 1942

Brig.-General C. L. Chennault
Peishiyi,
Chungking

Dear General Chennault,

Madame Kung and I have just learned with the deepest regret the passing of your dear father and hasten to express to you our heartfelt sympathies.

Though we did not have the pleasure of meeting him we know he must have been a charming gentleman to have a distinguished and likable son as you. He had lived to ripe old age and had the satisfaction, denied to many, of seeing his son make good in life. May this fact console you in your hour of grief.

> Yours sincerely,
> H. H. Kung[1]

The letter arrived on a rainy day as Chennault sat in his office. He stared out the window at the sheets of rain obscuring the foothills of the Himalayas and at the mud and water in the road. It was difficult for him to grasp that he could no longer communicate with his father—not that he had written that often to the old man. He had received perhaps two or three letters a year in the careful script that his father wrote in. But the fact that he was always there had made things at home seem stable and normal. Now, as he sat staring at the letter before him, he felt his throat constrict and his eyes burn with tears. There was so much he had wanted to tell his father about the long years in China and why he had stayed away from Louisiana so long. It had been difficult for the old man to understand why he had not come home to Nell and the children long before this. Chennault felt his father had never fully understood the war in China and why his son felt the need to fight in such a faraway land. He had tried to explain it during that Christmas at home in 1939, but he knew he had not done a good job of it when the old man simply looked at him and nodded slowly. Now he would never be able to talk to him at all. His father had lived to be eighty years old—a good long life.

As he fingered the edge of the letter lying on his desk, he remembered when his mother had died. He had been five years old. He and his younger brother Bill had been lost in the grief of her death. John Chennault had been unable to console his two sons for a time and it was not until five years later, when he married a schoolteacher, Lottie Barnes, that the boys had a home again. A farm girl herself, "Miss Lottie" had loved nature as young Claire had and she not only encouraged his love for the wilds and its creatures but also encouraged him in his schooling. When she died five years later it was as though his own mother had died again. He shook his head as he thought of them both—in another time and another place—so far removed from a mud hut in the rainy region of west China.

In August the B-25s began to hit Japanese shipping in the harbor at Haiphong. Picking up fighters and topping off with gas at the forward base of Nanning, they blasted the dock areas and sank shipping in the harbor—in spite of terrible weather. At the end of the month Chennault pulled the medium bombers back to Kunming and they began to hit at targets in northern Burma. On August 26 the mediums, escorted by the 74th's P-40s from Yunnanyi, bombed Lashio and received heavy opposition from Japanese fighters and antiaircraft fire. A few days later they returned to bomb Myitkyina, where the Japanese had based heavy concentrations of fighters and bombers.

As August dragged on mechanics and pilots sweltered in the sun and humid weather of the monsoons and just as quickly shivered in the drenching rains that hit each day. Everyone worked and flew in shorts and G.I. shoes, which remained caked with the cloying mud.

The dirt-and-crushed-rock fields at Hengyang and Kweilin were being hit regularly by Japanese bombs. Chennault asked the Chinese Army for work battalions and they supplied thousands of coolies for repair brigades. As soon as the Japanese bombed the strips, the coolies would fill up the bomb craters and smooth over the holes. On one day at Kweilin they filled up forty-five bomb craters in two hours.

There were no hangars or shelters for aircraft at either forward base. Trying to keep the handful of planes flying, mechanics worked on the planes at night with the aid of smoking kerosene lamps. Since there were no spare parts, they had to improvise everything. There were only two sets of tools that had belonged to the AVG mechanics. Records were kept on a battered typewriter borrowed from a missionary. The Chinese mechanics lived well, but the Americans grew weary of greasy pork, bean shoots, and rice. Pilots and ground crews came down with dysentery and jaundice, and malaria was something everyone learned to live with. Atabrine and quinine were the only available medicines and most Americans remained a sickly yellow color from the drugs. The only doctor was Colonel Tom Gentry and he was in Kunming.

The new crews from the Tenth Air Force in India were led on their missions by veterans like Tex Hill. Sick with malaria most of the summer, Hill nevertheless led his new pilots in constant attacks against enemy bombers—on daylight strafing missions and in night attacks. Alone, he once flew a single-plane night attack against Hankow to dive-bomb the airfield, keeping the Japanese off balance and unable to raid Hengyang that night. He was awarded the Silver Star for this mission.

Hill was helped in the defense of Hengyang by such veterans as "Ajax" Baumler and Johnny Alison, who teamed up to fly night interceptions—shooting down Japanese bombers in the bright moonlit nights over Hengyang. By the last of August the Japanese figured the loss ratio from all raids was becoming too high and that Hengyang and Kweilin were not worth the price they were paying in fighters and bombers and the raids slacked off.

But by this time the CATF was down to only a few remaining planes that were flyable and its pilots were exhausted. P-40s were flying on oil that had been refiltered until it was barely usable. Tires were in short supply and the few four-ply tires that did come over from India were so fragile that they sometimes blew out on the first landing on the sharp rocks of the Chinese airfields. Tail-wheel tires were also in short supply and pilots flew combat missions with rags stuck inside the casings. Engines quit on takeoff and several pilots made crash landings during combat because the old Allison engines just gave out. By the early part of September 1942, Chennault was down to thirty-eight pilots and thirty-four flyable P-40s spread out over four fighter squadrons and vast territory.

He got some relief in late September when a squadron of twenty P-40 pilots from Panama came in with some well-worn P-40K fighters and six more B-25 medium bombers. These pilots had been guarding the Panama Canal and were used to the heat and humidity of that area. Assimilated with the four squadrons of the 23rd Group, they were to remain the backbone of the CATF for the next year.

As the monsoon rains began to lessen, Chennault's B-25s began to attack targets in north Burma. On September 19 a squadron of B-25s, on a mission to bomb the town of Lungling, noticed a buildup of Japanese troops between Lashio and the Salween River. There had been no warning of this ground action and as a result the CATF was called upon to support Chinese armies in the area. The medium bombers and fighters hit supply depots and troop concentrations for eleven missions in a row and did considerable damage in the Wanting-Mengshih region.

Newspaper stories being released in the States made it sound as though the United States had a giant air force operating in China. A typical story ran in the New York *Times* on September 27:

> With the American Air Forces, in China, September 27 (AP)—Resuming their air offensive against the Japanese after a lapse of nearly a month, the American Air Force in China strafed troop columns in Southwest Yunnan Province yesterday after having made another of their attacks on Hanoi in French Indochina the day before, Lieut. Gen. Joseph W. Stilwell's headquarters announced today.

The American public, reeling under the bad news of Japanese landings on Guadalcanal, the fighting in the Aleutian Islands, and the war in Europe, had no way of knowing that the "Air Force" in China consisted of half a dozen medium bombers and half a hundred fighter planes. Stilwell—with the war in Burma stalemated—had little else in the way of good news to release from his headquarters in New Delhi.

Merian Cooper had been a great help to Chennault in planning "guerrilla" raids on the part of the CATF, but Cooper—who had quit Stilwell's staff to work with Chennault—had apparently incurred the wrath of both Stilwell and Bissell. Rumors of his impending removal had been filtering to Chennault by the CBI grapevine and he was not surprised to receive a letter from Bissell dated October 5 saying that he and Stilwell were "one hundred per cent in favor of a single command at Kunming and were equally in favor of that command being the CATF," but that the command would not be turned over to CATF until they had greater confidence in Chennault's staff than they had at present. Chennault knew he was talking about Cooper and was not amused when Bissell went on to say that "your present chief of staff has insufficient military background and experience properly to exercise his responsibility."[2] Angry as Chennault was, he could not do anything about the charge.

Cooper, who had a flare for the unexpected, organized a raid on October 25 against several large Japanese supply convoys that had arrived in Hong

Kong en route to Indochina and Rangoon. Twelve B-25s escorted by seven P-40s took off from Kweilin and plastered the Kowloon and Hong Kong docks with thirty thousand pounds of demolition and fragmentation bombs, heavily damaging the port facilities. The CATF planes were jumped by twenty-one Japanese interceptors but lost only one B-25 and a single P-40 in the running battle that ensued. The night of September 26, six B-25s returned unescorted from their first night mission of the war and did more damage to Hong Kong. Three more B-25s hit Canton the next day, doing extensive damage to the warehouse area.

Cooper was a rebel and as unorthodox as Chennault. In October, incensed at the delay in getting planes, spare parts, and supplies to the beleaguered CATF, he wrote a personal letter to Major General William Donovan, chief of the Office of Strategic Services, telling him about the plight of the CATF. Donovan, a close friend of President Roosevelt, circulated the letter around Washington. The War Department got wind of it and notified Stilwell. Cooper was ordered back to the States for "medical reasons." However, his "medical" reasons did not prevent him from returning to the Pacific theater where he served as an aide to General George Kenney.[3] Chennault's vigorous protests to the War Department were to no avail.

It was at this time, in early October, that Wendell L. Willkie, former candidate for the presidency in 1940 and presently a special envoy of President Roosevelt, visited China on a fact-finding tour.

Harrison Forman, reporter for the New York *Times,* wrote on October 5:

"Chungking, China, October 5—Wendell L. Willkie today held important conferences, visited three of China's "refugee" universities, made plans to go to the Chinese-Japanese front and kissed another girl.

Continuing a Sunday conference of three and a half hours with Generalissimo Chiang Kai-shek, he had a "heart-to-heart" talk with the Chinese leader.

Mr. Willkie saw Brig. Gen. Claire L. Chennault, American Army Air Force Commander in China, for a "down to brass tacks" discussion of the situation and he plans a similar meeting with Lieut. Gen. Joseph W. Stilwell.[4]

The New York *Times* version does not agree with Chennault's. In his autobiography, *Way of a Fighter,* published in 1949, he wrote:

"During his stay in Chungking, Willkie phoned CATF headquarters, then at Peishiyi, with a request to visit and chat confidentially with me. I told Willkie I could not see him until he secured Stilwell's approval. The next day, October 11, 1942, Willkie and Stilwell drove to Peishiyi in Stilwell's staff car. Stilwell said I had his permission to tell Willkie anything I chose. While Willkie and I talked for two hours, Stilwell sat in the outer office and waited."

It is possible that Willkie and Chennault had a brief discussion on October 4, but a lengthier one took place on the eighth. Chennault said Willkie—

"Genuinely shocked" by the discovery that Chennault was making his highly publicized raids against the Japanese with less than a dozen bombers and fifty fighters—asked him to state his case directly to the President in a letter that he could present to Roosevelt. Chennault knew a good thing when he saw it. Fed up with the stalemate of the Hump deliveries and what he perceived as Stilwell's and Bissell's efforts to hold down the air war in China, he relished the chance. Never one to worry about the chain of command—even when he was in the old Air Corps—he considered the end justified the means: winning the war. His letter to President Roosevelt was, to say the least, a classic:

Mr. Wendell Willkie,
Special Representative of the President
In his capacity as Commander in Chief
of the Armed Forces.

You have stated to me that you are the direct representative in the military, as well as a political sense, of the Commander in Chief of the United States Army, the President of the United States. You have ordered me to make a report directly to you on military operations in China against Japan. I herewith comply.

1. Japan can be defeated in China.

2. It can be defeated by an Air Force so small that in other theaters it would be called ridiculous.

3. I am confident that, given real authority in command of such an Air Force, I can cause the collapse of Japan. I believe I can do it in such a manner that the lives of hundreds of thousands of American soldiers and sailors will be saved, and that the cost to our country will be relatively small.

4. I speak with confidence, but, I believe, not with egotism. The reason for my confidence is based on the fact that since 1923 I have believed firmly in the possibility of Japan making war on the United States; I have devoted the best years of my military life to the study of this subject; I have for five years been unofficial advisor to the Chinese Air Force; in this capacity, I made war against Japan for over five years; for the last year I have commanded first the AVG, then the China Air Task Force; at no time in China have I had as many as fifty fighting planes in operation to meet the full fighting force of Japan; as Commander of the AVG and the CATF, I have never lost an air battle against the Japanese. This tiny fighter force under my Command has destroyed over three hundred Japanese aircraft confirmed and about three hundred more probably destroyed—I believe the total to be about six hundred—with the loss of twelve AVG pilots and four CATF pilots from enemy action. The bomber force of the CATF has consisted at maximum of eight medium bombers. With these I have made 25 raids

against Japanese installations, troops, and shipping, without the loss of either a man or plane through enemy action.

5. When I came to China the Chinese Air Force was under Italian advisors. Before America entered the war I had succeeded (because I believed we would fight the Axis powers and Japan), in having the Italians sent out of China. I believe I have the full confidence of the Generalissimo and all high Chinese leaders. If I have their confidence it is because (a) I have been a winning general, (b) I have never lied to the Chinese, and I have never promised to perform more than I believed capable of performance.

6. I am now confident that given full authority as the American military commander in China that I can not only bring about the downfall of Japan but that I can make the Chinese lasting friends with the United States. I am confident that I can create such good will that China will be a great and friendly trade market for generations.

7. The military task is a simple one. It has been complicated by unwieldy, illogical military organization and by men who do not understand aerial warfare in China.

8. To accomplish the downfall of Japan, I need only this very small American Air Force—105 fighter aircraft of modern design, 30 medium bombers, and in the last phase, some months from now 12 heavy bombers. The force must be constantly maintained at all times. We will have losses. These losses must be replaced. I consider 30 percent replacements in fighters and 20 percent in bombers sufficient.

9. My reason for stating that I can accomplish the overthrow of Japan is that I am confident this force can destroy the effectiveness of the Japanese Air Force, probably within six months, within one year at the outside. I am a professional fighter and this is my professional opinion. The facts on which this opinion is based are simple. Japan has only a limited production of aircraft. I can force that Japanese Air Force by aerial military maneuver to fight me in a position of my own selection. Having once fixed it in this position I can destroy its effectiveness. With its basic effective Air Force destroyed, our Navy can operate with freedom, and General MacArthur can push his offensive in the South West Pacific at will. Meanwhile, from the Eastern Chinese Air Bases, I will guarantee to destroy the principal industrial centers of Japan. No country is so peculiarly vulnerable to air attack. The cutting of the Japanese sea route to her newly conquered empire is a simple matter. Once the above two objectives are accomplished the complete military subjection of Japan is certain and easy.

10. To effectively maintain the small air force mentioned above, an aerial supply line must be built up between India and China. It is a simple statement of fact to say this aerial supply line will also be minute compared to the objectives to be accomplished. The full establishment

and maintenance of this aerial ferry route is child's play in comparison
with the difficulties overcome in establishing the Pan American South
American air line or its Atlantic and Pacific air lines. It only needs good
command—good management. The amount of freight to be carried over
this air line in order to maintain an air force is very small—the accompanying study will state the basic simplicity.

11. The present plan for the defense of this ferry line is that of the
standard orthodox, rigid military mind. It has no real military value. It
shows complete lack of conception of the true use of air power or even
of basic military strategy. I would defend this air line in the same way
that Scipio Africanus defended Rome, when Hannibal was at its very
gates. Scipio struck at Carthage, and the Carthaginians, by necessity,
had to call Hannibal and his Army back to Africa to defend Carthage.
In like manner, I would defend the ferry route by striking at the Japanese supply lines to the Southwest Pacific, and then hit Tokyo itself. The
Japanese Air Force by necessity would then be forced to fight in Eastern
China and over Tokyo. The Japanese have not the air power to fight
both over the ferry route in India, Burma and Yunnan, and over Tokyo
at the same time. No capable commander in history has ever adopted
the stolid plan of the present method of defending the ferry route. Grant
ordered Sherman to march through the heart of the South and destroy
Lee's supplies and cut Lee's lines of communications while he, Grant,
fixed Lee's Army in northern Virginia. Once Lee's supplies and lines of
communications were cut, Lee was defeated and the Confederacy was
ruined. I plan to do the same thing in China against Japan with air
power. Japan must hold Hong Kong, Shanghai, and the Yangtze Valley.
These are essential to hold Japan itself. I can force the Japanese Air
Force to fight in the defense of these objectives behind the best air
warning net of its kind in the world. With the use of these tactics, I am
confident that I can destroy Japanese aircraft at the rate of between 10
and 20 to one. When the Japanese Air Force refuses to come within my
warning net and fight, I will strike out with my medium bombers
against their sea supply line to the Southwest Pacific. In a few months
the enemy will lose so many aircraft that the aerial defense of Japan will
be negligible. I can then strike at Japan from Chuchow [Chuhsien] and
Lishui with heavy bombers. My air force can burn up Japan's two main
industrial areas—Tokyo and the Kobe, Osaka, Nagoya triangle—and
Japan will be unable to supply her armies in her newly conquered empire in China, Malaya, the Dutch East Indies, etc. with munitions of
war. The road is then open for the Chinese Army in China, for the
American Navy in the Pacific and for MacArthur to advance from his
Australian stronghold—all with comparatively slight cost.

12. While engaged in these operations, I will maintain full ground
installations for the eastern terminus of the ferry route in Yunnan, at

Kunming, Chanyi, Yunnanyi, etc. If a really major swift aerial movement is made by the Japanese across their staging route into Burma, to
attack the India–China air supply lines, then, acting on interior lines of
air communications, I can move back and again be within the warning
net which I have established in Yunnan, and meet the Japanese over
their Burma airfields and then and there destroy whatever force they
have sent against us.

My entire above plan is simple. It has been long thought out. I have
spent five years developing an air warning net and radio command service to fight this way. I have no doubt of my success.

13. However, in order to accomplish this aim, it is essential that I be
given complete freedom of fighting action, that I also be able to deal
directly with the Generalissimo and the Chinese forces. This latter I
know the Generalissimo desires. I would not make the above statements
so confidently if I had not, in my operations with the AVG never retreated one foot until the ground forces had fled behind me, leaving my
air bases exposed to ground attack. Only then did I retreat to again
destroy 20 Japanese planes for each one the AVG lost. Even then I
would not have been forced to retreat if I had had the necessary bombers and reconnaissance planes.

Given authority to report only to the Generalissimo, I intend to carry
out in China this combined ground and air action.

14. This plan I again repeat will enable the Chinese ground forces to
operate successfully, and most assuredly will permit MacArthur to successfully advance and will decisively aid the Navy's operations in the
Pacific. Moreover, it will make China our lasting friend for years after
the war.

> C. L. Chennault
> Brigadier General, AUS
> Commanding[5]

President Roosevelt was impressed. He had been reading newspaper reports about the exploits of the AVG and they had been among the few bright
spots in the war communiqués. He had long been an advocate of air power
and saw no reason why Chennault could not carry out his plans. Granted he
took the "I can cause the downfall of Japan" part as a bit of wishful thinking, he nevertheless read the rest of the letter with interest. He forwarded it
to the War Department where it caused a considerable reaction. Marshall
immediately contacted Stilwell and he, in turn, let Bissell know. Secretary of
War Stimson was annoyed, but there were a number of people in Washington
who agreed with Chennault—among them Roosevelt's trusted adviser Harry
Hopkins. In addition, there were Lauchlin Currie, Tommy Corcoran, T. V.
Soong, and Joe Alsop, who had been repatriated from a prisoner-of-war

camp in Hong Kong and was again writing a newspaper column in Washington.

The letter was followed up by a report to Secretary of the Navy Frank Knox by Chennault's old ally, Colonel James McHugh, naval attaché in Chungking. The Generalissimo—who had secretly wanted Chennault to replace Stilwell since his battles with his chief of staff over his handling of the Burma campaign—called the naval attaché in and he and Madame asked McHugh what he thought of the proposal. McHugh, having admired Chennault since the days at Nanking and Shanghai, was all for it. In his report he endorsed the suggestion that Stilwell be replaced and added that he considered Stilwell's attempt to recapture Burma strictly a personal ambition on the heels of a humiliating defeat. Furthermore, he stated, he considered that the effort to retake Burma would detract from Chennault's program to fight an air war. He added that the Generalissimo would be pleased with the removal of both Stilwell and Bissell "and their huge staffs." He emphasized that Chiang wanted Chennault to be in full control.

Knox passed the report on to Secretary Stimson, who immediately passed it on to General Marshall—who hit the ceiling. He contacted the Navy and McHugh, who was on his way home anyway, and told him he could no longer serve in China.

However, a copy of the document reached Roosevelt, who was receptive to Chennault's idea of concentrating air power on the Japanese from China and was already considering removing Stilwell—because of the pressure he had been receiving from T. V. Soong and others who wanted to placate Chiang. But Roosevelt did not want to antagonize his Secretary of War or his Chief of Staff. He had to wait for an opportune moment.

Seventeen

On October 21 the heavy bombers, the B-24 Liberators, were used for the first time. Six planes of the 436th Squadron from the 7th Bomb Group of the Tenth Air Force in India were flown to Chengtu, northwest of Chungking. They dropped bombs on the Lin-hsi coal mines in Hopeh Province near the city of Kuyeh. Although the bombs struck their target, not enough damage was done to flood the mines and stop production of coal.

In the meantime, Bissell was convinced that the Japanese were stockpiling planes at Lashio and a series of Japanese raids on Chabua, Dinjan, and Mohanbari in the Assam Valley on October 25 reinforced his view. Chennault had been sending photo recon planes over Lashio regularly and had seen no such buildup. He was convinced the enemy planes had come from fields in southern Burma, but Bissell insisted he pull his B-25s out of east China and attack Lashio. The east China bombing raids on Hong Kong and Canton had been very productive and this latest demand of Bissell's—without justification—made relations even worse between the two men.

Having been briefed by Stilwell on Chennault's writing directly to Roosevelt, Bissell was particularly critical of all of Chennault's operations and went out of his way to establish his own authority. He purposely assigned personnel to the CATF staff when he knew it was Army policy to let the commanding officer pick his own staff people. Even Hap Arnold, when sending out staff officers, played by the rules and only suggested positions for them. Aware of the view on the part of the China-based Air Force personnel that India was a plush base and that it was "short-stopping" supplies destined for the CATF, Bissell became defensive. It was no secret that Air Force people in India were being supplied regularly from the States. Pilots and air crews flying over the Hump brought reports that personnel stationed in India—particularly in New Delhi and Karachi—were living off the fat of the land. They had cheap liquor, the latest movies, ice cream, Stateside food, and even USO shows with pretty American girls. Ill fed and ill clothed and with no new planes or replacement parts, CATF morale dropped to a new low and the men made their feelings known.

Bissell wrote Chennault on November 22 a dispatch marked SECRET. In it he quoted from a report by someone he called an "impartial observer" that, while the morale of the CATF appeared high as a unit, the men were unhappy with the Tenth Air Force in India. He cited complaints by CATF men about shortages from India and general griping about the Tenth Air Force personnel living off the fat of the land while the CATF was literally starving in China. Like a schoolmaster lecturing a pupil, he said he thought Chennault should tell his people they were being well supplied from India and that personnel in India had as much to gripe about as did the CATF. He said dysentery was rampant in India and so was malaria.[1]

Chennault, barely able to choke down his rage, nevertheless wrote back that it was understandable that his men should voice complaints when cigarettes were scarce, a drink cost a fortune, rotation of personnel back to India and the United States was far behind schedule, promotions were delayed, and award of decorations was slow. He went on to cite lack of uniforms, insignia, PX supplies, and mail and signed the message curtly. He heard no more from Bissell on the subject.

T. V. Soong was the intermediary in all the negotiations between Washington and Chiang and between Marshall, Stimson, and Stilwell. Privately a Chennault backer, he still preserved an outward appearance of calm when dealing with Stilwell, Marshall, and Stimson. Both Marshall and Stimson repeatedly affirmed their support of Stilwell. In October Soong returned to Chungking. He knew on what side his bread was buttered and that the Generalissimo and Madame steadfastly supported Chennault's air plans for the defense of China.

Madame Chiang went to the United States in November and in New York had a meeting with the all-powerful Harry Hopkins. Hopkins was intrigued with the beautiful Mayling and during their talks she made it clear that she had no use for Stilwell but had the highest respect for Chennault's actions. Hopkins, also an admirer of Chennault, was further influenced.

Another friend was returning to China. Joe Alsop, Chennault's aide in AVG days, had been sent to Chungking by President Roosevelt to become the Lend-Lease representative there. It was good news for Chennault, who had always had a supporter in the gregarious Alsop.

Meanwhile the Allies had agreed that the campaign to retake Burma would start in February 1943, and, in India, Stilwell's high-priority project was to be the Chinese Army unit, the X Force, at Ramgarh. After considerable negotiation he and Washington had persuaded the Generalissimo to airlift forty-five thousand soldiers over the Hump from China for training. As a result Stilwell was having his usual battles with the British, who disliked having Chinese troops on Indian soil. Chinese General Ho Ying-chin, whom Stilwell also disliked and did not trust, was in charge of the Chinese armies on the Yunnan border, awaiting orders from Chiang to invade Burma when Stilwell did.

Stilwell, in spite of his annoyance over Chennault's letter to Roosevelt, was enough of a military strategist to realize the air war in China must be kept up. On November 22, in a radio to Marshall, he complained about what would happen if twelve transport planes were diverted to the Air Force after having been promised earlier for the support of Y Force (his designation for the Chinese armies under his command in northern Burma; they were named for Yunnan Force, the province from which they marched across the line into Burma). He asked for two fighter groups, one medium bomber group, and fifty transports to be sent at once to the CBI, and added that the 3,550 tons a month of Lend-Lease should be stepped up to 10,000 tons a month.[2]

The big problem concerning increased support for the CATF continued to be the Hump tonnage. In Washington, General Arnold—looking at the Hump tonnage figures—felt the only reasonable aid he could send Chennault would be one medium bomber squadron. Meanwhile, in China, Chennault continued to fight a battle for survival at the end of 1942. Operations had almost ceased because of shortages of everything. His fighter squadrons had to be pulled out of Kweilin, Hengyang, and Lingling, leaving these forward bases without protection. He even had to cut down his patrols and support for Chinese ground troops in western Yunnan. He knew it was time either to do something drastic or to quit in China—which he was constitutionally unable to do.

In India, Stilwell, insisting that a land route to China must be reopened, continued his demands in Washington and in Chungking that a two hundred-mile-long road be constructed through the jungles, over mountains, and across rivers from Ledo in India. The Chinese X Force, which he was training to invade Burma, was to march down this newly built road as it advanced southeast to join up with Y Force sometime after the beginning of 1943.

Chennault considered the Ledo Road a waste of time. Having flown over the rough terrain for years, he thought Stilwell had no conception of air transport: the troops could be transported or dropped as paratroops. In his opinion, the use of troops to build such a road was a waste of manpower that could be better used in building new airfields in Assam and China. He knew that Hump traffic was needed to solve the supply problem but he saw no reason why it could not be done with a massive airlift of matériel. Both Stilwell and Marshall disagreed, and Marshall backed Stilwell's ground approach. In view of the British lack of enthusiasm for having Chinese troops in India—which infuriated Chiang, who thought his offer was being spurned, thereby causing him to lose face—Chiang withdrew from the plan to invade

Burma with Y Force from Yunnan. He insisted the British Navy occupy the Bay of Bengal before he would consent to invade Burma from the north. The British had no such plans and had shown a reluctance to invade Burma from the start, being far more interested in protecting India and their far-flung colonies.

The Generalissimo was insisting more and more loudly to Washington that he considered offensive action in China to be the task of the Air Force—not a ground army.

Chennault wrote up a specific request for aircraft and sent it to the Generalissimo, who sent it to the British and to Stilwell's superiors in Washington. It consisted of a request for a hundred and five fighters, thirty medium bombers, and twelve heavy bombers, plus replacements. With these, he said, he could defeat Japan in the skies over China and Burma.

The Generalissimo's acceptance of Chennault's plan and his halting plans for an invasion of Burma on the ground put the ball in Washington's court. From a diplomatic position of strength, Chiang now could urge Washington to solve the China military problem by sending an air force. He would thus be relieved of the necessity to do anything himself in China and Stilwell would be left with no support by Chiang for his Burma campaign and a ground war.

Chennault wanted a separate air force in China. He had tired of the friction between himself and Bissell, in command of the Tenth Air Force, and wanted a free hand to run the air war in China. It was not an unreasonable suggestion, considering the special confidence he enjoyed with the Generalissimo, Madame, and T. V. Soong, and his fame as a hero to the Chinese people. He could expect to achieve far more than a stranger to that country and its customs. He also could assist the Gimo and Madame in reviving the dormant Chinese Air Force—with which he had been associated for so many years. The almost nonexistent Air Force had some trained pilots but no aircraft.

Chiang was in an excellent position to bargain because he expected that China would be the future site of Allied air operations against the Japanese homeland. When the Casablanca Conference was held by the Allies in January 1943, and Chiang realized that almost no time was devoted to the China theater of war, he could afford to be annoyed. While it was decided that the British would continue operations in southern Burma, in order to obtain some bases closer to the Japanese, it was also decided that Stilwell's major operations in northern Burma could not be undertaken until November 1943 —if then. About the only benefit to China was an agreement to reinforce the newly activated India-China Wing of the Air Transport Command.

After participating in the Casablanca Conference, General Arnold, in the company of Lt. Gen. Brehon B. Somervell and Field Marshal Sir John Dill, flew to New Delhi to see for himself what the problems were. He picked up Stilwell there and they both went on to Chungking to confer with the Generalissimo. Fed up with American promises that never came to fruition, Chiang demanded a separate air force for China with five hundred planes under Chennault's command and an increase in the Hump airlift to 10,000 tons a month.

Arnold wrote Marshall after the meeting that he felt the CATF could not afford to be independent of the Tenth Air Force in India because Chennault, while strong as a combat commander, was weak on administration. While opposing the separate air force, he promised Chiang that Chennault would get seventy-five more transport planes assigned to the ATC for Hump deliveries and the C-47s now flying would be replaced by the larger-capacity Curtiss C-46 Commando, plus four new four-engine C-87 transports. He also promised that the 308th Bomb Group (Heavy)—equipped with B-24 Liberators—would leave the United States soon and could be used for strikes against Japanese ports and ships and over strategic targets. He also, in principle, approved the plan to supply Chinese pilots with U.S. aircraft.

The Generalissimo, by now used to American promises, asked Arnold to carry a personal letter to President Roosevelt with his demands. Arnold had no choice. The letter repeated the demands for five hundred planes and the 10,000-ton Hump increase and Chiang's praise of Chennault as a combat commander and a man with whom Chiang could work with confidence.

Roosevelt, impressed with the letter, seemed at this time to be convinced that Chennault should have his own air force in China. Arnold got the message and informed Stilwell on February 19 that a decision had been made to organize AAF units in China into the Fourteenth Air Force, independent of Bissell's command, but under Stilwell as a theater commander. He added that additional staff would be sent to Chennault, who would be promoted to major general—as would Bissell. Chiang was to be notified of these developments. Roosevelt asked that the War Department send a draft of his reply to Chiang's letter, stating that a land route to China—the Ledo Road—should be opened and that five hundred planes would be sent for the new air force as soon as possible. Roosevelt also stated that he thought it would be possible, eventually, to increase Hump traffic to the desired 10,000 tons per month.

Chennault was elated. Though the United States Fourteenth Air Force was to be officially activated on March 10, the CATF was not to be assigned to the Fourteenth Air Force until April 24. In the meantime the CATF became a separate command with its operational sphere extended to include the area north of the Yangtze River. It was still to be supplied by the Tenth Air Force in India and the ATC Hump traffic would be its only limiting factor. Chennault had won his freedom to operate and the news brought a jump in CATF morale. The action by Washington also boosted the prestige of the Generalissimo.

Eighteen

General Stilwell was very unhappy with the turn of events that led to Chennault's having a clear field in which to operate in China. He was equally disappointed in the victory by Chiang, whom he constantly referred to in his diary as "The Peanut." What he probably did not realize was that he was talking about, and to, a head of state—not a battalion commander in the Chinese Army. Chiang may have been corrupt, arrogant, a politician, and he may have gone over Stilwell's head in issuing commands to generals of his Fifth and Sixth Armies, but he was Generalissimo Chiang Kai-shek and head of state of a nation of 400 million people. Stilwell's attitude, his choice of words when addressing Chiang, and his use of his military and Lend-Lease authority—like a big stick—was inexcusable. Stilwell had been sent to China as a chief of staff *under* Chiang, not as his commanding officer. In addition to arguing with Chiang, Stilwell constantly made demands upon T. V. Soong, China's representative in Washington. He considered Soong a messenger boy of Chiang's and treated him as such.

An example of his methods can be seen from his diaries:

"December 23—Gave T.V. the blast. A frank statement of maladministration that will ruin the project [the Burma offensive]. Naming names including the Peanut, and using veiled threats of the inevitable consequences. Demanded a commander [for Y Force] and some action. War ministry must be energized and Peanut must go to bat. Teevy says he'll work on the Peanut.''[1]

His opinion of the Chinese government can be summed up by one entry in his diary for January 19. After talking glowingly of the fight the Russians were putting up against Hitler's armies, he wrote: "Compare it with the Chinese cesspool. A gang of thugs with the one idea of perpetuating themselves and their machine. Money, influence, and position are the only considerations of the leaders. Intrigue, double-crossing, lying reports. Hands out for anything they can get; their only idea to let someone else do the fighting;

false propaganda on the 'heroic struggle'; indifference of 'leaders' to their men. Cowardice rampant, squeeze paramount, smuggling above duty, colossal ignorance and stupidity of staff, total inability to control factions and cliques, continuous oppression of masses. The only factor that saves them is the dumb compliance of the Lao pai hsing [the common people]. The 'Intellectuals' and the rich send their precious brats to the [United] States, and the farmer boys go out and get killed—without care, training or leadership. And we are maneuvered into the position of having to support this rotten regime and glorify its figurehead, the all-wise great patriot and soldier—Peanut. My God."²

In an undated diary entry in early February, after meeting with Chiang in Chungking, Stilwell wrote: "At last conference, I pinned Peanut on whether or not he would attack next fall, in case conditions limited naval support. He got mad as hell and said, 'Didn't I say I would?' He sent word by T.V. that I had embarrassed him publicly. He can go to hell; I have him on that point. Arnold and [Sir John] Dill [head of British joint staff mission in Washington] got a faint idea of conditions here and it made them sick."³

With the tacit support of his friends, George Marshall and Secretary of War Stimson, Stilwell obviously thought he could act as he wished. President Roosevelt thought his actions were unjustified and certainly in bad taste for a man in his position. He said so in a letter to George Marshall on March 8:

"Thank you for letting me see the copy of Stilwell's letter of February 9 . . . I have read this letter with a good deal of care and my first thought is that Stilwell has exactly the wrong approach in dealing with Generalissimo Chiang, who after all, cannot be expected, as a Chinese, to use the same methods that we do. When Stilwell speaks about the fact that the Generalissimo is very irritable and hard to handle, upping his demands, etc., he is, of course, correct, but when he speaks of talking to him in sterner tones, he goes about it just the wrong way.

"All of us must remember that the Generalissimo came up the hard way to become the undisputed ruler of four hundred million people—an enormously difficult job to attain any kind of unity from a diverse group of all kinds of leaders—military men, educators, scientists, public health people, engineers, all of them struggling for power and mastery, local or national, and to create in a very short time throughout China what it took us a couple of centuries to attain.

"Besides that, the Generalissimo finds it necessary to maintain his position of supremacy. You and I would do the same thing under the same circumstances. He is the Chief Executive as well as the Commander-in-Chief, and one cannot speak sternly to a man like that or exact commitments from him as we might do from the Sultan of Morocco . . ."⁴

Marshall later told the President that he had sent the pertinent passages of this letter to Stilwell, who interpreted them as a rebuke. Now that Roosevelt had laid down the rules—no more bargaining or debate in the approach to

China's problems, which previously had been condoned by both Marshall and Stimson—Stilwell was no longer to negotiate with Chiang. For the first time Stilwell realized that he was no longer to have a free hand in dealing with Chiang, that he was in disfavor at the White House, and that his days in the CBI were numbered.

None of this was known to Chennault. His regard for Chiang was the same as it had been since the early days in Shanghai. He regarded him as a head of state and his military commander. He had a great personal admiration for him—as he had for Madame. A single-minded man, Chennault remained loyal to Chiang as long as he lived—throughout World War II, the Communist-Nationalist war on the mainland later, and Chiang's regime as head of the Republic of Taiwan.

During all the terrible days of Shanghai, Nanking, Hankow, and the bombings of Chungking, Chennault never wavered in his loyalty—misplaced or not. Throughout the grim days of the AVG he continued to fight as a soldier and never questioned an order from Chiang. His job, as he saw it, was to do all in his power to help the Chinese win the war. He never deviated from that view or aim.

Now, in the spring of 1943, he was attempting to utilize the few bombers and fighters that were sent over the Hump from the Tenth Air Force. The Fourteenth Air Force got off to an inauspicious start. The American Air Force in China had been fighting a battle for survival since the beginning of 1943. Even the few medium bombers sent to Chennault had almost ceased flying because of fuel shortages. Fighter squadrons had to be pulled back of the advance bases at Kweilin, Lingling, and Hengyang in east China for maintenance and for the pilots to rest, leaving these areas practically undefended.

Because of bad weather, the fuel shortage, and a need for complete overhauling of planes, none of the squadrons could be returned to the eastern bases but remained in the area of Kunming and Yunnanyi. In late March, in spite of a lack of almost everything, Chennault managed to get off a series of missions to Lao-kai in Indochina which damaged phosphate mines in the area. The flights—bomb-carrying P-40s—were unchallenged by enemy fighters. About the only bright light that month was Chennault's promotion to major general.

The enemy attacked Lingling on April 1 but was turned back by P-40s of the 75th Fighter Squadron. In late April the 74th Fighter Squadron was conducting regular reconnaissance and strafing missions along the Burma Road from Lungling to Lashio from its base at Yunnanyi. On April 24, B-25s from Kunming struck into Burma and hit the Namtu mines. Two days later the enemy caught the 74th on the ground at Yunnanyi and destroyed five P-40s while damaging a number of others.

Several days later the Japanese caught Kunming off guard. The warning net had failed to pick up the incoming bombers, but a flight of P-40s from the 75th Squadron caught the twenty bombers coming in. The bombers dropped their loads on the airfield, doing considerable damage and slightly injuring Chennault's new chief of staff, Brigadier General Edgar D. Glenn, who had just arrived from New Delhi. The P-40s shot down ten of the attacking enemy fighter planes.

On April 20, while Chennault was busy with the arrival of his new staff officers at Kunming, he received a wire from Stilwell saying he would arrive at the field at 5 P.M. It turned out both were to go to Washington to confer with Roosevelt, Churchill and the Combined Chiefs of Staff at the Trident Conference in May.

Stilwell's version appeared in his diary under the date of April 18:

"Then the famous call to Washington. Peanut radioed Roosevelt that he and Chennault had been cooking up a plan that Chennault must come and tell him about. George [Marshall] tipped me off. I suggested that he call me, Bissell and Chennault in, [he] saying he was going to anyway. Roosevelt crossed Bissell off, and George told me to bring one of Bissell's staff. Then I taxed Chennault with the matter, and he knew nothing about it. No new plan and no visit to Washington. So Peanut is just talking about Chennault's 'six-months-to-drive-the-Japs-out-of-China' plan. I arranged for priority air travel, but luckily did not alert Win [Mrs. Stilwell]. Will see Peanut on Monday (4/19) and the thing may calm down. Must be in Washington by the end of the month, as George Marshall leaves soon after."[5]

Chennault said he did not know anything about the trip. He wrote:

"As he [Stilwell] stepped off the plane he looked at me in amazement.

" 'Where are your bags? Aren't you ready to go?' he growled.

" 'Go where?' I countered.

"We glared at each other silently for a moment. Then Stilwell beckoned me to follow him around behind the airplane's tail fin, out of earshot of the other officers present. I finally convinced Stilwell that I had not the slightest idea of where he was bound. He then explained that we had been summoned to Washington and intimated that he suspected it was the result of my finagling behind his back. He was leaving for India immediately and expected me to accompany him.

"I was taken completely by surprise. I got permission to confer with the Generalissimo in Chungking and agreed to meet Stilwell in Karachi in two days. I flew to Chungking early the next morning, but the Generalissimo was no help. He told me to present China's need for decisive military action, American supplies, and an air force free of Delhi control. I told him we already had a separate air force and most of the things we needed except actual delivery of supplies. I flew back to Kunming the same afternoon and kept my appointment with Stilwell in Karachi the next day, having flown 2,000 miles in two days."[6]

In the midst of the preparations for the Trident Conference, which was to meet in Washington the first week of May 1943, Roosevelt had received a request from Chiang that Chennault be called to Washington to explain a plan for an aerial offensive from China. In response, the War Department summoned both Chennault and Stilwell to appear before the Combined Chiefs of Staff at their May meeting. Stilwell and Chennault, in presentations broken at times by bitter exchanges, agreed only that there would eventually be massive air attacks against Japan from bases in China.

Stilwell continued to argue that the Hump flights could never be developed to a point where a land route to China would be unnecessary. He maintained that until the Ledo Road was completed Chinese land forces in Yunnan should be given the bulk of air freight in support of their conquest of northern Burma—an operation which should have first claim on available resources.

Chennault argued that the Burma campaign would be a long-drawn-out affair and that China might collapse before the road was completed. He argued that seizing a port city on the China coast would be a better way to get forces into China for the eventual attack against Japan. Every effort should be made to build up the airlift for support of the Fourteenth Air Force, which was in a position to do great damage to Japanese shipping and naval strength. He argued that development of the Assam Valley air bases in India should be given priority over the Ledo Road. The British agreed with him on the Assam bases; probably because of their long-range plans involving Bangkok, Malaya, and Singapore they were not ready to invade Burma.

T. V. Soong, speaking for the Chinese, said his nation could not wait for the completion of the Ledo Road. Chennault should be reinforced immediately and Hump tonnage greatly increased.

Getting down to specifics, Chennault estimated how many transport planes he would need for the required tonnage across the Hump. He said the Japanese were not eager to fight in the air in China and therefore "every effort should be exerted to make her fight there."[7]

His plan was geared to weather conditions that could be expected in east China beginning in July, when he proposed to take on the Japanese 3rd Air Division with his fighters. He said he would use B-25 bombers from Kweilin in late August to begin an anti-shipping campaign along the Yangtze River, along the China coast ports, and at Haiphong and Hainan Island. Later in the fall, he said, he would send the B-25s into the Formosa Strait to harass Japanese shipping. Late in the year he planned to send the heavy B-24 bombers to east China to help pound Formosa and the Shanghai-Nanking area. He estimated that by the end of the year he could start bombing the Japanese homeland. His revised needs in the way of aircraft now were seventy-five P-40s, seventy-five P-51s, forty-eight B-25s, thirty-five B-24s, and some photo reconnaissance planes. As for the tonnage across the Hump, he asked for 4,790 tons a month from July through September, and 7,129 tons thereafter.

At the conference, he described how it felt:

"Soon after arriving in Washington, I picked up Lt. Col. Harold 'Butch' Morgan, a recent arrival, who had been a mainstay of the 11th Bomb Squadron in China, and pressed him into service as an aide. Butch gave me the only staff help I got during that month of conferences. When the top secret sessions began, Butch was barred at the door, leaving me to participate without an aide. We made a ragged looking pair among the resplendent military finery of the Pentagon. I was one of the AVG who had been inducted into the Army without a uniform. The best I could muster was prewar olive-drab tunic, a gray wool shirt, and a black tie, both non-regulation. Butch had been in the CATF so long he owned only well-patched chino pants. We shared an office with Stilwell, whose party was larger than my entire China headquarters. The contrast was terrific. On one side sat Stilwell and his aides in freshly-pressed Palm Beach tan summer uniforms glittering with a fruit salad of ribbons. Across the room were the ragged representatives of the 14th."[8]

Stilwell wrote his version of the conference in his diary:

"[Washington] Continual concessions have confirmed Chiang Kai-shek in the opinion that all he needs to do is yell and we'll cave in. As we are doing. FDR had decided on an air effort in China before we reached Washington. This suited the British, who want no part of a fight for Burma. Why should they fight to build up China, if we can be euchered into bearing the brunt of the war against Japan? They'll get Burma back at the peace table anyway.

"Nobody was interested in the humdrum work of building a ground force but me. Chennault promised to drive the Japs right out of China in six months, so why not give him the stuff to do it? It was the short cut to victory.

"My point was that China was on the verge of collapse economically. That we could not afford to wait another year, that Yunnan was indispensable and that a force had to be built up to hold it. That if the Japs took Yunnan, the recapture of Burma would be meaningless. That any increased offensive that stung the Japs enough would bring a strong reaction that would wreck everything and put China out of the war. Witness the Chekiang campaign, brought on by the Jap belief that Tokyo was bombed from bases there. That the first essential step was to get a ground force capable of seizing and holding airbases, and opening communications to China from the outside world. Overruled. Churchill's idea was, so he said, that China must be helped and the only way to do it within the next few months was by air.

"At the same time they decided on Saucy [code name for the Burma invasion] they made it practically impossible for me to prepare the Y-Force, and then ordered it used in an offensive. But British reluctance caused the working of the directive to be so loose that it would be up to the commander as to what he could do. He could go the limit or he could quit at any time. With Wavell in command, failure was inevitable; he had nothing to offer at any meeting except protestations that the thing was impossible, hopeless, impractical. Churchill even spoke of it as silly. The Limeys all wanted to wait another year . . . , the four Jap divisions in Burma have them scared to death.

"The inevitable conclusion was that Churchill has Roosevelt in his pocket. That they are looking for an easy way, a short cut for England, and no attention must be diverted from the Continent at any cost. The Limeys are not interested in the war in the Pacific, and with the President hypnotized they are sitting pretty.

"Roosevelt wouldn't let me speak my piece. I interrupted twice, but Churchill kept pulling away from the subject, and it was impossible.

"So everything was thrown to the air offensive. FDR pulled 7,000 tons [monthly over the Hump] out of the air when told that 10,000 was impossible, and ordered that tonnage for July. First 4,750 [tons] for air [Fourteenth Air Force], then 2,250 for ground. They will do the Japs some damage but at the same time will so weaken the ground effort that it may fail. Then what the hell use is it to knock down a few Jap planes.

"Farewell lunch. Mr. Churchill: 'Mr. President, I cannot but believe that an all-wise Providence has draped these great events, at this critical period of the world's history, about your personality and your high office.' And Frank lapped it up.

"Henry Stimson and George Marshall were understanding. The War Department was O.K. Even the air was a bit fed up on Chennault. But what's the use when the World's Greatest Strategist is against you?"[9]

Chennault acknowledged the possibility of a Japanese offensive on the ground to occupy central China, but he said he did not think it would be any more successful than previous attempts. He probably shared the Generalissimo's belief that the "existing Chinese forces" could defend airfields in east China.

Stilwell had presented his side to the conference: that his mission was to increase the combat effectiveness of the Chinese Army. He said he was accomplishing that through the training at Ramgarh, the first thirty-division plan with troops at Kunming, and the second thirty-division plan, to be approved by Chiang.

He reminded the conference that he felt the Chinese were showing an increasing tendency to neglect their obligation to furnish manpower to equip and train and to continue to emphasize the need for air power. He said if they followed that course it would result in neglect of the ground war—the possession of bombing bases. He said the air war would cause some damage "but it will not be vital to the war effort."[10]

He reiterated that the only short cut to Japan was through China and that the Chinese must be held to their commitments.

He recommended that Chiang Kai-shek be reminded of the reason for the American presence in China and that he be held to his promise for manpower and training. He called for telling both the Chinese and British that they should be held to their commitments to invade Burma. He wanted the present Hump tonnage—three eighths for air and five eighths for all other needs—to remain unchanged. He wanted a corps of U.S. troops sent as soon as possible and a general strategic plan to be prepared and tied in with the operations of the Southwest Pacific.

The conference dragged on for days, but in the end the President had to decide the issues.

He could not rely on the Combined Chiefs of Staff because they could not agree among themselves. In the end he decided for himself. His decision was given to Stilwell by Marshall on May 3 in a memo:

"I talked to the President yesterday regarding China matters and found him completely set against any delay in Chennault's program. He had drawn the conclusion from his interview with you that the air exercises were, in effect, largely to be suspended while the more tedious ground buildup was being carried on. . . .

"The President accepted the proposition that necessary supplies for the Yunnan Force should be sent in, that he would handle Chiang Kai-shek, but stated that politically he must support Chiang Kai-shek and that, in the state of Chinese morale, the air program was therefore of great importance. . . ."[11]

An annex to the final paper of Trident set forth the projected strength of the Fourteenth Air Force. Chennault was to have, in addition to the 308th Bomb Group, a medium bombardment group, but he would not get it until ATC tonnage over the Hump reached 10,000 tons per month. His fighter command strength would be raised to two groups and the Chinese would get eighty fighter planes and forty medium bombers to operate under Chennault's command.

The President seems to have determined very quickly after getting the Generalissimo's letter, despite Marshall's already expressed opposition, that Chennault should be allowed to have his way on the question of a separate air force.

Chennault had won another battle—but not yet his private war with Stilwell and Marshall.

Nineteen

While Chennault was in Washington for the Trident Conference, Colonel Eugene Beebe was getting his B-24s of the 308th Bomb Group ready for combat in China. The 308th was now composed of four squadrons of heavy bombers from the 373rd, the 374th, the 375th, and the 425th Bomb Squadrons. They were being based at satellite fields around Kunming—Chengkung, Yankai, and Kunming itself. Chennault was slowly receiving a trickle of B-25 Mitchell bombers, which were being assimilated into the new 341st Bomb Group, made up of three squadrons of mediums—the 11th Bomb Squadron, the 22nd Bomb Squadron, and the 491st Bomb Squadron.

The 308th, by European and Pacific theater standards, was a tiny group, with scarcely more than five or six bombers to a squadron, but to Chennault the addition of a bomber force was a Godsend after the lean years of fighters only.

On May 4, gas and bombs having been stocked ahead of the mission, eighteen B-24s and twelve B-25s, escorted by twenty-four P-40s, staged the heaviest raids from China up to that date. The missions were also significant in that Chinese flew as copilots in the medium bombers for the first time.

The bombers flew to Lao-kai and then along the Red River to Hanoi, from where the mediums and fighters proceeded to Haiphong and the Liberators flew across the Gulf of Tonkin to bomb Sama Bay on the southern edge of Hainan Island. Clouds at Haiphong prevented the crews from seeing how much damage they did to the cement works, the primary target, and the harbor installations. At Sama Bay the heavy bombers did considerable damage to the airfield, coal docks, an oil refinery, and a fuel storage dump. One B-24 was badly hit by light antiaircraft fire and the crew jumped from it near Lao-kai on the return flight. One crewman was killed, but the first heavy bomber mission of the Fourteenth was considered a success.

The heavies struck the Tien Ho airdrome at Canton four days later and the bombs took out the main hangar and barracks areas. The flight was intercepted by twenty Japanese fighters, after the bomb runs, but P-40s from the forward base at Kweilin—led by Colonel "Casey" Vincent—shot down thirteen of them in a running battle.

Beebe, acting on orders from Chennault, began to make his B-24s self-supporting. He stripped the turrets from six of his twenty-four planes and used them for tankers—flying the Chabua–Kunming run across the Hump undefended.

Chennault had told the Trident Conference that his air force could effectively stop a Japanese ground offensive because he felt that any major offensive would have to utilize rivers. He said his planes could strafe and bomb enemy troop movement on water and he was proved right. The enemy began a ground offensive in the region of the rice bowl of China—the Yangtze Valley from north of Changsha toward Ichang—obviously intending to threaten Chungking. The Chinese, becoming alarmed when the Japanese approached with spearheads in the Ichang area, called for air support from the Americans. The battle area was out of range of the fighter aircraft so the B-24s were sent from Chengtu to bomb Japanese ground forces attempting to move west through the Yangtze Gorges. The B-24s continued to pound the enemy until the Japanese began to retreat, thus giving Chinese troops a boost in morale and enabling them to fight back. Enemy forces at other places along an offensive front also withdrew and the Chinese ground armies took heart. Following that victory at Ichang, the B-24s returned to hitting coastal shipping. Chennault returned from Washington to find the threat to Changsha and Chungking lessened. He continued to issue orders for his forward-based P-40s at Hengyang and Kweilin to hit enemy shipping on the Yangtze from Yoyang to Hankow with good results.

Chinese intelligence had been telling Chennault that the Japanese were going to make a major drive to capture the eastern fighter bases. He took them seriously but there was little he could do about it except keep as many fighters and medium bombers there as possible.

At the Trident Conference, as he had earlier, Stilwell had claimed that it would take fifty divisions to protect the east China bases, which were strung out over a vast area. Chennault later wrote that he thought that a strange statement considering Stilwell attempted the reconquest of Burma with only two Chinese divisions and three thousand American troops.[1] He had said right along that the combination of American air support and Chinese ground troops could defend the bases against all but a major enemy ground offensive. He thought that if the Japanese did mount a major offensive to take the bases the drain on their far-flung supply routes and battle lines in the rest of the Far East and Pacific would be worth the loss of the China bases. He later said he had assumed that the Chinese troops protecting the eastern bases would be supplied with American Lend-Lease equipment—small arms, ammunition, machine guns, mortars, and light artillery, all of which could be transported by air. He was not aware at the time that Stilwell bitterly opposed sending such Lend-Lease material to any Chinese force not under his direct supervision—no matter how desperate their struggle.[2]

On July 23 the Japanese sent air attacks against the eastern bases, driving against the Americans from both Hankow and Canton in a pincer action that saw much of the force aimed at the string of fields along the Peking–Hankow–Canton Railroad. Both Hengyang and Lingling were heavily hit, as was Kweilin. Casey Vincent wrote in his diary:

"July 24. What a day! Japanese came in from both the north and south. I sent six planes from here [Kweilin] to intercept over Ling-ling—which they did. Then the damn Zeros—eight of them—came up from Canton. We cleared the field and our pilots shot down seven of the eight Japanese planes. We lost one P-38 which had been jumped by two Zeros. Bonawitz and Barnes are missing from the flight at Lingling. Total for the day: about 10 Zeros and four Japanese bombers! Not a bad day's work. I didn't think they'd be back in the afternoon and they weren't."[3]

Six P-38s had been sent over the Hump from India in early July and were immediately sent on to the forward fighter bases. Their high ceiling made them valuable for high-altitude escort work and photo reconnaissance, but their rate of fuel consumption was so high that they did not prove practical for gas-scarce China. They were assigned to the 74th and 75th Fighter Squadrons and the one shot down on July 24 was the first combat loss. Two others were subsequently lost to weather and combat.

By the end of July Chennault was down to sixty-four planes for his four fighter squadrons, with only thirty-three at the forward bases of Hengyang and Kweilin. Most of his fighters were old, with the exception of six P-40Ks and eight P-40Ms that had arrived in July along with the six P-38s.

The Japanese also hit at the undefended and seldom-used satellite fields at Kienow, Chihkiang, Kanchow, and Shaoyang. They were heavily damaged but no planes or American personnel were there. The offensive continued for the next two days, until the Americans launched a counterattack against the big Japanese airfield at Hankow.

"We conducted a very successful mission against Hankow this morning," Casey wrote on July 26. "Our B-25s dropped bombs in the dispersal area—destroying at least ten Japanese planes on the ground. Our bombers were jumped by large number of Zeros before bombs were dropped! Bombers shot down five fighters. We lost one P-40."

As he had promised at the Trident Conference, Chennault began to concentrate on Japanese coastal shipping in late July. He sent the medium bombers to operate out of Kweilin and flew the B-24s out of Kunming to hit enemy shipping farther south near Hainan Island and off Indochina. He knew the shipping was a main artery of Japan's lifeblood and he also knew the enemy would be hurt if he could sink tankers and freighters running back and forth in the Formosa Strait. At the end of July his bombers, escorted by fighters, accounted for 42,000 tons of enemy tonnage sunk, and 35,000 more tons damaged. The weather turned worse in August and flying was held to a minimum until there was a break in the monsoon.

The Japanese had learned some valuable tricks from fighting Chennault in the past year and they decided to try a new tactic on the Americans. In August they came over the eastern fields at very high altitudes—higher than the P-40s could climb—and then dove on the Americans as they climbed to intercept. They would make one dive with their Zeros and then head for home after the attack. It was working. On August 20 they lost two Zeros that way but they shot down three P-40s. It was finally becoming evident to Chennault that the old reliable P-40 was outclassed and that the fighter squadrons badly needed the new P-51 Mustangs being used so successfully in other theaters of war.

The B-24s also began to run into determined opposition in late August. On August 21 fourteen Liberators of the 374th and 375th Bomb Squadrons from Kunming were to attack Hankow but were to rendezvous first with P-40 fighter escort over Hengyang. Before the bombers were due to arrive at Hengyang, Colonel Bruce Holloway, commander of the 23rd Fighter Group, sent his fighters up to do battle with a flight of enemy fighters. After their air battle Holloway called his planes down for refueling but could get only twelve back up for the escort duty. The B-24s missed Hengyang altogether and, accustomed to flying unescorted missions into Indochina, went on to Hankow. There they were met by a hoard of enemy planes—numbering anywhere from sixty to ninety fighters. The Japanese had a field day against the heavy bombers, protected only by their own turrets and waist gunners. The enemy fighters shot down the lead B-24, which carried Major Bruce Beat, squadron leader, and wounded the pilots of the two other lead planes. The battle lasted nearly half an hour and one B-24 crashed with three of its crew dead and two wounded. Another was forced down at Lingling. By the time the other eleven reached Kweilin, ten were badly damaged and one tail gunner had been killed and four pilots wounded plus the ten crewmen killed on Major Beat's plane. The heavy bombers had inflicted severe damage to the attacking planes, but no accurate count had been possible in the running fight. The size of the defending force gave rise to speculation that the enemy had known of the bombing raid in advance.

U.S. naval intelligence had been assigned to China by this time and Admiral Milton Miles, then in command of intelligence forces in China, told about the war on Japanese spies in his excellent book, *A Different Kind of War*. He said that when one of his agents—Lieutenant Colonel B. T. ("Banks") Holcomb, U. S. Marine Corps—arrived in Kunming late that spring to head up the radio intercept program, he told Miles he could follow Chennault's planes from Kunming all the way to the intended target by the radio stations that went on the air to report them to the Japanese.

The loss of the two Liberators on the August 21 Hankow raid made it obvious that the bombers must not fly without fighter escort—something Chennault had preached for years. However, the 308th Bomb Group had not learned that yet.

The rest of the squadrons of the 308th went back to Hankow for revenge. On August 24 seven B-24s from the 373rd Squadron and seven from the 425th Squadron, based at Kunming, headed for Hankow. But the 373rd got lost in bad weather and returned to base, leaving the 425th to go on alone. The 425th bombed the airfield, doing heavy damage, but was jumped by forty enemy fighters and encountered heavy antiaircraft fire. In a running battle that raged for forty-five minutes, the enemy fighters attacked the big Liberators—shooting down four of the heavies before the remaining three staggered back to Kweilin. These three were badly damaged; one pilot and one crewman were dead and six more men were wounded. To make matters worse, one of the surviving planes crashed the next day on the way back to Kunming, killing ten men and injuring two more. Of the seven planes that had left Kunming for Hankow, only two returned and, of the seventy men on the planes, more than fifty were killed, injured, or missing.

Stilwell, at this time, was still trying to prevent Chennault from operating as an independent commander. He asked Marshall for a theater air officer to command both the Tenth and the Fourteenth Air Forces.[4] Chennault's position at the moment, in view of his relationship with Chiang and his recent support by Roosevelt, made him politically safe from Stilwell. But Marshall and Arnold—looking for the next best thing—decided it was possible to appoint a senior air officer to "coordinate" air operations in the CBI. It was decided to suggest to Chiang that Major General George E. Stratemeyer, General Arnold's chief of staff, be sent to the CBI with a small staff to "coordinate all air corps matters relating to administration, transportation, logistics of supply, maintenance and training."[5] The Generalissimo replied with some proposals of his own: that Bissell be recalled, that Chennault be named Air Chief of Staff, China Theater—on a par with and completely independent of Stilwell. President Roosevelt, on receiving Chiang's proposals, was agreeable to the "independent command from Stilwell," but when he asked Marshall how he felt about it, Marshall reverted to character and claimed Chennault was not good at handling logistics and was too closely aligned with the Generalissimo to properly represent United States interests.[6]

Marshall could see the handwriting on the wall for Stilwell and strongly opposed any recall of his friend. The President, not wanting to intimidate his Chief of Staff, let the matter drop for the moment. But he did approve making Chennault Chief of Staff, Chinese Air Force—which officially gave him direct access to Chiang. Bissell, much to Chennault's relief, was recalled to the United States, where he eventually became Assistant Chief of Staff,

G-2, War Department General Staff. Brigadier General Howard G. Davidson was named commander of the Tenth Air Force in India.

Command problems were a major stumbling block in the CBI theater. The location in New Delhi of British and Indian authorities, of the U. S. Services of Supply, of Stilwell's rear echelon, of the British Army GHQ, and of Air Headquarters, India Command, RAF, made New Delhi the only logical choice for the headquarters of Stratemeyer's staff. Almost simultaneously with his assignment to New Delhi came plans, determined upon at the Quadrant Conference in Quebec in August 1943, for even more far-reaching organizational changes in Asia. As the time grew closer for offensive action in Burma the need for closer cooperation among the Allies and for the creation of a unified command with a Supreme Allied commander became obvious, but the selection of such an individual was a genuine problem. A British commander for the entire theater would not be acceptable to the Chinese. An American commander might please the Chinese, but the British would not agree to such a plan. A Chinese commander was never seriously considered. As usual, politics determined the choice in an already complicated setup. The Southeast Asia Command (SEAC) was established at Quebec and Lord Louis Mountbatten was named Supreme Allied Commander. From the operational sphere of SEAC, however, China, Indochina, and India were excluded. Mountbatten would have no control over American-trained Chinese ground forces except through Stilwell as chief of staff of the Chinese Army. This meant that the ultimate authority rested with Generalissimo Chiang Kai-shek. Although SEAC did not include India, the major part of its assigned forces were stationed there. Mountbatten's command did not include the huge Indian Army.

Stilwell, however, was to continue in his capacity as commanding general of U. S. Army forces in the CBI. It is understandable if one becomes confused as to just what Stratemeyer's position was. It was planned that he would be in command of all Army Air Force units assigned to SEAC. On August 28, General Arnold wrote to Stilwell, Stratemeyer, and Chennault, asking each to do his best to make an unwieldy organization function. The exact place Stratemeyer had in relation to his commanders became more and more vague and it became clear to all that he was assuming more responsibilities as a quasi-ambassador. But it was also clear that his duties involved giving tactical and strategic support to Stilwell's Burma campaign and concentrating on Chennault's logistical problems. Another of his duties, as set down in a letter from Marshall to Stilwell on July 20, was to train both Chinese and American personnel.[7]

As soon as Stratemeyer arrived in India in early August he began to concentrate on providing more aircraft to Chennault. In mid-August he sent additional P-38s to China—the 449th Squadron of the 51st Fighter Group, now part of the Fourteenth Air Force. He began work on the long-proposed plan to integrate into the Fourteenth Air Force Chinese planes and pilots

trained with Lend-Lease funds. Many Chinese pilots had by now been
trained in the States and had returned to the CBI. Named the Chinese-
American Composite Wing, the organization was set up so that, for each
position in the wing, a Chinese and an American would work together. The
new wing was to be trained at Karachi and report to Chennault by October,
1943.

Chennault—now that he was Chief of Staff of the Chinese Air Force—was
presented by the Chinese with a newly constructed tile-roofed house close to
the airfield at Kunming. He was (unofficially) told that, if he chose to stay in
China after the war was won, it was to be his home forever.

The relaxed, informal days of the AVG and CATF were gone. Chennault
was enmeshed in the piles of paperwork that traditionally befall a commanding general of an air force, although the Fourteenth was the smallest air force
the United States had.

Living with him in his new home were Tom Gentry, his new chief of staff,
"Buzz" Glenn, and Captain Joe Alsop, who had finally made it back to work
with Chennault. Alsop functioned as a mess officer as well as acting as an
aide. The dachshund, Joe, still ran the house. For his staff car, Chennault
still had the Buick Paul Frillman had "liberated" from Rangoon—now a
battered wreck from the Kunming roads and constant Japanese bombardment. His personal plane had been upgraded from the dilapidated Beechcraft
of AVG days but was nevertheless an old C-47 that had been put together
from salvage parts by CATF mechanics. However, he was blessed with excellent personal pilots such as "Tex" Carlton and Al Nowak. Also his old
"Three Men on a Flying Trapeze" pal from early Air Corps days, Luke
Williamson, had returned to the CBI as commander of the 322nd Troop
Carrier Squadron.

With the first days of fall, Chennault spent as much of his free time as
possible hunting doves and teal by the lake near the field. He said some of the
finest breakfasts he could remember from those days were those of broiled
teal and black coffee. Louisiana friends on the State Game Commission kept
him supplied with cases of canned oysters, with which he concocted dove
pies. His cook grew okra in the garden and he received a sack of corn meal
from home which kept the staff supplied with hot corn-bread sticks. He was
able to get all the hot preserved peppers and hot sauces he required from
Madame Chiang and her sisters in Chungking.

By the end of the year, all six of his sons had jobs in the various services.
Jack was commander of a fighter group in the Aleutians; Max was an air
traffic controller in the Air Transport Command; Pat was a P-51 pilot in
England; Pug was an Air Corps radio mechanic; Bob was an aviation cadet;
and Dink was aboard the U.S.S. Helena, a crusier, in the Solomons. Mail
from home—from Nell and his two daughters—was mostly about the war
effort.

Chennault's working day began early, after a dawn breakfast, when he answered the most urgent radio messages. After that he plunged into the mass of correspondence. Tom Trumble, who had served as his secretary since the AVG days, once described how Chennault would nap after work:

"One of the things the General always did was take a short nap at noon, after lunch. It was always routine with him that he'd eat his lunch, then Major Shu would slip back to the interpreter's office and take a little nap, the General had a chair in there. He always slept sitting in a chair. He'd smoke a cigarette and then he'd put it out, and his head would just drop like this. At those times, I would either put Joe Dash up on the davenport we had there or hold him on my lap to keep him quiet.

"It would be about 20 or 25 minutes, you wouldn't hear a sound in that office. The General would be sitting on his chair, absolutely out, relaxed. All of a sudden I'd hear him clear his throat. He'd light a Camel. He wouldn't say a word. He'd drag deeply on that Camel, look far, far away and it just seemed as if he was gradually recollecting himself and coming back. Then he'd shake himself a little bit, get up on his feet, then I'd go get Major Shu, and then we were back in shape again."[8]

After work he would either hunt or play badminton with Glenn, Gentry, or Alsop. On some days he played baseball—either pitching or as umpire for games with his men. There was no rank involved in those games in Kunming and many a private challenged his calls as an umpire just as strongly as a fellow general would. Many times the offended team booed him loudly for his calls and a slight smile would flicker across his face at the catcalls.

His office was filled with a steady stream of high military brass and VIP civilian visitors. He was constantly asked for interviews by correspondents from the American wire services, by those from Europe and the Near East, and by staff writers on the major newspapers. Editors and publishers of book publishing houses in the United States bombarded him with requests to sign contracts for the exclusive story on the American Volunteer Group and his life story. He politely turned them all down with the excuse that he had a war to fight and asked them to contact him after the hostilities had ended. Some of his correspondence was concerned with stating that AVG impostors had no official connection with the former volunteers. So many people claimed in the media to be former Flying Tigers that it was becoming an annoyance. Colonel Robert Scott had returned to the States and had written a book about his exploits with the AVG and CATF. He had entitled it *God Is My Co-Pilot* and Hollywood had purchased the movie rights. Chennault was not happy with the idea of being in a movie about the AVG but had agreed that Scott had a right to write about him as commander of the AVG. He was certain Stilwell would seize upon his participation in any movie as a chance to criticize him. He wrote to Scott on November 7:

"I am sorry that you are not satisfied with the part which I agreed to play in the picture *God Is My Co-Pilot.* I hoped that I had made my views clear to you in my previous letter. I am still wholly occupied with fighting the enemy and do not desire to have my name used in such a way as to popularize a book or picture—since the book is your story and not mine, I do not see the necessity for my appearance on the screen for more than three minutes. I am besieged with enemies other than the Japanese as it is and the additional charge that I was seeking publicity might be decisive. However, in view of the earnestness of your request, I will authorize you and Warner Brothers to increase the time from three minutes to five minutes. I must insist upon the other conditions which I imposed." He was only depicted for a few minutes by actor Raymond Massey.

He heard regularly from a number of ex-AVG pilots and ground personnel —all of whom seemed ready to return to the Far East to work. George Paxton wrote from New York that he was with American Export Airlines at La Guardia Field on Long Island and was involved with Parker Dupouy and Bob Neale in a book being written by a Captain Robert Hotz called *With General Chennault: The Story of the Flying Tigers.* Hotz, a former New York *Herald Tribune* writer, was a captain in the Air Transport Command. Paxton was busy trying to form a Flying Tiger Association and to organize other ex-AVG people into putting out an AVG yearbook.

In December Chennault found out—with a shock—that he was to be the subject of a cover story in *Time* magazine. Fame had indeed come to the retired Air Corps captain who only a few years earlier had been buried in a dusty training field in Yunnan, literally unknown to the millions of people at home.

By the middle of October the first increments of the newly activated Chinese-American Composite Wing (CACW) moved to China—constituting the first heavy reinforcement the Fourteenth had received since the B-24s of the 308th Bomb Group had arrived during the summer. The CACW consisted of the 3rd and 5th Fighter Groups and the 1st Bombardment Group (Medium) —B-25s—and was stationed in Kunming.

The Japanese had begun an offensive in the north and activity had begun to increase in the Hankow area. Also, now that the monsoon weather had cleared again, the Japanese were busy pouring additional fighters and bombers into the fields at Canton and in Indochina. Reports filtered in from Chinese intelligence that the enemy was building up considerable strength on the ground in both the Myitkyina area of north Burma and on the west bank of the Salween River in west China. Chennault dreaded the announcement that these two offensives would be launched simultaneously. His thinly stretched Fourteenth would be hard pressed to meet the threats on all fronts.

The Japanese had been hurt by the strikes against their coastal shipping. Vital supplies for their ground forces in Burma and Indochina had ended up on the bottom of the Formosa Strait and the South China Sea in the past few months and they were determined to stop further attacks by taking the U.S.

bases. B-25s of the 11th Bomb Squadron under Lieutenant Colonel Morris Taber had been hitting shipping all the way up the coast to Shanghai. Coolies had completed the advance base of Suichwan in east China and it permitted the medium bombers far greater range.

The Japanese knew they also needed to neutralize Kunming because the B-24s stationed there had been laying mines in Haiphong Harbor and blasting port facilities at Hainan Island. In addition the B-24s had been flying sorties against ground troops west of the Salween.

Chennault gave the 308th Group a chance to get even for the loss of their planes and crews at Hankow by letting them fly decoy missions over the Hump. The Japanese fighters had been shooting down two or three unarmed ATC transports a day in late October. The ATC had been using the huge four-engine C-87—the transport version of the Consolidated B-24 bomber. Chennault sent a flight of B-24s with instructions to fly a loose, ragged formation over the southern route of the Hump. The Japanese fighters had been attacking from their bases in the Myitkyina area. The B-24s of the 308th Group took along extra ammunition. The Japanese, mistaking the silhouettes for the unarmed transports, fell for the trap. The B-24s, using highly concentrated firepower from turrets and waist guns, knocked down eight attacking fighters. The Japanese became more cautious about attacking transports thereafter.

In east China the Fourteenth Air Force was busy lending air support to Chinese ground forces against Japanese who were attacking in the Tungting Lake area near Changsha. In late November the Fourteenth made its first attack on the island of Formosa—hitting Shinchiku on the northern part of the big island. Casey Vincent, commander of the fighter forces, had received reinforcements in the form of another medium bomber squadron of the CACW as well as twelve old, worn P-51s to replace the outmoded P-40s. His aerial reconnaissance had shown seventy-five enemy bombers on the Formosan base and he scheduled a daylight surprise strafing and bombing raid for November 25. Eight P-51s, eight P-38s, and fourteen B-25s were to attack under the command of Tex Hill. They caught the Japanese by surprise and the P-38s—going first—knocked down fifteen of the twenty enemy fighters that tried to scramble to intercept. The B-25s went in at 1,000 feet and dropped fragmentation bombs on the airfield. The P-51s flew escort for the bombers, then went on strafing missions. Without the loss of a single Fourteenth plane, the attackers destroyed forty-two enemy planes.

As the year wound down, the Fourteenth planes in the east were increasingly called upon to lend assistance to Chinese ground forces in the Changsha area. The Japanese stepped up their attack on the eastern bases while the situation in the west remained virtually unchanged.

The size of the operational theater in China—plus the arrival of some additional units—led to some reorganizational changes by Chennault at the end of the year. He set up a provisional forward echelon under Casey Vincent which was to operate east of the 108th meridian; no comparable organization existed in Yunnan to the west. Transfer of the full 51st Fighter Group to the Fourteenth, the arrival of the remainder of the 341st Bomb Group (Medium), and the presence of three CACW squadrons (with three more due shortly) made the need for regular lower echelons of command imperative. The necessity to keep both bombers and fighters in each of the two main combat areas made it impossible to maintain a bomber and a fighter wing. Consequently, on December 23, 1943, Chennault activated the 68th and 69th Composite Wings, the 68th under Vincent and the 69th under Colonel John Kennedy to the west of the 108th meridian. CACW units were assigned 68th Wing for operations, and the wing missions were—to all intents and purposes—the same as had been assigned previously to the eastern and western forces. It was also decided by Chennault that as of March 1, 1944, the Fourteenth would take over from the Service of Supply in India responsibility for the construction and maintenance of airfields in China.

Twenty

By this time the war in Europe had progressed enough so that the Allies could reasonably predict the defeat of Germany, which they estimated would be in the fall of 1944. General Arnold submitted a plan to the Combined Chiefs of Staff to bomb Japan with the new long-range B-29s. He said the big planes—which would be supported by C-87s from the Calcutta area of India—would be supplied to China in ten groups of twenty-eight aircraft each. He called it the "Air Plan for the Defeat of Japan."

Again it had seemed to Americans at the Quadrant Conference, that the British were not too eager for an offensive in Burma for the purpose of opening a road to China, which they did not seem to want that badly as an ally. President Roosevelt, as he had at Trident, emphasized the need to retake Burma in order to keep Chiang in the war. The British seemed far more interested in retaking Singapore, where they had a vested interest. The target date for the plan to defeat Japan was tentatively set for six months after the defeat of Germany and the Combined Chiefs approved a plan to begin the ground march on Japan from the east through the Marshall and Gilbert Islands. This was to be done while steadily improving the air power in China and the Chinese armies. As one of their first priorities, the Combined Chiefs discussed the completion of the Ledo Road, being pushed through the jungles of north Burma from Ledo, India. It was to link up with the Burma Road in the vicinity of Bhamo when completed. The Combined Chiefs were anxious to begin using the road as a supply artery to China, supplementing the supplies being carried over the Hump by the ATC.

After the conference General Marshall attempted to explain Stilwell's role under the new setup. The Quadrant decisions were, Marshall said, "really just an affirmation of the Trident decisions," which called for an invasion of Burma in mid-February 1944 and the taking of Myitkyina to broaden the air route to China. It was also decided to enlarge the Fourteenth Air Force and to train and equip Chinese forces. The creation of SEAC simply meant that there were now three geographical theaters, all combined in one operational theater. Command responsibilities under SEAC were extremely complicated. The whole command had been set up for political motives because of India's place in the British Empire and because of Chiang Kai-shek's situation.

Marshall reminded Stilwell that the British were America's principal ally and that he would have to get on well with Mountbatten, who, Marshall said, would be a "breath of fresh air." Stilwell, with his Yonkers, New York, upbringing and inferiority complex in the face of anything approaching British aristocracy, would soon alienate Mountbatten by his sarcasm and obstinance.

Stilwell knew there would be the inevitable Japanese offensive to try and take the east China airfields as Chennault's planes sank more and more enemy shipping and began to bomb closer to Japan. He proposed to Chiang that he organize an offensive in east China to forestall that attack. Neither Stilwell nor Chennault knew that Chiang had no intention of supplying Lend-Lease arms to his Chinese commanders that far east. On the other hand, Stilwell—with his lack of support from the President and with no power to bargain with Chiang—also knew he would probably be held responsible for the defense of the east China bases. His dislike for the Air Force was apparent again in an entry in his "Black Book" of September 12:

"Now with Project 8 [for Hump tonnage increases] in view, the development of the Chinese Army will be a secondary consideration. The air will get all the supplies and we will be left to struggle along in the mud unaided. But they'll expect us to damn well produce a force that can protect the fancy boys while they do their spectacular stuff."[1]

The Americans, and indeed the rest of the world, knew very little about the Communist Chinese armies in north China. From time to time there had been periodic clashes between the Communists and the Nationalists, but little about them was known outside of Nationalist inner circles in Chungking. The last one had been in the Yangtze Valley in 1941 and had been hushed up. The New Fourth Army—a Communist force—had been fighting a guerrilla action against the Japanese, and Chiang, possibly fearing the Fourth was getting too close to Shanghai, ordered it back up north of the Yangtze. The Fourth Army had begun its march when fighting broke out and Chiang claimed it was revolting against government troops. The fight was bloody, and the Communists later claimed they lost five thousand killed. However, the Fourth Army had by no means been destroyed and many troops escaped into Kiangsi Province to regroup. Chiang—convinced that the Communists were trying to mutiny—ordered the Fourth's designation erased from the Nationalist Goverment Order of Battle, arrested the commander, General Yeh T'ing, and imprisoned him in Chungking. Relations had been strained, to say the least, from that day forward.

So when Stilwell proposed that Chiang give some of his Lend-Lease aid to the Communists to help him fight the Japanese, there was more to the request than met the eye. To Americans watching the war in China from the Pentagon or New Delhi, it would seem that the war effort would benefit if all of China's strength could be directed against the Japanese, instead of part of it being devoted to containing, and sometimes fighting, the Communists.

While Chiang was thinking this proposal over, Madame decided it was time to throw her support behind Stilwell. She called him to Chungking and invited him to a luncheon with herself and Madame H. H. Kung to show their cooperation with his efforts. He reacted favorably and asked her to help him with his proposals to Chiang.

What he proposed, specifically, was that Y Force get first priority—with a target date of December 1—and that a reorganization of the thirty divisions in the Kweilin area begin immediately. Chiang stalled on Y Force but hinted that some action might be taken to capture Ichang and the Wuchang area.

Stilwell thought the time had come—possibly he took Madame Chiang's change of heart as a good sign that things were changing—to give Chiang a comprehensive letter on his views of China and its military problems. It was a lengthy document and he sent a copy to Madame Chiang. In essence it said that sixty reorganized divisions would strengthen Chiang's command. He sent a summary of this program to Secretary of War Stimson, but Stimson knew Stilwell had no power to negotiate with Chiang and was not overly impressed.

In the meantime, Chennault had been complaining, rightfully, that he was not getting anywhere near what he had been promised in the way of supplies and replacements. In a letter to Roosevelt he told the President he was fighting against heavy odds. Two squadrons of B-25s were being held in India by Stratemeyer and Chennault knew it. So did Chiang. The President apologized to Madame Chiang, through a memo to Stilwell, and said the replacements for the Fourteenth were on the way. T. V. Soong—annoyed at the delays in getting supplies to Chennault—began a campaign to have Stilwell recalled. Stilwell finally realized he was unable to do anything to improve the combat readiness of the Chinese armies in Yunnan and east China.

"I have about reached the limit of what I can do," he wrote in his diary.[2]

The Japanese, fully aware that the B-29s had been made operational, were fearful that they would be sent to China. This—in the winter of 1943–44—was the reason for their buildup of ground forces in eastern and central China. They were right. The U. S. Air Force did plan to send the B-29 Superforts to China. The B-29s would have been used earlier in North Africa and Europe had they been completed on schedule. But they were finally made combat ready in time to be used in the Pacific and in China.

The Japanese had been shaken up by Chennault's Thanksgiving Day raid on Formosa far more than the American command realized. The Japanese knew the American Air Force was now at liberty to bomb their shipping at will from a number of bases in China. The Imperial General Headquarters of the Japanese Army decided the China airfields had to go. Their Eleventh Army had been moving into the rice-bowl area of Tungting Lake toward the town of Ch'ang-te while the weather was bad in late November. But when the weather cleared in December, U.S. fighters and bombers from Hengyang and Lingling took off in support of Chinese divisions guarding the Ch'ang-te area. The Eleventh Army withdrew under the constant air attacks and counterattacks by the Chinese Army. Chennault and his Air Force intelligence were heartened by the withdrawal and misread the reason for the pull-out. Actually the Japanese had ordered the withdrawal of the Eleventh Army because the high command wanted it to join other elements of the Japanese Army in a mass ground offensive it was planning in the Changsha region—as was later learned from Japanese war records.

Chennault had based some of his plans for current and future operations of the Fourteenth on his past record of ground support. He had successfully bombed and strafed the Japanese on the west bank of the Salween River in the spring of '42 and they had not crossed the Salween. In May 1943 his planes had bombed the Japanese in the Yangtze Gorges and the enemy had fallen back. Now, after the Japanese had retreated once again, Chennault believed he could keep them out of east China with the Fourteenth and the existing Chinese ground force.

He divided up the China theater into his two areas—east and west of the 108th meridian—because of several factors, weather conditions being one of them. From January until June weather is good in the western portion, then steadily grows worse until summer. In the east flying weather is generally good from July to December. Therefore he planned to fly most of his missions from January to June 1944 in the west in support of Stilwell's Burma campaign and in defense against Japanese planes hitting the Hump airfields from Burma and Thailand. From July to December he would hit enemy shipping and planes in the east. To supply his operation in 1944, he requested supplies over the Hump in the following numbers:

	EASTERN AREA TONNAGE	WESTERN AREA TONNAGE
January	1,900	6,900
February	2,100	6,900
March	2,300	6,900
April	2,700	5,400
May	4,500	3,400
June	6,200	2,700[3]

Late in 1943, Allied successes elsewhere encouraged Chennault to believe that the War Department might come up with more resources against Japan, so he drew up a comprehensive plan for the use of an expanded Air Force in

China. He knew his plan would depend upon increased tonnages over the Hump and on improvement in the ground supply lines from Kunming to the eastern base of Kweilin, but he was confident both could be achieved. His plan called for much heavier and increased strikes against enemy merchant shipping and the Japanese Air Force. He also projected long-range bombing against the homeland of Japan from bases in China. For this projection he estimated he would need six fighter groups, two medium groups, and three heavy groups.

When the plan was submitted to Stratemeyer in late November, Stratemeyer said he doubted the Hump tonnage could support the plan. Further, he revealed that plans were being made in Washington to send very-long-range (VLR) bombers to China with fighters to support them, and these new planes would be controlled directly from Washington. Implementation of the VLR plan, he told Chennault, would take precedence over claims of the Fourteenth, but the VLR program would approximate the last phase of Chennault's plan—bombing the Japanese homeland. Minor portions of Chennault's plan, such as the improvement of the Kütsing–Tuhshan bottleneck on the Kunming–Kweilin supply line, were approved by Stratemeyer. Chennault was keenly disappointed that the crucial blows against Japan would not be made under his direction and he was also displeased that the plan to base the new VLR B-29 bombers in India and stage them through Chengtu—a Chinese base—would saddle the Fourteenth with a new program of airfield construction and supply. He was also worried that—even though he had been told that the B-29s would haul their own bombs and gas over the Hump—the Fourteenth would have some of its gas supplies diverted to the VLR program.

General Arnold had called in Brigadier General Kenneth B. Wolfe on September 20, 1943, and asked him to come up with a plan calculated to "initiate strategic bombardment of Japan with the maximum of available B-29s at the earliest possible date."[4] Wolfe had been in on the early development of the Superfort and its production program and expected to have a force of a hundred and fifty B-29s and three hundred crews ready by March 1, 1944—and another three hundred planes and four hundred and fifty crews by September. He planned to organize these into a bomber command with two wings of four combat groups each. Stilwell would provide bases in China and India. Supply at these bases would be by the B-29s themselves—aided by the Fourteenth's 308th Bomb Group and reinforced by twenty C-87s.

In December, still receiving far less than he needed in the way of Hump supplies, Chennault had written one of these personal letters to Roosevelt, which did not endear him to either Marshall or Arnold. The President—knowing of the impending B-29 project and Wolfe's plans—nevertheless wrote Marshall: "I am still pretty thoroughly disgusted with the India-China matters. The last straw was the report from Arnold that he could not get the B-29s operating out of China until March or April of next year. Everything seems to go wrong. But the worst thing is that we are falling down on our promises [to Chiang] every single time. We have not fulfilled one of them yet. I do not see why we have to use B-29s. We have several other types of bombing planes."⁵

Chennault, in his conversations with Roosevelt following the Trident Conference in Washington, said Roosevelt had asked him to write him "from time to time and let me know how things are getting along."

"Do you mean you want me to write you personally?" Chennault asked.

"Yes, I do," the President replied.

Chennault remembered: "During the next 18 months I wrote a half-dozen personal letters to the President fulfilling his request and received personal notes of encouragement from him. Some of my letters found their way to the War Department again, and for this alleged breach of military protocol, Gen. Marshall has never forgiven me. To him it was convincing proof that I was intriguing against his old friend, Stilwell."⁶

Arnold—at Marshall's request—replied to Roosevelt, explaining the difficulties in getting any new combat plane into action and offering to divert B-24s to Chennault; but, he also explained, only the B-29 could hit directly at Japan.

Following the Cairo Conference, in November and December 1943, attended by Roosevelt, Churchill, and Chiang Kai-shek, the B-29 project, named "Matterhorn," was approved. General Arnold asked a specific committee—composed of military as well as civilian special consultants—to come up with a study of "analysis of strategic targets in Japan," the destruction of which might knock Japan out of the war.⁷ The committee came up with the finding that the most harm could be done to Japan by disrupting its production of such basic materials as steel.

Two thirds of all steel was produced from coke that came from a limited number of ovens concentrated in Kyushu, Manchuria, and Korea. Since the B-29s from China could not reach either Manchuria or Korea, Kyushu seemed like the logical choice. The planners had selected Chengtu, north of Chungking, in Szechwan Province as a base from which B-29s could fly and not be in danger from Japanese ground attack.

When Chennault heard about the B-29 program and suspected he was going to be bypassed, he wrote to Brigadier General Eugene C. Beebe of SEAC in New Delhi:

"Frankly, I am much disturbed by the plan of operations laid down for the project by the Chiefs of Staff in Washington. As you know, the plan still calls for sending heavily loaded bombers at rather low altitudes across a wide belt of enemy held territory where there are many fighter bases. The risk strikes me as extremely serious and totally unnecessary. I spoke my mind about it, first to Strat, and later at Cairo, where the representatives of the Washington planners appeared surprised to learn that the enemy fighter bases actually existed. I do not, unfortunately, seem to have made as much of an impression as I could wish. Yet I am not content to let the matter rest, for I foresee unpleasant consequences if the present plan is adhered to.

"If you agree with me, I am in hopes that your opinion will carry the necessary weight with the authorities. As coming from a specialist in heavy bombardment, with a distinguished record here in China, your views can hardly be ignored.

"I may add that I am also worried by the apparent intention to divide control of the Matterhorn Project and the 14th Air Force. As I remembered in the Plan of Air Operations which you saw in Delhi, the operations planned under the Matterhorn Project and the operations of the 14th Air Force should be regarded as a boxer's right and left. Without the close coordination which can only be afforded by unified command, neither will achieve maximum effectiveness. Timing will be wrong. The blows of one will not prepare for and increase the force of the blows of the other. The fullest protection against enemy counter-operations will not be afforded. Moreover, I am afraid that if the present plan for Matterhorn is not altered, and difficulties are encountered, the 14th Air Force will immediately be converted into a sort of glorified Fighter Wing to protect the Matterhorn operations. This will of course mean abandonment of the complementary offensive operations by the 14th Air Force which I now plan."[8]

Beebe, while sympathetic to Chennault's views, would not commit himself to taking sides. Chennault—feeling the issue was important to the Fourteenth—wrote General Arnold on February 9:

Dear General Arnold:

Arrangements for command of the Matterhorn Project seem to be completed, but the War Department has not yet taken final action. Before that occurs, I feel I ought to present to you personally certain points which, it seems to me, may materially affect the Project's future.

As you know, I have already had a number of most satisfactory talks with K. B. Wolfe, in whom I believe you have found an outstanding leader for your great enterprise. Whatever happens, I look forward to working closely with him, but in the first place, so far as I can understand the plan, immediate authority over the Project will be rather vaguely dispersed between Strat and me, with the last word resting with Strat. This is unnecessary. It is cumbersome and inefficient. And worst of all, it amounts to a system of divided command of air operations in China. The whole weight of my experience here is on the side of the conclusion that the peculiar local tactical situation gives no room for divided command. At best, it will diminish the total force of our blows against the enemy. At worst, in the event of the Matterhorn Project provoking really determined Japanese counter-operations, I am afraid that divided command may prove downright dangerous.

In the second place, I wonder whether it is necessary to have all

Matterhorn missions actually scheduled by the Joint Chiefs of Staff. I recognize that you in Washington must exercise a pretty thorough supervision, in order to carry out your fine conception of several coordinated B-29 groups simultaneously striking at Japan from different points. I realize, of course, that there may be cases when it will be desirable to order a specific mission at a specified time, so that a blow from China, for example, may follow up a blow from the Aleutians. But in view of the importance of prevailing weather conditions, the local tactical situation and other purely local factors, I feel that some latitude should be left the commander in the field. As I see it, you should be the quarterback, calling the signals, while the commander in the field should be the runner, free to choose how best to carry the ball. I believe this would be accomplished if the Joint Chiefs of Staff, as a rule, prescribed general objectives and established priorities, leaving the field commander to set the missions up.

Furthermore, in this area at least, I think the field commander should have some freedom, within the framework of the Joint Chiefs' directives, to set up an occasional mission not on the Washington list. For instance, the great staging areas on Formosa are more immediately vital to the enemy war effort than any industrial installations on the Japanese islands. If the 14th Air Force is strengthened as I hope it will be, I intend to attempt to deny use of these staging areas to the enemy. If the course of the attempt should reveal that only the B-29s could deliver the finishing blow, it would seem to me sensible to send them in for the kill. But this will hardly be possible, if the question has to be referred to Washington and debated back and forth by cable. Then too there is the problem of Japanese counter-operations. While it is obvious that in principle the B-29s should be strictly reserved for such missions as those against the Japanese islands and Formosa, in practice it might become necessary to use their power to deliver an enormous weight of bombs, to pulverize Hankow or other major bases of a Japanese offensive. The entire success of the Project might hang on such a quick, temporary diversion of the B-29s from their main task. The success of the Project is my first consideration. I hope you will accept and consider these suggestions as being made with no other idea in mind, but that of adapting the Project to the peculiar Chinese conditions which I know from long observation.[9]

Arnold, having been through the same discussion with General Kenney, wrote back on February 25 in a letter marked SECRET:

My Dear Chennault:

I should like to extend my congratulations to you and your command for the fine work that you have been doing against Japanese shipping. I know it must be gratifying to you as it is to me to see the results of operations for which you have laboriously prepared.

Your letter of February 9 raised the question of the command arrangements for the B-29 groups of the Matterhorn Project. This is a problem to which a great deal of careful study has been given and I shall tell you quite frankly the policies being formulated here in Washington on this subject.

You are not the first Air Force commander to raise this subject. Nearly every Air Force commander in every theater of war has advanced convincing reasons for the direct command and control of the B-29 units in his theater. You have indicated half a dozen reasons why the Air Forces should be placed under your control in order to exploit local opportunities or meet local situations—so has each of the other Air Force commanders who has raised his voice on this matter. Collectively you all prove again that if the B-29s are to really concentrate their efforts in a determined mass operation against a selected system of objectives, regardless of tempting local plums, they must be controlled by an agency which has a world-wide and not a local perspective. This is no criticism of you or any other Air Force commander nor is it a new observation. The best commanders everywhere, motivated by the finest of principles, are always bound to see the general situation through glasses prescribed by the local optician.

The command arrangement for the employment of the B-29s is not intended to militate against you or any other of the Air Force commanders. I fully expect that the concept of centralized control on a global basis will be applied to all the VLR bombers wherever they may be based. I think you would be the first to agree that if you did command the B-29s and planned a projected operation against a vital target in Japan, you would be quick to object to the right of some other Air Force commander to abandon his share in operations against the same targets in order to exploit a local opportunity which seemed most tempting to him.

One of the principal reasons why the heavy bombers will not be placed under the control of local Air Force commanders is in order to exploit their mobility. It is quite possible that the B-29s of the Matterhorn Project may have to operate once or twice from bases in Ceylon against targets in the Netherlands East Indies. Again, as other bases become available, it may be necessary to shift temporarily, or permanently, a part of the force in order to bear more directly on the vital Japanese targets. This can be achieved only through retention of centralized authority.

This concept of control has been applied elsewhere with success. For instance, the 15th Air Force operating from Italy is not under the command of the Mediterranean Air Force Commander but is under the operational command of Spaatz whose primary headquarters is in England. This command arrangement was set up primarily to insure the concerted efforts of the 15th Air Force with those of the Eighth Air Force against strategic targets in Germany rather than local targets in Italy. The local U.S. Air Commander in Italy is, on the other hand, fully responsible for the administrative and logistical support of the 15th Air Force, just as I shall expect you to be responsible for the support of the XX Bomber Command in China.

If I am to function as the executor for the Joint Chiefs of Staff with regard to the B-29s, I expect to designate Strat as my representative in the China-Burma-India area. He will not have unqualified command of the force but will simply be my representative to carry out the directives of the Joint Chiefs of Staff. He will, of course, function administratively under Gen. Stilwell, who will be responsible for providing logistical and administrative support from the primary base areas. . . .[10]

Chennault knew when there was no use in discussing the issue any further. The B-29s were coming to China and he would have to make the best of it. On March 30 he wrote Arnold:

Dear General Arnold:

This will acknowledge your letter of February 25, concerning the command of the Matterhorn Project.

As I am sure you understand, my only object in writing you was to place before you opinions on a subject of great importance to you, which were based on my experience here. I wanted you to have all the facts before you when you made your decision. I am glad to have your clear explanation of the problem, and I shall, of course, cooperate closely with Strat, whom I regard not only as your representative but also as an old friend, and shall endeavor to carry out to the best of my ability the responsibilities which rest upon me personally.

With kindest personal regards, I am,

> Most sincerely yours,
> C. L. Chennault
> Major General, USA
> Commanding[11]

Twenty-one

In addition to the supply problems over the Hump, Chennault had a ground supply problem to east China as the spring of 1944 wore on. In order to maintain the east China airfields he needed to develop a system of moving 10,000 tons a month of gas, bombs, ammunition, spare parts, and other supplies down a highway from its starting point north of Kunming. The carefully hoarded caches of gas stored up by the Chinese years ago for the lean times ahead had long ago been depleted. Chennault had fallen back on them for hard times, but there had been just too many hard times. The Kütsing–Tuhshan road wound down from Yunnan Province through Kweichow Province and into Kwangsi, twisting through the rugged Kweichow Mountains. The road was little more than a dirt trail in many places and the eight hundred alcohol- and charcoal-burning Chinese trucks that were used to carry supplies were obsolete when they started. The fleet of battered vehicles was only able to move 2,300 tons a month over the route. Chennault had appealed to Stilwell over and over to assign modern trucks as part of Lend-Lease supplies, but no new trucks ever showed up. Nor were labor crews ever sent over from India to build a proper road to the east China bases. Most were busy building the Ledo Road through the jungles of Burma. The lack of equipment to help with a land route to east China, where most of the fighting was being done, seemed strange in light of the fact that the taking of Myitkyina was to open up a land route to China. This would be of little use if supplies never reached the fighting areas. Supply in China fell under the authority of the Service of Supply (SOS), responsibility for which was directly under Stilwell. Having decided there was nothing he could do to bolster Chinese armies in east China, Stilwell ignored the supply problem in the same area. Shipments of alcohol as well as spare parts for the old trucks were held up until the highway supply system was falling apart by December of 1943. The only help that arrived for the road supply came from China

Defense Supplies and the Foreign Economic Administration (FEA) in Washington, which provided spare parts and repair facilities. Chennault—realizing he would get help only from this quarter—sent Doreen Lonberg, who had been a personal secretary since AVG days, to Washington to coordinate activities between the Fourteenth and the FEA.

Whiting Willauer, who had earlier been in China Defense Supplies in Washington and who had been helpful to Chennault from the early days, was made head of the China Division of FEA. Chennault was delighted and wrote to congratulate him on his new post.

A strong memo to Stilwell in December having produced no results, Chennault went to New Delhi in February to argue his case. CBI headquarters sent Colonel Maurice Sheehan over and he did what he could to iron out the supply bottleneck, but there was little he could do in the long run as Stilwell banned the shipment of all vehicles to China and diverted alcohol supplies to the Burma area. He said the supply route to east China was a Chinese problem.[1]

The Fourteenth—growing in numbers each day as more and more personnel were assigned to China—nevertheless fought its war with about half the normal personnel and with about one fourth the supplies allocated to a normal air force. The Chinese took care of all the housekeeping work that would have been performed by Americans in any other theater. Chinese did the cooking, built the airfields, and ran the aircraft repair factories in Kunming and Kweilin. They also acted as security guards. The Chinese War Service Corps—set up by Madame Chiang and run by General Jerry Huang—fed the Americans in China. Feeding Americans was a tremendous job for Chinese, who lived on a sparse diet of rice and noodles. Americans ate more meat in a single day than a Chinese family ate in a year. Eventually livestock—slaughtered for meat—ran out and water buffalo had to be substituted. Chickens could not lay enough eggs to keep Americans happy. The diet was not always appetizing to the foreigners, but the Chinese kept the Americans alive and fighting.

Since no bulldozers could be flown over the Hump, the Chinese built all the airfields, including the huge runways for the B-29s, by hand. Hundreds of thousands of coolies swarmed over the fields, breaking and strewing crushed rocks over the strip. The work was done by old men, old women, and young women with babies in slings on their backs.

Chennault wanted to build a rest camp close to a lake in the mountains near Kunming for the pilots and air crews, who needed rest from the constant grind of combat missions. In India, combat crews of the Tenth Air Force had been routinely sent to Kashmir, high in the mountains, for their R and R. CBI headquarters in New Dehli turned down Chennault's request. But a group of Kunming bankers, headed by Dr. Y. T. Miao, bought the land near the lake, began construction of the rest camp, and charged the Fourteenth one Chinese dollar for leasing it.

The Chinese were constantly bringing back downed airmen after they had been given up for dead. They were returned through the lines in the Hankow area, and even when crews went down in the seas near Hong Kong and Hainan Island, junks would show up and fish the men from the water. They would end up back at bases in east China or Kunming months later, thinner from the long marches, but safe. Chennault had asked the Chinese to make silk flags—called "blood chits"—that could be worn on the backs of leather jackets. On the flags was written in Chinese, and occasionally in Burmese, the fact that the owner was an American flier and needed to be gotten back to friendly lines.

Chennault's disappointment at learning from Stratemeyer in November that the B-29s would be staged at Chengtu and would depend upon the Fourteenth for supply was offset in January by the arrival in China of elements of the 341st Bombardment Group. In February a second contingent of the CACW arrived with 1st Bomb Squadron (M) and the 7th and 8th Fighter Squadrons, but they bought only eighteen P-40s and thirty-three B-25s.

The weather in east China was terrible in January, February, and March and little flying was done against the Japanese, who were piling up supplies and troops for the expected offensive.

Stilwell, contrary to Chennault's belief, had been concerned about the east China bases. General Ho, the Chinese Army Chief of Staff, had proposed that forty-five Chinese divisions be used to form what he called a C Force to extend from the Yangtze River in the north down a line to south China. Stilwell was all for it and proposed to call it Z Force for Zebra. He sent Brigadier General Thomas Arms from the Y Force Training Center in Yunnan to open up an Infantry Training Center at Kweilin. It was opened in December 1943, with the Generalissimo and General Pai Chung-hsi of the National Military Council as honorary commanders. General Arms estimated that the center might be able to turn out 4,800 officers from the infantry and 2,730 officers from other branches as graduates by May 1944. However, the War Department in Washington decided that equipment for Z Force be kept at the 10 percent level—effectively killing the project.[2]

In the meantime, Stilwell was expending his efforts on the upcoming invasion of Burma with his Chinese forces who had been trained in India. He would be assisted by the British and American forces under General Frank Merrill. One of his biggest problems was in trying to ensure that the Y Force (Chinese armies in Yunnan) would join him in the Burma invasion. The Generalissimo had not committed his troops to the battle plan as yet. Stilwell appealed through Marshall to the President and the President, in January, began to hint to Chiang that Lend-Lease to China might cease if the Y Force were not used against the Japanese.

Chiang had just asked the American government for a billion-dollar loan and had asked that the United States pay for the use of Chengtu airfield for the B-29s. It seemed to Roosevelt and others that Chiang was blackmailing them. He was. The Generalissimo stated that unless the loan was forthcoming and if the United States failed to finance the Chengtu project the Chinese would stop providing food and housing for American forces after March 1944. Chennault knew nothing of this—not being privy to exchanges between Chiang and Roosevelt. It was a ticklish period for U.S.-China relations. Roosevelt decided to stay calm; he discussed the proposal with the Treasury Department and a series of letters and memos began to pass from Washington to Chungking through United States Ambassador Clarence Gauss. Payment by the Americans for Chinese services in China—such as rental on bases like Chengtu and the feeding and housing of U.S. personnel —had to come from India. It was usually in Chinese currency, which was printed in the United States and was highly inflated: when shipments of money were made, the Chinese currency was measured in tonnage rather than by dollar bills. Chennault once complained that it took 4,500 gallons of critically needed gas to fly one day's airlift of Chinese currency.

Chennault, becoming thoroughly fed up with the stalling in India and seeing the huge Japanese build up in east China, spent most of his days at his desk buried under an avalanche of radiograms and mail. At night he either played gin rummy with Buzz Glenn or had friends over to dinner. The Carneys and the Sutters—his longtime friends from AVG days and before— had fallen upon hard times. Harry Sutter, the Swiss who had been employed by the Chinese Aeronautical Commission, was accused of smuggling some vital supplies over the Hump. The Criminal Investigation Division of the U. S. Army had questioned him at length but had not been able to find enough evidence to prosecute him. His wife Kasey was still living in Kunming with their two children, a boy and a girl, ages five and seven, and she frequently attended dinners at Chennault's. Boatner Carney, an instructor who had been with Chennault since the days in Hankow and who later joined him in the AVG, had killed a man in a drunken card game. The Chinese intended to put him in prison, but Chennault interceded with the Generalissimo and he was deported to the States. His Chinese wife Rose stayed behind in Kunming. Rose was a beautiful woman with a mysterious past, an excellent businesswoman who was constantly involved with selling goods to the Americans. She had been married to a Chinese years before and had a son who lived with her father in Hong Kong. An old friend of Chennault's, she was seen at his house for dinners and ran errands for him in the city.

Joe Alsop and Tom Gentry were his constant companions at the house, and Colonel Dave Barrett, who was a close friend of Kasey Sutter as well, came down frequently from Chungking to stay overnight.

Barrett was stationed at Kweilin in March 1944 as G-2 in the headquarters of Z Force. At dinner on the twenty-fifth he told Chennault confidentially that he had just been ordered by Brigadier General Thomas Hearn,

Stilwell's chief of staff in China, to report to Chungking. It seemed John Paton Davies, Jr., Stilwell's political adviser, had written to the State Department suggesting that a consulate general be opened in the territory of the Chinese Communists and that a military mission be sent to them. With a long history of service in China—particularly as a military attaché and one who spoke flawless Peking Chinese—Barrett had been named by Stilwell to head the mission. He was excited by the chance to see the Communists in person. Chennault too was fascinated by the idea that any American would be allowed to travel to that part of China. Barrett promised to keep him advised of the progress of the mission. Since it was primarily a State Department plan, Barrett did not consider it a secret military matter and had no qualms about discussing it with his longtime friend Chennault. Chennault's only feelings about the Communist Chinese at that time were that they were on different sides politically from the Generalissimo. He would have welcomed their entry into the war in order to protect his east China bases.

The Generalissimo sent a message to Roosevelt on March 17 that some of his troops had been bombed by Soviet planes near Mongolia and that he did not think this could have been possible without some sort of arrangement with the Japanese. Something else for Roosevelt to think about. In addition, Chiang told Roosevelt that the Chinese Communists seemed to be gathering their strength for an uprising in Shensi Province—something he hinted might be tied in with a Soviet-Japanese alliance.

Chennault, becoming thoroughly fed up with the stalling in India and seeing the huge Japanese buildup in east China, wrote a strong letter to Stilwell on April 8. In the lengthy letter he laid the facts on the line. He told Stilwell he knew from his reconnaissance that the enemy now had within range of his bases 1,170 aircraft. He also said, in no uncertain terms, that the disposition of the "enemy's ground forces in China is also more threatening than has been the case since Pearl Harbor." He went on to describe troop movements in east China in detail. He said he was sure Stilwell shared his view that the Japanese were preparing two major offensives in China. "In considering the likelihood of effective resistance to these anticipated offensives," he wrote, "I need not point out to you the underlying weakness of the Chinese armies."

He went on to say that from the foregoing it was apparent that the Fourteenth was going to be called upon to fly missions vastly greater in scope than the mere defense of the Hump, support of ground operations in Burma, and attacks upon targets of opportunity. He reminded Stilwell that he and Arnold had saddled the Fourteenth with the fighter protection of the upcoming B-29 program at Chengtu and added that, in order to accomplish that mission, it was essential that they hold on to his forward bases. He added that Chiang had asked for air support for his armies in the upcoming defense against the expected Japanese offensive and said that, while "air support alone may not be the best way of strengthening the Chinese armies, as matters stood, it was the only way.

"The plain fact is," he wrote, "that with circumstances as they are now, the combined air forces in China cannot conceivably meet such demands, even by abandoning all such activities as our fruitful and effective anti-shipping operations." He pointed to the shortage in tons delivered by the ATC over the Hump. He said the incoming supplies were about half of what he needed to maintain combat efficiency and that the reserve situation was critical.

He suggested several alternatives:

1. Restore cuts in Hump tonnage that had been made in April. (SEAC had diverted transports from the Hump to support Burma-India operations.)

2. Improve the Yunnan-east China communications and transportation system.

3. Temporarily divert Matterhorn Project air transport capacity to building minimum stockage levels at critical eastern and northern air bases to ensure a defense against an offensive.

4. Prepare to use B-29s for tactical rather than strategic purposes in case of an offensive, using the B-29s to hit Japanese bases in east and south China.

"If none of the above courses recommend themselves," he wrote, "it would appear necessary to inform the Generalissimo that, owing to pressure of the Burma operations and the Matterhorn Project on the China supply line, he can no longer depend on effective air support for his armies in the anticipated offensive; and to advise the appropriate authorities in Washington that the security of China as a base for Matterhorn and other military operations against Japan may be in doubt.

"I deeply regret the necessity of confronting you with this problem," he added, "when you are already so heavily and importantly engaged. But the purpose of your campaign in Burma is, after all, to open a better supply line to China; and as I have said, I believe the security of China itself is now in jeopardy. I am confident that the danger can be averted for the present by placing the air forces in China on a sound footing. I earnestly trust that you will take measures to this end. And I beg you to believe that, in saying we do not now have a reasonable chance of success in the great tasks confronting us, I am stating a simple truth in conservative language."

Stilwell—at the beginning of April—had decided to risk everything on a push for Myitkyina. He knew the monsoons were about to start again and he had better start before them. Chennault's letter reached him at an awkward time. The Japanese were putting pressure on India, and Mountbatten—who was Stilwell's boss—had diverted twenty transports from flying the Hump to help his forces.

Stilwell told Chennault that until the India problem improved he saw no possibility of increasing the flow of supplies. "You will simply have to cut down on activity to the point where you can be sure of reasonable reserves for an emergency," he wrote.[3]

Chennault—desperate for help in any form—was furious. "If Stilwell's neglect of the Hump seemed strange," he later wrote, "his studied indifference to the China internal supply problem was incredible."

What was even more incredible, Stilwell added a warning to Chennault not to send any gloomy estimate of the situation to the Generalissimo.[4]

Chennault was very concerned with the developments of the Japanese offensive. On April 15 he sent a letter to the Gimo which ended with the warning:

". . . Under the circumstances, therefore, it is necessary to inform Your Excellency that the combined air forces in China, excluding the VLR [B-29] Project, may not be able to withstand the Japanese air offensive and will certainly be unable to afford air support to the Chinese ground forces over the areas and on the scale desired. In order to put the air forces on a footing to accomplish these missions, drastic measures to provide them with adequate supplies and adequate strength must be taken. As the Japanese threat appears to be immediate, such measures should be taken without further delay."[5]

The Generalissimo sent a copy around to General Hearn in Chungking, but Hearn was ill and the copy went to his vice chief of staff, General Benjamin Ferris. Circulated among Stilwell's staff officers in Chungking, Chennault's letter drew emphatic dissents from them.[6]

But in New Delhi, Stratemeyer apparently took Chennault's warning at face value and discussed it with Stilwell. Stilwell—aware that the B-29s had received the highest priority—sent an order to Chennault which reached him on April 26 and stated that his primary mission was to defend Chengtu "even at the expense of shipping strikes and support of the Chinese ground forces, dependent upon Japanese reaction to operations from the Chengtu area."[7]

General Arnold had allocated two hundred fighter aircraft—mostly P-51s—for the defense of the B-29 staging fields at Chengtu, but Chennault, already engaged in trying to stop the Japanese on a wide front in east and north China, was startled that Stilwell would order him to defend such a remote field and ignore the rest of the offensive. Chengtu itself was in no danger. He wired Stilwell:

"I have been advised by letter from Stratemeyer that . . . the primary mission of the 14th Air Force is changed from the defence of the Eastern Terminals of the Air Transport Route and air support of the Chinese ground armies, to the defense of the Chengtu area. . . . I respectfully request reconsideration of this decision and also request clarification of the note of April 17 which states 'General Stratemeyer has authority to limit the scope of fighter operations in case of emergency.' It is not clear to me just who will determine what constitutes an emergency, but in any case, I have certain responsibilities . . . and most sincerely trust that my hands will not be tied by requiring me to contact General Stratemeyer in the event an emergency exists.

"Such an event requires prompt action and particularly so in matters of air warfare. These instructions create a division of responsibility which I am reluctant to believe was your intent and furthermore it is contrary to your agreement with the Chinese government with reference to command of air units in China.

"Defence of the Chengtu area gives me no concern and I must assure you that with the 200 fighters such as have been provided, there is no problem in that area. Chengtu receives two hours warning and the Chinese American Wing is now in position east and north of Chungking. These forces constitute an exceptionally strong outer defense of the area.

"This matter reaches me at a time when I am busily engaged in trying to stem the Japanese invasion in the Yellow River area and preparing to support Dorn [Brigadier General Frank Dorn, Commander Y Force] in his impending operations [Salween River] and Chinese armies in Hunan. Defense of the Chengtu area is child's play compared to the more difficult problems that confront us. In times like these I need your support and most of your confidence. I trust that I will be so honored."[8]

Stilwell, as sarcastic as ever, wired back from his jungle headquarters in Burma, where he was marching toward Myitkyina:

"I am glad to hear that the defense of Chengtu is child's play. I had gathered from your letter of April 8 that the security of China as a base for Matterhorn and other military operations against Japan might be in doubt. It is a relief to know that we have no problems at Chengtu and under these circumstances of course the question of action in emergency will not arise. Until it does, there is no intention of limiting the scope of your operations in any way."[9]

This gave Chennault temporary operational freedom—which was already guaranteed him under his position of Chief of Staff to Chiang. But Stilwell still refused to declare there was an emergency under which he, as U.S. theater commander, could release supplies that were being stockpiled for the B-29 program to Chennault in his emergency.

As April wound down, the defense of Honan Province seemed a lost cause. The Generalissimo was truly alarmed when his commanders began to fall back and he ordered them to plug the gap in the Tungkuan Pass, whose fall would open the way to Sian.

As Japanese armored forces approached the plains of Honan, Chennault tried in vain to get reinforcements from Stilwell. He sent his chief of staff, General Glenn, to India to try to appeal to Stilwell personally to declare an emergency in east China and to allocate supplies and equipment. Glenn could not find Stilwell, though he personally flew a light reconnaissance plane to the jungles of northern Burma to look for him. Stilwell did not

25. Chennault directs operations at his field command post near Kweilen in east China, 1944. (U.S. Air Force Photo)

26. Chennault reviews the military situation in east China with noted radio commentator Lowell Thomas, Kunming, 1944. (U.S. Air Force Photo)

27. Colonel Tex Hill greets Chennault on the latter's arrival in New Orleans, 1945. (Courtesy of Tex Hill)

28. Chennault and his wife Anna at an American Legion party, Shanghai, 1947. (China *Post* Archives)

29. A Nationalist Chinese soldier guards a CAT plane as it is loaded in north China, 1948. (CAT Photo)

30. Nationalist troops being transported to Taiwan. (CAT Photo)

31. Cessna 195s, used by CAT for short flights in China and on Taiwan. (CAT Photo)

32. CAT C-47s and C-46s being repaired at the maintenance base at Tainan, Taiwan, 1952. (Author's Photo)

33. Jim Brennan, CAT vice president of finance, giving the victory sign as CAT is awarded custody of the CNAC/CATC aircraft at Hong Kong, 1953. (Author's Photo)

34. One of the CNAC/CATC planes being loaded aboard a barge en route to the U.S. aircraft carrier *Cape Esperance* in Hong Kong Harbor. (Author's Photo)

35. Whiting Willauer, left, and Al Cox, the president and vice president, respectively, of CAT. (Author's Photo)

36. Chennault as chairman of the board of CAT, Hong Kong, 1953.
(Author's Photo)

maintain radio contact with his Burmese headquarters at Shaduzup while he was on combat patrols. Glenn finally gave up and returned to China.[10]

Bogged down in his offensive against Myitkyina and irritated that Chennault had sent his estimate of the air situation to the Generalissimo on April 15, Stilwell asked for an explanation.

Chennault replied that he was Chief of Staff of the Chinese Air Force, which gave him direct access to the Generalissimo, and added that he had addressed the estimate to General Hearn but that Hearn was ill. Stilwell concluded that Chennault had been insubordinate and should be relieved.[11]

Obviously under stress in his jungle campaign, Stilwell wrote:

"Chennault (stated): The Chinese ground forces can protect the bases with the help of the 14th AF. . . . Chennault has assured the Generalissimo that air power is the answer. He has told him that if the 14th is supported, he can effectively prevent a Jap invasion. Now he realizes it can't be done, and he's trying to prepare an out for himself by claiming that with a little more, which we won't give him, he can still do it. He tries to duck the consequences of having sold the wrong bill of goods, and put the blame on those who pointed out the danger long ago and tried to apply the remedy. He has failed to damage the Jap supply line. He has not caused any Jap withdrawals. On the contrary, our preparations have exactly what I prophesized, ie, drawn a Jap reaction, which he now acknowledges the ground forces can't handle, even with the total air support he asked for and got."[12]

Stilwell continued to ignore, or was unaware of, the cuts in Hump tonnage to Chennault—February down to 6,844 tons; March down to 4,735 tons; and April dangerously close to the March figures. Chennault had repeatedly told Stilwell he would need 10,000 tons a month to contain the Japanese. Also Stilwell either did not pay any attention to Chennault's combat reports or did not care to acknowledge them. In January the Fourteenth B-24s and B-25s had sunk 56,000 tons of Japanese shipping off the coast of south China, and in February they sank 65,000 tons. The Japanese—in deciding to take the east China bases—knew how effective Chennault had been in damaging their supply lines, if Stilwell did not.

All evidence now pointed to the largest and most ambitious military operations the Japanese had ever considered in China. The appearance of Japanese ground forces, long kept in Manchuria, pointed to a campaign with far-reaching objectives. If the Japanese offensive were successful it would make an overland transportation route from Peking to Indochina feasible and would eliminate all the bases from which Chennault could operate against enemy shipping. It could render the China coast useless as a base for later Allied amphibious landings and it could eliminate the Chinese armies in east China—leaving the way open to the downfall of Chungking and the Nationalists.

But Stilwell was far more interested in obtaining a promise from Chiang to commit his Y Force to an attack on Burma to open up a ground route to China—if there were any China left.

Chennault had no other choice than to try to defend China with what he had. CACW units were prepared for a move against Japanese forces in the bend of the Yellow River up north. They would be moved to Chinese Air Force bases. The remaining squadrons of the 68th Composite Wing were scattered at various fighter fields to intercept possible attacks from north, east, and south. Elements of the 69th Wing were called to help support Y Force in the invasion of Burma and were based in Kunming, but Chennault appealed to Stilwell to postpone the offensive so he could utilize the 69th Wing in the defense of east China. Stilwell ignored him and the offensive in Burma began as anticipated. For the next three months the 69th Wing was to fight a losing battle against overwhelming odds in the air as well as in supporting ground troops.

Chennault—realizing he was going to get no help from Stilwell or CBI headquarters in New Delhi—moved four fighter squadrons of the 68th Composite Wing and one medium bomber squadron (the 11th) to the Chinese Air Force bases at Liangshan, Enshih, Nancheng, and Sian on April 8. They would operate with two fighter squadrons of the Chinese Air Force flying old P-40s. His orders to them were to defend as many cities in range of the Japanese planes as possible; attack enemy traffic on the Yellow and the Yangtze rivers; and destroy the railroad from Hankow north to Sinyang. In addition they were to attack rail junctions and enemy airfields.

Hoping to get some help from Chiang, he flew to Chungking, but there he found the Generalissimo and the Chinese high command more interested in the upcoming assault on Burma. He flew back to Kunming and ordered the Liberators of the 308th Bomb Group to hit at the Yellow River bridges. He sent a few P-51s with Tex Hill to Chengtu, both to escort the heavy bombers and to strike at river and highway bridges. On April 25 twenty-seven B-24s, led by Lieutenant Colonel James Averill and escorted by ten Mustangs, hit rail and highway bridges north of Chenghsien. The next day twenty-four Liberators, escorted by ten P-51s and twelve of the first P-47 Thunderbolts to arrive in China, struck at Chungmow.

By this time the medium bombers and fighters of the headquarters squadron of the CACW had arrived. The 2nd Bombardment Squadron was commanded by Colonel Winslow Morse and four squadrons of the 3rd Fighter Group were under the command of Colonel Alan Bennett.

The Japanese—aided by light and medium tanks and dive bombers—had begun moving south and west on April 17 and 19. On May 3 the B-25s scored direct hits on the Yellow River bridges earlier damaged by the B-24s. The Japanese apparently had not expected much opposition from the air and the fighters and medium bombers were able to strafe Japanese troops on the major highways in daylight, causing much damage. The B-24s of the 308th were used for missions for which they were never designed as they flew strafing sorties against cavalry and armored forces. The B-24 gunners in turrets and waist guns sprayed the enemy with .50-caliber machine-gun fire.

The CACW—originally scheduled to stay in the Chengtu area for a month —stayed on through June and never did move back south. The Japanese began to rebuild the railroad north of Sinyang, which had been breached by Fourteenth bombs. A massive battle was being waged in the Ichang area of the Yangtze River and the CACW was soon called upon to deliver air support to the Chinese armies there. In June more fighters from the 26th Squadron arrived at Liangshan to help out. They bagged twenty-two enemy locomotives on their first strafing mission.

By the end of May the Japanese ground offensive was fully under way south of the Yangtze. The Chinese became confused by the size of the offensive and did not realize that Changsha was the main objective until it was too late to defend it.

In the west, the mission of Y Force was to drive down the Burma Road, taking Tengchung, Lungling, Mengshih, and Pingka, and eventually to meet with the other attacking forces in Burma. The mission of the 69th Wing was to give tactical support to the attackers, isolate the battlefields, and provide air supply. Final word on the selection of targets was to be given by Brigadier General Frank Dorn, commander of Y Force, from his headquarters at Paoshan. A forward echelon of the 69th Wing was set up May 2, at a new field near Yunnanyi, with Major A. B. Black in command. Air support was to be given by the 22nd Bomb Squadron of medium bombers and the 25th Fighter Squadron. The 27th Troop Carrier Squadron—recently arrived from India—was attached to the 69th Wing for air-dropping supplies. The 308th Bomb Group from Kunming was being called upon to help hit targets with the heavy bombers. They would all do what they could to help the ground forces until August, when the combined Chinese and Americans would take the town of Myitkyina.

Twenty-two

In June Stilwell suddenly came out of his jungle headquarters and flew to Chungking to confer on what he finally perceived to be an emergency in China. On June 6, on his way back, he stopped off at the Fourteenth Air Force headquarters in Kunming and announced he would spend thirty minutes discussing the east China base problems with Chennault. Chennault appealed to Stilwell to boost the Fourteenth Hump tonnage to 11,000 tons a month, to drastically help increase the land supply route from Yunnan to the east China bases, and to authorize one B-29 mission to Hankow, the key to Japan's supply line in east China. Stilwell stated that nothing could halt the Japanese drive in east China and he refused to order the mobilization of forces available in the CBI to meet the threat. He did increase the Hump tonnage allotment to the Fourteenth to 10,000 tons and agreed to assign the 7th Bomb Group in India to flying the gas to east China. Chennault said later that Stilwell refused to do anything about strengthening the ground link to east China—without which the Hump tonnage increase meant little.[1]

Stilwell actually cut down on the efficiency of the ground supply route, Chennault later said, by insisting the Y Force get a priority on alcohol fuel. Instead of authorizing Brigadier General K. B. Wolfe, commander of Matterhorn in Calcutta, to fly a mission to flatten Hankow, Stilwell forwarded Chennault's request to the Joint Chiefs of Staff, who did nothing. Chennault appealed directly to General Arnold, who replied that he would not authorize any B-29 mission to a target that could be reached by B-24s. (Later, however, Arnold authorized the first B-29 mission in the Far East to Bangkok, which had been bombed by B-24s of the RAF, the Tenth Air Force in India, and the B-24s of the Fourteenth.)

On June 8, three months after Chennault's strong warning of the massive Japanese offensive, Stilwell finally declared an emergency in east China.

Changsha fell to the Japanese a few days later, on June 18, which touched off a wave of panic in Chungking.

Tex Hill kept his fighters at Hengyang—just south of Changsha—as long as he could to get in some last-minute strafing raids against Japanese troops. But he was forced to pull out on June 26 as the armored columns swept up to Hengyang—though not in time to keep the Americans from blowing up the base. The fighters retired to Lingling, a hundred miles to the south.

Expecting the B-29s to start flying from China any day, Chennault had sent two hundred fighters to be based at the fields around Chengtu—Fenghuanshan, Shwangliu, Pengchiachiang, and Kwanghan. The Generalissimo consented to improve a number of other China bases to receive the Superforts—the fields at Chengkung and Luliang near Kunming, Kweilin and Liuchow in Kwangsi Province, and Hsincheng and Suichwan in Kiangsi Province.

The B-29s flew their first combat mission in the CBI the morning of June 5 from their home base at Calcutta. The XX Bomber Command had been set up with General Wolfe as its head. The target was the Makasan railway shops at Bangkok—a 2,000-mile round-trip mission. A total of a hundred and twelve B-29s were assigned to the flight, leaving from a number of bases in India. One bomber, commanded by Major John B. Keller, crashed on takeoff at Chakulia, killing all the crew except one man. Fourteen other Superforts were forced to abort for a variety of mechanical reasons and several more failed to reach the target. The weather was cloudy and the planes bombed from 25,000 feet. Much of the bombing was by radar—the first time for many of the bombardiers—and the results were spotty. The antiaircraft fire, though heavy, was inaccurate at that altitude and only a handful of enemy fighters came up to intercept.

The monsoon was just starting and the weather proved more of an obstacle than the enemy. The crew parachuted out of one B-29 heading for Kunming and were brought in later by the Chinese. One crash-landed at Dum-Dum Airfield and twelve others landed at the wrong bases. Two planes ditched in the Bay of Bengal and nine crewmen were rescued from one. The other ditched in rough water and the pilot and radio operator were killed on impact. Ten other crewmen took to rafts and the next day picked up two more men who had spent the night floating in the water. All were finally rescued.

The planes were still returning to their India bases when General Wolfe received an urgent wire from General Arnold that a flight of B-29s was urgently needed to hit the Japanese homeland in order to take some of the pressure off Chennault's eastern bases. Apparently Chennault's appeal had finally reached other than deaf ears.

Wolfe said he could put fifty B-29s over a Japan target by June 15 if he could stockpile enough gas at Chengtu. Arnold wanted more planes than that for the first raid on the Japanese homeland and Wolfe finally said he could do it if he stepped up the Hump traffic and cut down on the gas allotment for the 312th Fighter Wing, which infuriated Chennault. The theory all along on the XX Bomber Command was that it would be self-supporting, that it would fly its own supplies in from Calcutta for each raid. Like so many other plans made in the Pentagon, it did not work out in practice in China. The XX soon discovered that the B-29 was not as good at carrying gas as it was at carrying bombs, which were easier to load than gasoline. It soon turned out that the XX was depending upon the old workhorse C-46s of the ATC, which cut into the tonnage allocated to the Fourteenth.

The P-47 Thunderbolts that had been sent to Chennault to help defend Chengtu turned out to consume 50 percent more gas than did the P-51 Mustangs—another drain on Chennault's forces.

Staging of the B-29s from Calcutta to the forward areas of Chengtu and other fields began on June 13 for the big raid on Japan. Wolfe sent ninety-two Superforts to China. Only seventy-nine arrived. One was lost en route and the rest turned back for mechanical reasons. Yawata—home of the Imperial Iron and Steel Works—was the designated target. The B-29s arrived in China battle-loaded with bombs and ammunition. All they needed was to be refueled. Bombay tanks had been installed for the long haul. To be along on the first major bombing raid of the war on Japan, every VIP and correspondent who could hitched a ride on the Superforts. There were more staff and general air officers in Chengtu than in Calcutta by the time the mission left. Takeoff time was set for 4:30 P.M. in order to get the planes over the target in darkness. Of the seventy-five B-29s that were ordered off, sixty-eight took to the air. One crashed on takeoff, but the crew was not injured.

Chennault, whose losses over the years had been to combat, was appalled at the waste of men and equipment from noncombat causes.

At eleven thirty-eight that night the first plane released its bomb load over the target. Bombing was ordered for between 8,000 and 10,000 feet for the first group and from 14,000 to 18,000 feet for the second group. The Japanese had been alerted to the mission and the city of Yawata was completely blacked out. The first bombs dropped set fires, which also helped to obscure the target. Only fifteen bombardiers dropped their bombs visually, the rest bombed by radar—never an accurate system from any altitude. While the correspondents wrote glowing accounts of the big air battles when they returned, the Air Force crews reported little activity. Only sixteen enemy fighters were sighted and only a few fired at the bombers—with no damage. The antiaircraft fire was light and also did no damage. One plane had crashed on the way back and killed the crew, six others had jettisoned their bomb loads because of mechanical difficulties, and the only combat loss was from a plane that set down at Neisiang, a Chinese field near the Japanese lines. The enemy fighter planes strafed the plane and destroyed it, wounding two of the crew.

The XX had lost four planes and fifty-five men with not much enemy activity. In addition, the photo recon missions flown over Yawata by the Fourteenth on June 18 showed that very little damage had been done by the Superforts. Only one hit was made on a powerhouse and some industrial areas. The steel industry, the primary target, was untouched.[2]

Arnold—aware of the public relations value of the China-based B-29 missions on the Japanese homeland—wired Wolfe two days after the Yawata mission that it was "essential" that he keep up the pressure against Japan.[3]

Arnold was personally commander of the B-29s and it was his first combat command. In World War I he had been assigned to a desk in Washington in spite of strenuous efforts to get overseas. Now, in World War II, he had seen younger officers in his Air Force go on to glory as combat commanders. The XX was formed with a charter on April 10, 1944, with terms that stated: "A strategic Army Air Force, designated the Twentieth, was to be established, to operate directly under the Joint Chiefs of Staff, with the Commanding General, AAF (Arnold) as executive agent to implement their directives for the employment of VLR bombers."

In addition, Arnold had direct communication with VLR commanders in the field "advising appropriate theater commanders of communications thus exchanged."[4]

In his directive to Wolfe, Arnold stressed that objectives of the upcoming raid were to be a major daylight attack on Anshan in Manchuria, and a strike against Palembang in Sumatra from Ceylon. Wolfe answered that he only had 5,000 gallons of gas at Chengtu on June 21 and that he could not make the Anshan mission until August 10. Arnold could not wait that long and on June 27 ordered Wolfe to attack Anshan with a hundred B-29s between July 20 and 30. In the meantime he wanted a fifteen-plane raid against Japan between July 1 and 10. He urged Wolfe to step up the C-46 Hump run and his own B-29 tanker capacity. He had shown no such concern over Chennault's supplies in the past.

Wolfe did not think Arnold had a firm grasp of the problems of getting supplies into China and, in order to fulfill Arnold's planned missions, he asked for a flat guarantee of ATC Hump tonnage. Then he set up the Anshan mission for fifty B-29s, not the hundred that Arnold had asked for. Wolfe was suddenly ordered to Washington to take over an "important command assignment" and he left two days later. This left Brigadier General LaVerne Saunders in charge, a man Arnold obviously thought would follow his orders to the letter.

The change in command had no effect on the July missions because twenty-four B-29s had left for Chengtu and Kwanghan in China and eighteen of these took off on July 7. Eleven planes bombed Sasebo in Japan and individual B-29s hit at Omuta and Tobata. Two others with mechanical trouble turned back—one of them attempting to bomb Hankow but missing by twenty miles. The antiaircraft fire over the Japanese targets was light and only eight enemy fighters attacked the planes, causing only minor damage. All twenty-four planes returned to India.

Saunders would have much preferred a night raid on Anshan but, remembering what had happened to his predecessor, agreed to Arnold's demand for a hundred-plane daylight precision attack in July. The ATC did its best and managed a banner month in July for gas. By July 26, a hundred and six B-29s had landed at Chinese forward bases. The primary target was the Showa Steel Works at Anshan. The monsoon was on in earnest and D day for the mission was moved up to July 29. The heavy rain mired the field at Kwanghan and the 444th Group was unable to take off, but the other three groups managed to get seventy-two planes up. Of that force, sixty B-29s managed to get over Anshan. The planes went in on a clear day at 25,000 feet, but the first wave dropped its bombs on a by-products plant just off the aiming point and the smoke from that obscured the main target. The flak was heavy but did not cause much damage to the heavy bombers—probably because the 200-mph speed on the bombing run made it difficult for enemy gunners to judge properly. Enemy fighters did no damage over the target area and the only combat loss was to a B-29 that was jumped by enemy fighters over China on the way back, eight of the crew bailed out over China and were brought back to Chengtu by Chinese guerrillas a month later. Comparison of strike photos taken at the time and Fourteenth photos taken on August 4 indicated that considerable damage had been done to Anshan.

Chennault never subscribed to the use of B-29s in China and often battled with the XX for gas and other supplies.

"My pleas," he wrote, "were to hit targets affecting shipping, where the Japanese were already on the verge of a critical shortage, rather than the steel and coke plants the Washington bosses fancied. Inroads on steel production might not have been seriously felt for as long as two years."

He was backed up after the war by a study done by the U.S. Strategic Bombing Survey, which concluded that the "aviation gasolene and supplies used by the B-29s might have been more profitably allocated to an expansion of the tactical and anti-shipping operations of the 14th Air Force." That is exactly what Chennault had been advocating for the previous year, but neither Arnold, Marshall, nor Stilwell agreed.

As approved by the Quadrant Conference in Quebec in August 1943, several pipelines were being constructed: one into the Assam Valley in India from Calcutta and another six-inch thin-walled pipeline from Ledo in India along the route of the Ledo Road into northern Burma. The pipe was transportable by air and had been dropped to labor battalions building the road. Two pipelines were to be extended into China: one carrying aviation gasoline and the other fuel for trucks. Construction had begun in November 1943 but it was to be a long time before the fuel reached China.

Stilwell's troops reached Myitkyina on May 17, and correspondents with him spread the news that the theater commander had achieved a great victory. But after seizing the airstrip west of the town Stilwell's forces failed to take the town itself. The failure was blamed on exhaustion of his troops, inexperience, low morale, and the failure to properly coordinate reinforcements by air. Whatever the reasons, the enemy, now forewarned, was able to dig in and the war settled down to a long siege.[5] During this time—which lasted almost three months—air support for Stilwell was delivered by the Tenth Air Force.

When Stilwell, the Chinese, British, and other American forces finally succeeded in retaking Myitkyina in August, elements of the Fourteenth Air Force had also been involved. Feeling his troops needed a rest after the long siege, Stilwell prepared to establish a defensive position along the Taungni–Kazu line, about twenty miles south of the town of Mogaung in north Burma. The decision to halt there was a disappointment to the Generalissimo. Earlier in the spring he had been persuaded to commit his 50,000-man Y Force under General Dorn to the Burma campaign. Stilwell had expected to take Myitkyina without much opposition and Chiang had counted on connecting up with his other Chinese X Force troops advancing along the Ledo Road. Already fed up with Stilwell, he decided to halt his Y Force when he discovered Stilwell had ceased to advance. As a result, a stalemate began which was to last until October.

In east China, meanwhile, Chennault had his hands full. Long before Myitkyina was besieged by Stilwell, the Japanese Army was well on its way to taking the Hengyang–Kweilin–Nanning line of airfields.

Chennault had finally got his five-hundred-plane air force, but not in time to conduct offensive air tactics. Because of the huge Japanese offensive, he found himself almost totally committed to defensive action. In addition to the forces tied down along the Salween front, much of his air force in China had to be used to defend the B-29 bases at Chengtu.

For support of the Chinese armies in the Hengyang–Kweilin area he had the veteran AVG and CATC pilots Casey Vincent and Tex Hill to keep his fighters flying. And he had the B-24s of the 308th Bomb Group, the B-25s of the 11th and 491st Bomb Squadrons, and the planes of the 118th Tactical Recon Squadron. As elements of the CACW, the 5th Fighter Group with P-40s and the 3rd and 4th Bomb Squadrons with the B-25s were also there.

Casey Vincent became a brigadier general on June 23, making him the second youngest general in the U. S. Army, but despite his age he was an old man by combat experience. All of the above units—as well as the 322nd Troop Carrier Squadron and the 21st Photo Squadron—were assigned to Vincent as a special task force. Chennault issued him orders and his priorities were: first, enemy aircraft; second, shipping on rivers and lakes in the Hankow region; and third, troops, trains, camps, motor vehicles, bridges, and river crossings. Strikes against any other types of targets—however inviting—were forbidden because of gas shortages.[6]

So the East China Task Force began to buckle down for the final defense of the forward bases.

Twenty-three

Casey Vincent's job in east China was an almost impossible one. Lifting the morale of the Chinese ground armies by air support was about all he could do in the long run. He sent his planes out every day to bomb and strafe Japanese troops, but it was hopeless. The weather was miserable and his P-51s had to strafe and bomb beneath hundred-foot ceilings. The planes flew so many sorties per day that armorers rushed out and hung new loads of fragmentation and demolition bombs on the wing racks as soon as the Mustangs landed. Pilots had just enough time to run to the alert shack and report on the last mission before they were briefed on the next run and were back in the cockpits.

Vincent wrote on June 20:

"Things really took a turn for the worse today. The Japanese are darn close to Hengyang. I am evacuating that base tomorrow. Demolition will follow soon after. I had to send George McMillan word to get ready also. I'm moving him to Kanchow soon—then to here. God, I will hate to evacuate this place! I can't get any support from the people at the 14th Air Force Headquarters. Either they don't know how serious the situation is—or they don't care. My request for six transports was refused with a very nasty wire. I sent one back saying if they couldn't trust my decisions, they could relieve me—and I meant it! We are out of touch with our liaison teams in the field—no information for the last twelve hours. Apparently, the Chinese may try to make a stand at Hengyang. As for us, we'll 'fire and fall back!' "[1]

Changsha had fallen to the Japanese troops two days earlier. Hengyang was vitally important to the Japanese as well as to the Chinese and Americans, for the city controlled the main lines of communication leading from Hankow to Nanning. Its position was exceptionally strong and it was thought that the well-staffed Chinese garrison there might be able to halt the Japanese drive. If they did, it would be an important morale factor to the

Chinese. If the city fell, the southern half of the Hankow–Hanoi axis would be doomed.

During the first week in July the Fourteenth, performing superbly, staggered the Japanese despite a major effort by their Air Force to defend the Japanese Army lines of communication. There was some indication that the Japanese were preparing to withdraw from Hengyang and the lines of civilians seeking to escape to the south paused in their flight; some of them even turned back toward Hengyang. But the Fourteenth had used up virtually all its fuel at the forward bases. The prospects for holding Hengyang appeared bleak.

In mid-June Chennault received some much-needed help from the States in the form of radar-equipped B-24s that were capable of bombing Japanese shipping from an altitude as low as a hundred feet above the surface of the sea. In a letter to Chennault, General Arnold had said a few months earlier:

"The project of 14 LAB [low-altitude bombardment] equipped B-24 aircraft is progressing according to schedule and should depart here before 15 April 1944. As you probably know, the low altitude bombsight has paid dividends . . . on shipping attacks. Your LAB equipment will be considerably more flexible because of a slight modification which will enable you to do area bombing in darkness or above clouds up to 15,000 feet. While this is not the primary function of the equipment, and it is not nearly so accurate at medium as at low altitudes, you may be able to accomplish something with it in that respect, if you insist upon a fine state of training for the crews and select proper targets."[2]

In one of the most secret operations of the war, a group of B-24s had been separated from the heavy bombardment training command in the American West in the early spring of 1944 and sent for special training to Langley Field, Virginia. There the pilots and bombardiers—in specially equipped Liberators with the Plexiglas noses completely blacked out—were taught to bomb "blind" at targets anchored in the Potomac River at a hundred-foot altitude.

The Air Force had discovered how to utilize the highly successful Norden bombsight tied in with a small auxiliary radarscope in the nose of each bomber. This small scope—working off a large search radarscope in the waist of the plane—substituted radar traces on a screen for the cross hairs of the Norden sight. The training aimed at making these crews adept at hidding Japanese shipping in the South China Sea and in the Strait of Formosa by attacking at night. The Japanese knew the U. S. Navy had radar on its ships but had no idea bombers could use it to bomb in almost total darkness. Had Chennault received the full extent of gasoline and supplies he needed in east China, the special Liberators could have done considerably more hurt to the enemy than they did. As it was, these Liberators, operating out of Kweilin in June, were averaging 900 tons of enemy shipping sunk per mission. Chennault described their operations:

"Their record of getting the most results from the least supplies was fantastically good. During a four month period, they sank a ton of Japanese shipping for every 2½ pounds of bombs dropped and every two gallons of gas their planes burned. The first week in July, gas reserved in the east fell so low I had to order these B-24s back to Kunming and stop anti-shipping operations just when the pay-off promised to reach new peaks."[3]

The Japanese were truly shocked by the appearance of the radar-equipped planes in June. Unable to believe the Americans had such a weapon, the Japanese Navy blacked out its fighting ships in darkness and simply assumed the American fliers could not see them. A lone B-24 of the 425th Bomb Squadron, 308th Bomb Group, commanded by pilot Jay E. Levan and operating out of the forward base at Liuchow, encountered a huge radar "blip" on the screen of the search radar. Unsure of what it was, the crew made a run on the target in total darkness. The bombardier, John D. Shytle, dropped two 1,000-pound bombs with delayed fuses and the bombs hit just below the waterline of what turned out to be a *Nagano*-class heavy cruiser. At the explosions, the Japanese turned on their lights and opened up with an awesome array of firepower. The B-24 made two more attack runs at low altitude, dropping two more bombs. The huge cruiser began to burn while the Liberator circled out a distance of several miles. After talking it over, the crew decided to make one more run to try to sink the cruiser, but while they were getting ready for the final attack the huge naval vessel suddenly capsized and sank—ending one of the most epic feats of the war.

On June 20, Henry Wallace, Vice President of the United States, arrived in Chungking as a special emissary of President Roosevelt. Wallace wanted to find out what was going on in east China. Brigadier General Benjamin Ferris, Stilwell's vice chief of staff, met him, along with Chennault. Suspecting Stilwell would try to get to Wallace first with his version of the feud, Chennault beat him to the gun by assigning First Lieutenant Joe Alsop—who had known Wallace both professionally and socially in Washington—to him as an "air aide." It worked. Stilwell had planned to have Wallace met by an itinerary committee composed of Ferris and John P. Davies, his political adviser. Ferris later wrote Stilwell a report that indicated what the State Department wanted to pass on to Wallace. The suggestions from the State Department referred several times to the desirability of the Communist and Nationalist forces fighting together against the Japanese, instead of against each other. Also—to give an indication of State Department thinking in June 1944—the need for better Sino-Soviet understanding was stressed.[4]

During the next few days Wallace was involved in meetings in Chungking with the Generalissimo and with Chennault's people in Kunming.

Ferris and John Service (who was with the State Department in Chungking as political adviser to Ferris) were allowed to give their views on sending an observer group to the Chinese Communists. Headquarters of the CBI was not invited to attend these discussions and Wallace did not try to obtain Stilwell's views on any subject.[5]

Wallace's party flew on to east China, where they met with Casey Vincent —fighting desperately to hold off the Japanese ground attack. Vincent, on June 27, wrote in his diary:

"It certainly felt odd for me, a young squirt of a Brigadier General, to be at the head of the table with the Vice President of the United States sitting on my right! Others at the head table were Ambassador T. V. Soong, John Carter Vincent, John Davies, Brigadier General Richard Lindsey, Art Ringwalt (local U.S. Consul), and Colonel Bob Pugh. Chinese Generals Pai Chung Shih and Chang Fah Kwei met the Vice President later in my office. Mr. Wallace, like me, tried to pin them down, but they wouldn't be pinned. I gave the Vice President the unvarnished truth—that, barring a miracle, the Japanese will have all of east China by July 15! I saw the Vice President off for Chengtu in the afternoon."[6]

After weighing the comments by the Generalissimo and Alsop on Stilwell, Wallace decided to recommend that he be recalled. He later said his first impulse was to replace Stilwell with Chennault, but Alsop convinced him that neither Marshall nor Arnold would approve and that Chennault could not leave China—where he was needed. Wallace finally told Roosevelt he felt Stilwell was unsuited to his post and recommended the appointment of another general officer of the highest merit who could win the Generalissimo's confidence. Wallace also told the President that he should take immediate steps to prevent the deterioration of the situation in east China or be prepared to accept the loss of China as a base from which to launch or support U.S. operations in the Pacific.[7]

He recommended that a joint American-Chinese guerrilla offensive be launched in east China to avert the loss of Chennault's bases. He said the military situation in east China was not hopeless and that the joint venture might even improve U.S. relations with China.

In the meantime, General Marshall—in London for a meeting of the Combined Chiefs of Staff—was told by General Sir Alan Brooke, Chief of the Imperial General Staff, that Stilwell would have to be relieved as Mountbatten's deputy because he did not get along with Mountbatten's commanders in chief or with the British in Burma. Stilwell's personality was still his chief handicap.

Marshall, stubborn to the end, had no intention of letting his old friend be recalled. As Army Chief of Staff, he swung considerable weight with the Joint Chiefs. He told them that Chennault's air offensive in China and the huge ATC airlift he said was supporting it were a waste of the nation's resources. He then added that the Allies had been handicapped in Europe— in the Rome breakthrough—because air transports and crews were tied up trying to aid Chennault in his efforts to stop eight Japanese divisions by tactical air. He then prevailed upon the Chiefs to study the question of sending Stilwell up to the China theater.[8]

Weighing the talk by Brooke and knowing of the recommendations by Wallace to have Stilwell recalled, Marshall then asked Stilwell for comments on the possibility of being named to command the China forces. He said that the pressure was on to increase Hump tonnage to Chennault and asked what Stilwell thought of transferring his principal efforts to "the rehabilitation and, in effect, the direction of the leadership of the Chinese forces in China proper."[9] It was somewhat too late to ask.

Stilwell was not enthusiastic about the idea. Marshall intended to promote him to a four-star general if he chose the command but did not tell him, lest it influence his decision.

Stilwell came up with a number of reasons why he would have difficulty in giving up his command:

"It is a difficult matter to find a man to command U.S., British and Chinese units acceptably," he wrote Marshall. "Supposing a steady, seasoned senior man can be found for this job, and I go to China. The G-Mo is scared, but he is still driving from the backseat, both on the Salween and Hunan. If the President were to send him a very stiff message, emphasizing our investment and interest in China, and also the serious pass to which China has come due to neglect of the Army, and insisting that desperate cases require desperate remedies, the G-Mo might be forced to give me a command job. I believe the Chinese Army would accept me . . . without complete authority over the Army, I would not attempt the job. . . . The communists should also participate in Shansi, but unless the G-Mo makes an agreement with them, they won't. Two years ago they offered to fight with me. They might listen now. . . ."

Marshall and the Joint Chiefs then tried to persuade the President to convince the Generalissimo to accept Stilwell as his field commander and Roosevelt sent such a message to Chiang on July 6. Chiang, neither liking nor wanting Stilwell, agreed in principle at first but brought up the fact that Chinese troops were not commanded in the same manner as foreign troops and that such a move would cause "misunderstanding and confusion." He asked for an influential personal representative who enjoyed Roosevelt's complete confidence to be dispatched to Chungking to be between himself and Stilwell "to enhance the cooperation between China and America."[10]

In east China the Japanese intensified their attacks along a wide front. In mid-June American Marines had successfully landed on Saipan with massive casualties, and construction had begun on airstrips for B-29s that were now within reach of the Japanese homeland.

Casey Vincent finally ran out of gas. During the second week of July no resupply came in from western bases. Chennault was desperately trying to get allocations of emergency gas from Stilwell but was getting no reply to his

messages. On July 12 the 491st Bomb Squadron of the CACW, fearful of
being overrun by the enemy, withdrew on its emergency gas and temporarily
left Liuchow for the Salween front. Air operations were drastically cut after
the B-25s left, and between the seventeenth and the twenty-fourth of July the
68th Composite Wing was practically grounded.

On August 8, Hengyang fell. A long-anticipated Japanese drive from Canton north along the Canton–Hankow Railway suddenly turned west—from
where it had been heading for Hengyang—and made for the American base
at Liuchow. A short time later the northern force of Japanese troops came
down the railroad toward Kweilin. It was obvious to Chennault that in only
a few weeks east China would be completely isolated. The air warning system—so painfully built up in earlier years—had collapsed, with the result
that both airstrips at Liuchow and Kweilin were badly exposed to the enemy.

Casey Vincent was thrown into the defense now of Liuchow. If his job
seemed hopeless it was not because he and Chennault had not tried. His
planes of the forward echelon, from May 26 through August 1, had flown
5,287 sorties, over 4,000 of them by fighter aircraft. A total of 1,164 tons of
bombs had been dropped, and more than a million rounds of ammunition
had been expended, chiefly in strafing attacks. Out of an overall strength of
about a hundred and fifty aircraft, forty-three had been lost. It was estimated
by Chennault that his task force had accounted for 595 enemy trucks, 14
bridges, approximately 13,000 enemy casualties, 114 Japanese aircraft, and
more than 1,000 small boats.

After the fall of Hengyang, there was a move on the part of one of the
Chinese Army commanders, Marshal Li Chi-shen, to send a message to the
Americans that he wanted to defect from Chiang's command. In effect he
wanted—with the support of the provinces of Kwangtung, Kwangsi, Hunan,
Fukien, Anhwei, Szechwan, Yunnan, and Sikang—to set up his own govern-
ment and he demanded the resignation of Chiang Kai-shek.

Stilwell's reaction—considering his hatred of Chiang—was predictable.

"Hooray for crime!" he wrote in his diary. "Lucky I prepared the ground
months ago."

He sent orders to General Timberman: "Our policy is to lay off the internal affairs of China, but we now have a big stake in this business and must
keep ourselves informed. Listen to any proposition that may be made but do
not make any commitments nor even express any opinion. Just say you will
forward any messages proposed."[11]

The American Embassy in Chungking kept a discreet silence and Ambassador Gauss told State Department personnel at Kweilin to deal with Chinese simply as "local" authorities. It was suddenly easy to see why the
Generalissimo had been loath to send arms to Marshal Li Chi-shen.

John Service was in Yenan with Colonel Dave Barrett's military observers,
code-named the Dixie Mission, to study the Chinese Communists. He made
discreet inquiries as to whether the Chinese Communists were in with Mar-

shal Li. He found that they were neither in with him nor knew anything about the attempted coup. He also decided that the northern Nationalist war commanders were solidly behind the Generalissimo.

Chennault—trying to find any way possible of keeping the Japanese from taking the last east China bases—was in favor of sending arms quickly to General Hsueh Yueh, commander of the IX War Area, who had been fighting fiercely to hold back the Japanese in the Kweilin region. He knew Hsueh was not in favor with the Generalissimo but at the moment didn't care what was going on politically. He was in danger of losing Kweilin and Liuchow—his biggest and best forward bases. He wired Hearn:

"I would be willing to contribute one thousand tons my tonnage for bringing light machine guns, grenades, demolitions and so forth as would contribute to the effectiveness of Gen. Hsueh Yueh's army. I would not be interested in turning this over to the Minister of War because the chances are great that it would never reach Hsueh Yueh whom [sic] I believe will fight if given the bare essentials. Suggest that you discuss this with Timberman [Brigadier General Thomas S. Timberman] who gave me the impression that he was convinced we must do something quick."

Hearn got in touch with Stilwell, who told Hearn:

"The time for halfway measures has passed. Any more free gifts such as this will surely delay the major decisions and play into the hands of the gang [Nationalists]. The cards have been put on the table and the answer has not been given. Until it is given, let them stew."

Hearn then radioed Chennault:

"Your proposition to divert one thousand tons from air force allotment to ground force supplies in order to retake Hengyang has been given the best treatment in this shop. We find after investigation that one thousand tons is sufficient to equip only one army with a very limited quantity of infantry weapons, a small amount of signal and demolition equipment with sufficient transportation to haul but one unit of fire. Stilwell also sent us his views on your proposal. He agrees, in order to restore the situation in the east, an operation is required. He is working on a proposition which might give this spot a real face lifting and is loath to commit himself to any definite line of action right now. Consequently we must hold off in making any proffers of help to the ground troops until things precipitate a bit more. Realizing the press of time, sorry had to hold up on this non-committal answer until heard from boss man."

Nothing was done to help the Chinese armies of General Hsueh, who was then within ten miles of the main Japanese force.

Chiang was insisting that if Stilwell was named the field commander the Chinese Communists could not be subject to Stilwell's authority unless they agreed to obey the administrative and military orders of the Chinese Nationalist Government; that Stilwell's title, function, and relationship to the Generalissimo be clearly defined; and that distribution and disposal of Lend-Lease material in China be placed under Chiang's control.

As for a personal representative of Roosevelt to deal with Chiang, the Joint Chiefs had at last settled upon Major General Patrick J. Hurley, who had a distinguished career in law, politics, and diplomacy. He had carried out a number of diplomatic missions for Roosevelt, all of them successful. His name was placed before the Generalissimo, who tentatively approved it along with the stipulation that there be "thorough preparation and mature consideration" before Stilwell was given command.

The President told Hurley his mission was to promote harmonious relations between Chiang and Stilwell and to facilitate Stilwell's exercise of command of the Chinese armies. Hurley was ordered to Chungking via Moscow to discuss Sino-Soviet relations first. While he was en route to Chungking the Operations Division of the War Department suggested that the CBI be divided into two geopolitical areas, China and India-Burma, and that Lend-Lease be removed from Stilwell's control. This was done partly to relieve Stilwell of the Lend-Lease problem and to free him for field command. On August 7, Stilwell was promoted to full general. On September 8, Hurley took up his role as negotiator.

Twenty-four

R oosevelt—having received Chennault's letters on the east China crisis and having talked to Wallace at length—turned to the Joint Chiefs of Staff for advice. He was told Stilwell was the only officer capable of stemming the tide in China. Realizing he had to do something rapidly, he sent the following message to Chiang Kai-shek on July 6. It had been prepared by the War Department and signed by Roosevelt.

"I think I am fully aware of your feelings regarding General Stilwell, nevertheless . . . I know of no other man who has the ability, the force and the determination to offset the disaster which now threatens China and our over-all plans for the conquest of Japan. I am promoting Stilwell to the rank of full General and I recommend for your most urgent consideration that you recall him from Burma and place him directly under you in command of all Chinese and American forces and that you charge him with full responsibility and authority for the coordination and direction of the operations required to stem the tide of the enemy's advances."[1]

Marshall informed Stilwell of the message sent to Chiang by the President and warned him to avoid giving further offense to the Generalissimo if he wanted to be left in command of the China theater.

In looking for a start on his new job, Stilwell went back into CBI headquarters files and dug out the Plan and Staff studies done by a group of officers—including Colonel Dean Rusk—as a basis for what he would present to the Generalissimo. The geography and contending forces had been worked out in the summer and were still applicable.

Stilwell and Hurley arrived in Chungking on September 6 to begin their talks with Chiang Kai-shek. Chiang's first points were that in the past Stilwell's work had been 100 percent military but under the new job his work would be 60 percent military and 40 percent political. Stilwell would receive his orders from Chiang through the National Military Council. If Stilwell wanted to use Communist troops, these troops would have to recognize the authority of the National Council as well.

All during this conference, at which T. V. Soong was also present, Stilwell received reports from field commanders of the collapse of Chinese forces in east China and of trouble on the Salween front. Hurley and Stilwell rejoined the conference on September 12 after preparing an agenda, which had been requested by Chiang. By September 13, Hurley had prepared an order for the Generalissimo that gave Stilwell sweeping powers—an authorization to reward and punish Chinese officers. He could appoint and relieve them, all in conformity with Chinese law, and could issue orders for the operations of both ground and air forces of the Republic of China. Notification of such authorization was to be sent to all Chinese commanders. Stilwell requested and was granted authority to reorganize the Chinese armies defeated in east China.

While the Chinese considered the issues presented, Stilwell went to east China to see what he could do. The President had told Chiang that Stilwell was to command both Nationalist and Communist forces. The War Department told Stilwell that it contemplated giving Lend-Lease material to a Chinese army that would include both Communist and Nationalist troops.[2] Stilwell wrote in his diary on September 12:

"Chiang Kai-shek agrees to appoint Joseph W. Stilwell and give him his 'full confidence.' Dickering proceeds. T.V. is back in the game. Hurley has agenda ready, so maybe we can get down to cases now. Papers again. Pat [Hurley] is in p.m. Rather discouraged—G-Mo very difficult, says he must control Lend-lease and that I have more real control in China than he has. Wants to dicker about powers for me. Thinking about a diagram to show my authority. Bad news from Timberman. Collapse. Decided to go to Kweilin and see about it."

In Kweilin, Stilwell found things collapsing. Chennault had joined his flight in Kunming and the two of them toured the base, which had grown to three bomber fields and a fighter strip. Chennault was sick that the huge base had to be abandoned. A description of the day appears in Casey Vincent's *Fire and Fall Back:*

"On the morning of 14 September, Generals Stilwell and Chennault came to Kweilin for a last conference with Casey and Chinese General Chang Fah Kwei. Stilwell approved the final decision—'Blow it and get out.' "

All but one or two trucks had pulled out in the dusk while the last planes were still loading cargo. Colonels, lieutenant colonels, and majors worked alongside junior officers and GIs of all grades, hoisting generators, tires, duffel bags, and other gear into the waiting planes. It was fully dark by the time the last load was aboard and airborne.

Only two planes were left on the flight line—Casey's B-25 and a C-47 transport for his staff and General Timberman.

Demolition began at midnight. A red glow in the sky behind the mountains to the east signaled the burning of a satellite field. Rolling rumbles came over the hills as the bombs "let go" on the distant runways.

The shacks and hostels at the Kweilin base were tucked away in the arroyos and clefts of the Kwangsi hills. Demolition crews had set up a barrel of gasoline in each building. With a helper holding a flashlight beam on the target, a sergeant would fire his carbine into the barrel. When enough gasoline had trickled through the holes to fill the room with fumes, the sergeant would fire again and the room would explode with a roaring flash. Flames rippled through thatched roofs and poured into adjacent rooms like racing water. One by one, the buildings went up until the whole field blazed.

Just before dawn demolition men began "blowing" the airstrips—leaving one temporarily for the two remaining planes to use.

As the gray light of morning crept over the hills, Casey Vincent and Tex Hill finished packing. They found they had a stock of six bottles of bourbon, so they took it along. Vincent stuffed a pillow slip into his bag. "My wife, Peggy, gave me that," he said, "and I'll be damned if I'll leave it for the Japanese." When they arrived at their B-25, Vincent took the pilot's seat. Tex crouched down behind him. Also aboard was *Time* correspondent Theodore H. ("Teddy") White.

As soon as the C-47 transport carrying General Timberman and the staff people was airborne, Vincent took off. It was 5:30 A.M. as he circled over the burning field and headed for Liuchow.

Colonel Waldo Kennerson and Major George Hightower remained behind with one demolition team and an oral directive from Vincent to "blow the last runway—make sure no American strays are left behind—then, get in your car and truck."

Chennault was later to write:

"Four days later, on September 17, after he was thoroughly convinced east China was hopelessly lost, Stilwell authorized air delivery of 500 tons of American arms and ammunition to the Chinese armies defending Kweilin. This was the first American aid to the Chinese armies in the east except for the few 75 mm shells and belts of .50 caliber machine gun ammunition the 14th dropped into Hengyang."

On the morning of September 15 Stilwell left for Chungking. In his diary he wrote:

"Off at 8:10 a.m. Chennault reports Chow Chih-jou [commander of the Chinese Air Force] is not cooperating, refused gas to United States planes from common stock. Maybe they are learning at last in the 14th Air Force. Chungking. G-Mo calling for me. Took Hurley down at 12:00, one and a half hours of crap and nonsense. Wants to withdraw from Lungling, the crazy little bastard! So either X Force attacks in one week or he pulls out. Usual cockeyed reasons and idiotic tactical and strategic conceptions. He is impossible."

This was in reference to Chiang's demand that, unless Stilwell get his X

Force Chinese troops moving from below Myitkyina to Bhamo within a week, he was going to withdraw his Y Force troops from Burma to the east bank of the Salween River.

The next day Stilwell reported the progress—or lack of it—in his diary:

"September 16. the G-mo insists on control of Lend-lease. Our stuff, that we are giving him. T.V. says we must remember the 'dignity' of a great nation, which would be 'affronted' if I controlled the distribution. Pat [Hurley] told him 'horsefeathers.' Remember, Dr. Soong, that is our property. We made it and we own it, and we can give it to whom we please. (We must not look, while the customer puts his hand in our cash register, for fear we will offend his 'dignity.') Pat said there were 130 million Americans whose dignity also entered the case, as well as the 'dignity' of their children and their children's children, who would have to pay the bill. Hooray for Pat! I am sunk. The Reds will get nothing. Only the G-mo's henchmen will be supplied, and my troops will suck the hind tit. 4 p.m. Plain talk with T. V. Soong, all about the situation. He is appalled at gap between our conception of field commander and the G-mo's. I proposed Chen Cheng for minister of war, Pai Chung-hsi as chief of staff. Gave T.V. the works in plain words. I do not want the God-awful job, but if I take it I must have full authority. Two hour bellyache."[3]

It is not surprising Chiang Kai-shek was annoyed with Stilwell. Naming his Minister of War and Chief of Staff was hardly what Marshall meant when he advised Stilwell not to offend the Generalissimo.

Falling back on his old custom of going over everyone's head to talk to the Army Chief of Staff, Stilwell appealed directly to Marshall—neglecting to send copies of his correspondence to either Hurley or Chiang. He reported his conversation with Chiang about the withdrawal of the Y Force from the Salween and said he was appalled at Chiang's actions. He intimated that the plan to withdraw the Y Force was intended to mean a withdrawal and an effort to sabotage the Burma campaign. He added that Chiang would "not listen to reason."

Stilwell's message reached Marshall in Quebec where he was attending the Octagon Conference with Roosevelt and Churchill. He repeated Stilwell's message to the Combined Chiefs of Staff on September 16 and drafted a message to be sent to Chiang over Roosevelt's signature.

After reading the last reports on the situation in China, my chiefs of staff and I are convinced that you are faced in the near future with the disaster I have feared. The men of your "Yoke" Forces crossing the Salween have fought with great courage and rendered invaluable assistance to the campaign in north Burma. But we feel that unless they are reinforced and supported with your every capacity, you cannot expect to reap any fruits from their sacrifices, which will be valueless unless they go on to assist in opening the Burma Road. Furthermore, any pause in your attack across the Salween or suggestion of withdrawal is exactly what the Jap has been striving to cause you to do by his operations in eastern China. He knows that if you continue to attack, cooperating with Mountbatten's coming offensive, the land line to China will be opened early in 1945 and the continued resistance of China and maintenance of your control will be assured. On the other hand, if you do not provide manpower for your divisions in north Burma, and if you fail to send reinforcements to the Salween forces and withdraw these armies, we will lose all chances of opening land communications with China and immediately jeopardize the air route over the Hump. For this you must yourself be prepared to accept the consequences and assume the personal responsiblity.

I have urged time and again in recent months that you take drastic action to resist the disaster which has been moving closer to China and to you. Now, when you have not yet placed General Stilwell in command of all forces in China, we are faced with loss of a critical area in east China with possible catastrophic consequences. The Japanese capture of Kweilin will place the Kunming air terminal under the menace of constant attack, reducing the Hump tonnage and possibly severing the air route.

Even though we are rolling the enemy back in defeat all over the world, this will not help the situation in China for a considerable time. The advance of our forces across the Pacific is swift. But this advance will be too late for China unless you act now and vigorously. Only drastic and immediate action on your part alone can be in time to preserve the fruits of your long years of struggle and the effort we have been able to make to support you. Otherwise, political and military considerations alike are going to be swallowed in military disaster. The Prime Minister and I have just decided in Quebec to press vigorously the operations to open the land line to China on the assumption that you would continue an unremitting attack from the Salween side. I am certain that the only thing you can now do in an attempt to prevent the Jap from achieving his objectives in China is to reinforce your Salween armies immediately and press their offensive, while at once placing General Stilwell in unrestricted command of all your forces. The action I am asking you to take will fortify us in our decision and in the continued efforts the United States proposes to take to maintain and increase our aid to you. This we are doing when we are fighting two other great campaigns in Europe and across the Pacific. I trust that your far-sighted vision, which has guided and inspired your people in this war, will realize the necessity for immediate action. In this message I have expressed my thoughts with complete frankness because it appears plainly evident to all of us here that all your and our efforts to save China are to be lost by further delays.

Roosevelt[4]

The message was sent—no one later was sure why—to Stilwell rather than Hurley. The original message was, in rough form, a typewritten draft proposal by the War Department with penciled changes in Marshall's handwriting. With it went a note to Stilwell saying that the President's note was "in effect an answer to your CFB 22638 of 15 September."[5]

Stilwell looked at the President's message and noted in his diary that it was "hot as a firecracker." He decided to deliver it himself. He knew exactly what he was doing. In his diary for that day he wrote: "Mark this day in red on the calendar of life. At long, at long last, FDR has finally spoken plain words and plenty of them, with a firecracker in every sentence. 'Get busy or else.' A hot firecracker. I handed this bundle of paprika to the Peanut and then sank back with a sigh. The harpoon hit the little bugger right in the solar plexus and went right through him. It was a clean hit, but beyond turning green and losing the power of speech, he did not bat an eye. He just said to me, 'I understand' and sat in silence, jiggling one foot. We are now a long way from the 'tribal chieftain' bawling out. Two long years lost, but at least FDR's eyes have been opened and he has thrown a good hefty punch. . . . I . . . came home. Pretty sight crossing the river: lights all on in Chungking."

Stilwell, understanding the Chinese and speaking the language, must have known he had caused the Generalissimo a great deal of loss of face. Hurley later wrote that he remembers the occasion vividly. He said Stilwell had shown him the message and Hurley said, upon reading it, that it appeared to be an ultimatum and that he suggested Stilwell let him paraphrase the message to the Generalissimo. Hurley also said that a tea-drinking ceremony was observed first, then Stilwell rose, said he had a message from the President for the Generalissimo, and gave it to General Chu Shih-ming to translate. This was in particularly bad taste because Chu was a powerful Chinese whom Stilwell considered a possible successor to Chiang.

Hurley, realizing this, quickly got up and took the message from General Chu and handed the Chinese portion of it to the Generalissimo—with the excuse that it would save time if the Generalissimo read it himself.

Chiang knew that Stilwell had intentionally engineered an attempt to humiliate him publicly. It took him a few days to contain his wrath. He thought Stilwell was not above having sent the message to himself just to humiliate him. Hurley later said the same thought occurred to him. T. V. Soong, to whom Stilwell had so harshly spoken his "plain talk" a few days before, asked Hurley pointedly if Stilwell had done just that. Hurley refused to ask Stilwell.[6]

Stilwell, apparently unable to understand that he had humiliated the ruler of a nation, suggested to Hurley on September 23 that he be sent to the Chinese Communists with proposals that they accept the authority of the Generalissimo and Stilwell's command of their forces in return for a promise to equip five divisions; and, second, that Chiang be given control of Lend-Lease material on the understanding that X and Y Forces in Burma enjoy first priority. Hurley—with this obviously conciliatory message in his hand—went to Chiang. He was told in no uncertain terms that Stilwell would have to go. Two days later Hurley received a message from Chiang Kai-shek, for transmission to President Roosevelt, formally requesting that Stilwell be recalled. Chiang said he was willing to place an American officer in command of the Chinese-American forces in China, but "I cannot confer this heavy responsibility upon General Stilwell, and will have to ask for his resignation as chief of staff of the China Theater and his relief from duty in this area."[7]

On October 5, Roosevelt asked Chiang to reconsider. The Generalissimo had no such intention. On October 9 he sent another message, through Hurley, to Roosevelt, charging that Stilwell had sacrificed east China for the sake of his campaign in Burma—a charge that Chennault had long made. On October 11, Hurley advised Roosevelt: "If you sustain Stilwell in this controversy, you will lose Chiang Kai-shek and possibly . . . China with him." The President replied next day with a request for Chiang's choice of a successor. The Generalissimo, Hurley replied, wanted Eisenhower, but since that was obviously not possible, he would take either Generals Alexander Patch, Albert Wedemeyer, or Walter Krueger.

Stilwell, knowing now he had enraged the Generalissimo and waiting for new developments, got into another dispute with Chennault. The previous May the Joint Chiefs had ordered Stilwell to begin accumulating gasoline for support of Pacific operations—with a target date of November 1944. Because Chennault needed all the gas he could get in the summer of 1944, not much was done about it, but in August the Joint Chiefs held Chennault's Hump tonnage at the 10,000-ton level in order that the CBI might begin building up the stockpile that had been ordered in May. It was agreed that if emergencies occurred Stilwell might allow gasoline to be taken from the stockpile. On September 27, Stilwell authorized Chennault—who was certainly having an emergency in east China—to borrow 1,000 tons from the stockpile. At the end of the month the CBI headquarters totaled up the gas and said Chennault had overdrawn the allotment by 2,400 tons. Headquarters arbitrarily decided to even the score by cutting Chennault's October allocation to 7,600 tons. Chennault protested vehemently. He was fighting to keep Liuchow from falling into enemy hands and had asked General Stratemeyer for the gas—which Stratemeyer had so authorized. Stilwell, unable to let it go without pulling rank, wired Chennault:

"Unauthorized use of theater stockpile reserves particularly when done by an officer of your rank set a poor example for junior officers and is prejudicial to proper military discipline. Your failure to make prompt report or bring matter to my attention has resulted in my making commitments in support of Pacific aid which are now embarrassing. Such procedure is not consonant with rank and position you hold."

The President's decision finally came. On October 18 he replied to the Generalissimo that Stilwell would at once be recalled. Stilwell wrote in his diary: "October 19, THE AXE FALLS. Radio from George Marshall. I am 'recalled.' Sultan in temporary command. Wedemeyer to command U.S. troops in China. CBI split. So FDR has quit. Everybody is horrified about Washington."

Everybody but the Fourteenth Air Force. In Kunming, Chennault was jubilant. His old enemy had been vanquished.

Major General Albert Wedemeyer was transferred from Mountbatten's staff and assigned to head the new China theater. Major General Daniel Sultan commanded the new India-Burma theater.

Chennault was later to write of Stilwell's departure:

"I was not sorry to see Stilwell go. . . . Stilwell's abrupt exit cleared the way for the first effective top level Sino-American military cooperation of the war. So marked was the change, that less than six months after Stilwell left, Wedemeyer and his Chief field commander, Maj. General Robert McClure, had forged a genuine Sino-American ground army team on a basis that Stilwell contended was impossible. . . . Stilwell always thought of himself as a field commander. He seemed most happy and effective when plying that trade. Stilwell was personally brave, enjoyed the rigors of field campaigning, and had the rare quality of being able to lead men under enemy fire. . . . This was an ideal temperament for a division commander, but hardly the viewpoint of a competent theater commander. There was considerable truth, along with the malice, in the oft-repeated description of Stilwell as 'The best four-star battalion commander in the Army.' "

Stilwell remained only forty-eight hours in the CBI after his recall. Profane and arrogant to the last, on October 20 he wrote in his diary: ". . . The Peanut offers me China's highest decoration. Told him to stick it up his ————."[8]

Before he left, he ordered the return to Washington of John Service, who had just returned with Dave Barrett from the Dixie Mission in Yenan, to argue successfully for opening relations with the Communists. He was angry at Hurley and wrote that he had been "Hurleyed out of China." He never admitted that his great and good friend Marshall might have been wrong in assigning him to the theater in the first place. Never, for the rest of his life, did he admit in the slightest that he might have been personally responsible for the failure of his mission to China. Never did he consider the China-Burma-India theater of war as an air operation. It may never have occurred to him that there was any significance in the fact that, when he was assigned to the CBI in May 1942, and after the defeat of Burma, U.S. air personnel in the CBI numbered 3,000 officers and men and the ground forces numbered a grand total of 94. When he was relieved, in October 1944, Air Force personnel in the theater had reached a total of 78,037 and the ground forces 24,995.[9]

General Marshall—who had ample reason to fear that Stilwell's acid tongue and bad temper would further hinder Chinese-American relations—had him flown home as quickly as possible. There he was told, in no uncertain terms, to keep his mouth shut. While the press made a hero of "Vinegar Joe" Stilwell, courageous Yankee general who had battled alone against the wily Orientals, the Administration and War Department knew when to keep him under wraps. There was no welcoming committee and the War Department kept him out of sight. Neither Marshall nor Stimson met him on his arrival.

He was subsequently made commander of the Army Ground Forces on January 23, 1945, and remained in that training post until June 23. He then took command of the Tenth Army on Okinawa—where he finished the war waiting to invade the Japanese homeland, while the B-29s of the Air Force he hated made that invasion unnecessary.

Twenty-five

With the departure of Stilwell and the arrival of General Wedemeyer, on October 31, 1944, Chennault began to hope that a solution to the defense of east China might be found. In his headquarters in Kunming, the arrival of clear fall weather and blue skies seemed an omen of good luck.

Roosevelt and the Joint Chiefs—learning a hard lesson from Stilwell's relations with the Generalissimo—had given Wedemeyer a new set of mission and roles. They were:

(a) Your mission with respect to Chinese forces is to advise and assist the Generalissimo in the conduct of military operations against the Japanese.

(b) Your primary mission as to U.S. Combat forces under your command is to carry out air operations from China. In addition you will continue to assist the Chinese air and ground forces in operations, training and in logistical support.

(c) You will not employ United States resources for suppression of civil strife except insofar as necessary to protect United States lives and property.[1]

The Joint Chiefs told him he was Commanding General, United States Forces, China Theater, and then they "authorized" him to accept the position of Chief of Staff to the Generalissimo. Wedemeyer and the Gimo quickly established an easy and pleasant personal relationship. Unlike Stilwell's acerbic personality, Wedemeyer's tact, his disarming personality, and his regard for amenities made his advice palatable to Chiang. Wedemeyer had the same relationship with Chennault.

One of the first things he did upon taking command was to notify the Combined Chiefs and the Supreme Commander, Southeast Asia, that a large part of the Chinese force fighting in Burma was urgently needed to fight the

Japanese in east China. Mountbatten protested, but the move was made by air in spite of his objections.

The transport planes moved two Chinese divisions, the New Sixth Army headquarters, a heavy mortar company, a signal company, and two portable surgical hospitals in what was called "Operation Grubworm." The whole operation was carried out by the ATC and Combat Cargo, temporarily attached to the Fourteenth Air Force, in less than a month. Chennault had tried to tell Stilwell—before the Ledo Road was begun—that Chinese armies could be moved by air but had been ignored. In the Grubworm, the ATC and air commando squadrons made 1,328 flights and hauled 25,095 Chinese soldiers, 396 American soldiers, 1,596 pack animals (horses and mules), 42 jeeps, 48 75-mm. howitzers, 48 4.2-mm. mortars and 48 antitank guns in what must be regarded as one of the major transport achievements of the war.[2]

When Wedemeyer and Chennault began to push for an offensive to seize the initiative in China in November 1944, the Fourteenth Air Force had a total personnel strength of 17,473 men, and there were 535 fighter planes, 109 medium bombers, and 47 heavy bombers (B-24s). The Hump tonnage for gasoline—which for two years Chennault had battled Stilwell to raise to 10,000 tons per month, and which seldom happened—rose dramatically from 14,792 tons that month to 23,888 by January 1945. By June the Hump tonnage had reached unprecedented totals of 55,386 tons and by July 71,042.

In November of 1944 the Fourteenth Air Force consisted of thirty-six combat squadrons, grouped under the 68th and 69th Composite Wings, the Chinese-American Composite Wing, and the 312th Fighter Wing. Chennault had stationed the 69th Wing—which was composed of 51st Fighter Group and the 341st Bomb Group (M)—in Kunming. Its mission was to defend the Hump route and southwest China. He had given the 68th Composite Wing —composed of the 23rd Fighter Group and the 118th Tactical Recon Squadron—the job of supporting Chinese ground forces along the Hankow–Canton railway and maintaining a counter area campaign. The Chinese-American Composite Wing—made up of the 3rd Fighter Group, the 5th Fighter Group, and the 1st Bomb Group (M)—was assigned the combat area of central China, the regions of the Yellow River and as far east as the Nanking-Shanghai area. The 312th Fighter Wing, made up of the 311th Fighter Group with three squadrons—once saddled with the defense of Chengtu by Stilwell—was now assigned to interdict the railways of north and east China. In order to help it do that, Chennault assigned the 409th Bomb Squadron (M) and later, B-24s of the 308th Bomb Group to bomb railroads.

Although the Fourteenth—with its beefed-up strength—looked good, it was reinforced at a time when the Japanese had taken just about all of east China.

Chennault had his last look at the big forward base at Liuchow on November 6:

"Luke Williamson flew me down to Liuchow early in November for a final look at the east. Heavy clouds blanketed the east and we slipped into Liuchow under an 800 foot ceiling in heavy rain. The Japanese were less than 50 miles away. It looked as though the weather might allow the Japanese the final triumph of catching our planes on the ground at Liuchow. On the night of November 7, Casey Vincent's men began putting the torch to our base at Liuchow. The next day, with the ceiling still sagging down below the surrounding peaks, the flag was hauled down, and the planes took off for the last time. The last plane off was a silver P-51 flown by Casey, replacing a sick fighter pilot who had to be evacuated by transport. Weather was so bad that three fighter planes spun in and crashed before they reached west China bases. That night the Japanese cut the railroad 30 miles to the west of Liuchow and three days later occupied the city."[3]

Not only had the Japanese moved south from Hankow to overrun the forward bases at Hengyang, Kweilin, Liuchow, and finally Nanning, but they had surrounded other advance fields at Suichwan, Kanchow, Namyung, and Kulong. To combat the advances and in hopes of holding the airfields east of the Japanese corridor, Chennault in November organized the East China Air Task Force. Under this plan, designated Strongpoint, he divided the 68th Composite. The 75th and 76th Fighter Squadrons remained west of the corridor, while the 74th Fighter Squadron and the 118th Tactical Reconnaissance Squadron were located east of it. These two squadrons were strengthened by a detachment of Liberators from the 308th Bomb Group, the 21st Photo Squadron, and a couple of transports. Though small, the task force was versatile and effective.

The first units of the new task force reached Suichwan on November 12 and the B-24s immediately began recon flights. The Fourteenth planned to drop 1,000 tons of supplies to General Hsueh, who was fighting the Japanese fiercely, near Suichwan, but the government in Chungking refused to let the supplies go to him because Chiang feared him as a political and military rival. Hsueh had no choice but to retreat and the Fourteenth gave him close air support as the battle progressed. Then the weather turned bad and no air support was possible. The Japanese took advantage of that and, on January 27, Suichwan was captured. Kanchow fell on February 7, and Kulong and Namyung were soon to fall. Strongpoint was over by mid-February, and the squadrons reported back to Kunming, but the operation was a valiant try, and all in all 747 sorties had been flown by the four fighter squadrons and 110 tons of bombs were dropped. Fighters of the task force shot down or destroyed on the ground three hundred and twelve enemy planes and lost no planes themselves. However, thirteen P-51s were shot down by ground fire or were lost to mechanical failure or weather. While the operation did not succeed in stopping the Japanese ground forces, it did manage to pin down the Japanese Air Force in east China.

In November the Japanese continued their drive and many in China thought this move was preparatory to taking Kweiyang and ultimately Kunming.

Wedemeyer did not think so. He did not think the Japanese intended to end the war in China by defeating Chiang Kai-shek's government in Chungking. Rather, he thought the Japanese were attempting to set up an inner zone of defense in east China as a buffer against future inroads by American forces in the Pacific. Such a zone would comprise the home islands of Japan, Formosa, Hainan Island, and a wide belt of the Chinese mainland running from Korea to Indochina. From that stronghold, he reasoned, the Japanese intended to put up a fight against American forces coming in from the sea and against Chennault's fighters and bombers operating from west China. He figured the Japanese would then try to control everything east of a line from Peking down through Hankow and to Nanning—essentially a railroad line— and to hold key railroads, airfields, waterways, and highways.

While Stilwell had given little more than lip service to Chennault's pleas for B-29 support in hitting the big Japanese supply bases in east China, Wedemeyer strongly endorsed the idea of an attack on Hankow. He communicated with Curtis LeMay, commanding general of the XX Bomber Command, and requested the B-29s run hundred-plane missions against Hankow. LeMay, who knew Wedemeyer commanded only in China and that the B-29s were headquartered in the India-Burma theater, questioned Wedemeyer's authority. Washington—acting on the Joint Chiefs' decision to allow theater commanders to divert B-29s from strategic to tactical operations should the occasion demand—upheld Wedemeyer's authority.

LeMay conferred with Wedemeyer at Chungking and with Chennault at Kunming and they worked out a coordinated strike. The Fourteenth Air Force would hit at Hankow-area airfields an hour after the big Superforts plastered Hankow itself. Targets for the B-29s were the extensive dock and storage area along the Yangtze River.

On December 18, LeMay got eighty-four planes armed with incendiary bombs over the target. There were some mix-ups in the plans, but much damage was done to the big city. Chennault said the raid "destroyed Hankow as a major base" and wrote:

"The December 18 attack of the Superforts was the first mass fire-bomb raid they attempted. LeMay was thoroughly impressed by the results of this weapon against an Asiatic city. When he moved on to command the entire B-29 attack on Japan from the Marianas, LeMay switched from high-altitude daylight attacks with high explosives to the devastating mass fire-bomb night raids that burned the guts out of Japan. . . ."[4]

Chennault's plans were to keep the enemy air force pinned down in east China. He figured if he could sustain air superiority he might be able to hold the Japanese ground armies where they were and at least contribute to the Allied war in the Pacific. By now the Allies had reached the Philippines and it would not be long before planes would be hitting Japan from a number of bases.

All of the Fourteenth was active at this point, but the 312th Fighter Wing, now that it no longer needed to remain in the Chengtu area, was free to bomb and strafe all the way east to Peking. Under Brigadier General Russell Randall, the P-51s of his command began in November to hit the enemy fields at Anyang, Yüncheng, Süchow, and Chuchiatai.

By mid-February 1945 the Japanese Air Force in east China showed signs of weakening. All through January and February the fighters of the CACW flew daily sorties against the ammunition dumps at Wuchang and Hankow. The planes struck at bridges, railroads, canals, rivers, vehicles on highways, and locomotives. In February, Chinese intelligence reported that a hundred and forty-two locomotives had been destroyed and thirty-seven bridges knocked out.

Both Tex Hill and Casey Vincent completed their combat tours and Vincent departed for the United States on December 13 with a note: "Left Kunming today for the United States of America, Finis Chinese-Burma-India Tour! Finis Diary!" Chennault felt the departure keenly. The war was indeed winding down.

He heard regularly from members of both the AVG and the Fourteenth who had gone home and felt they had to keep the "Old Man" posted on the latest events. George "Pappy" Paxton, one of the original AVG pilots, was busy with a few others in trying to organize a Flying Tiger Association. He wrote Chennault constantly—some letters six or seven pages long—with all the latest news. William Pawley, who was named Ambassador to Peru by the President, tried to get into the AVG act by offering a $10,000 "gift" to start the organization at a dinner in New York. Told about it, Chennault sent a telegram to Paxton:

"Will not accept membership in any organization with Pawley who was never member of AVG and who failed to serve us in the most critical hour. Best wishes to all others."

Paxton circulated the telegram to other AVG people and Pawley's gift was turned down. As Paxton said in a letter, without Chennault there could be no Flying Tiger Association. The AVG men were having trouble convincing the military that their AVG time should be credited toward military time (they never did) and Chennault joined the controversy. He wrote Paxton:

Dear Pappy:

You are undoubtedly receiving many inquiries regarding credit for time with AVG in the Army readjustment program. I have also been asked for information on this subject and others, to which I am unable to find the answers. As most of these questions are subject to War Department decisions, I have drawn up a letter asking for official War Department clarification, and am inclosing it for your approval before it is sent forward. I believe most of the questions have been covered, but if you think of more which should be incorporated please re-write the letter. If you do send the one inclosed I suggest that your committee authenticate it and take any of these subjects up with their congressmen if it is found that they will need to be pushed through legislature.

There has been no official notification from the War Department on the wearing of our AVG pin, but that will no doubt take a little time.

You will be pleased to hear that "Black" McGarry was finally rescued. I saw him and had a short talk with him before he left for home. He was anxious to get back into combat but I vetoed that, at least until he has had a chance to visit his family and get a rest.

With very best personal regards and good wishes, I am

> Most sincerely,
> C. L. Chennault
> Major General, USA
> Commanding

By February 16, Air Force headquarters in Kunming had finished totaling the combat record of the Fourteenth for the year 1944, and in spite of Japanese victories in east China, Chennault's planes had killed 33,450 Japanese troops, destroyed 494 planes, and sunk 640,900 tons of enemy shipping. Liberators of the 308th Bomb Group kept operating off the coast that final spring of the war, but it was the fighter planes that did much of the damage to shipping as well as to enemy planes and airfields. Chennault knew he could run fifty fighter missions on the gasoline it took to run several B-24 sea sweeps.

Fighter planes that spring knocked out 512 enemy planes and bombed radar stations, coastal defenses, troop garrisons, and supply dumps from Shanghai to Hong Kong without loss of a single pilot in air combat. Much of the success of these missions was due to two lieutenant colonels—John C. "Pappy" Herbst and Edward O. McComas, commanding officers of the 74th Fighter and 118th Tactical Recon Squadron respectively. Chennault talked about them in his *Way of a Fighter.*

"Operating from the eastern-pocket, Herbst and McComas led attacks that cleaned out enemy air strength at Canton, Hong Kong and the Yangtze River fields from Hankow to Nanking. Herbst's treatment of enemy planes over Canton compared with the early CATF victories over the same area. In three attacks Herbst's Mustangs shot down 38 enemy planes over the city. One dawn attack caught enemy pilots at breakfast in lighted barracks with mechanics warming up planes on the flight line. Chinese reported 40 pilots and 100 mechanics killed by strafing. In the final blow at Canton, Herbst led 16 Mustangs over the city at 15,000 feet and circled insultingly until the Japanese fighters took off and climbed to that altitude. The Mustangs sent 13 enemy fighters flaming into the city, scattered the rest and then went down on the deck to strafe the airfields until their ammunition was exhausted. Gas dumps were fired, planes burned, barracks and control towers wrecked, and the enemy so demoralized that for months afterward not even a recon plane was based on any of Canton's three major fields.

"Nothing in all these attacks, however, could compare with our first strikes on Shanghai. The enemy had a network of five fields around the city and used them as major staging bases in air movements between the Asiatic mainland and Japan. The Japanese considered the Shanghai fields well beyond our fighter range. Their defenses were far from alert.

"The Shanghai strikes were the valedictory to China of 'Pappy' Herbst. This smashing fellow, officially grounded from all combat missions since early fall, had shot 11 Japanese planes out of the air on flights that were officially logged as 'administrative' or 'training' flights. Pappy's idea of a training flight was to take a new pilot on his wing to beat-up Amoy and Swatow airdromes, where the Japanese always kept a half-dozen fighters. 'Pappy' once flew a mustang from one of the pocket fields to Chihkiang for major repairs to its armament. Only three of the six machine guns would fire. On the way he ran into two flights of eight Oscars. 'Pappy' shot down both Japanese formation leaders but was badly shot up by the remaining Japs. He finally found himself fighting with only one gun working and half blinded by blood flowing from deep cuts in his head caused by broken glass when enemy gunfire shattered his canopy. 'Pappy' landed at Chihkiang to become the only pilot I know of who won a Silver Star and Purple Heart on an 'administrative' flight.

" 'Pappy' planned the Shanghai strikes on the basis of his experience in the pocket fields. By using a staging field which was less than 100 miles from the big enemy air base at Nanchang, the Mustangs would have ample fuel to fight over Shanghai. Herbst was officially forbidden to fly combat missions, so he flew to Shanghai as an 'observer' and shot down the only two enemy planes to get into the air. Lt. Col. Charles Older, a veteran of the AVG, led the Shanghai strike.

"Sixteen Mustangs, flying less than 200 feet above the ground all the way from Nanchang, streaked in over Shanghai on January 17 to catch the enemy by complete surprise. Mechanics were working on planes. Fighters were parked in neat rows before the hangars. Flak-gun positions were unmanned, and the guns were still swathed in their canvas covers. Three bombers fleeing a Superfortress strike on Formosa were circling for a landing when the Mustangs opened fire, sending the bombers crashing into the city. A total of 73 planes was burned on the ground as the Mustangs strafed until ammunition was exhausted. Not until the sixth or seventh pass did a few scattered flak guns open fire. Two fighters that managed to take off after the attack began were picked off by 'observer' Herbst, circling at 5,000 feet like a hawk over a chicken yard. Not one American plane was damaged. Two days later another strike found the enemy better prepared. They lost 25 more planes with four Mustangs downed by flak. All the downed American pilots were rescued by the Chinese New Fourth Army."⁵

On March 9 thirty-one Liberators, with an escort of twelve P-51s from the 311th Fighter Group, took off from a forward field to bomb the railroad assembly and repair shops at Sinkiang in Shansi Province. The Japanese had been hauling damaged locomotives there for repair. The big bombers hit the marshaling yards, severely damaging tracks and warehouses. Another raid on March 16 by Liberators of the 308th Bomb Group did the same sort of damage to Shih-chia-chuang. The heavy bombers attacked railroad yards at Tsinan on March 23 and damaged a bridge over the Yellow River.

By April the heavy bombers of the 308th were transferred to India to help ferry supplies and gas over the Hump, thus ending their combat role in China. Chennault later spoke of their record:

"They took the heaviest combat losses of any group in China," he said of the 308th, "and often broke my heart by burning thousands of gallons of gas only to dump their bombs in rice paddy mud far from the target. However, their bombing of Vinh railroad shops in Indochina, the Kowloon and Kaitak docks at Hong Kong, and the shipping off Saigon were superb jobs unmatched anywhere. When the Army Air Forces Headquarters in Washington tallied the bombing accuracy of every heavy bomb group in combat, I was astonished to find that the 308th led them all."

Meanwhile the 341st Bomb Group and the 51st Fighter Group were operating in Indochina and inflicting enough damage in the period March through May to permanently stop the flow of traffic from Vinh to the border of China.

Wedemeyer's trained Chinese armies began, in April, to attack the Japanese in the area of Chihkiang, on the western edge of Hunan Province. The enemy had localized its advance to this sector and Wedemeyer thought his well-equipped and well-trained forces could stop the advance there. The troops were again airlifted to the war area.

It was in April 1945 that Chennault began to realize there was a move afoot to remove him.

Twenty-six

Colonel Dave Barrett came down to Kunming in April to spend a few days with Chennault. After a dinner party attended by Kasey Sutter, Rose Carney, Joe Alsop, and Buzz Glenn, along with several Chinese Air Force officers and their wives, Barrett asked Chennault if they could speak privately. They took their drinks into Chennault's bedroom and closed the door. The only one with them was Joe, the dachshund.

Barrett began the conversation by reminding Chennault that he had been an attaché and military intelligence officer in China for many years and that he heard a great many things. Chennault said he knew that.

Barrett then told Chennault he had got himself involved in some murky dealings between the Office of Strategic Services (the forerunner of the modern CIA) and General Wedemeyer. As commanding officer of the Dixie Mission, Barrett's party of Army and State Department observers had spent almost four months with the Communist Chinese in Yenan. The purpose of the mission, Barrett said, was to try to convince the Communists that they had a stake in joining with the Nationalists in fighting the Japanese.

Barrett said he had been put in for promotion to the rank of brigadier general by Wedemeyer for his role in leading the mission until it was discovered that some OSS negotiations with the Communists had blown up in the faces of all concerned and that he was being partly blamed for the fiasco—although he had known nothing about the negotiations. He said that while Wedemeyer, Hurley, and Major General Robert B. McClure, Wedemeyer's chief of staff, had been engaged in the proposals and negotiations, the Office of Strategic Services, under General William Donovan, had been contemplating far-reaching negotiations with the Chinese Communists. McClure asked Barrett to present a plan he had for cooperation between the Communists and the Nationalists. McClure's plan, Barrett told Chennault, was to be presented simply for the Communists' reaction and was not a formal proposition by the United States Government. Barrett was also carrying a message from Hurley to the Communists. With Barrett on the plane was Colonel Willis H. Bird of the OSS. Apparently neither Hurley nor Wedemeyer knew of Bird's mission.

While in Yenan, Bird presented a comprehensive plan to the Communists from his superiors in Washington. Barrett was unaware of Bird's plan. Among other things, it was to: equip units assisting and protecting OSS men in sabotage work; supply points of attack to be selected by Wedemeyer; provide equipment for up to 25,000 guerrillas; set up a school for arms, demolition, and communications; set up an intelligence radio network in cooperation with the Eighth Route Army of the Communists, to supply 100,000 single-shot pistols to the People's Militia, and, when required by Wedemeyer for strategic uses, attain complete cooperation of the Communists' 650,000-soldier army and the People's Militia of 2.5 million.[1]

In the meantime, whether or not aware of what was being undertaken by the OSS, McClure had instructed Barrett to deliver to the Communists his own plan and Hurley's, for cooperation between themselves and the Nationalists. As far as both McClure and Hurley knew, Barrett was on the trip to deliver their message. On December 16, Chou En-lai, who was essentially a Foreign Minister for the Communists, wrote his answer to that message to Hurley. It was that negotiations between the Communists and Nationalists were at an end. Hurley was puzzled. It was not until the middle of January— while visiting with the Generalissimo—that he learned what had happened from the U. S. Navy Group in Chungking, the arm of U.S. intelligence. The Communists had let slip the proposed plan presented by Bird to offer U.S. paratroopers to help lead Communist guerrillas. In effect this would have meant recognition of the Communists and have given them their objective— the destruction of the Nationalists and the gain of Lend-Lease from the United States. At the same time there were reports of clashes in the Yenan area between Nationalists and Communists. It looked as if the Communist leadership was considering war.

Barrett told Chennault this had badly shaken up Washington, and Marshall immediately ordered Wedemeyer to make an investigation. Apparently it had also infuriated the Generalissimo. In his report to Marshall on January 27, Wedemeyer said he had informed all the officers in his command that "we must support the Chinese National Government" and that no negotiation of any kind was to be carried out with any Chinese without the approval of Chiang Kai-shek. Wedemeyer said he had not known that Colonel Bird had accompanied Barrett to Yenan and he knew nothing of Bird's message. He apologized to Marshall for the incident and said he was sorry his people had become involved in such a delicate situation. Barrett said negotiations between the Nationalists and Communists had resumed on January 24, so the breach was not permanent, but that his promotion had been canceled by Marshall, and Wedemeyer called Barrett in and told him the reasons for the cancellation even though Barrett was an innocent victim. During the discussion with Barrett, Wedemeyer said there would be no more activities involving U.S. personnel dealing with the Chinese in any way. He told Barrett he knew Chennault had dropped military supplies to General Hsueh Yueh in east China months before and that it was just another example of unilateral action on the part of U.S. commanders. He added that General Hsueh was not in the good graces of the Generalissimo and that Marshall had been notified of the incident.

General Wedemeyer—in a letter explaining his stand to Lieutenant General John E. Hull, assistant chief of staff, Operations Division, War Department—said of the political activities of U.S. personnel in China: "I rather question the Navy's concern about the Chinese attitude. Miles [Admiral Milton Miles, commanding the Navy intelligence operation] has been Santa Claus out here for a long time and just between you and me, Chennault has given supplies to a certain war lord friend without accounting for them."

Chennault had indeed dropped 75-mm. shells and belts of .50-caliber ammo to General Hsueh during the battle for Hengyang and had thought nothing of it.

Sitting on a chair with his feet propped on the bed, Chennault sipped his drink and nodded slowly to Barrett. They both knew Marshall had been smarting about Chennault since the Stilwell recall and did not need much of an excuse to act against him. Chennault thanked Barrett and told him he was extremely sorry about Barrett's loss of his star. They both drank to that and went back to the dinner party.

Meanwhile the battle for Chihkiang was in full swing. The Japanese had driven down from Paoching with three flanking movements—the first from Yüankiang, a hundred and eighty miles to the northeast, the second from the Sinhwa area, and the third from Sinning. The Japanese had 60,000 troops and expected hardly any resistance from an ill-equipped Chinese force of 100,000 soldiers. However, this time Wedemeyer had flown in the Chinese New Sixth Army—trained in Burma and outfitted with the best equipment. For air support, there was the Fourteenth Air Force's 5th Fighter Group and the 3rd and 4th Bomb Squadrons (M) of the CACW.

The battle raged for nearly two months and the .50-caliber machine guns of the Fourteenth may have been a major factor in lending aid to the Chinese ground forces. As a result of the new morale of the Chinese ground forces and the close air support, the Japanese, for the first time, were decisively beaten on the ground. By May 15 they were in full retreat.

It was the turning of the tide, and by the end of the week the enemy was also moving back in the Indochina area. By June the Japanese had made it clear they would not move south of the Yellow River, and by the end of that month their troops began to evacuate the area south of Shanghai.

A reorganization of the Army Air Forces on the Asiatic mainland had been under consideration for some time and Stratemeyer contributed to the thinking in Washington in January 1945 when he drafted a proposal to move all the Air Force units from India and Burma to China at the earliest possible time after the liberation of Burma. It was proposed that an Air Force headquarters in China would command both the Tenth and Fourteenth Air Forces. This proposal received the approval of Wedemeyer in a meeting in Myitkina in the middle of January. Stratemeyer and General Sultan approved it. When the plan was submitted to Chennault, he opposed it on the basis that logistics could never support such a massive infusion of personnel into China.

Knowing Chennault was totally opposed to the plan, Wedemeyer took with him to Washington, in March, Colonel Howard Means as Chennault's personal representative and Stratemeyer's chief of staff, Brigadier General Charles B. Stone. Means's argument in Washington was the same as Chennault's, but he was countered by a promise that the Hump tonnage would be considerably increased by the addition of many C-87s. Washington seemed to think the plan feasible. The special mission returned to the CBI with no written directive but convinced Washington was committed to moving Stratemeyer's headquarters and the Tenth Air Force to China.

Stratemeyer estimated that by July the Air Force mission in the Southeast Asia Command would be terminated and that its air units would be sent to China. The Tenth Air Force would then be assigned to the area south and west of Chihkiang, while the Fourteenth was to be based in Chengtu. The Fourteenth was to be reorganized as a bomber command and charged with strategic operations. Stratemeyer would then become the new theater commander with his headquarters close to Wedemeyer in Chungking. All this was predicated on Stratemeyer's estimates that there would be a sufficient increase in the tonnage of supplies over the Hump.

On May 3 the city of Rangoon fell to Allied troops. Although there were still some pockets of resistance left in northern Burma, the campaign there was finally over.

On May 5, Wedemeyer gave the orders for the Tenth Air Force to move to China but almost immediately reversed his decision. Chennault gave the reasons why:

"This entire plan was allegedly drawn up in Washington during the planning conferences on China. Actually it was written in Stratemeyer's Calcutta headquarters by officers, headed by Brig. Gen. Charles Bertody Stone III, none of whom had had a day's experience in China. It was rubber-stamped in Washington and on May 1 became China Theater policy in a general order establishing Stratemeyer's Chungking headquarters and moving the 10th and 14th.

"The 14th began the dreary move to Chengtu early in May. Truck headquarters was packed in shipping crates, truck convoys were already moving north, and the first echelons had arrived in Chengtu when we received a sudden order to suspend movement. Air Transport Command had announced to Wedemeyer that they would be unable to deliver the promised tonnages. Wedemeyer called a conference of statistical officers at Chungking to work out new allocations. Instead of a statistical officer, Stratemeyer sent his chief of staff, Stone. Stone tried to slip through Kunming unbeknownst to me by omitting his plane from operations and gas-receipt records. Naturally I learned of his transit and sent Brig. Gen. Albert Hegenberger, who had succeeded Glenn as my chief of staff, and Captain Joe Alsop to Chungking to match Stone.

"The routine conference soon changed to a battle royal. The 14th representatives demonstrated that the Stratemeyer plan was based on an absurd logistical foundation and could not possibly be executed with the supplies actually available. When the battle was joined, Hegnberger and Alsop, ably assisted by Lt. Frank Kravis, our statistical representative, uncovered evidence of the loosest sort of logistical planning. The gravest error had been committed in computing the cost of delivering supplies from the airlift terminals in western China to the Chinese ground armies in East China. The scene of the planned offensive for the summer of 1945 was some 1,500 miles east of the major cluster of Hump terminals around Kunming. Only 20 percent of the Hump tonnage had been allotted for delivery of these supplies over this 1,500 mile stretch. Actual practice proved that 50 percent of Hump tonnage was consumed in this Intra-China haul. I arrived for the final day of the conference and demonstrated that execution of the Stratemeyer plan would actually produce 50 percent less air combat operation than the 14th was then providing.

"Wedemeyer was shocked. He called on his staff to refute our arguments. They sat silent. One general gruffly announced he was not concerned with logistics. Wedemeyer was thoroughly disgusted with his staff. I am unaware of what Wedemeyer said to them after that session, but he issued an immediate order suspending all movement of Air Force troops and wrote Marshall that it was impossible to execute China air plan approved by Washington under current conditions.

"After he had digested the results of the Chungking conferences, Wedemeyer requested 14th headquarters to move to Chungking where it could also function as his air staff. Wedemeyer busied himself with finding quarters in Chungking for me and my staff. Wedemeyer also called on Col. Howard Means and Cap. Joe Alsop, both of the 14th Air Force plans section, to rewrite the China Theater logistical tables.

"On May 29, I received the following message from Wedemeyer indicating that the shift of 14th headquarters to Chungking was still planned: 'Permanent house for you and part of your staff will not be ready until about June 20. Available on June 1 is house complete with essential furniture, houseboys and cooks for either Hegenberger or yourself and approximately 12 officers. This can be used until your permanent house is ready.'

"Wedemeyer's reversal was a smashing victory for the 14th. It left Stratemeyer in an embarrassing position. His defeat at Chungking became an open secret with the suspension of all movement orders. Stratemeyer's promotion to lieutenant general had been rushed through the Senate on the basis of his new command. He had three stars but no command to justify them. Arnold and Marshall might have to answer embarrassing questions from senators if the word got around. Stratemeyer asked Wedemeyer to accompany him to Manila, where Gen. Arnold was inspecting the Far Eastern Air Force. Wedemeyer declined and suggested that Stratemeyer take me as China Theater air representative. Stratemeyer politely rejected that offer and finally flew to Manila alone to meet Arnold. Radiograms flashed between Manila and Washington. Stratemeyer sped back to Chungking with a letter from Arnold to Wedemeyer.

"On June 20, the day my Chungking house was supposed to be ready, Wedemeyer called an extraordinary conference at Chengtu of all American generals in China. It was strictly an 'ears alone' affair. Aides and stenographers were barred. Only generals were admitted, and there was no record made of the proceedings. The proceedings were short and simple.

"Wedemeyer read Arnold's special-delivery letter stating that it was the wish of Marshall and Arnold that reorganization of the China air forces be carried out as planned 'regardless of the consequences.' That phrase burned in my memory. I could hardly believe that they would commit such a bald statement to paper. But there it was. They were determined to get rid of me at all costs. Wedemeyer made it clear he had no choice but to accede to Marshall and Arnold's 'wishes.' Neither had the power to issue orders to Wedemeyer, but he was a junior theater commander, owned his military eminence to Marshall, and could hardly openly defy him when the issue had been made so plain in Arnold's letter. Marshall, basing his stand on Stilwell's information, was determined to remove me from any responsible post in China.

"I flew back to Kunming with a bitter, bitter taste in my mouth. I thought of all the grim years behind me and the first bright glimmerings of victory now visible on the horizon."[2]

Arnold had no intention of becoming involved in a feud with Marshall or the other general officers of the Joint Chiefs, and when Stratemeyer arrived in China he carried a letter from Arnold to Wedemeyer that stated:

"General Chennault has been in China for a long period of time fighting a defensive war with minimum resources. The meagerness of supplies and the resulting guerilla type of warfare must change to a modern style of striking, offensive air power. I firmly believe that the quickest and most effective thorough way to change air warfare in your theater, employing modern offensive tactics and techniques, is to change commanders. I would appreciate your concurrence in General Chennault's early withdrawal from the China Theater. He should take advantage of the retirement privileges now available to physically disqualified officers that make their pay not subject to income tax. Otherwise he may be reduced and put back on the retired list at his permanent rank."[3]

Just to make sure Arnold's letter got Wedemeyer's attention, it had been preceded by a message to Wedemeyer on June 8 from Marshall, expressing surprise that Wedemeyer's original plan had been dropped and that Stratemeyer had not yet assumed command. Marshall also said that Stratemeyer's promotion had already been put through and that it was on the basis of his being used in China that he was being promoted.

On June 20, Wedemeyer told Marshall he would go along with his recommendations on the organization of his air forces and that Stratemeyer would command the China theater Air Forces. Under him, Chennault would command the Strategic Air Force and Major General Howard Davidson would command the Tactical Air Force. Chennault, fed up with the whole game by now, tendered his request for retirement on July 6. Stratemeyer promptly approved it and appointed General Stone as Chennault's successor in command of the Fourteenth Air Force.

News of Chennault's resignation hit China like a bomb. For the next several days he was inundated with personal messages from all over China.

From the provincial government of Yunnan, Chennault was told the road from Kunming to the airfield had just been officially named the General Chennault Road.

From his old comrade General Hsueh, commanding general of the Ninth War Zone, he received a cable expressing dismay at his resignation and adding that his service to the people of China would be remembered "in all the days to come."

General Tu Yu-ming, commanding general of the Kunming Defense Force, wired him that he was shocked beyond description at the news.

There were messages of condolence from T. L. Wang, director of the Ministry of Information, and his old friend General C. J. Chow, director of the Chinese Aeronautical Commission. He immediately answered both with his thanks.

Asked to make a statement to the Chinese press, Chennault released a memo through the Fourteenth Air Force Public Information Office that was a routine announcement of his resignation and his appreciation of the help the Chinese people had been to him in fighting their common enemy.

He was presented by General Wedemeyer with an oak leaf cluster to his Distinguished Service Medal at a ceremony in Chungking. The banquet was given by Chiang Kai-shek, who presented Chennault with China's highest honor—the Grand Cordon of the White Sun and Blue Sky—and was visibly distressed that he was leaving. Chiang had been unable to stop the changes in the U. S. Air Force in China. Taking Chennault's hand, he said, through Major P. Y. Shu: "I am truly sorry for this. If Madame Chiang were here [she was in Brazil], she would be able to make things clearer. I hope you understand." Chennault said he did.

General Wedemeyer later said:

"General Chennault enjoyed the confidence and respect of the Chinese officials, both military and civil, and the Chinese people love and respect him also. Actually, he was a national hero, and I believe deservedly so."

Chennault's farewell to the wartime capital of Chungking and its people was something that those there to see it would never forget. The Generalissimo gave his personal car and driver to Chennault to drive into the streets of the bombed city. The people had walked for days from the small towns and surrounding cities in the area to say good-bye to "Old Leatherface," as they fondly called him. "Chen-au-duh" was the way his name was phonetically transliterated into Chinese.

The people—literally millions of them—would not let the driver control the car and the chauffeur finally turned off the key and let the throngs push the car. They pushed it for hours up the narrow cobblestone streets and up the city's steep hills. It was a foggy day and the air was filled with the acrid smoke of thousands of exploding firecrackers. Chennault could see nothing but a sea of Chinese faces as far as he looked. The throng pushed the car into the center of a square and in the humid heat of the July day millions of Chinese came to bid farewell to the man they believed had saved China from her enemy.

All that morning and far into the afternoon, people filed up to a wooden platform decorated with flowers and the insignia of the Flying Tigers and the Fourteenth Air Force and covered with an arch of pine branches and flowers. They brought gifts of precious stones, jade, lacquerware, antiques, and paintings. There were hand-painted scrolls and banners with the sentiments of the city, village, or group they represented. In a touching gesture, the Chinese moved up in single file to shake hands with Chennault—a decidedly un-Chinese custom. Chennault stood alone on the platform, tears running down his weatherbeaten face at the honor.

After Chungking, he made the rounds of the military bases in China—Paishiyi, Sian, Chengtu, Luliang, and Kunming—to say good-bye to his men. Everywhere he went the Chinese turned out in droves to see him and to wave good-bye. In Kunming, Jerry Huang, who had fed and housed the Americans for years, said to Chennault: "No foreigner since Marco Polo has so endeared himself to the Chinese."

On July 31 he received his orders from Air Force headquarters:

Subject: Orders
To: Maj. Gen. Claire L. Chennault 010 090 USA, Hq 14th, APO 627.

1. Effective 1 August 1945, you are relieved from assignment to and duty with the 14th Air Force APO 627, China Theater, and from further assignment to the China Theater. You will proceed to the United

States in accordance with travel orders issued by the 14th Air Force, reporting upon arrival to the Commanding General, AAF.

2. EDCMR 10 August 1945.

3. Priority for movement to the United States by air is CI-US-I-10623-AAF.

By Command of Lieutenant General Wedemeyer

His headquarters staff came down to the field to see him off and his personal pilot, Tex Carlton, a veteran of two China tours, was in command of the C-47 that was to take him to India and from there on to the United States.

On August 1, 1945, Chennault looked out the window of the plane as hundreds of thousands of Chinese lined both sides of the runway to watch his plane take off. In the last three years his Fourteenth Air Force—under the most trying conditions—had destroyed more than 2,600 enemy aircraft, while losing 500 from all combat causes; had sunk or damaged 2,230,000 tons of enemy merchant vessels and 44 naval ships; and killed more than 66,700 enemy troops—with the smallest and most remote air force in the war.

The C-47 droned down the crushed-rock strip and lifted off into the haze of a summer morning. More than eight years after he had landed in Shanghai in 1937—as a retired captain coming to China to advise the Chinese Air Force—Major General Claire Chennault was going home.

PART III

Twenty-seven

Chennault left China emotionally drained and physically exhausted. Although a Protestant, he stopped in Rome for a brief audience with the Pope, then paused in London to visit an old friend, Sir Charles Portal, Chief Air Marshal of the RAF, whom he had known in India. After brief stops at Iceland and Labrador he landed at Mitchell Field, Long Island.

The Air Force—as it did all men returning from overseas combat zones—sent him to a hospital for a checkup. He was transferred to a hospital in Miami where he spent several weeks recuperating. His bronchitis had got no better and he had lost some weight.

From there he went home to Waterproof. All his sons were away in the service and Nell was almost alone in the big house. Irene, his son Jack's wife, was staying with her. In the hot, humid weather Chennault tried fishing on the Tensas River but the fishing was slow. He had forgotten how enervating the weather could be in July and August in Louisiana.

Some of his old friends, including Governor James Noe, called upon him one day to suggest that Chennault consider running for governor. Chennault was flattered but told them he did not feel qualified, having no political experience. They then suggested he run for United States senator. He again declined but did say he would consider the post of state game director—which was a political appointee job. Noe and the rest thought the post not prestigious enough. They apparently did not realize Chennault was quite serious about the job.

In August the atom bomb was dropped on Hiroshima and a few days later a second one on Nagasaki. Chennault, reading the newspaper on the porch of the house in Waterproof, was elated. His men in China would be spared additional fighting. The Japanese surrendered a few days later and Chennault became depressed at the thought he would not be in at the end. He wrote later in *Way of a Fighter:*

"I left China full of anger and disappointment. For eight long years my sole ambition was to defeat the Japanese, and now I was deprived of participating in that final victory. On VJ Day it was my fondest hope to be aboard the battleship *Missouri* in Tokyo Bay and watch the Japanese formally acknowledge their defeat."

No one invited him. What was even more galling was to learn that Stilwell had been brought up from Okinawa to participate in the ceremonies.

He tried keeping himself busy around the house but the inactivity made him restless. Men were being discharged every day from nearby bases and coming home to cities and small towns in Louisiana. The college campuses were filling up with veterans on the GI bill, and most people were suddenly concerned with "getting back to normal." A retired major general was no more important than a discharged corporal.

His relationship with Nell had been deteriorating for a long time. The longer he had stayed in China the fewer letters he had written home. Over the years she had also written him less frequently. Her letters had been concerned with news of the children at first but later, as they left school one by one, even this news had been missing. She had been greatly concerned over the safety of her sons in the service, but they had all come through the war safely. She had drawn into herself more and more as she realized her husband was not coming home from China but was probably going to stay until the war was over. Though there was no way she could have known of his relationships with women in that far land, she must have suspected them. She devoted most of her time to her church and charitable organizations.

She had put on a great deal of weight over the years and Chennault found her cold and distant when he arrived home. It was apparent she wanted nothing to do with him physically and Chennault, secretly, was rather glad. He felt guilty that he had slept with Kasey Sutter and Rose Carney regularly over the years—as well as having occasional affairs with a number of Chinese women. He knew he should have been more faithful to Nell, but he rationalized it by attributing his affairs to wartime and the great distance from home.

Nell solved the problem. She wanted to discuss the possibility of a divorce and he was receptive to the idea. He suggested she talk to their family lawyer and see if he could draw up satisfactory papers. She agreed.

Suddenly he wanted to get away and be with people with whom he could talk about familiar things—China, the war, and flying. He knew his former secretary, Doreen Lonberg, was working for the Foreign Economic Administration. He phoned and asked her to reserve a hotel room for him in Washington. He left the following day, August 20. He did not blame Nell. Eight years away from home was a long time. She had been a good and faithful wife and they had eight grown children to show for the marriage.

He was happy to see Doreen and they immediately looked up as many friends from China as they could. He had vague plans to return to China and attempt to start an airline. He told Doreen that while still in China he had discussed starting a provincial airline with Lung Yun, governor of Yunnan Province, once the war ended. Yun had brought in Dr. Y. T. Miao, a prominent Kunming businessman and government economist, to talk about postwar possibilities in that area. Yunnan had long been an isolated province and only with the war had it developed links to the outside world. Yun and Miao were concerned that it would once more recede into a backwater when hostilities were over. Chennault had said he would see what he could do in the United States to find financial backing for such an endeavor. He had not realized at the time that he would be seriously considering the idea in the fall of 1945.

He was notified by his old friend Admiral Milton Miles of his award of the Navy Distinguished Service Medal. He went over to the Navy Department for the award ceremonies. He was happy and proud at the presentation. It brought to more than a dozen his major decorations, which now consisted of the Army Distinguished Service Medal with Oak Leaf Cluster (meaning he was awarded two); the Navy Distinguished Service Medal; the Legion of Merit; the Distinguished Flying Cross with Oak Leaf Cluster; the Air Medal with Oak Leaf Cluster; the Chinese order of the Blue Sky and White Sun; the Chinese order of the Celestial Banner; the Chinese Long Sword of Distinguished Commander; the Chinese order of Cloud and Banner; the Order of the British Empire Commander; the Polish order of Polonia Restituta; the French Legion of Honor; and the French Croix de Guerre with Palm.

Whiting Willauer had returned from the Philippines and they met for lunch. Willauer was very interested in Chennault's plans to start an airline in Yunnan and they discussed Willauer's concerns about procurement of strategic materials in the Far East and postwar planning. Willauer had left his post as director of the Far East and Special Territories Branch of the Foreign Economic Administration in Chungking and had gone to the Philippines on a mission of economic intelligence. He had returned a few weeks earlier and had joined Thomas Corcoran and his brother David in their law firm. The Corcoran brothers and William S. Youngman, a partner, had formed a company named Rio Cathay S.A.—a Panamanian corporation formed to look into the possibilities of business ventures in South America and China. Willauer had taken on the job of investigating airline possibilities in China. He needed financial backing—as did Chennault—but he realized Chennault had connections in the upper levels of the Nationalist government that he did not have. Rio Cathay arranged with Pennsylvania Central Airlines (PCA) for a fee of $50,000 to fund preliminary work on Willauer's airline scheme. While making arrangements for the China trip, Willauer approached Chennault and suggested he join the Rio Cathay group. Chennault told Willauer about his own plans to start an airline in west China but had to admit that this plan seemed less likely to succeed now because his key supporter, Governor Lung Yun of Yunnan Province, had been overthrown. The Chinese Central Government would probably be opposed to any greater autonomy on the part of Yunnan. Chennault and Willauer finally decided to merge their two ventures and Rio Cathay then secured $35,000 from PCA for Chennault. The necessary financial arrangements completed that fall in Washington, the two men left for Shanghai in December 1945 to begin new lives in China.

Willauer had an interesting background. A 1928 graduate of Princeton, he later attended Harvard Law School. He had married a socially prominent and wealthy woman, Louise Russell, whose maternal grandfather had been the founder of Union Carbide. He worked as a lawyer in Washington before the war—with the Civil Aeronautics Board and later with the Department of Justice, where he was assigned to cases involving subversive activities. He had a reserve commission in naval intelligence, but an old injury kept him out of the service. He got a job with China Defense Supplies through his old Princeton roommate, Howard Corcoran (brother of Tommy and David). There he had worked with T. V. Soong and with other Americans at setting up Chennault's AVG and later had gone to China with FEA, where he had been so much help to Chennault and the Fourteenth. It was a logical partnership.

"Old China hands" of prewar China would not have recognized the huge city at the mouth of the Whangpoo River. The city was hopelessly overcrowded. Inflation was soaring and the American military was in evidence throughout the port—Marines walked the streets and U.S. warships anchored in the river. American officers had taken over the French Club and General Wedemeyer had set up his headquarters in the old British quarters at the Cathay Hotel. Extraterritoriality no longer existed and the Chinese now ran their own companies and industries, while foreign firms hired experienced Chinese to front for their operations.

While Willauer set about finding lodgings, Chennault went to take a look at his old haunts. He later wrote:

"I retraced in a few weeks the course of my original three-year trek up the Yangtze River from Shanghai through Nanking and Hankow to Chungking. The scenes of devastation and famine I encountered were appalling even to a seasoned observer of China's sorrows. In the former Japanese-held corridor running south from Hankow every major city except Changsha had been completely destroyed. Half of Changsha was in ruins. Kweilin, Liuchow, Lingling, and Hengyang were blackened acres of rubble—scorched by the Chinese, pounded by our bombs, and then wrecked again by the Japanese as they retreated. All the smaller villages and towns had been burned to the ground.

"This was not an ordinary famine caused by a single year's crop failure. This was permanent disaster with no relief in sight. The Japanese had stripped the countryside bare of food during their retreat. Now Chinese were stripping bark from trees and eating boiled weeds. Rice straw was considered a delicacy. Clay was sold in the markets, as its addition to these nutritionless messes gave them sufficient bulk to ease hunger pangs in Chinese stomachs. Not even stray dogs or rats prowled the ruined cities. All had long since been eaten by the starving people. Japanese slaughter of oxen and water buffalo for food and gobbling of surplus seed stores left Chinese farmers without the means to start a new crop. Families yoked themselves in buffalo harness and tried to drag heavy wooden plows and harrows through thick rice-paddy mud, but their half-starved bodies were not equal to the task. All of this was in an area that normally produced surplus rice to feed half of China.

"During my journey I talked with many of the Chinese leaders I had known in the war years. The Generalissimo and Madame Chiang were back in Nanking, where I had first met them eight years before.

"Everywhere I went in China I heard the same story. Transportation was the most acute need. More than half of the prewar tonnage of river shipping had been sunk during the war. Timber to build new boats had to be imported. Without exports flowing out of China imports were impossible. Railroads were so badly wrecked that a return to normal operations would have required from three to five years of concentrated effort unhampered by civil war. Roads were in bad repair and there were few serviceable trucks. Air lift was pitifully small. There were only forty commercial transport planes in all China. The 120 transports given to the Chinese Air Force at the end of the war were too busy supplying Chinese armies in the field to be used for relief work.

"What little transportation remained moved at the pace of a coolie's trot or oxen's plodding. Lack of any modern transportation had paralyzed trade and prevented effective relief operations. Economic life of China was skidding backward at a quickening pace. Only in a few coastal cities was there any trade. United Nations relief supplies were flowing across the Pacific into a bottleneck at Chinese ports. Vital goods were piled high in coastal warehouses, unable to move inland, while millions of people in the interior died of disease and starvation."[1]

Chennault's visit with the Generalissimo and Madame was emotional. The Generalissimo—not one to show emotion at any occasion—warmly shook Chennault's hand and through Madame said he had not expected Chennault back after the hostilities. Chennault said he had not been able to forget the Chinese people and he knew the country was devastated by the war and he had come back to see what he could do to help. He then discussed forming an airline that would aid their people by flying in relief supplies and that could help the general economy by providing air transport. Madame was also touched at seeing her old friend and told him she and the Generalissimo would do all they could to help him. She said her brother, T. V. Soong, was now a high government official in banking circles and advised Chennault to see him. She added that Chennault's old associate, General Chou Chih-jou, was still director of the Aeronautical Commission. She suggested he see him and also Yu Fei-peng, Minister of Communications. Chennault had already earned his $35,000 advance from Rio Cathay.

Madame Chiang gave him a letter of support which he took back to Shanghai and gave to Willauer. Chennault set up a luncheon meeting with Madame and Willauer was ecstatic. He wrote to his wife: "We have been promised the full cooperation of Madame Chiang. We have been enthusiastically received everywhere with our idea of really making an overall approach to the air transport problem."[2]

But it was not to be as easy as it first looked. Nothing in China ever was. CNAC was still in operation and had expanded since the war. It had thirty C-47s and a few C-46s and was now jointly owned by the Chinese government and Pan American World Airways. The American company owned only 20 percent, however. Then there was a totally owned government airline—Central Air Transport Corporation (CATC)—that was already flying routes with twelve C-47s. The two companies were owned by powerful Chinese interests, both in and out of the Nationalist Government. Each had its lobbying group putting pressure on the Executive Yuan and the Ministry of Communication, which approved airline applications.

Chennault had almost exhausted his contacts by the end of January 1946. There were elements of the Nationalist Government that opposed the intrusion of any foreigners into the airline business in China and even American advisers to the Chinese government advised against airline expansion. They counseled that expansion threatened to involve foreign exchange costs beyond what the government could afford.

While in the United States, Chennault had talked at length with New York Mayor Fiorello La Guardia, a former flier. He had spoken of his hopes of starting an airline in China, and when La Guardia became director general of the United Nations Relief and Rehabilitation Administration (UNRRA) in 1946, he remembered their conversation. The answer to Chennault's and Willauer's problems came when the UNRRA director of operations in China, Colonel Ralph W. Olmstead, suddenly asked the two to come up with a plan for an airline that could carry to stricken areas of China relief supplies that had been piling up on the docks of Chinese ports. Neither CNAC nor CATC was able to handle the loads in addition to heavy passenger traffic. Olmstead had instructions from La Guardia to deal with Chennault. On February 6, 1946, Chennault proposed that "Chennault Airline" carry the relief supplies from the ports to interior destinations and operate commercial cargo flights on its way back. UNRRA—through its Chinese branch, CNRRA—was to supply the funds necessary to purchase the aircraft and equipment, and Chennault and Willauer were to supply the working capital and the experience and would operate the airline.

That was only the beginning. The airline had to be licensed by the Ministry of Communications (MOC) and Chennault had to use all his clout to convince Yu Fei-peng the airline was needed. It took the combined pressure of Madame Chiang and T. V. Soong to do it. There was still a great deal of opposition from certain segments of the factionalized Nationalist Government.

Willauer, meanwhile, threw all his administrative know-how into proving that CNAC could fill only a small part of China's freight needs and that a new, vital airline was needed. He convinced powerful opponents in the government that American adviser Arthur Young's argument against allocating more foreign exchange would not apply in the case of their new airline because the foreign exchange would be supplied by UNRRA. In spite of the powerful support given Chennault and Willauer, it was late April before MOC gave tentative approval for the new airline.

As usual, graft played a large part in the UNRRA-CNRRA picture in China. Relief supplies arriving by ship at ports such as Shanghai, Canton, and Hong Kong were piling up by the day. Tons of much-needed supplies— tractors, trucks, and rice—remained uncollected because there was no transportation available to pick it up. A few boats ran the supplies upriver from Shanghai to Nanking and on, but for the most part the supplies lay where they were delivered. CNRRA was a ripe plum for the politicians. Under the agreement with UNRRA, CNRRA was the distribution agent for supplies totaling nearly a billion dollars in American money. It was inevitable that much of it ended up on the black market and in centers of political power— especially in the big cities such as Shanghai.

In China, Deputy Director of UNRRA Henry T. Samson wrote at the time: "It is a heartbreaking task to try and get CNRRA supplies from the docks of Shanghai into the hands of the starving millions back in the province of the interior. The bottleneck is transport—any transport. The problem is graft—keeping CNRRA supplies off the Chinese black market."[3]

CNRRA also wanted to control the operation of the new airline—along with all distribution. Both Olmstead and Willauer were convinced that some of the opposition to the airline was politically inspired by Communist elements in the government, although they were never able to prove it. Both felt that the Communists were trying to undermine the Nationalist Government at all costs, and hindering the relief program would serve their purposes. Neither Chennault nor Willauer believed in the current view—held by many in the State Department and elsewhere in the United States—that the Chinese Communists were simply "agrarian reformers." Willauer wrote his wife that spring that he felt the Communists traditionally came up with such a popular program as agrarian reform as a way to gain a footing, but "Lord help those objectives once control is established. . . ." The United States should develop "a positive, long range policy of moral and material support to China, which is publicly announced, and which will be given almost the dignity of a treaty."

Chennault, as a military man, already saw the implications of the Communist-Nationalist fighting in north China. At the time he wrote:

"The Russians are well aware, even if most Americans are not, of the strategic implications of China. North China and Manchuria were the industrial bases that furnished more than one-third of all Japanese war production. From air bases built for the Americans during the last war at Chengtu, Sian and Lanchow in northwest China, all of the vast Russian industry east of the Ural Mountains is open to air attack. From these same bases and dozens of others in North China, the slender thread of Russian communications between eastern and western Siberia could be snapped by even a small air force. With North China controlled by a government friendly to the United States, Russia's only access to these would be across a thousand miles of Turkestan desert. As a result of the communist sweep in China, many of these vital fields are already in the hands of Chinese communists."[4]

When the Japanese surrendered in August 1945 the Chinese Communists occupied only a small portion of China. By the fall of 1946 they had begun a race to occupy as much territory as possible before anyone stepped in to stop them. Chu Teh, commander of the Communist forces, had ordered the surrender of Japanese armies in areas adjacent to his control in north China. General Douglas MacArthur, as Supreme Allied Commander, told Chiang Kai-shek to issue an order to the Chinese Communists to remain at their posts and await further orders. The Communists ignored that order and it was not long before Chinese Communist troops were pouring into Manchuria. This move must have been agreed to by the Russians because the Communist armies were receiving Japanese arms that had been surrendered to the Russians. The Chinese Nationalist forces were in south and west China when the war ended and far from the big eastern ports and cities.

Fortunately for Chiang Kai-shek's forces, General Wedemeyer diagnosed the race for Japanese arms for what it was and set up an Allied airlift to leapfrog Nationalist troops and occupy key cities and establish communication lines. U. S. Navy vessels later moved more Nationalist troops to occupy vital ports in Manchuria. Wedemeyer seemed to be one of the few military commanders who was thinking politically as well as militarily at the time. He was concerned about the Communist Chinese drive to occupy key areas in east china and about Russia's intentions in China. He asked the War Department to send seven U.S. divisions to set up a barrier through north China and Manchuria. The Joint Chiefs replied that the seven divisions were not available.[5]

Manchuria, strategically, was the key area—especially since it had been occupied by Russian troops after the surrender. The U.S.S.R. had declared war on the Japanese only a few weeks before they surrendered in August 1945. In the fall and winter following that occupation, the Russians removed tremendous amounts of Japanese industrial matériel as spoils of war. They also remained in Manchuria beyond the originally scheduled day for their departure—December 3, 1945. They did not leave until February 1, 1946. The Chinese Communists benefited from the Russian occupation of Manchuria as they ended up with most of the Japanese arms. As a result, skirmishes began to break out between the Communists and the Nationalists all along a wide front in northern China and eventually a civil war began in earnest.

Until late in 1945—and until Chennault and Willauer arrived back in Shanghai to start their airline—it was the official policy of the United States to support the Chinese Nationalist Government. But factions in the State Department—particularly John C. Vincent, head of the China desk, and Owen Lattimore, longtime political adviser in China—had been telling President Truman that the U.S. policy of aiding Chiang's government would trigger Russian aid to the Chinese Communists, thus causing a division in China. Both urged that China be unified under a coalition government—with the Chinese Communists having considerable power within that coalition.[6]

In November 1945 the Joint Chiefs of Staff ordered Wedemeyer to cease military aid to China "if evidence compels the United States government to believe that any Chinese troops receiving such aid are using it to support any government which the United States cannot accept, to conduct civil war, or for aggressive or coercive purposes."[7]

In other words the United States would send aid to Chiang, but not if it was to be used to fight a civil war. The U.S. policy had gradually turned to one of intervention in the political affairs of China. In late November, Vincent called for a truce between the Nationalists and the Communists in China and his suggestion was backed by Secretary of State James Byrnes.

General Hurley had been in China as ambassador since his days as a negotiator for President Roosevelt, but he had returned to Washington in the fall of 1945 for consultation. He was asked to return to China by President Truman and Secretary of State Byrnes. A struggle between Hurley and the State Department had been going on for some time. He wanted to continue the American policy of supporting the Nationalists, and members of the Department in China—notably John Davies and John Service—wanted more support for the Communists. Hurley had previously relieved both Davies and Service of their duties in the China theater—Davies having been transferred to the U. S. Embassy in Moscow, and Service back to the Washington office.

Within the State Department in Washington, many changes had been taking place among those responsible for the conduct of Far Eastern affairs. The post of Undersecretary of State had been taken over by Dean Acheson, and Vincent was director of the Office of Far Eastern Affairs. John Service was in the personnel section but was subsequently transferred to Tokyo to be a diplomatic adviser to General MacArthur.

Unable to get a clear and positive description of American policy in China —where he was supposed to continue negotiations with the Communists in Yenan—Hurley became frustrated. He returned to his home in Sante Fe, New Mexico, and on November 25 he offered to resign his post but was turned down by Byrnes. He went back to Washington to discuss the issue in person. Two days later President Truman accepted his resignation. Hurley resigned because he was constantly opposed by career men in the State Department while trying to carry out the stated policy of the United States in China. In his resignation he stated:

"I requested the relief of career men who were opposing the American policy in the Chinese Theater of War. These professional diplomats were returned to Washington and placed in the Chinese and Far Eastern divisions of the State Department as my supervisors. Some of these same career men whom I relieved have been assigned as advisors to the Supreme Commander in Asia. In such positions most of them have continued to side with the Communist armed party and at times with the Imperialist bloc against American policy. This, Mr. President, is an outline of one of the reasons why American foreign policy announced by the highest authority is rendered ineffective by another section of diplomatic officials."[8]

When President Truman announced Hurley's resignation on November 27, he appointed General George C. Marshall as his personal representative to China to continue the negotiations between the Nationalists and Communists begun by Hurley.

It was unfortunate, according to Wedemeyer, that Marshall never had either the time or the inclination or the "opportunity to study the methods of Communism; and he had implicitly believed the reports of his old friend, Gen. Stilwell who ascribed all ills of China to the government of Chiang Kai-shek. . . ."[9]

Marshall's directive, ostensibly from President Truman, was one he could never have accomplished, even if he had been a diplomat. The directive advocated a coalition government for China: "The United States is cognizant," it read, "that the present National Government of China is a 'one party' government and believes that peace, unity and democratic reform in China will be furthered if the basis of this government is broadened to include other political elements in the country."[10]

Marshall was directed to secure unity in a country that was engaged in a civil war, but he was not allowed to put down any rebellion by armed force. He must obtain "peace and unity." In order to get that peace he would have to yield to Communist demands and to that Chiang Kai-shek certainly would not consent.

Who drew up that directive? Then Undersecretary of State Acheson testified later:

"At the end of November 1945, Secretary Byrnes and General Marshall met. This was after Marshall was asked to go to China. Secretary Byrnes read him a memorandum suggesting an outline of instructions for him. General Marshall did not approve of it. He said he would wish to try his own hand, assisted by some of his associates, in drafting the instructions. This he did; and a draft was prepared by him in conjunction with four generals, who were working very closely with him."[11]

Marshall arrived in Chungking on December 20, 1945. Chennault and Willauer landed in Shanghai a month later to begin their airline negotiations. Chennault's old nemesis, Marshall, was, in effect, administrating his own U.S. policy in China.

Twenty-eight

While Tom Corcoran did much of the spadework in Washington to try to grease the skids of approval for the new airline, Chennault and Willauer kept at it in China. It was not until October 25, 1946 that Chennault and Willauer signed the contract with CNRRA that created CNRRA Air Transport.

UNRRA allocated $2 million to CNRRA for the purchase of aircraft and supplies. In addition, it would allocate an additional $1.8 million for foreign exchange. This was to be used to pay salaries of foreign personnel and to purchase the necessary imports for an airline, such as aviation gasoline and spare parts. The new airline—with the initials CAT (Civil Air Transport)—would carry the relief supplies for CNRRA from port cities to the interior and would be allowed to charge regular commercial cargo rates for the empty space on returning flights. The agreement with CNRRA stipulated that CAT would be paid forty-six cents per ton-mile for the first 10 percent of cargo flown each month, and ninety cents for the remainder. Chennault and Willauer had to furnish $1 million for working capital. In addition they were given an option to buy the aircraft at cost plus 10 percent.

They immediately began to hire pilots and attempt to find aircraft. They ran into opposition almost immediately in the form of a smear campaign by both CNAC and CATC. Through advertising pressure and stories in both the Chinese- and English-language press, CNAC and CATC circulated stories that the new line was out to make money and was a strictly commercial operation—not a famine relief airline. Corcoran had been optimistic about financial support from Rio Cathay and Penn Central Airlines, but suddenly he wired Chennault and Willauer that financial backing had been withdrawn.

During the summer Chennault made an emergency trip to the United States to drum up the much-needed capital. Meeting with no success in

Washington, he went, in desperation, to one of the only friends he knew who was doing well in the aviation business—former AVG pilot Bob Prescott. Prescott had organized the Flying Tiger Airline in California, a cargo line that had developed into a going business. Prescott, after a quick trip to China with Chennault, agreed to invest an initial $20,000 providing he was given 24 percent interest in the airline. He sent his brother George, an accountant, out to work for CAT as a comptroller. George was sitting in the lobby of the Hotel Manila on October 25 when he was suddenly struck in the head by a stray .45-caliber bullet fired by a Filipino gangster involved in a gang war in the lobby. He died instantly. This unfortunate accident must have seemed like an omen to Prescott, who immediately pulled out of the airline venture.

Nell had written Chennault that the divorce settlement had been concluded and that the family lawyer wanted them both to appear at the proceedings. He flew down from Los Angeles and signed the papers in Waterproof.

The settlement included $250 per month to Nell—to be paid out of his retirement pay as a major general. In addition, he signed over rights to nearly a dozen lots in Raven's Wood and Consuelo Plantations in Concordia Parish, together with all the buildings and improvements on the property known as the "Home Place." He retained half interest in the Lamond Place, with all its buildings, of which Nell was granted the use as long as she lived or until she remarried. He gave her $10,000 cash and two notes for $5,000 each, payable in two years. He agreed not to change the beneficiary of his $10,000 veteran's life insurance policy provided she paid the premiums. There was a settlement of jointly owned stock—in Prudential Building Association, General Motors, Paramount Pictures—and some additional life insurance policies, which went to Nell. After signing over the cash in a joint checking account to Nell and giving her a $10,000 Victory Bond, Chennault caught a plane back to the West Coast—considerably poorer, but a single man.

Willauer, far more of a businessman than Chennault, realized they had an airline franchise to sell and quickly went to Chinese backers. He looked up a wartime associate from Chungking days, L. K. Taylor, and Wang Wen-san, manager of the Kincheng Bank. They put together a group of investors and offered a loan of $250,000 in Chinese money. In exchange the Chinese wanted a 42 percent share of the airline. Willauer, desperate for backing, had no choice but to agree.

This did not set well with Corcoran, who immediately wrote to Willauer that he and his backers had already spent $120,000 on the airline operation so far and had worked hard to obtain the contract with CNRRA. When Chennault had agreed to pay Prescott 24 percent of the airline for his investment, that meant that he and Willauer retained 38.5 percent and the rest went to Corcoran and his associates—37.5 percent. Under the new terms with the Chinese backers, Corcoran would have to be satisfied with 28.5 percent interest—which did not amuse him. He insisted on his original share.

Willauer—exhausted from his scramble to find money and his constant negotiations—felt the people in Washington had no idea what a task he and Chennault had. He wrote Corcoran a heated letter in which he told him how necessary the Chinese support was and that he did not think Corcoran had any idea of the value of Chennault in the overall operation.

"I am sick and tired of what appears to be a failure to appreciate General Chennault's position with reference to the job which has been accomplished in establishing CNRRA Air Transport as a going concern," he wrote. "I insist he be given a one third share of the American interest in CNRRA Air Transport, or any successor, without any reservations of any kind whatsoever."[1]

Corcoran, back in the busy world of Washington politics, realized he might have been a bit harsh and dropped his demands for his original share of stock.

Chiang Kai-shek gave his support to the new airline but, though it was welcome, it did not do much more than give tacit approval. Chiang, the consummate politician, had to run his factionalized government as best he could and, like a juggler, he had to keep as many balls in the air at one time as possible. He had to soothe the backers of CNAC and CATC as well as approve of CAT.

It was necessary to get good pilots and Chennault spread the word that he wanted to hire men. Doreen, in Washington, established a CAT office and began to recruit pilots and ground personnel. A few Army Air Force squadrons were still operating and Chennault contacted Colonel Richard Wise, who had served with him in the Fourteenth, and talked him into taking detached service. Wise joined CAT as operations manager and was successful in talking a number of pilots of the 322nd Troop Carrier Squadron at Peking to take their discharges and join CAT. Signed up were Harry Cockrell, Stuart Dew, Paul Holden, and Frank Hughes. Chennault's old associate in the Fourteenth, Charles ("Chuck") Hunter, joined CAT as an assistant to Wise. Also hired from the Air Corps was Major Kenneth Buchanan, who had been an air inspector for the ATC in Shanghai and was taken on as chief pilot. John Williams, Chennault's longtime communications chief during the AVG, CATF, and Fourteenth days, was hired to set up communications. They found two ex-Navy pilots in Shanghai, Weldon Bigony and Willis Hobbs, and from the Marine Corps Air Wing at Tsingtao, CAT recruited Robert Rousselot, Lawrence Buol, Var Green, and Lewis Burridge.

Chennault put them right to work. He handed Burridge and Green a certified check for $500 for expenses and sent them off to the Philippines where there were five surplus C-47s that could be purchased with CNRRA funds. On January 27, Cockrell, Dew, Holden, Green, and Burridge landed the five planes at Lunghwa Field in Shanghai—bringing to China the first planes of the new CAT airline.

Three days later a C-47 piloted by Frank Hughes and Doug Smith—with Chennault along on CAT's inaugural flight—took off from Shanghai for Canton with a load of CNRRA supplies and a jeep. CAT was in business.

Flying across uncharted China was "old hat" for Chennault but to the new pilots the flights presented problems. The country lacked almost every feature considered necessary for safe commercial flying. There were almost no suitable airfields, and communications—particularly air-to-ground communications—were virtually nonexistent. There were almost no navigational aids and maintenance facilities were primitive at best.

A few weeks earlier three CNAC planes, carrying passengers and freight, had crashed in dense fog at Shanghai on Christmas Day, killing seventy-two people. An investigation had been ordered immediately by the Ministry of Communication. The Chinese press got into the act and the pages were filled with accusations of pilot error and mismanagement. As if that were not enough to discourage the public from flying, a CNAC C-46, carrying forty-six people, slammed into a mountain near Tsingtao on January 5, 1947, killing all aboard. When two more CNAC planes crashed in the next several weeks, CNAC temporarily suspended all passenger flights. It was not a good atmosphere in which to begin a new airline.

Chennault decided to base the airline operations in Canton, as it was closest to the famine areas of the interior, and in early February CAT personnel—who now numbered 158 people—began to set up permanent facilities at Tien Ho Airport. Chennault found it ironic to be operating out of a field that such a short time ago had housed the Japanese fighters and bombers that had been striking at his bases in east China. Two additional C-47s arrived that month and flying began in earnest. In March, CAT obtained its first C-46s—four of a fleet of seventeen that were to make up the workhorses of the airline. Chennault had asked his daughter Peggy Sue's husband, Bob Lee—who had been in the aviation purchasing business—to look at a fleet of surplus C-46s stored in Hawaii. Lee reported they were in mint condition but neglected to tell Chennault they had been stored in preserved condition—with the engines packed in grease. The price, however, was excellent and Chennault immediately obtained the CNRRA funds for their purchase. However, the crews he sent down to pick up the planes had to wait months for them to be readied—while the pilots enjoyed themselves, on salary and $10 per diem, on the beaches. The first four C-46s, flown by Dick Rossi (AVG), Joe Rosbert (AVG and CNAC), Robert Conrath, and Ozzie Young, arrived in Canton on March 2.

Chennault maintained a house in Shanghai, which he preferred to Canton. He began to collect a retinue of old friends around him, many of them from the days in Kunming. Kasey Sutter had moved to Shanghai with her two children and Rose Carney also was back. P. Y. Shu, now discharged from the Chinese Air Force, went to work for CAT as a personal aide to Chennault. P.Y.'s services as an interpreter had always been welcomed by Chennault and he became a trusted friend—having been through the wars, literally, with Chennault. With some of the same servants he had in Kunming and his faithful dachshund Joe, Chennault was indeed back home.

CAT set up an office on the Bund, the main business thoroughfare in Shanghai, and Chennault used it as his headquarters. Hardly a day passed when some old friend did not drop in for a visit. Admiral Miles surprised Chennault one day by telephoning and setting up a lunch. He was commanding a Navy cruiser that was anchored in the river.

The airline was doing well for a new operation. In March the line flew 91,343 ton-miles of mostly CNRRA relief supplies and 14,589 ton-miles of mail.[2] The planes flew medical supplies to a leper hospital in Nanchang; seeds for spring planting in the Yangtze Valley; displaced persons who needed to be flown back to homes deserted during the war; sheep to the northwestern province of Kansu—everything flyable. Chennault, for the first time since leaving China in 1945, was happy. He wrote:

"After so many years of experience with the airplane as a means of destruction, it is indeed a pleasure for me to use it for constructive purposes by which it can build up a country instead of smashing it flat."[3]

But by April it was clear that—even with the constant flying—CAT was not making enough on the relief cargo. Chennault and Willauer went to Nanking to see Chiang Kai-shek, who agreed to an amendment of the contract that would permit CAT to carry cargo on China's approved import list. The new agreement—plus new mail contracts—helped the increase in ton-miles, which jumped to 386,343 in May and 322,820 in June. By July 1 there were 385 people working for the airline and CAT was making money. The line would fly anything anywhere and began to earn the reputation that later made it famous. It was not without incidents, however, and Russian fighter planes occasionally "buzzed" the silver CAT transports as they flew cargo missions to north China. On one occasion a C-46 was hit by machine gun fire, and photos taken by the pilot showed it to be a Bell P-63 that had been Lend-Leased to Russia by the American government.

The C-46s and C-47s of CAT were flying into the old Fourteenth fields at Liuchow, Hengyang, Sian, Kunming, and Lanchow—bringing medicine, food, farm equipment, and Chinese bank notes. Herds of cows and sheep were airlifted into those eastern areas where all cattle had been slaughtered years before. On return flights the planes carried tung oil, hog bristles, raw cotton and wool, tobacco, silk, and tea. Yunnan hams and beef were delivered by CAT to Shanghai and melons from Kansu were on the tables of eastern port cities a day after being flown from the interior.

While the new airline had been slowly making progess, General Marshall had been sent by President Truman to try to negotiate a peaceful settlement between the two warring factions of China's government. So far the Nationalists had been winning their battles against the Communists. Early in 1946, Marshall had arranged for a committee of three—consisting of a Nationalist, a Communist, and an American—which would attempt to set up a truce between the two forces. A headquarters was to be set up in Peking for the purpose of carrying out cease-fire agreements and in the meantime hostilities were to be frozen. In spite of his belief that the Communists could not be trusted the Generalissimo went along with a suggestion by Marshall that a coalition government might be formed. Following the cease-fire and the conclusion of agreements on the reorganization of the government and integration of the Communist forces into the Nationalist Army, Marshall thought that peaceful reconstruction had arrived at last.

He left for consultation with President Truman in March 1946 and while he was gone the Communists poured troops into Manchuria, which had been under Japanese control for fifteen years. Chiang's forces felt this was a violation of the cease-fire agreement, and after the Communists had attacked and occupied Changchun on April 15 seven Nationalist divisions were transported to the area by U.S. forces. Chiang personally went to take charge, and on May 19 his forces defeated the Communists at Szepingkai and, a few days later, at Changchun.

Marshall returned from the States in time to find Nationalist troops heading for Harbin and Kirin. He immediately called for a truce, and Chiang—though he was winning—complied with the request. This was a crucial truce because the Nationalists were winning and the Communists had not yet had time to train troops in the use of their newly acquired Japanese arms. The truce was signed on June 26 and hostilities ceased in Manchuria—allowing the Communists to regroup and rearm.

But by August fighting had begun to break out along a "truce" line and Chiang issued a statement blaming the Communists for the breakdown in negotiations. He said the Communists would have to "give up their policy to use armed force to seize political power, to overthrow the government and to install a totalitarian regime."[4]

Chennault described the impasse:

"North of Hankow some 200,000 government troops had surrounded 70,000 Communist troops and were beginning a methodical job of extermination. The Communists appealed to Marshall on the basis of his truce proposal, and arrangements were made for fighting to cease while the Communists marched out of the trap and on to Shantung Province, where a large Communist offensive began about a year later. On the East River near Canton, some 100,000 Communist troops were trapped by government forces. The truce teams effected their release and allowed the Communists to march unmolested to Bias Bay where they boarded junks and sailed to Shantung. The worst fiasco was at Kalgan Pass. This gap in the North China Mountains is a historic gateway between China and Manchuria. At the end of the war there were no organized Communists in Manchuria. Chinese Communists flocked from their base in Northwest China through the Kalgan Pass to join the Russian troops in Manchuria. When the Chinese Government troops occupied Manchuria, they found the great industrial centers stripped bare of machinery and the tremendous arsenals of the famed Japanese Kwantung Army empty. There was no trace of either the Kwantung Army or its equipment."[5]

Fighting commenced in the fall and by October 10 the Nationalists captured Kalgan. Despite all, Marshall continued to hope for a coalition government and as late as December 1 he warned Chiang that it was imperative that "efforts be made to bring them [the Communists] into the government."[6]

Chou En-lai then sent a message to Marshall setting forth his terms for a renewal of negotiations. The terms called for the dissolution of the National Assembly and the relocation of all Chinese troops to where they had been on January 13, 1946—when the Communists had all the advantages.

Marshall was still hoping for the impossible—peace between two bitter enemies—when Truman announced Marshall had terminated his mission and would be named Secretary of State. He left China on January 8, 1947, his fifteen-month mission to China a complete failure. Chennault wrote:

"When his coalition plans collapsed and fighting flared again, Marshall finally gave up his China venture. He returned to the United States with a 'plague on both your houses' speech that was a remarkable confession that his early profession of faith in the integrity of the Communists was not justified by their subsequent actions."[7]

Marshall could not have won in China. When an agreement was signed between the Nationalist and American governments on August 30, 1946, for the sale of American surplus property located in India, China, and on seventeen Pacific islands, with an estimated procurement value of $900 million, the Chinese Communists were vehement in their denunciation of American aid to the Nationalists. They attacked Marshall for presuming to mediate between two Chinese parties while the United States furnished war supplies on a grand scale to one of the parties. Marshall himself recognized how untenable his position was. He took pains to explain to Chou En-lai that the surplus property did not contain military matériel but consisted mainly of machinery, vehicles, and communications equipment which would be of use in the recovery of the Chinese economy. The Communists simply ignored this explanation. To prove his impartiality toward both sides, Marshall advised the American government to stop issuing licenses for the export to China of military equipment; in late September shipments of combat items from the Pacific area to China were halted.

Those were crucial years. China's plight was so bad that even the New York *Times* reported on June 22, 1947, that the guns of the Nationalists' armies were so worn and burned that "bullets fell through them to the ground." The Communists, on the other hand, were well supplied by the Soviet Union.[8]

Chennault wrote shortly after Marshall's departure from China:

"I believe the State Department has the cart before the horse. Military aid should have top priority. Without a military decision, there can never be the internal stability required for any effective reforms. Last March when the Marshall plan for China was presented to Congress, I was appalled to note that only 1/6 of the program was devoted to the military aid so desperately needed. . . . I told Congress last March that unless effective military aid was immediately forthcoming for China, the Chinese Communists would overrun Manchuria and be well on their way to taking all of North China within six months."[9]

Marshall's mission did a great deal for the Communists and very little for Chiang's forces. When Marshall arrived, the Communists occupied a very small portion of China with an army that consisted of less than 300,000 badly equipped troops. When he was recalled by Truman after fifteen months at the task, the Communist armies had grown to more than two million relatively well-equipped soldiers.[10]

By the winter of 1947–48 these Communist armies began their inexorable movement south in a massive offensive against Chiang's forces. The Generalissimo watched as the Communists gradually surrounded his outnumbered garrisons. By November his troops in Mukden were threatened and he pulled his troops from Kirin and Changchun to reinforce that city.

The original contract CAT had with CNRRA stipulated that operations were permitted as long as CNRRA was still operating. Now—with CNRRA about to be dissolved at the end of 1947—Chennault and Willauer began to push for contract renewal by the Nationalist Government. They got a break when the province of Yunnan bought 7 percent of the CAT stock and lobbying in Nanking by Wang Wen-san and other Chinese stockholders brought in additional stockholders. In January, Chennault and Willauer signed a draft agreement for continued operation of the airline.

The threatening situation in north China was certainly one reason why the Nationalist Government agreed to renew CAT's contract. When the agreement was signed, the Ministry of Communications officials made it clear they expected CAT to begin carrying military supplies—food and soldiers—to Manchuria. In January, CAT signed a contract to airlift 7,000 government technicians and their families from beleaguered Mukden to Peking.

Chennault could take pride in what CAT had done in 1947. The airline had flown nearly two million miles and had carried almost seven million tons of cargo. Chennault and Willauer had paid off the monies advanced by UNRRA and they owned an airline with nineteen planes and 822 employees. Chennault was now ready to go to war for Chiang Kai-shek—for the second time.

Twenty-nine

In the spring of 1947, Chennault settled into a routine of social life in Shanghai. His old friend General P. T. Wong insisted he accept a large house on Hungjao Road as a gift. Chennault did not want to accept it—considering it too large—and finally paid Wong what he figured was a reasonable amount from CAT funds, with Willauer's concurrence.

Friends from the AVG and Fourteenth days were showing up in Shanghai, many to work for CAT. Doreen Lonberg returned from Washington to take a job with the airline. Chennault saw a great deal of her and they attended many social functions together.

"Whitey" Willauer's wife Louise arrived from the States, and they stayed with Chennault until they found a house. Chennault still saw Kasey Sutter and it seemed to be a foregone conclusion among his close friends that he would eventually marry her. Another companion on many social occasions was an attractive girl named Anna Chen, a Central News Agency reporter who had first interviewed Chennault in Kunming in 1943. He had seen her at press conferences occasionally and when he returned to Shanghai with Willauer in December 1945 she was one of the CNA reporters who had asked for an interview. Her older sister, Cynthia, had been a nurse with the Fourteenth in Kunming and their father was with the Chinese consulate in San Francisco. It was rumored she had been married, but her husband, if any, was not in evidence. Since his return to Shanghai, Chennault had spent much time with her—finally suggesting she take a job with CAT.

In August the public relations officer for the airline, Clyde Farnsworth, had published a *CAT Bulletin.* The newsy, personalized little magazine started out as a mimeographed sheet concerned with the doings of the airline. It went to the employees as well as to a number of outsiders. Anna was given a job editing the magazine but kept her free-lance writing job with CNA.

Chennault, having been divorced for more than a year—and essentially a single man for almost ten years—was seriously thinking of remarrying. As a result, his personal life was becoming somewhat complicated. Always fond of women, his social life now became hectic. His old friend Tom Gentry, former flight surgeon of the AVG and the Fourteenth, returned to Shanghai and moved in with Chennault until he could find quarters. Gentry, a slow-speaking Southerner, was someone in whom Chennault could confide but was not much help with his advice. To Gentry, all Chennault's women friends were appealing. He had just married a spectacular-looking Southeast Asian woman named Ugette who probably contributed to Chennault's desire for a wife.

In the spring Rose Carney, with whom Chennault had been associating for years, had shown up at the house Chennault and the Willauers were sharing. Louise later wrote:

"On the occasions Rose came to the house on Hungjao Road to see the General in 1947, she was accompanied by several Chinese women and a little boy. I did not take a good look at her or the others because the General had so many callers that all I needed to know was whether they were expected or not. . . .

"She was brought to my attention sometime during that spring by Kasey, who was the General's most constant companion at the time. Kasey told me that Rose had arrived in Shanghai with a little boy whom she claimed was the General's son, and then asked me what I would do if Rose presented me with the boy. I burst out laughing, and asked why she would do such a thing even if the child were the General's, which I refused to believe.

"Kasey explained that I would be presented with the child because I was living in the same house with the General, which I gathered was a very logical reason from a Chinese point of view. I then asked how she knew this was going to happen, and she said that Rose had called at her house when she first arrived in town, as her own friendship with the General was common knowledge and because she had known Rose in Kunming."[1]

Louise went on to write that she told Kasey she would demand a blood test to see who the father was and said her bluff worked. Rose did not come to see her and Kasey did not mention the subject again. But Louise said she had discussed the matter with Chennault and he did not deny being the father. Louise said he told her he would like to have the boy called Joe—as he had never had a son by that name.

She added:

"I had a feeling that the same trick would be pulled on Anna as had been tried on me, so I warned her to expect a call from Rose after she and the General were married, and I told her how I had handled it. I did not then know that the General had admitted the child to be his.

"Rose was eventually paid $10,000, and at the time she agreed not to claim that the child was the General's. The papers to do with the transaction stated that the money was to put the kid through college, and that the General made the gift of his own free will for friendship's sake in gratitude to Rose for the good job she had done running the hostel in Kunming.

"It all should have ended and been forgotten, but several years later I heard that Rose turned up in Hong Kong with a son with the name of Chennault."[2]

If that were true, the son never surfaced in China or the United States.

As the fall wore on Chennault and Anna were seen together more and more often. Chennault told close friends he had decided to marry and everyone seemed to know but his partner Willauer, who had written to Louise on September 7:

"The General still puts it down as a foregone conclusion that he is going to marry Kasey. I am pretty sure that if Anna did not have a husband who would not divorce her, the General would choose Anna. The latter has been around a lot, and I think she is pretty much O.K. Yesterday was the General's 57th birthday. He tried to keep it a secret, but the Chinese papers wrote a big story about it, and he got presents from all over China, all of which really tickled the hell out of him. In one of the stories it said that he was going to marry a Chinese girl, and this morning the United Press got me out of bed to deny a Chinese story in one of the smaller papers that he had married Anna on his birthday. Maybe he should of, but anyhow he didn't."[3]

Chennault and Anna did marry, on Sunday afternoon, December 21, at Chennault's house. It was a small ceremony since they could not be married in a church. Anna was Catholic and the Church did not recognize divorce. Chennault, a Baptist, would not be converted to Catholicism so they agreed to the simple wedding. Anna's parents flew in from San Francisco, as did her sister Cynthia. Chennault's best man was Tom Gentry. Also at the wedding were Mr. and Mrs. P. Y. Shu, Whitey and Louise Willauer, and George Yeh, the Vice Minister of Finance.

Louise wrote her parents in the United States after the ceremony:

"We are all pleased about the General's marriage. He was lonely and needed a wife and constant companion. It is not incongruous for a Chinese girl to marry a man as much older as the General is than she [she was twenty-three and Chennault was fifty-seven], as it is usually the parents who do the choosing and financial security is the first consideration. Anna seems as genuinely in love with him as he is with her. I wrote the children about the wedding, but I suppose the rest of you probably haven't seen their letters and will want to hear about it also.

"The General and Anna had been contemplating marriage for some time, but actually made the decision and set the date very suddenly. Anna's family left for Hong Kong on Wednesday and on Thursday Anna telephoned them to come on back to Shanghai as she was to be married on Sunday. The General said that he isn't getting any younger and that if he was going to be married, why wait, and besides someone had given him a big wild goose which wouldn't keep any longer than Sunday!—not to mention the fact that he would have had to ask everyone in China if he had any other kind of a wedding. . . .

"Fortunately the ceremony was delayed because we had to wait for the Vice Minister of Finance who flew down from Nanking and whose plane was late. But at last he arrived and everything was ready. The General, Tom Gentry, the minister who was to perform the ceremony, and I retired to the porch to wait beside the Victrola for the signal that the bride and her father were at the door. The solemn moment came. The door swung open. Tom turned the Victrola up as loud as it could go and set the needle on the record. And out came a Hill Billy tune! The General, being deaf, squared his shoulders and started off at the first bar, but Tom grabbed him and we tried again. Someone had mixed up the records, we will never know who, and it took three tries to find Lohengrin.

"From then on everything went smoothly except for the . . . bride's father being taken ill and put to bed. We drank tea and ate wedding cake and toasted the bride and groom in champagne and then went home to change our clothes for the wedding banquet which was served at 7:30 and which was plainly insulting if you wished to consider the staff of servants as devoted retainers who wanted to show their Master that his happiness was also theirs after having served him for many years. The only good thing about it was the wild goose which had not been bought by the cook. Besides that we had some gumbo which was so greasy the General apologized for it, and he was not copying the Chinese custom where the host criticizes the food for not being worthy of his distinguished guests, some poorly cooked vegetables and apple pie.

"The General, being the General, and a man of military habit, went to work at the usual time, 8:00 the next morning, and it had only been with difficulty that Tom and I had persuaded him to give up his usual Sunday morning hunting on the day of the wedding."[4]

Not much prevented Chennault from hunting.

CAT began its military airlift in earnest on January 18, 1948. Mukden was besieged and it was necessary to bring food and supplies into the city and to evacuate people on the return flight. It was bitterly cold in Manchuria and passengers had to wait in the subzero cold and wind for coolies to unload the C-46s before they could board.

Chennault sent operations officer Dave Stauffer to the beleaguered city to set up ground facilities for an airlift. There was not much with which to work—only a windswept half-mile runway and some abandoned hangars. Stauffer installed VHF radio in a broken-down bus and at least had air-to-ground communications. The ground personnel stayed in the Railway Hotel.

CAT pilots flew a steady airlift, bringing in flour and other foodstuffs through the antiaircraft fire from the Communists, who completely surrounded the city. Planes taking off had to stay over the field and circle upward to avoid flak from guns on the outskirts of the city. Arriving planes had to remain in a small pattern high over the field, then dive down in tight circles to get in safely.

As the airlift progressed everyone, including the administrative staff, became involved in the war. Several CAT employees, including traffic manager James Stewart, were trapped on the ground at Linfen in south Shansi Province when the Communists attacked the city in March. The Chinese Air Force was little help in getting them out with light aircraft—as the Nationalist pilots knew what would happen to them if they were caught on the ground in a Communist area. Willauer, who had gone to Peking to ask for CAF help, gave up and returned to Shanghai. As the fighting got worse, Erik Shilling, one of Chennault's original AVG pilots who had come back to fly for the "Old Man," volunteered to go in and pick up the employees. With a C-46, piloted by Jim Bledsoe, circling overhead to keep the Communists occupied, Shilling slipped in at low altitude in a single-engine L-5 observation plane that had arrived disassembled from Shanghai and rescued Stewart and several Chinese employees.

The city of Weihsien was the setting for the next CAT drama. In April, Lew Burridge and John Plank flew a C-46 into the besieged town in an effort to find out how serious the blockade was. Staying overnight, they were caught by a Communist attack. The Reds captured the airfield where the CAT plane sat and the two pilots had to radio for help. Burridge cleared a small landing strip on a playground in hope that another light plane could pick them up. CAT asked the Navy and Marines for help—since the two pilots were noncombatant American citizens—and Vice Admiral Oscar Badger sent a Marine Corps reconnaissance airplane with CAT markings on it. Pilot Dick Kruske flew the small plane into the makeshift strip and just made it. However, on the way out, carrying Burridge, he hit a building and demolished the plane. Neither pilot was seriously hurt. While the Communists continued to attack the city, Bob Rousselot circled in a C-47, dropping flares and beer bottles that whistled like bombs as they fell. Early the next day Willauer flew over the city to try to locate the two downed pilots. He returned to Tsingtao and gathered two observation planes—the CAT L-5 and another Piper Cub. By the following afternoon both Burridge and Kruske had been flown out by Roger Fay, but on the return trip pilot Ed Trout broke a prop on the L-5 while landing. Marsh Stayner, an ex-Marine pilot, flew in with the Piper Cub and washed out the landing gear. Plank, Trout, and Stayner had to stay another night under siege, but the next day they managed to fix the damaged Cub and Stayner and Trout got out.

Rousselot came back for Plank in the L-5, forgetting that he weighed almost two hundred pounds. Realizing he could not get Plank out, Rousselot tried a takeoff carrying a smaller Chinese radio operator. The plane hit a telephone pole and crashed, killing a spectator. The pilot and his passenger were not seriously injured. Stayner came in later in the Cub and Plank flew it out alone, but Kruske arrived with another light plane to pick up Stayner. Now Rousselot was the only one left behind.

That night everybody got into the act. Realizing they had to try to pin down the attacking Communists in order to keep Rousselot safe, CAT personnel loaded down a C-47 with flares and bombs to drop over the city.

If the situation had not been so serious the following day, it might have been considered a comedy of errors. Stayner cracked up a light plane coming in to pick up Rousselot and Kruske damaged the L-5 following him in. Now there were three CAT pilots waiting to be rescued. While Willauer, Burridge, and Var Green dropped hand grenades and rifle ammunition to government troops within the city that night, the three pilots worked on the damaged planes. By the following morning Stayner and Kruske flew out in one light plane, leaving only Rousselot to spend a final night. Stayner picked him up on the morning of April 16.

Rumors of CAT's participation in combat spread around through the Marine Corps and Air Corps units in the area and it was not long before the State Department sent CAT a sharp warning about dropping bombs and flares in support of Chinese military operations. The threat was that such actions in the future would result in the loss of passports.

The military airlift and rescue flights were harrowing to the air crews, but the airline was making money. In April, CAT flew 3,161,625 ton-miles. Chennault and Willauer were now able to pay off the $250,000 loan to their Chinese backers and to send additional funds to the United States for Corcoran and his associates. In June, Chennault and Willauer concluded negotiations with the Jardine Aircraft Maintenance Company of Hong Kong to do CAT engine maintenance, so that the engines would no longer have to be crated and shipped to the States for work.

The Communists continued to move south and Shantung Province now became the scene of heavy fighting. Chiang decided to make a stand at the city of Tsinan on the Yellow River in west central Shantung Province. CAT suffered its first casualties on July 29 when pilot Clyde Tarbet, copilot Har Yung-shing, and radio operator Chan Wing-king were killed on takeoff at Tsinan after dropping off troops who had been airlifted to defend the city. Erik Shilling flew into the city, which was then under heavy enemy fire, and took out about half the CAT staff. Burridge flew in the next day and with bullets whining through the fuselage managed to evacuate the rest of the CAT personnel as Red soldiers came onto the field. By this time Chennault was beginning to feel he had his old combat command back. It was "just like old times," he told Willauer.

Cities began to fall like dominoes. By October 29, CAT abandoned the base at Mukden and several days later the Nationalist garrison there surrendered to the Communists.

In Nanking, the Nationalist capital, Chiang feared the worst. He decided to make another stand at Hsüchow, a hundred and seventy-five miles to the north. He felt he could deploy his armored forces there and successfully hold back the Communist tide. The battle began on November 8 and CAT—together with CNAC and CATC—flew in rice and ammunition to Hsüchow and flew out wounded. Tom Gentry went along on the flights to do what he could in the way of first aid to the wounded, but many were beyond help by the time they were loaded onto planes.

By the end of November the situation was so bad at Hsüchow that CAT had to abandon the field. Fear-crazed soldiers fleeing the Communists swarmed onto the field, pushing the wounded aside to get on the planes. Nationalist troops were surrendering by the thousands. The city fell on December 1.

Chiang Kai-shek began to think seriously that he might lose the mainland and to look at Taiwan as a place to move the government treasury. The last act was about to be played on mainland China and CAT was to be a big part of it.

37. Chennault and author Jack Samson hunting pheasant on Taiwan in 1951. (Author's Photo)

38. Joe, Chennault's faithful dachshund, hunting with his master, 1953. (Author's Photo)

39. Anna and Claire Chennault in Taipei, April 1952, with their daughters
Cynthia Louise (left) and Claire Anna. (Courtesy of Sue Buol Hacker)

40. Chennault holds his daughter Claire Anna on her third birthday, Taipei, 1952. (Courtesy of Sue Buol Hacker)

41. Chiang Kai-shek reviewing his troops, Taipei, 1953. (Author's Photo)

42. Flak-damaged C-119 at Cat Bi airfield near Haiphong, French Indochina, April 1954. Damage is similar to plane in which CAT pilot Paul Holden was wounded. (Author's Photo)

43. Pilot James B. McGovern at Cat Bi airfield, March 25, 1954, shortly before being shot down over Dienbienphu while on a CAT mission. (Courtesy of E. C. Kirkpatrick)

44. CAT pilot Bob Snoddy just prior to his death on a covert flight over Manchuria. (CAT Photo)

45. Chennault's sons and daughters by his first wife Nell, taken several months before his death in 1958. *(Left to right)* Rosemary, Max *(standing)*, Pat, Jack, David *(rear)*, Charles *(front)*, Peggy, and Robert.

46. Chennault's casket moving through Arlington National Cemetery. Pallbearers *(left to right)*, Whiting Willauer *(rear side of caisson)*, General Nathan Twining, Ambassador Holington Tong *(rear side of caisson)*, General Carl A. Spaatz, General Albert Wedemeyer, and General Charles B. Stone. (Fourteenth Air Force Association)

47. Anna Chennault at her husband's casket at Arlington National Cemetery. Jack Chennault stands behind her. (Fourteenth Air Force Association)

Thirty

In March 1948, Chennault had been invited to address the House of Representatives on United States foreign policy. He outlined the history of aggression in China by the Japanese and talked about the Communist-Nationalist war. He warned of Russian support for the Chinese Communists.

"Russia violated her treaty of amity and friendship with China," he said. "Under terms of this treaty, which China was compelled to sign under the Yalta Agreement, Russia agreed to respect the sovereignty of the Nationalist Government of China. She has repeatedly and consistently aided the Communists who are in open, armed rebellion against the recognized government," he warned.

He went on to say that, though the major portions of the five northeast provinces that formed Manchuria were under the control of the Communists, he did not feel it was too late to step in and help the Nationalist Government, our longtime ally.

"Our aid must be substantial, adequate for their needs, if it is to serve as the inspiration for all-out national resistance to Communism. Our aid must also be immediate, for time has now become of paramount importance. Continued delay in furnishing aid will result in material and spiritual losses which may never be regained. If we delay until Manchuria is definitely lost, the effect upon Chinese morale will be very bad."[1]

He was thanked by the senators and representatives with a standing ovation. Whatever conclusion they came to, however, was too late.

When Chennault returned to China—convinced the United States was going to do nothing in time to save the Chinese mainland—he began to think about organizing another AVG. Remembering how his AVG had stopped Japanese ground forces at the Salween and later in the gorges of the Yangtze, he talked the plan over with Chiang Kai-shek. Chiang—weary of the continued fighting and exhausted by requests for help that never materialized—

told Chennault China could no longer afford to back such a plan and that it would have to be funded by the United States. The word had got around quickly, however, and Chennault began to receive queries from former fighter pilots.

The rumors hit Washington, and Secretary of Defense James Forrestal, one of the men who believed the United States should do something militarily to help China, suggested to Secretary of State Marshall that they explore the possibility of reinstating an AVG. The reaction on the part of Marshall to Chennault's becoming involved in the fighting in Asia again was predictable.

Professor William Leary, in his excellent book about CAT, *Perilous Missions,* wrote:

"Alarm bells began to clang in Foggy Bottom following the Forrestal-Marshall encounter. Assistant Secretary [William Walton] Butterworth hastened to prepare a memorandum that set forth State's objections to an American volunteer force for China. 'The formation of an AVG,' he wrote on November 29, 1948, 'with or without U.S. Government support or tacit approval, would have serious implications for our policy in China, the position of U.S. nationals there and our relations vis-a-vis the USSR. Such an organization would be viewed by people around the world as direct American intervention in the civil war, a policy 'which we have consistently and scrupulously avoided.' It could also have adverse effects on American nationals residing in areas that were or might later fall under Communist control. Further, Butterworth raised the specter of Russian backing for a 'Soviet Volunteer Group,' leading to aerial combat between American and Soviet fliers over Chinese territory. 'It would therefore appear,' the assistant secretary concluded, 'that the formation at this time of an AVG in China would carry with it all the disadvantages of open American intervention in China's civil war and none of the possible advantages. For it is obvious that, while such a group could provide considerable annoyance for the Communists, it could not turn the tide in favor of the Nationalist forces.'

"Later in the week, Brigadier General Marshall S. Carter, special assistant to Secretary Marshall, asked Butterworth 'what the Department is doing to stop the formation of a revived AVG.' Nothing, Butterworth replied. The subject had never been raised, formally or informally, so it seemed best to ignore the 'rumors.' 'It is extremely unlikely,' he reassured Carter, 'that General Chennault would attempt to take unilateral action in the matter without first obtaining at least the tacit consent of the Government, for without such consent he could not be assured of receiving continuing supplies and material for the operation.' "[2]

With help from Washington impossible, Chennault reluctantly abandoned the plan.

Deprived of moral and material support from the United States, the Nationalist forces had been forced to give up the ancient capital of Peking in January 1949.

But not everyone in the United States was unaware of Nationalist China's plight. The State Department had not been able to deceive a number of congressmen and military men. On February 7 a group of fifty-one members of the U.S. House of Representatives sent a letter to President Truman which declared that the undersigned members of the House of Representatives were deeply disturbed by what was happening in China. Listed were the names of the legislators—among them a young congressman named Richard M. Nixon.

Chennault and CAT were busy trying to help the battered Nationalists hang on to the city of Taiyüan. There Marshal Yen Hsi-shan, a sixty-five-year-old veteran of the Japanese wars and now of the Communist campaign, was holding out in a city surrounded by Red troops. Still thinking of the Japanese war, he had called for Chennault to come and help him under command of a two-hundred-plane air force. Chennault replied that he could not bring an air force but he would do what he could. CAT was now using Tsingtao as its major base in order to get supplies to Marshal Yen. The city needed two hundred tons of food a day to survive and CAT had been able to maintain this level of supply up through December 1948. With the fall of Tientsin, the tonnage began to drop off. Chennault, in desperation, went to his old friend General Chow Chih-jou, commander of the Chinese Air Force. On January 8, CAT received the word that the Chinese Air Force wanted the airline to go to work for them.

Chennault, Willauer, Bob Rousselot, and Joe Rosbert sat down with the Chinese Air Force and planned Project Demonstration. Ten P-47N fighter bombers, with ten volunteer CAT pilots with fighter experience, hired "temporarily" by the Chinese government, were to be staged at Sian. After several practice flights they were to drop napalm on the Communist troops, thereby both relieving Yen's besieged troops and at the same time giving the Chinese Air Force a practical demonstration of the use of napalm.

Just before dispatching the mission Chennault had second thoughts about pulling it off without at least the unofficial approval of the United States Government. He had been in China too long to expect the State Department to ignore this one. On January 12 he sent Willauer to Shanghai to get the tacit approval of Consul General John M. Cabot. Cabot's reply was never recorded, but it is not difficult to imagine what it was. Willauer jotted in his pocket diary: "No demonstration."[3]

CAT continued the airlift to Taiyüan. In order to help CAT get in and out, Yen constructed two airfields—simple dirt strips—on the west bank of the Fen River close to the town. They were well within range of the Communist mortars, but the Red gunners needed several minutes to adjust the mortars each time, so a plane could land, shove out rice, and take off between bursts. Roy Watts landed his C-46 on January 14 and got off again, but not before being bracketed by three mortar rounds. Two days later Ernie Loane took off with mortar hits two hundred feet behind the aircraft. These young American pilots continued to fly in and out of Taiyüan in one of the most heroic—if least known—airlifts in history.

Willauer was determined to get in to talk with Marshal Yen and on January 26 he and Bob Rousselot flew in in a C-46 carrying TNT and detonator caps for the Nationalists. Immediately after landing, the plane came under mortar fire and Rousselot taxied it up under a cliff for protection. Willauer drove into town and apologized to Yen for the failure of Project Demonstration, but he urged the old warrior to hold on and said that help was coming from the United States. He told Yen a "popular movement," supported by such well-known figures as Senator Arthur Vandenberg, Representative Walter Judd, former ambassador to Russia William Bullitt, and Paul Hoffman, director of the Economic Cooperation Administration, was being organized. He urged the marshal to abandon the doomed city and to use the TNT to blow up the factories so that they could not fall into the hands of the Communists. Yen was adamantly opposed to this course of action, so Willauer and Rousselot took off amid mortar bursts and flew back to Tsingtao.

The courageous CAT crews continued the airlift through January but, on February 10, CAT ran out of gasoline at Tsingtao. Yen, in desperation, radioed that his troops were starving and when no help came he flew out himself and went to Tsingtao to talk with CAT members and Navy commander Admiral Badger. Badger said he would try to do what he could about the gas shortage and in the meantime ordered U. S. Marines ashore on a "training exercise" to raise Chinese morale.

The old marshal flew on to Nanking to plead personally with Chiang Kai-shek for help, and there he was able to borrow 700,000 gallons of gas from the Chinese Air Force. It was to be shipped from Shanghai to Tsingtao and should last CAT through March.

The airlift started again as soon as the gas began to arrive and CAT pilots were flying as many as eighteen hours a day. On March 3, Randall Richardson, a former AVG and CNAC pilot, logged twenty-one hours and forty-five minutes carrying supplies into the shell-pocked strips. When James P. McGovern, a former Fourteenth Air Force P-51 fighter pilot, landed on the Taiyüan field on March 8 an engine froze up. John Plank flew in to let McGovern and both crews fly out with his plane while he spent a night under fire. Norm Schwartz flew in the next day with a supply of rice and a new engine—plus four mechanics. That same day Plank and the four mechanics flew out in the repaired plane, probably setting a record for a C-46 engine change.

In spite of the courageous stand by the old marshal and his men—plus the heroic efforts of the CAT pilots and crews—the Communists began a determined attack on April 16. Marshal Yen, who had been flown out a few days earlier for a conference in Nanking, was determined to get back to his men.

Burridge would not let the old man parachute in, at his age, because the airfields had been closed. On April 24, after bitter fighting in the streets of the city, Taiyüan fell.

Chennault, expecting Mao's forces to move down the old route the Japanese had used—from Changsha to Canton—left orders with the CAT personnel to evacuate the airline's base at Canton if that happened. In fact, he told Willauer, if it happened, "This might be considered the signal for the liquidation of CAT."⁴

In a last desperate effort to get aid for the battered Nationalist Chinese Government, Chennault left for the United States the following week. It was the beginning of May 1949. Aided by Tommy Corcoran in Washington, Chennault—though nothing concrete had come from his appeals to the House of Representatives and various committees on foreign policy—still hoped for some support for his plan, one of many floating around Capitol Hill at the time, to help anti-Communist forces in China.

He was to find his help from an unexpected source—the Central Intelligence Agency.

Thirty-one

Chennault's book, *Way of a Fighter*, had just been published by G. P. Putnam's Sons of New York. The "autobiography" had been written by Robert Hotz, a former newspaperman and Air Force officer who had served in China. In 1943 he had also written *With General Chennault: The Story of the Flying Tigers*, with the help of ex-AVG pilots George Paxton, Parker Dupouy, and Robert Neale.

Doreen Lonberg had returned to Washington to work in the CAT office there and, with her help and that of Corcoran, Chennault began a campaign to gain support for Chiang and the Nationalist Chinese. The book was sent to every influential person in Washington and particularly to the military, where—for the most part—it was well received.

Chennault embarked upon a tour—testifying before congressional committees, making speeches, and giving interviews. At a hearing before the Senate Armed Services Committee on May 3 he urged that the United States send a military mission to China where American advisers would serve with the Chinese down to the company level. He urged an air combat arm and said that CAT, CNAC, and CATC could provide the logistical support. Seeking to allay fears that he would profit from this arrangement, he told the committee: "I am not advocating any aid here for the benefit of my airline. I have offered to give up my interests in the airline, resign my position with it, if my recommendations for aid are carried out and if I can be used personally in the program."[1]

Chennault appeared before several hearings at the State Department and though Secretary of State Dean Acheson had no real interest in Asia he assigned Dean Rusk, his undersecretary, to hear Chennault. One of General Stilwell's former staff officers, Rusk had a fossilized view of both Chennault and the Nationalists and was unimpressed with Chennault's plan. He sent the plan on to the embassy in China where Ambassador John Leighton

Stuart, himself an old China hand, dismissed it as impractical and of doubtful value. Dean Acheson, testifying at a closed session of the House Committee on Foreign Affairs, effectively ended the discussion of Chennault's plan when he said he would not ask Congress for money for something the State Department considered to be impossible.

Tom Corcoran arranged a meeting between Chennault and Rear Admiral Roscoe Hillenkoetter, director of the CIA, which, in 1947, had been entrusted by the National Security Council with the responsibility for covert activities. The CIA replaced the old Office of Strategic Services—General William Donovan's OSS. Hillenkoetter was attentive and congenial, but the meeting produced little in the way of concrete developments. However, Chennault's old friend Paul Helliwell, who had been in the Kunming division of the OSS, was now in the CIA and was impressed with both Chennault and his plans. He recommended to another friend, Frank Wisner, head of the Office of Policy Coordination (OPC, the government's covert action arm), that he get in touch with Chennault about the possibility of using CAT as a front for clandestine operations. Wisner, a Virginian and new head of OPC since September 1948, had already begun to consider plans for covert operations in the Far East. He was delighted to hear Chennault had a concrete proposal for China and he and several associates met with Chennault in his hotel room on May 9. Wisner was impressed by Chennault's personality and with his dynamic approach to the problems in the Far East. He came away from the meeting with a plan to ensure the airline's financial future by a loan from the Economic Cooperation Administration.[2] Chennault, seeing he was not getting very far with pleas for economic and military aid to Chiang's government, figured that at least aid to CAT would be the next best thing. The size of the amount frightened off a lot of those in OPC who might have been willing to gamble on CAT. Talk of the loan died down temporarily.

Meanwhile in China, despite the deteriorating military situation, Willauer was fighting to keep CAT in business. The number of flying hours and ton-miles dropped off in May, but operations picked up some when CAT established a base at Lanchow in north China and service began between there and Sining in late May. Pilot Sterling Bemis inaugurated the first flight to Ninghsia on May 15, and in the south CAT contracted with the Chinese Army to fly silver dollars of the Army payroll to such points as Chungking and Hengyang.

On June 19, CAT had its first light-plane casualties. Ed Norwich and two Chinese passengers were killed when one of CAT's Cessna 195s crashed in a sudden sandstorm in the rough terrain outside Lanchow. Three of the light planes—purchased some months before—had inaugurated flights in north China in May.

Willauer finally managed to get some business out of flying tin from Yunnan Province down to French Indochina, a project he had been working on for more than a year. The French gave permission for CAT to fly into Haiphong and built gasoline storage tanks at the port. CAT sent one of its two French-speaking employees, Frank Guberlet, there as operations manager. During June, CAT flew thirty-three trips in a three-day period and airlifted 165 tons of tin from Mengtze to Haiphong.

However, the Communists were moving south in an inexorable wave. Sian was occupied in May by a 150,000-man army and Red troops began a march toward Lanchow. The Nationalists fought bravely near Sian and temporarily won a victory when their cavalry drove the Communists back. But the Reds, now 200,000 strong, regrouped and by August were advancing upon Lanchow—the CAT base—in three columns.

Then, on August 5, the State Department issued a White Paper on China, edited by Philip Jessup, deputy U.S. delegate to the United Nations. On July 27, Secretary of State Dean Acheson had announced that the entire United States Far Eastern policy would be reviewed. A nongovernment counsel was to consist of Jessup and others—assisted by such Department of State personnel as George Kennan and Walton Butterworth.

The White Paper, consisting of 1,054 pages, outlined in detail all the Nationalist Chinese failures over past years and all the supposed reasons why the United States should no longer support Chiang's government.

The timing of the document was extremely damaging and jarred the morale of the Nationalists. It could only aid the Communists in their conquest of China. Jessup rejected a strong plea from Chennault, who argued that the release of the White Paper now would undermine the Nationalist Government in her struggle with the Chinese Communists.[3]

The White Paper provoked a storm of protest in the United States. William Bullitt, former ambassador to Russia, wrote Jessup that the U.S. view of how China was conquered by the Communists was "proof of the lengths to which our government officials will go to protect their vested interests in their own mistakes. To publish an inquest on a faithful ally—not yet dead but fighting in despair to preserve its national independence—is incompatible with any standard of decent conduct. And our Department of State has done this not to serve a national American interest, but to serve domestic political expediency."[4]

Ambassador Stuart, who spent a lifetime in China, wrote: "The White [Paper] served to inform the world that the Nationalists in the opinion of the United States Government, had lost the 'Civil War.' Without admitting any mistakes in United States policy, it tried to place all the blame upon the Nationalist Government of China. United States policy, it claimed, had been in no way responsible for the 'ominous result.' By implication it announced that the United States support of the National Government and the efforts of the United States toward survival of that government were at an end."[5]

In the United States conservative circles were furious. The American China Policy Association, Inc., of New York, whose president was William

Loeb and which boasted of a large membership of Republicans and other conservatives—such as Clare Booth Luce and Max Eastman—immediately published an analysis of the White Paper in which it pointed out a long list (thirty-nine) of discrepancies. Its vice president, Alfred Kohlberg, sent them to Chennault. In the statement on the White Paper the ACPA charged, among other things:

That President Roosevelt's telegrams to Chiang Kai-shek were either omitted, extracted, or taken out of context; Wendell Willkie's 1942 mission to China was not referred to nor was his report included; many agreements made at the Cairo Conference of December 1, 1943—pledges by Roosevelt and Churchill to Chiang Kai-shek—were omitted.

Among the thirty-nine discrepancies listed were the omission of Roosevelt's offer to Stalin of access to the port of Dairen in Manchuria; Henry Wallace's report to Roosevelt after his trip to China in July 1944 was not referred to; Ambassador Hurley's reports on the general situation in China during 1944–45 were omitted; coded documents called for by Ambassador Hurley on his public appearance before the Senate Foreign Committee in December 1945 were omitted. Hurley had said these documents would clearly show the change of the State Department policy in favor of the Communists.

Other charges were that Stilwell's opinions of Chiang were included but that Hurley's reports of Chiang's analysis of Stilwell's charges were left out. Reports of Wedemeyer during the period he was theater commander in China (October 1944 to Spring 1946) were omitted except for extracts, understood to be taken out of context. These reports contained reports of murders of isolated American troops by Chinese Communists. It was noted that, while Chennault commanded our Air Forces in China, all his reports were omitted from the White Paper but all of Stilwell's reports on the Chinese armies in the war area of China proper were included. Notice #16 of the Chinese Politburo, the top Communist committee, adopted in March 1946, revealed that the Communists planned to use General Marshall as a cat's-paw to secure truces while they obtained arms and training from the Soviets. This paper was omitted from the White Paper.

The statement wound up by saying:

"The White Paper's Revelation of American pressure on Chiang to form a coalition with the Communists, the State Department's desertion of his Government when he failed to do so and our refusal of his suggestions that the whole question be left to popular elections, must cause other nations faced by the possibility of Communist conquest to wonder just how far they may trust the United States. Prime Minister Nehru expressed that doubt to an American correspondent last fall. He well may wonder whether additional White Papers justifying the abandonment of our other Allies (Poland and the Baltic Republics) will be issued and whether later White Papers on the Philippines, India, Europe, etc. will, in turn, follow their abandonment.

"The omission from the White Paper of essential documentary material discredits the good faith of the State Department and of the Government and people of the United States, and seriously undermines the confidence of our allies in Europe in our policy there.

"The whole Truman Doctrine for the containing of Communism is put in jeopardy by this partisan performance by our State Department."[6]

Chennault, elated that someone in the States agreed with him, wrote Kohlberg on August 26, thanking him for sending him ACPA's statements on the White Paper. He added this:

"There is another curious omission among the many 'omissions' of important documents from the White Paper. In July 1945, when Stilwell was in command of the 10th Army at Okinawa, he prepared and forwarded to Washington a plan for landing the 10th Army on the northern coast of Kiangsu Province where he would be joined by two to three hundred thousand Communists. He proposed to arm and train these Communist troops and then turn south to capture Shanghai. This would have placed the Communists in control of Shanghai and the entire Yangtze Valley as far west as Ichang and would have bottled the Nationalist Government in Szechwan Province on V-J Day. This plan was forwarded to both the Ambassador and the Commander of the China Theater in China for submission to Chiang Kai-shek and the Nationalist Government. It arrived in China about the last of July and created a terrific storm—Chiang Kai-shek refused to see any American for several days. We now know that this plan reached China only two weeks before Japan unconditionally surrendered and we also know that the capture of Shanghai by the Communist troops could have had no bearing on ending the war with Japan. Obviously the only objective of the plan was to place the Communists in control of China's biggest seaport and largest city."[7]

Willauer—just as CAT's business in Yunnan had begun to bring in money —was faced with the collapse of his new venture. On September 2 the Minister of Communications issued secret orders to CAT to evacuate Kunming within forty-eight hours; the message was later rescinded, but it shook up Willauer. He was becoming weary of Nationalist defeats and Communist victories—as was everyone else on the Nationalist side. He wrote Louise:

"I do wish the U.S. would get a move on. There are lots of these people who will fight if we can get to them before the last vestige of their morale is gone. Everywhere you go, there is this awful depression. It is killing the spirit of the boys in the airline, of our servants, of everyone. The God damned State Department ought to be taken out one by one and hung."[8]

Anna had given birth to a daughter, Claire Anna, in February 1948. Now she had beome pregnant again, and with the fall of the mainland imminent in the fall of 1949 Chennault planned to have her and the child move to For-

mosa. The seat of the Nationalist Government had already been moved there
—as had most of the wealthy and influential Chinese of the government.
CAT had been busy flying personnel to Taipei for months and there was a
long waiting list of people associated with the government who wanted to be
evacuated. As is the case in most wars, the persons with the most political
connections and money got the first airline seats.

As the Communists moved south, CAT was involved in every sort of
mission. On October 9, Nationalist troops pulled out of Kükong, north of
Canton, and the Chinese defenses of the British crown colony of Hong Kong
began to crumble. Willauer sent word to CAT personnel at the big base at
Canton to evacuate key office personnel—which was done—but security
guards at White Cloud Airport seized personnel director Reese Bradburn
and traffic manager Arthur Fung and held them for ransom. Willauer and
financial adviser Jim Brennan gathered up what Hong Kong dollars they
could and, with Bob Rousselot flying a C-47, flew the ransom money to
Canton. The two men were released—along with nearly eighty Chinese employees.

The Office of Policy Coordination of the CIA in Washington, under Wisner, had decided to at least experiment with CAT—as a prelude to investing
major funding—by assigning some agency personnel to the airline. Al Cox, a
former OSS agent who had served in China in 1945 organizing guerrilla
forces, was sent to Hong Kong in late October. His title was vague but he
was to work as an assistant to Willauer and Chennault, in addition to trying
to set up guerrilla units on the mainland. He arrived just in time to be
involved in supervising the rescue of CAT personnel from Canton. He must
have felt right at home—with his intelligence and guerrilla background.
CAT now began to set up a headquarters in Hong Kong. The British crown
colony was jammed to the breaking point with refugees of every nationality
fleeing the Chinese Communists. There were "stateless" persons of every
race and political persuasion trying to find work and quarters in a city normally a quiet British port.

Chennault had to call on every influential Chinese he knew to get housing
for CAT personnel, who numbered about three thousand. Willauer leased a
river steamer and that served for some, but it was not large enough. Office
space was at a premium and each afternoon the executives of CAT would
meet for discussions on the mezzanine of the Gloucester Hotel. The British
government did not allow the installation of private radio facilities, so Chennault had to make do with a radio station for the airline at Portuguese
Macao down the China coast—not a satisfactory arrangement at all. Currency was a terrible problem and the airline was forced to operate with a
mixture of Hong Kong dollars, American money, gold bars, silver dollars,
pounds, and French francs. It was a nightmare.

The Nationalists were putting up the best fight possible and a few seasoned
commanders, such as General Pai Chung-shih, the governor of Kwangsi

Province, actually drove the Communists back in battles during early October. He sent Communist General Lin Piao reeling back from Hengyang to Changsha.

CAT suffered its third fatal accident on November 8, as pilot Norman Jones was killed in the crash of a C-47 in the Indochina jungle while flying a load of tin from Mengtze to Haiphong. Copilot M. H. Kung parachuted to safety, but flight operator K. V. Chin was missing.

Another accident happened on December 6 when Jim McGovern had to make an emergency landing near Liuchow. Nobody was injured, but the Communists captured McGovern and his crew. At that time McGovern weighed three hundred pounds and just feeding him was a problem for the Reds.

On November 20, Chennault flew to Seoul, Korea—where there were ominous signs of Communist troop movements along the 38th parallel in that country—for a meeting with General MacArthur and Korean President Syngman Rhee about contingency plans to contain Communist troops should they invade South Korea.

It was now only a matter of time before the mainland fell. Back in April, Chiang had ordered the government's treasury—gold and silver estimated at U.S. $335 million—and selected air and naval units moved to Taiwan, the Chinese name for Formosa. He was to follow shortly with his staff. On November 29, CAT evacuated Chungking, flying people to Taipei. Based in Hong Kong since the fall of Shanghai in May, both CNAC and CATC had been expected to help in the evacuation of the old wartime capital. The defection of the general managers of both airlines to Peking with twelve aircraft and crews in November was a shock to both CAT and the Nationalist Government. CAT was swamped with cries for help from Chungking and had to charter extra planes from Pacific Overseas Airways Siam, Hong Kong Airways, and Cathay Pacific Airways to help carry the evacuees. The last three planes out carried the last of the CAT personnel and AP correspondent Spencer Moosa.

The two defecting airlines left seventy-one planes—including modern Convairs and DC-4s—on the ground in Hong Kong, and the Communists immediately filed claims of ownership with the British as property of the Chinese People's Republic.

Chennault was alarmed to think that Communists would get control of the aircraft and use them either to bomb the Nationalist Government on Taiwan or to drop paratroops. He and Willauer went to Taipei to talk with Chiang Kai-shek, who had set up his government headquarters in Taipei, the new capital of the big island. Chennault proposed that CAT act as an agent for the Nationalist Government with authority to change title to the CNAC and CATF aircraft on the ground in Hong Kong so as to prevent the Communists from taking possession. On November 11 the Chinese Civil Aeronautics Commission suspended the CNAC and CATF registration certificates of the aircraft. CAT hired a squad of Sikhs to guard the aircraft and Willauer—just to make sure the Communists didn't take off in the planes—led a group of CAT employees to the area on Kai Tak Airfield and let all the air out of the tires. The British—nervously watching Communist troops surround Hong Kong—were anything but happy at CAT's intervention. However, the governor of the crown colony, Alexander Grantham, announced on November 17 that no aircraft would be allowed to leave Hong Kong for the mainland until the Chinese-British agreement had been clarified. CAT was ordered to remove the Sikh guards; when they left, Communist former employees of both CNAC and CATF took possession of the planes, promising to maintain physical possession until the British government formally recognized the new Chinese government in Peking. The British—not wanting to further antagonize the Communists—did nothing to prevent the former employees from holding the planes.

Chennault realized the only chance to keep the aircraft out of Communist hands was to transfer the planes to American ownership. Tom Corcoran set up an American company to represent CAT in an effort to keep the planes from the Communists and to recover them for CAT. The purposes of this operation was to both keep the planes from the Communists and recover all the assets of the two Chinese airlines. The stockholders of the newly organized company, Civil Air Transport, Inc. (CATI), were Chennault, Willauer, Tom Corcoran, David Corcoran, Bill Youngman, another partner, and Jim Brennan. Chennault and Willauer proposed to the Chinese on Taiwan a plan to purchase from CNAC and the Chinese government the CATC aircraft. The Chinese agreed to the transaction and Willauer signed, on behalf of Chennault and himself, a promissory note for $4.75 million—and the legal battle for the aircraft was on.

In London, William Donovan, now a senior partner in the law firm hired by Tom Corcoran to represent CATI, informed the British that Americans had purchased CNAC and CATC. In Washington, Corcoran was busy trying to secure American registration for the planes. The one big problem was that Pan American World Airways still owned 20 percent of CNAC and would protest the transfer of registration. And that registration had to be in American hands to establish clear title. William Bond, vice president of Pan Am, was not enthused about selling the shares of stock to Chennault and Willauer, but neither did he want the planes to fall into the hands of the Reds. On December 20 he and T. V. Soong, representing the Nationalist Government, sold the shares to the newly formed corporation for $1.25 million and the CAA immediately granted American registration to the planes in Hong Kong.[9]

While lawyers for CAT and the Communists began to prepare for a battle royal, CAT continued to fly evacuees to Taiwan. Kunming was being evacuated in early January 1950 and the tin lift from there and Mengtze to Haiphong was coming to a close. Chennault decided to try to fly the 472 tons of tin stored at Mengtze to Hainan Island before the city fell to the Communists, but he was too late. The last planes were leaving but pilot Bob Buol, for some unknown reason, decided to spend the night in Mengtze rather than stay at the field. Fighting broke out at the field about midnight and pilot Bill Welk flew in to try to pick up Buol. Communist machine-gun fire struck his plane while taxiing and slugs hit copilot Henry Davis in the leg. Welk poured the power to the plane and took off as fast as he could. Buol was captured the following day and sentenced to prison.

Almost all of the mainland had fallen by this time and CAT—after losing a great deal of equipment and all its bases in China—was nearly broke. Willauer left Hong Kong for the States during the holiday season to try to get CIA backing for the sinking airline, and as 1949 came to a close Chennault flew to Taipei where he and Anna—six months' pregnant with their second child—had taken a house at number 12 Wuchang Villa. In spite of its financial problems, Chennault could be proud of his airline's record in its three years on the mainland. Through the hectic days of the fighting CAT had flown almost 60 million ton-miles and had carried nearly 300,000 passengers. If it had not been a business success, the struggling airline had at least been an example of heroic efforts on the part of a lot of people.

Thirty-two

The Nationalist Chinese were not firmly entrenched on Taiwan. They were unwelcome guests to the native Taiwanese people, who had been occupied by the Japanese since 1895. The language taught in the schools had been Japanese and the Taiwanese were not receptive to the Nationalists, who insisted Chinese now be taught. There were a number of revolts in the latter part of 1949, but Chiang—who needed a sanctuary and was in no mood to tolerate any nonsense from any minority—ruthlessly quelled the Taiwanese opposition.

He received no support in his stand on the island from the United States. In December the Department of State wrote its foreign personnel that Taiwan's "control by the Communist forces would not imperil our position in the Far East."[1] Secretary of State Acheson told a *Time* magazine correspondent in December 1949, "What we must do now is shake loose from the Chinese Nationalists. It will be harder to make that necessary break with them if we go to Formosa."

President Truman was firm in his resolve not to help the Nationalists on their island bastion when he said, "The United States Government will not provide military aid or advice to Chinese forces on Formosa."[2]

In January, Great Britain, Norway, Finland, Sweden, and Switzerland recognized the Communist regime at Peking. The U. S. State Department received a rude shock when, in that same month, the Chinese Communists seized American consular property in Peking in violation of treaty rights. Acheson explained the removal thus: "Our people are leaving because the normal and accepted standards of international conduct have not been observed by the Chinese Communist authorities in their treatment of our representatives and because they have, in effect, even been summarily ejected from their offices in Peiping."[3]

A lively debate now began in parts of Congress and in the press about the wisdom of any steps that might further weaken the Nationalist Government on Taiwan. Ex-President Herbert Hoover—when asked by Senator William Knowland for his views on the situation—said the United States should not only continue to recognize the Nationalists, but that we should back it fully, even to giving it naval support.

Chennault, after reading his statement, wrote Hoover in January 1950 to thank him for expressing his views and detailing the importance of Formosa to the United States.

Chennault's views were not shared by the State Department or the President. On December 30, 1949, President Truman announced that United States occupation of Formosa was not advisable and again, on January 5, 1950, he stated categorically, ". . . The United States Government will not provide military aid or advice to Chinese Forces on Formosa."

It was only after the outbreak of hostilities in Korea in June 1950—and the subsequent entrance of Chinese Communist forces against American troops in that conflict—that the United States was again forced to reverse its policy toward China. Formosa now became strategic to our war in Korea and on June 27, 1950, Truman made it clear that any attack on Formosa by the Communists would be considered an attack upon the United States. He sent the United States Seventh Fleet to the Formosa Strait and the South China Sea and ordered it to prevent any attack on the big island. He also called on the Nationalists to cease any and all operations against the Communists on the nearby mainland. The Nationalist garrisons on the tiny, rocky islands of Quemoy and Matsu were literally in sight of the mainland. Sporadic shelling across the strait had been taking place.

But in January 1950, while the United States was still officially considering abandoning the Nationalists, the outlook for Chiang's forces as well as for Chennault was bleak. With nowhere else to go, CAT joined the Nationalist Chinese on Taiwan, began a schedule of round-the-island flights to help Taiwan business, and inaugurated Taipei–Hong Kong–Haiphong and Taipei–Manila flights. All the planes in the CAT fleet were switched to U.S. registry, the ownership shown as Civil Air Transport, Inc.

By March 1950, CAT was at its lowest point since being organized in 1946. The airline was down to 124 foreign employees, many of them on leave without pay. With its mainland routes gone and the Yunnan–Haiphong tin run closed, CAT desperately needed business. Joe Rosbert had been made director of operations and the line hired Hugh Grundy as chief engineer.

In Shanghai in the spring of 1949, Chennault had purchased a surplus American LST to house aircraft maintenance equipment—a 328-foot, 2,500-ton craft. It was purchased just as the U. S. Navy had designed it, but as CAT gradually lost one base after another, repair and maintenance shops were gradually moved aboard it and she was repainted. It was moved down to Canton in September and the machinery and shops from Canton were loaded aboard. With CAT heavy equipment—and the personal effects of

CAT personnel—aboard, the LST was moved down to Hainan Island as the south China area fell to the Communists. In January she was sailed—in terrible weather and loaded down to the waterline—to Kaohiung on the south tip of Taiwan. The name of the port had been changed from Takao, a Japanese naval base and a former target of the Fourteenth Air Force.

The LST, accompanied by a supply barge, constituted a floating maintenance and supply base that could not be equaled in the region. On it were propeller, woodworking, paint and fabric, communications, instrument, sheet metal, blasting, electroplating, engine, welding, and hydraulic shops— all gleaming, spotless, and running like Swiss watches. Approximately two hundred and fifty men worked aboard the LST and the marine crew consisted of thirty-three people. Grundy established a land maintenance base at Tainan just to the south. Living conditions on this fully equipped maintenance field were Spartan for the approximately four hundred men and twenty foreign supervisory personnel working there. As CAT tried to keep its planes in the air and sought desperately for new business, financial expert Jim Brennan cut expenses to a minimum and put through stringent economic measures—even to the extent of drawing upon $29,000 from Willauer's personal funds and $25,000 from Chennault's without notifying them in advance. Chennault was furious and talked about filing embezzlement charges against Brennan.[4] Things were to get worse. The airline lost $671,000 in the first three months of 1950.

Chennault and Willauer spent considerable time in Washington in the search for backing; they dealt with Corcoran, Donovan, and Wisner of the OPC. It is not clear how it was done, because records on OPC and CIA dealings are seldom available, but in March the CIA finally decided to support CAT. The State Department and the Defense Department—plus the Joint Chiefs of Staff—ratified the decision on March 13.[5]

The situation in the Far East—with mainland China gone and Ho Chi Minh's activities in Indochina becoming more serious—apparently spurred the CIA to do something concrete. While the United States still had not reversed its policy on the Nationalists on Taiwan, covert activities were permissible. The CIA was beginning to act as it did in later years—unilaterally. The agency's bankers advanced CAT $350,000 on March 24, to clear up bills such as payroll, gasoline debts, and supply bills. In addition, $400,000 was to be paid to fund operating deficits until mid-June. The bankers— "undisclosed principals" in CIA parlance—would then have the option to purchase the airline for $1 million.[6]

With money finally coming in, Chennault had two reasons to celebrate. The other reason was that he had just become a father—again. Anna had given birth to another girl, Cynthia Louise, who immediately became "Cindy Lou" in Chennault's Louisiana accent. The little girl was named for Anna's sister Cynthia, who had married Dr. Richard Lee and who also lived in Taipei. Both the Lees worked in the medical department of CAT. Anna wanted to keep busy, so Chennault assigned her a job as coeditor of the airline magazine, the *CAT Bulletin*. The publication, now being printed as a regular magazine, was half in Chinese and half in English, requiring two editors. Now that the CIA was involved in the operation, it began to send employees over to work in the airline. They needed "front" jobs and so were assigned to the traffic and sales, public relations, and financial divisions of the company. One such employee, Stuart McFadden, became the public relations officer and a coeditor of the *Bulletin*. The magazine was edited in Taipei, where Anna had a small office with four to five people helping her, but printing facilities were almost nonexistent in Taipei and the *Bulletin* was a struggling operation. Later in the year it was decided to have it printed in Tokyo.

The infusion of CIA personnel into the airline was done so slowly and so subtly that many regular employees never suspected the company was becoming a front for covert activities. To look legitimate, CAT continued its regular commercial operations and many employees had no idea it was anything but a cargo and passenger airline.

Hainan Island fell on April 24. The Communists came across the strait from China on junks and swept away the disorganized Nationalist forces. CAT evacuated its base there, abandoning valuable radio equipment. Invasion jitters now hit Taiwan and even Chennault made arrangements with the U. S. Air Force to park about twenty C-46s on Guam in case the island fell.

For all his dislike of the Japanese—after ten years of fighting them on the Chinese mainland—Chennault knew the airline needed to gain a foothold in Japan and he began to explore the possibilities of service to that country and to South Korea. In April he entered into negotiations with Korean National Airlines (KNA) to set up joint operations of domestic and international routes. CAT opened an office in the newly built Readers Digest Building in Tokyo, a glass and brick edifice close to the moat of the Imperial Palace. Burridge was put in charge of the office and immediately set up traffic, sales, and financial operations there. In the first part of June, Bob Rousselot made the inaugural flight of air freight service between Taipei and Tokyo.

On May 31, Jim McGovern was released by the Reds at Hong Kong—weighing sixty pounds less than he did when he was forced to land near Liuchow. He wore a ragged-looking beard and was rather unkempt. Chennault laughed when they met in Taipei, saying it must have been rough for the Communists to have to feed McGovern all that time and their armies too. After a few weeks of rest and food McGovern went back to flying for Chief Pilot Rousselot—in the best tradition of CAT.

The U. S. State Department showed signs of waking up to the Communist threat in the Far East and military assistance programs were being initiated for Indonesia, the Philippines, Burma, Indochina, and Thailand. About the same time Wisner of the OPC informed the State Department that the CIA intended to purchase CAT as a bulwark against Communism in the Orient.

On June 25 the United States learned what Chennault had been preaching right along: that the Communists indeed had plans for the conquest of the Far East. North Korean troops poured across the 38th parallel into South Korea and the Korean War was on. Chiang offered 33,000 troops to fight with United Nations forces in Korea, but the State Department continued to look upon the Nationalists with some suspicion and Truman did not accept the offer. Apparently he felt the Nationalists forces might provoke the Chinese Communists to enter the war.

On June 28, CIA Director Hillenkoetter approved the purchase of CAT. A holding company of three employees of the financial section of CAT, Inc., together with a CIA employee of CAT, became the majority and controlling interest in CAT, Inc.'s seven-man Board of Directors—thus ensuring policy control.

The $1 million payment to CAT's owners paid off the original Chinese investors for their 22 percent stock holding. Chennault and Willauer got back their money that had been spent by Brennan. Corcoran and Youngman asked for $100,000 for what they claimed was six years of "legal work" for CAT, and the balance of $700,000 was roughly divided among Willauer (17.64), Chennault (14.46), Rio Cathay (Corcoran and Youngman—28.88), Brennan (8.46), and the rest in smaller shares to Wang Wen-san, L. K. Taylor, and other minor Chinese investors.[7]

The financial arrangements made Chennault happy, because the airline would have folded in late spring if it had been left to its own devices. He wrote Corcoran:

"I am quite satisfied with the airline solution arranged by Whitey, you and other associates. It is far better than piecemeal liquidation or pinching down to a size that would satisfy our current operational requirements. We could not operate a competitive airline with our aircraft, and we don't have the capital to buy modern transports."

The new arrangements also provided for Chennault to be made chairman of the board of the new company. The CIA realized it would have to get along with the Nationalist Chinese if the aircraft were to carry the Nationalist flag on their tails and the agency also knew that only Chennault could negotiate with Chiang Kai-shek.

Willauer became president of the new company and Brennan a financial vice president. Hugh Grundy remained chief engineer, Joe Rosbert remained as director of operations, and Bob Rousselot became chief pilot. Two of the higher-echelon CIA employees took over administrative posts in the airline —Al Cox as vice president for management and Bob Terhaar as treasurer.

Although Chennault had a high-sounding title, he really had very little to do with the day-to-day operation of the airline. The CIA knew he was needed as liaison with the Nationalists but it also distrusted his close ties to Chiang. By its very nature, the CIA was involved in a number of covert operations it would rather the Nationalists not know about. It was attempting to organize on the mainland anti-Communist forces who were not necessarily Nationalist sympathizers; these were known covertly as a "Third Force." The CIA figured that if Chennault knew about this arm of the operation he might leak the information to Chiang—as well he might have, considering their long association. So he was not brought in on the top-secret decisions regarding covert operations with a Third Force, but he did know of covert operations involving CAT aircraft.

It was necessary to make flights to the Chinese mainland for a number of intelligence purposes. There were still Nationalist pockets of resistance in China—though not many—and the CIA wanted to establish contact with these. In addition, scattered remnants of Nationalist armies were still in such places as northern Burma where they had been driven by the Communist armies in Yunnan. It was necessary to maintain contact with them. Under the command of General Li Mi were a force of some 1,500 men of the former Nationalist 97th Division. He recruited other Nationalist soldiers who had fled south and by mid-1950 had managed to build up his forces to about 4,000 troops. They were not well armed but they had enough arms to be a threat to Burma. They lived off the land—plus making a living in the opium trade.

CIA's CAT planes were designated to make these flights. It was obvious they could not take off from such civilian bases as Taipei and Hong Kong with the easily spotted Nationalist flags on the tails of the silver C-46s and C-47s. A number of CAT planes were painted olive drab at the big maintenance base at Tainan. Easily detachable flags were designed so that they could be used for airways flights but could be taken off at military bases. It was necessary to make flights into Communist-held territory from bases where the planes could not be observed by prying civilian eyes. Air bases such as Kadena on Okinawa, Tachikawa near Tokyo, and U.S. bases in South Korea were used as takeoff points. A number of CAT pilots with long experience in China were interviewed by CIA operatives and by Cox for jobs flying these missions. A navigator, Cyril ("Pinky") Pinkava, who had considerable experience over China, was hired and prepared for the long, dangerous flights. In true CIA fashion, all markings were removed from the crew's clothing and no identifying rings or watches were worn. The men were well armed with side arms and the planes were equipped with automatic rifles and machine guns. Each man carried the customary lethal pill in case of capture. It at least gave him an option. Object of the missions was to drop leaflets, radio equipment, and other supplies to agents on the mainland; to bring in agents—either by landing or by dropping them in by parachute—and to pick up agents who wished to come out. The latter missions were especially dangerous, as no one ever knew when a trap was being set.

The Korean War, as expected by Chennault and Willauer, brought a considerable amount of military contract work to CAT as a carrier of equipment to the war zone. These flights were completely separate from the covert CIA operations. CAT used its silver-colored as well as its olive-drab aircraft with the Nationalist flag painted on the tail. The contract flights, however, gave the covert side of the airline a good opportunity to fly from military bases in Japan and Korea with their unmarked planes. The flags could be painted out on any of the military fields and put back on after the secret flights.

By August 1950, CAT had secured a contract with the Far East Air Material Command (FEAMCOM) to carry cargo and personnel about the Far East. Rousselot called back as many pilots as he could from the leave on which they had been placed after the fall of the Chinese mainland in late 1949 and by September CAT was back to twenty-five flight crews.

At the same time the military contract flights were flying military supplies to Korea and wounded soldiers back to military hospitals in Japan, Cox had convinced the CIA to allow three C-46s to operate out of Tachikawa Air Force base near Tokyo.

Chennault, celebrating his sixtieth birthday quietly in Taipei, felt that he was at least contributing to the anti-Communist fight with his military flights for FEAMCOM and his covert missions to the Chinese mainland.

In November the Chinese Communists entered the Korean War and American and South Korean casualties began to escalate. CAT C-46s assisted in the evacuation of wounded from Yonpo, losing one C-46 in the process. The next day another CAT C-46, piloted by Bob Heising, struck the side of Mount Fuji in Japan at the 8,000-foot level. The pilot must have been blown off course by high-altitude winds, as Fuji is the only high mountain in Japan and every pilot knew it well. Killed were Heising, copilot Jimmy Chang, and radio operator T. W. Wen.

CAT was contributing greatly to the Korean War. It carried 27,000 tons of supplies and thousands of wounded; at the same time its covert flights allowed the OPC to carry hundreds of agents from CIA training bases throughout the Far East.

As for its commercial operations elsewhere, the airline owed its existence to Chennault's relationship to Chiang Kai-shek. Most Chinese officials on Taiwan were never able to differentiate between CAT and CAT, Inc., and as a result confusion arose over a number of technical matters. Chennault *was* CAT—in the minds of most Chinese. It was necessary to maintain this relationship in an airline that flew the Chinese flag under a Chinese charter, no matter who the actual owners were. Willauer wrote:

"The extraordinary loyalties of the flight operations personnel of the airline ran to him [Chennault] personally and his presence in Formosa was an indispensable factor in the confidence of the Chinese Government [in CAT]."[8]

As the Korean War rolled on, the disguised operations of CAT in the Far East expanded rapidly. The CIA itself was mushrooming into a large agency.

General Walter Bedell Smith took over its directorship and its budget was expanded.

The CIA, hoping to divert the Communists' attention away from their forces pouring down through North Korea and across the 38th parallel, decided to arm part of General Li Mi's ragged troops in Burma. It was hoped they could cause enough diversion by an attack against the Yunnan border to cause the Communists to pull some troops from Korea. CAT was chosen to supply the operation. The OPC deal was coordinated through a "front" company, Sea Supply, in Bangkok, and flights began from Okinawa where arms were picked up and air-dropped to Li Mi's troops. The Nationalist troops marched northward through the Burmese jungles and invaded Yunnan in early May. Arms were air-dropped all along the route by C46s and C-47s flown by Rousselot, Robert ("Dutch") Brongersma, Charlie Hays, Bob Snoddy, and Harold Wells. Chennault went to Okinawa where the briefings took place and instructed the Air Force on jungle conditions along the Yunnanese border—his old stamping ground south of Kunming. Li Mi ran into stiff resistance on the part of Communist troops in Yunnan and was driven back into the Burmese jungles a month later, but it had at least been a valiant effort on the part of CAT.

The Communists knew all about the covert operation and—after Li Mi's defeat—protested vigorously to the Burmese government, which in turn filed an official protest with Washington. In what was the beginning of years of official denial on the part of the United States Government in cases of CIA activity, Secretary of State Dean Rusk blithely denied to U.S. Ambassador to Burma David Kay (who just happened to know nothing about the operation because he had not been briefed about it) that the government had any connection with the operation that was delivering arms to Nationalist forces in Burma. The CIA even went so far—in answering British charges that it had intervened in Burma—as to imply that there was some American civilian support of the Nationalists in Burma, possibly connected with Chennault. Some reporters in the Far East were not fooled by the denials, and reports of covert CIA activity began to appear in American newspapers. The CIA couldn't have cared less. Such newspaper stories only lived for a day or so in the media around the world and were forgotten shortly afterward.

Al Cox was stationed in Hong Kong and, while his position with CAT gave him considerable work, his covert operations on the mainland were his primary job. Assisted by Conrad La Geaux, Stuart McFadden, and Bob Terhaar, he was responsible for connecting the mainland guerrillas in China with the Nationalist forces on Taiwan. The Nationalists claimed they had a million guerrillas in China who were ready and willing to fight the Communists. Chennault thought so too, and made speeches and wrote articles in late 1951 and early 1952 using that figure. The actual number was probably considerably less and not all those dissidents were Nationalist sympathizers. Chennault—because of his unique position of having access to Nationalist intelligence information through his association with the Generalissimo and his CAT-OPC connections—was in a good position to coordinate activities between guerrilla operations on the mainland and Taiwan. He lived and operated out of his home in Wuchang Villa, which was a housing complex about ten minutes by car from downtown Taipei. His neighbors included Admiral Charles M. Cooke, retired commander of the U. S. Seventh Fleet and military adviser to the Nationalists, and Colonel Raymond Peers, former World War II OSS commander in Burma and head of almost six hundred employees of several branches of the CIA on Taiwan. Support of the pro-Nationalists had transformed Taiwan into an armed camp of CIA activities by the spring of 1951. A Far Eastern Division of OPC had been located on the island to provide guerrilla training, logistical support, overflight capabilities, facilities for propaganda coverage of the mainland by radio and leaflet balloon, and other tasks. Because of his many years on the mainland and his close ties to the top Nationalists, Chennault was constantly consulted by the OPC—particularly on flying matters concerning weather conditions and terrain on the mainland. His home was a thoroughfare for people stopping in for information at all hours. It was a problem to keep up with who was who in the intelligence business. Innumerable employees of Western Enterprises —a fictional company that provided commercial cover for CIA employees— called on him daily.

Bob Rousselot was Chennault's right hand and the key link between CAT and the CIA for covert missions. Assigned a task by Chennault or Al Cox, Rousselot would take charge of operational planning and the selection of crew. A former Marine combat pilot, he had joined CAT in Shanghai and became chief pilot in 1948. He was the kind of steady flier Chennault liked, and both he and Willauer entrusted the tall, handsome ex-Marine with all sorts of responsible tasks for the airline. For the covert flights Rousselot looked for capable, responsible men who would complete a mission if at all possible but would abort when necessary. Although a CIA case officer could veto his choice of crew, this seldom happened.

The overflight missions performed by CAT were volunteer missions and not all company pilots participated. The additional pay was welcome and perhaps two thirds to three quarters of the pilots flew these covert flights at one time or another. The most dangerous flights were assigned to a hard core of experienced pilots—Rousselot, Norman Schwartz, Bob Snoddy, Eddie Sims, Merril Johnson, Bill Welk, Paul Holden, and Roy Watts. Pinky Pinkava was the navigator on the hazardous flights.

Many of the flights were "routine" leaflet drops along the China coast and posed very little risk. The Chinese Communists had few planes and what MIG fighters they had were employed in the Korean War far to the north. Antiaircraft fire was confined to large cities and military bases. However, the flights involving agent drops and agent pickups were very risky. CAT planes were used on most of the flights, but now and then an Air Force four-engine plane would be used. CAT finally purchased a four-engine DC-4 early in 1952 and this was used at all other times as the flagship of the airline's commercial operation—flying from Bangkok to Tokyo via Hong Kong and Taipei. The Nationalist Government was informed of these flights and both Chiang and Madame knew of each mission. Several times they personally thanked the crews. Some of these flights dropped agents into the far reaches of western China and took as long as fourteen hours flying time.

While some members of the foreign press were aware that there were rumors of clandestine operations by CAT, very few stories detailing such movements appeared. The brightly painted CAT aircraft, with the colorful Nationalist flag on the tail, were everyday sights at airfields throughout the Far East. It was a busy cargo and passenger line and routinely flew correspondents back and forth between Asiatic cities as part of its regular service. The traffic, sales, and booking offices were located in the busy sections of Tokyo, Taipei, Hong Kong, and Bangkok and the line certainly had the appearance of a normal commercial operation.

But its operations were well known to the Communists. There is no doubt that some employees who were flying covert missions let slip a few vital secrets without realizing what the consequences would be. In any war there are casualties.

The CIA was still attempting to supply guerrillas in the Third Force on the mainland—those guerrillas not in sympathy with the Communists, but also not loyal to the Nationalist Government. Such missions by CAT—in cooperation with the U. S. Air Force—could not be flown from Taiwan because of Nationalist Government sensitivity. So they were flown from military bases to the north—Tachikawa in Japan and fields such as Kimpo Air Base in Seoul, Korea.

Norm Schwartz and Bob Snoddy were assigned to fly these missions in the spring and summer of 1952 in a specially outfitted C-47 with a tail number that could not be read except from very close up. The Air Force also assigned them a special four-engine B-17 that was flown by Snoddy, a World War II Navy B-24 pilot.

Flying agents into west and north China was not a very complicated procedure. Bringing them out could be. Most agents were dropped in at night by parachute. It was necessary to land in order to pick them up—until OPC came up with a new device for snatching them off the ground. Two poles were set in the ground and a wire was strung between them. A harness was attached to the wire and a man was strapped into this harness. Theoretically —for it had not yet been tried in China—a plane would approach the wire at slightly above stalling speed and a line with a hook would catch the wire and jerk the man into the air.

On November 29, 1952, the CIA decided to try the system in Manchuria, and Schwartz and Snoddy were sent, along with two intelligence officers, John Downey and Richard Fecteau, to pick up an agent. The agent, Li

Chun-ying, who had been dropped into Manchuria in October, had signaled he wanted to come out. The four men took off from Seoul in the special C-47. As it approached the pickup wire just above the ground in the darkness, the Communists opened fire and both Snoddy and Schwartz were killed almost instantly by machine guns. The plane cartwheeled across the ground and Downey and Fecteau were pulled from the wreckage, badly injured. The Communists had learned of the mission ahead of time and were ready. The CIA learned through agents on the mainland that Downey was sentenced to life imprisonment and Fecteau to twenty years in prison.

When the plane did not return, CAT immediately—through its public relations office—put out a release that one of its planes was missing on a routine flight from Korea to Japan and a massive sea search was started. The Communists, who knew better, never said a word, apparently preferring to let the lesson sink in. CAT security and the CIA thoroughly investigated recent activity of both the pilots—hoping to come up with a clue to the security risk. It could have been in many places. Both pilots were popular and in the previous months had been to a number of parties where a casual word could have been picked up. In Tokyo there were numerous agents operating in and about the homes of CAT personnel—as there were in Hong Kong. Most of the CAT pilots were single (Snoddy was married) and most had girl friends over much of the Orient. It was like looking for the proverbial needle in the haystack.

The United States Government never admitted the death of either Snoddy or Schwartz. They were both buried by the Communists in unmarked graves in Manchuria. Fecteau was quietly released from prison by the Communists in 1971—after serving nineteen of his twenty-year sentence. President Richard M. Nixon, on his 1971 visit to Peking, discussed the Downey case with the Communists and later said at a press conference in February 1973 that Downey had been a CIA agent whose *military* plane had been *forced down* in Chinese territory. Satisfied with the admission, the Communists set Downey free on March 12, 1973.[9] The release got little publicity. After the men were shot down Chennault personally consoled Snoddy's wife Charlotte, who was pregnant with their first child, and recommended to the CIA that in the future only single pilots be used on the covert flights if possible.

On July 28, 1952, the British Privy Council in London ruled that the seventy-one aircraft that had been impounded in Hong Kong since 1949 rightfully belonged to CAT and not to the Communists. Chennault was jubilant. The planes were in terrible shape after the long wait on the cement ramps of Kai Tak Airfield in the humid weather of Hong Kong, but the victory was still sweet. The CIA had not lain idle while the case was being argued in London, for as soon as the decision was reached an escort carrier, the USS *Cape Esperance,* moved into Hong Kong Harbor and tied up alongside the Kowloon docks. Any foreign correspondents who doubted the airline had connections with the intelligence community had only to ask how a civilian airline suddenly ordered an aircraft carrier to tote away its aircraft.

In a matter of days the carrier, with its huge loading cranes, lifted the seventy-one aircraft onto the decks and sailed off. The planes were to be sold in the States and elsewhere after being reconditioned.

Chennault, questioned in New Orleans in October, talked a bit about the disposition of the planes. He had been to South America to see if they could be sold to airlines there.

With the settlement of the case, the Chinese on Taiwan immediately pressed Chennault and Willauer for payment of the $4.75 million in promissory notes that had been signed by Willauer at the time of the original purchase of the CNAC planes in December 1949. Unable to differentiate between CAT and CAT, Inc., the government on Taiwan became stubborn when the officers of CATI tried to explain the new setup. CATI had advanced over $10 million in counterclaims against the government—including $3 million for foreign exchange that had been promised but not given on the mainland, plus $2.5 million for legal and other expenses connected with the recovery of CNAC/CATC assets. Willauer told the Nationalists that CATI had sold only fifteen of the seventy-one aircraft so far and that the money from that sale had been used for legal expenses, for removing the planes from Hong Kong, and for renovating the aircraft for sale. CATI's partners had already spent $500,000 and $2.9 million more was expected to go for getting the remaining planes in shape for resale. The Chinese were offered two choices: they could wait until all the planes were sold and take their share of the profits then or they could accept $1.2 million in cash for a complete settlement. The Chinese—still unable to differentiate between CAT and CATI—refused to negotiate and the whole thing became a political football.[10]

Chennault, as chairman of the board, was involved in political decisions between CAT and the Nationalists and with the Communist threat. He was no longer involved with the financial troubles of CAT since selling his shares to the OPC. On a regular salary with enough money to purchase outright the house in Taipei and another big home in Monroe, Louisiana, for Anna and the two girls, he was free to concentrate on lectures, articles, and interviews. He made frequent trips to the States to appear on radio shows and to give talks. His only connection with CAT now was in the covert operations and those took on a new aspect as the war in Indochina warmed up with the siege of Dienbienphu.

Thirty-three

While Chennault was involved, in the summer of 1953 with a lecture tour in the States on the imminent threat of Communist domination of Asia, the situation in Indochina continued to worsen.

French colonial rule in that land was rapidly coming to an end. Communist troops surrounded the French on the Plaine de Jarres and the French Air Force was called upon to drop food and ammunition to their men. The Air Force was understaffed and without sufficient planes—having only forty-nine C-47s and a few German JU-52 transports. The French appealed to the United States for some large transports and the word reached President Eisenhower by April 23. He discussed the French predicament with Secretary of State John Foster Dulles. Dulles talked to his brother Allen, who had just taken over as director of the CIA, and Allen contacted Cox in Hong Kong. He told Cox the French were concerned with the situation in Laos and wanted to borrow heavy transports to fly tanks and other heavy equipment there. It would require the use of the C-119 "Flying Boxcar" and Dulles was concerned about sending regular U. S. Air Force crews there to fly the big planes. Such an action might have international repercussions. Cox assured Dulles CAT pilots on Taiwan were able to fly the planes and could do so on a "volunteer" basis—thus avoiding embarrassment to the French.

Chennault flew back from the States in time to get in on the last-minute briefings to the pilots and was on hand at the airfield in Taipei to see pilots Felix Smith, Gene Babel, Harold Wells, Steve Kusak, E. G. Kane, and N. N. Forte fly down from Tokyo to join Paul Holden, Eddie Sims, George Kelle, Pinky Pinkava, Bill Welk, and Monson Shaver. The pilots were given a thorough briefing by Chennault on the terrain and weather conditions of Indochina—his old AVG and Fourteenth Air Force stamping ground—and Bob Rousselot spoke to them on the flight characteristics of the big Flying

Boxcars before flying to Clark Air Force Base in the Philippines for a quick seventy-two-hour checkout in the cumbersome C-119. There members of the 483rd Troop Carrier Wing were getting six of the big planes ready for work in Indochina by removing all American markings on the planes and paintings on the insignia of the French Air Force. Eighteen U.S. Air Force mechanics accompanied the CAT pilots on the trip, dressed in civilian clothes. Operation Squaw left on May 5 for Indochina.

For the next few months the CAT pilots flew missions deep into Laos, dropping huge parcels of ammunition, mortars, howitzers, and tanks from the cavernous bellies of the boxcars. They were escorted by French fighters which strafed and dropped napalm on the Communist troops of General Giap.

The main Communist forces returned to their bases in Tonkin in June, leaving guerrilla units to fight the French, who still depended upon French Air Force air drops to supply them. Squaw lasted until July 16, when the CAT pilots pulled out, but few suspected they would be called back again.

In the fall the French—wanting to lure the Communist Vietminh troops into a major battle where French heavy firepower might be fully utilized—dropped paratroopers into Dienbienphu, two hundred and twenty miles behind enemy lines and about a dozen miles from the border of Laos. They believed the troops could be well supplied by air drops from the French Air Force. The U. S. Air Force agreed to charter C-119s to the French provided they were flown by French crews. By December the French crews had flown in barbed wire, howitzers, tents, and a considerable amount of ammunition. The planes were originally to have been withdrawn in December, but the Communists moved in several divisions of Vietminh troops and it was decided to leave the C-119s there through January 1954.

The French crews were exhausted from flying continuous missions, and once again the French asked for help. CAT was called upon once more. Washington contacted Cox again and twenty-one pilots were checked out in the C-119s at Ashiya Air Base in Japan, but it was not until March that the French contracted for twenty-four CAT pilots to fly the Boxcars—again painted with the colors of the French Air Force. The contract said the pilots would fly missions of a logistical nature—"exclusive of any combat missions. Bombardment and dropping napalm will never be required" was the wording of the agreement.[1]

In addition to the same pilots who had flown the earlier Squaw missions, there were Hugh Hicks, Neese Hicks, Roy Watts, A. L. Judkins, Hugh Marsh, Tom Sailer, M. K. Clough, and—back for more combat after his years with the AVG and CNAC—Erik Shilling. Their job was to supply Dienbienphu from Cat Bi Airport, located just to the southeast of Haiphong and one and a half hours flying time away.

The French were dug in close to an airstrip and were surrounded by barbed wire. The Communists had brought up a dozen 105-mm. howitzers and trained them on the airstrip, but there did not seem to be any antiaircraft guns in the vicinity. The pilots considered the air supply drops would be routine.

The battle for Dienbienphu began in earnest on March 13 with a bombardment of the French positions. The CAT crews had begun to supply the French when it was suddenly discovered that Chinese troops had joined the fight and had brought in sixty-four 37-mm. antiaircraft guns to join some General Giap had installed previously and had hidden in caves.

The CAT pilots—who had been flying two three-hour round trips per day in the C-119s, which dropped seven tons on each mission—were making the drops from an altitude of 4,000 to 5,000 feet. On March 24 the Communists opened up with intense antiaircraft fire, knocking down a French C-47 on March 26 and two more the following day. The French raised the altitude of the drops to 6,500 feet, but at that altitude half of the cargo landed outside the drop zone.

CAT crews made eighty-seven drops over the zone during the rest of the month but, though they suffered no casualties, their planes became pockmarked with flak holes and scars from .50-caliber ground fire. By early April, CAT crews began to complain that the rigid 10 A.M. to 3 P.M. drop schedule gave the Communists too much of an advantage to get ready for the drops and also that the French had provided no air cover as promised. The French increased their flak suppression flights and things improved a bit. By April 15 the crews were dropping 137 tons a day.

On April 24, Paul Holden received a flak fragment in his right arm and was flown to Clark Air Force Base, where surgeons managed to save his arm. He returned to duty several months later.

By the end of April, CAT pilots had completed 428 missions—flying through flak that was as bad as anything some pilots had seen over Germany in World War II. It took three minutes to make the flight over the airstrip at Dienbienphu and that time seemed like three hours. The C-119s took sixty direct hits without being disabled enough to crash.

By May the weather was beginning to cloud up as the monsoons began. On May 6, Jim McGovern and Wallace Buford began a spiral down into the beleaguered airstrip in their C-119 to drop an artillery piece. The heavy plane dove down through a curtain of intense flak and a piece struck the left engine. McGovern feathered the engine as another burst struck the tail section. He started the damaged left engine, hoping for enough power to gain control. The plane slipped off and began to lose altitude. Steve Kusak, in radio contact from another C-119, told McGovern to bail out, but the big man—dubbed "Earthquake McGoon" because of his 270-pound frame— apparently did not want to walk out as he had the last time he was captured. He told Kusak he didn't want to do "all that walking again" and would stick to the plane. The big flying boxcar struck the side of a hill with one wing tip and cartwheeled across the slope in flames. McGovern and Buford were killed instantly. Dienbienphu surrendered to the Communists the next day.

McGovern's death came as a blow to Chennault. The big man had been a P-51 fighter pilot in the Fourteenth Air Force and one of his "boys." He wrote a story for *Look* magazine a few months later about McGovern's death and it was reprinted in the *Reader's Digest*. In the article Chennault suggested forming a new American Volunteer Group to fight in Asia. The response was immediate. Young men from all over the United States wrote him to volunteer their services. Some were fighter pilots and some were simply boys eager to fight the Communists.

Whatever Chennault had hoped to accomplish by the story was quickly discouraged by the State Department, which showed no great enthusiasm for another AVG. Chennault finally abandoned the plan—though he did so reluctantly.

He and Anna were spending more time in Monroe now that the two little girls were growing. On his trips back to Taiwan he again became immersed in the myriad tangles of CAT's relationship to the Nationalist Government and was called upon to act as liaison between the line and the Chinese. Always eager to spend time hunting, he frequently flew down to Tainan with several friends and his son Dink, who had come to work for CAT as a security man. Chennault's other constant hunting companion was burly Gene Verschaer, a Belgian, who was CAT's chief of security officer on Taiwan. The endless sugar cane fields of southern Taiwan were filled with ring-neck pheasants and waterfowl. Chennault, who could walk tirelessly all day, loved to move along the edge of the canebrakes where the colorful cocks would suddenly flush into the air, giving him a clear shot at the spectacular birds. Joe, his faithful dachshund, had grown old and fat in Taipei, and though he would have loved to accompany his master on these hunts, Chennault took along Fatty, one of Joe's offspring, to retrieve the birds.

In the evening he and his hunting friends would take the birds to a local restaurant where the native cooks would prepare them. Chennault always brought along several jars of sauces from Szechwan and a jar of his own hot peppers from Louisiana. He never tired of inviting unsuspecting strangers to try the peppers and always laughed until the tears ran down his cheeks as the victim choked and gasped for breath at the searing pain.

After the meal he would sit back at the table with the ever present cigarette dangling from the side of his mouth and tell hunting and fishing stories. As the lights flickered on the bamboo curtains of the restaurant and the sounds of clattering dishes being washed echoed from the kitchen, he would sip his bourbon and recall the olden days afield. Verschaer once asked him if he did much fishing. Chennault said he had not had a chance to do much in China and there were no fish to speak of on Taiwan—except for carp raised in the many farm ponds. Then he remembered a trip taken years ago when he was in the Army Air Corps and flying the air mail across the West, as many service pilots had done in the late 1920s and early 1930s.

He said he had been flying in an open-cockpit DH-4 biplane with a Liberty engine and had made the flight from El Paso, Texas, to Phoenix, Arizona, many times before. The country around the Gila River in southwestern New Mexico was spectacular and in the many times he had flown over the rugged Gila Valley he had wanted to land and try fishing the river for trout. He stowed a flyrod in the plane and on one particularly beautiful spring day he could no longer resist the temptation; he landed the plane in the bottom of the Gila Canyon, on a narrow strip of land close to the water. He got out and, assembling the bamboo flyrod, began to cast for trout.

The sun was hot and the sky a clear blue as he spent several happy hours catching the beautiful native trout of the clear river—before realizing he had better be about his official business. He disassembled the rod and hung his string of glistening trout on a hook in the cockpit for later eating. A stiff crosswind had come up and when he tried to take off a gust caught the craft in the narrow canyon, causing Chennault to hook the undercarriage on a large boulder and flip the plane over on its back. He received a deep cut in his forehead. He said he hung upside down in the cockpit, the string of wet trout slapping him in the face, while he hoped the plane would not catch fire. When it did not, he lowered himself to the ground and surveyed the damage. There was nothing he could do. He shouldered the mail sack and, with his flyrod and trout in the other hand, began to climb out of the steep canyon.

When night fell he built a fire, cooked the trout, and curled up to sleep in the lee of a boulder on the mesa above the canyon. He had picked a remote area to land and it was not until the following day that he walked into a ranch a number of miles across the flats. The rancher and his wife were startled to see a leather-jacketed stranger, wearing a black mustache and helmet and goggles, knock at their door. When they heard his story they made him comfortable and he called the base to report that he had made a forced landing—not unusual in those days—but that he was all right and had the mail. The rancher's wife washed the gash in his forehead and put on a bandage. Chennault—that night years later in Tainan—grinned as he took a sip of his drink and said it had been difficult trying to convince the Air Corps investigating team it was sheer coincidence that he crashed right beside a prime trout stream.

There were thousands of ducks in the small farm ponds near Tainan, and Chennault and Verschaer would walk up to one side of the pond while Dink and a Chinese colonel, P. Y. Li, approached from another. As the ducks climbed for altitude, all the gunners got shots and the air was filled with tumbling teal, mallards, pintails, and widgeon. Chennault brought back dozens of ducks and pheasants to Taipei where he and Anna would invite friends in for wild game dinners.

Although Dienbienphu had fallen, CAT continued supply flights in Indo-china. The French left the country after the Geneva Agreement was signed in July 1954 and the Vietminh occupied all of the country north of the 17th parallel. South of that, the country was administered by the government of Ngo Dinh Diem and an agreement allowed people to move freely between the two zones. There were Nationalist Chinese in North Vietnam who wanted to be expatriated before the Communists took over and CAT was asked to fly these people out. Pilots John Plank and Harry Cockrell flew a month-long series of missions to evacuate refugees from Hanoi and Saigon. There were French who wanted to leave Indochina now that their forces had surrendered, and Chennault negotiated with the French to charter CAT planes for an airlift. Dealing with the French civil authorities was difficult, but CAT set up Operation Cognac and, from August to October, flew 19,808 men, women, and children out of North Vietnam.[2]

In addition to the refugee flights, CAT cooperated with the CIA's Saigon Military Mission (SMM), which had been set up after the fall of Dienbien-phu to organize resistance to the Vietminh. CAT pilots supplied planes for SMM agents who wanted to travel from South to North Vietnam and they carried such paramilitary supplies as radios, guns and ammunition, and ex-plosives. As 1954 wound down CAT played a decreasing role in Indochina, but the original CAT crews who flew in the troubled land were a prelude to operations by their successors—pilots of Air America—who played such a vital and bloody role in the Vietnam conflict.

Chiang Kai-shek asked Chennault to help evacuate the remnants of Gen-eral Li Mi's troops from Burma. CAT flew out almost two thousand soldiers and more than three hundred dependents in late 1953. Now, in 1954, CAT, operating out of Thailand, brought out almost three thousand more soldiers —all poorly armed and in rags—and more than five hundred dependents. All were flown to Taiwan, where they received a tumultuous welcome.

Willauer, who had been having problems with the CIA management about how to run the airline, had become more and more alienated from it as time wore on. He believed in autonomy for the personnel who were working in Asia as a way of life he and Chennault had learned since 1946—but the CIA believed in a tight control of airline operations. There were a number of arguments and, when Willauer's youngest son, Tommy, was killed in an accident in Massachusetts in the summer of 1953, Willauer suffered a severe embolism from the shock. He severed his connections with CAT in the spring of 1954 and, following a lengthy recovery, was named ambassador to Honduras. He did not return to the Far East. Cox was named by the CIA to succeed him as president. Chennault continued to serve as chairman of the board.

After McGovern and Buford were killed over Dienbienphu, CAT suffered its second fatal crash in its charter operation when a C-47 on charter to Sea Supply in Bangkok crashed into the Gulf of Siam. Returning from a night parachute operation in October 1954, the plane struck the water while coming in for a landing and killed copilot Y. C. Kan, radio operator Y. Z. Chen, CIA Agent Jim McCarthy, Jr., and three Thai policemen. The pilot, Harry Kaffenberger, survived the crash.

Cox was having some trouble over renewing CAT's franchise with the Nationalist Government. The franchise—which had been arranged in 1946 by Chennault and Willauer—was necessary if the airline was to be licensed under the Ministry of Communications. With the company divided into segments and CIA-owned, the Chinese were leery of its politics and on March 31 canceled the old franchise. It was a shock to both Cox and the CIA, and it now fell to Cox to come up with a new plan that would keep the Nationalist Government happy. In the States, George A. Doole, Jr., an experienced airline executive and longtime CIA employee, had been named by the CIA to be responsible for CAT and he and Cox did not get along well. The people in Washington had no real knowledge of how Americans worked with the Chinese and the CIA handled correspondence with the Nationalists in a heavy-handed manner. When the Nationalists wrote CATI and demanded immediate settlement of indebtedness based on assessment of $5.2 million in company assets, the CIA suggested the Chinese and CATI divide equally the remaining CNAC/CATC planes, real estate, and a bank balance of $215,000. The Chinese were not interested. CATI offered $1.2 million in cash plus real estate on Taiwan as a settlement, and sent Chennault to explain the offer to Chiang. He was cordial to his old friend but was suspicious about the CIA in Washington. Chennault told Willauer at a board meeting: "He was not happy about the proposed settlement, but I am sure I convinced him that the net worth of CATI is far below the reports."

The Chinese continued to hold out for a better deal—assuming CATI was far more valuable than it was. In July the CIA, irritated at the Chinese refusal to negotiate, appointed Doole vice president, vice chairman of the board, and chief executive officer in the United States.[3] He immediately began to put the pressure on Cox to do something with the Nationalists. Afraid of Chennault's great strength as a figurehead and conscious of his strong connections with Chiang, Doole did not attempt to pressure Chennault, but he did lean heavily on Cox—who had been drinking excessively and was weary of the battles in Washington. By September, when Cox had come up with no results, Doole came to Taipei to see what was going on. With the help of Corcoran in Washington and the intervention of the State Department, the CATI account was settled with the Chinese. It amounted to about $2 million to the Nationalists. The extremely complicated settlement included real estate on Taiwan and property in Hong Kong that had formerly belonged to CNAC and CATC. Chennault was not completely happy with the final settlement and wrote Willauer, ironically:

"I hope this will be a lesson to both you and me never to intervene in the future when we learn that an airline is defecting to the Communists."[4]

Chennault had pulled the coals out of the fire, as usual, by going to Chiang and Madame at the last minute. After Doole had left for Washington, believing he had been responsible for the settlement, Chennault told Corcoran:

"Mr. Doole is completely confident that he obtained government approval practically as a result of his own efforts. As a matter of fact, he would still be sitting here for a much longer time had it not been for the calls made by Al Cox and me on Madame Chiang and my calls alone on the Generalissimo, Premier and the governor."[5]

But the controversy had been destructive to the airline and Cox was on his way out as a result. He was called to the States in December and was informed he was being removed as president of CAT effective December 31, 1954. Both Chennault and Corcoran were shocked at the ruthless way in which the firing had been carried out, and Chennault—at the time—decided he wanted little more to do with an organization that operated in such a manner.

Doole returned to the Far East and appointed Hugh Grundy, an excellent engineer but a cold, impersonal man, to the job of president. Morale of the airline hit a new low with all of the original officers except Chennault gone, and the flying personnel began to look for jobs elsewhere.

Pilot Bob Buol—who had been captured by the Communists in Mengtze in January 1950—was suddenly released in September 1955. His wife Sue, whom Chennault had hired as a personal secretary when Buol was captured, and several CAT pilots met the gaunt pilot as he was released in Hong Kong's New Territories. It was a joyous reunion, but unfortunately for Buol, who had been on a lean diet of rice and vegetables for years, the sudden change to Western opulence was too much. He died less than a year later of a heart attack.

Though Chennault remained on the books of the airline as chairman of the board, he did very little for the company from then on, spending much of the year in Louisiana. During a routine physical examination at Walter Reed Hospital in Washington less than a year later—in the spring of 1956—doctors found a malignant tumor in his left lung.

Bill Leary, in *Perilous Missions,* tells us what happened to CAT:

"CAT continued to operate its unique combination of normal commercial business and clandestine missions under the new [CIA] managerial team. Major covert projects in the late 1950s involved aerial assistance to dissident forces in Indonesia and Tibet. With increasing American involvement in Southeast Asia during the 1960s, the CIA rapidly expanded its air properties to cope with a variety of new tasks. Operating under the name of Air America, the agency's air force dropped rice and guns and transported supplies and troops to a thirty six thousand man army of Hmong tribesmen and their three hundred American case officers in the not-so-secret war in Laos. Air America also flew rescue missions for downed American military pilots, contracted with U. S. Government agencies for overt commercial work in support of the war effort, and undertook numerous deeply secret ('black') flights throughout Southeast Asia and into China.

"The CIA relegated CAT to a 'cover' role during the 1960s. Serving as an international flag carrier for the Republic of China, the airline used a single Convair 880 jet transport (later replaced by a Boeing 727) to operate commercial passenger service along routes extending from Tokyo to Bangkok. CAT also maintained several DC-4s and C-46s for domestic service on Taiwan and for charter flights. An accident involving the airline's jet transport, and the subsequent controversy over responsibility, finally put CAT out of business in 1968."[6]

Thirty-four

During that spring of 1956, Chennault's bronchitis grew worse. He continued to smoke his two packs of Camels a day and his cough—which he attributed to a "smoker's cough" he had had for years—became a constant source of annoyance.

He and Anna took a vacation trip to Lake Louise in Canada in June and on the drive back to Monroe Anna noticed that he began having headaches at night. After a consultation with his doctors, it was decided he needed an operation to remove the infected lung tissue and the surgery was scheduled for August 29, 1957.

Chennault spent the following month in his garden in Monroe, growing vegetables and beds of flowers—jade magnolia, daffodils, jonquils, hyacinth, violets, and pansies. He faced the operation in the same spirit of calm strength with which he had faced all the crises of his life. On the night before the operation he wrote Anna:

"I have no doubt that I will survive the operation tomorrow and live for many years with you and our beloved daughters. However, as you know, all things are in the hands of the Supreme Being and no one can know when he will be called back to the place whence he came.

"If it should happen that I cannot see or be with you in the flesh again, I do want you to know and remember I shall always be with you and the girls in the spirit. I love you and them as much as anyone can love and I believe love will endure beyond the grave.

"Do remember and teach our girls the true principles of life—to be moral, to be honest, loyal and kind to all who need kindness. Live within your means, envy no one, enjoy both the comforts and the privations of life on this earth.

"Be humble and work hard at anything you choose for a profession. Much love to you and our girls. . . ."

Chennault was on the operating table for three hours while the doctors at Walter Reed removed most of his left lung. They were cautiously optimistic about his chance for recovery. The biopsy had shown malignancy of the tissue removed.

Two months later Chennault, Anna, and the girls were back in Taipei. He was strong enough to attend meetings at the CAT office and a few luncheons with friends in the city. He went to several Masonic meetings—something he had not been able to do on the mainland. He had become a master Mason in Texas while in the Army Air Corps, but because of his travels had not been able to attend meetings until he moved to Taiwan.

Joe, the family dachshund, became ill while they were in the States, and Chennault reached home the day after the little dog died. Anna said it was the only time she had ever seen Chennault weep. He buried his dog—which had been with him throughout the AVG and Fourteenth Air Force days—on a small hill overlooking the Tamsui River near Taipei.

The family spent Christmas at number 12 Wuchang Villa and Chennault was strong enough to go hunting near Tainan once more. In the spring he moved the family back to Monroe where his garden needed planting. As the days grew warmer, he fished in the Tensas River with his old friend Jim Noe, and in the warm evenings they sat on the porch of the "fishing shack" near the river and drank bourbon in tall glasses. It was as happy a time as Chennault could remember. He wrote many letters to friends in Washington and to members of Congress, stressing the need for vigilance against Communism in Asia and calling for support for the Nationalist Government on Taiwan.

Both the AVG and the Fourteenth Air Force veterans had formed organizations and Chennault attended the AVG convention in Ojai, California— thoroughly enjoying his reunion with his old P-40 pilots and ground crews of the Burma and Kunming days.

The Fourteenth Air Force convention was attended by men who had served with him from July 1942, when the China Air Task Force was activated, up through July 1943, when the Fourteenth came into being, and on until the end of World War II. Chennault had been able to attend a number of their conventions since the Fourteenth Air Force Association had been formed and each year looked forward to being with his "boys." That year more men than ever came to see the "Old Man."

Chennault had given up cigarettes on doctors' orders but still smoked a battered pipe he carried clenched between his teeth. His regular checkup in June proved negative and, though he tired easily, he continued to work in the garden and to fish regularly. He and Anna took a trip to Europe where they visited Paris, and later Chennault had a chance to see old RAF friends in London. But by the time he returned to the States he knew something was wrong. He was constantly tired and slept restlessly. Thirteen months after his first operation the doctors found a malignant spot in the lung cavity.

They discussed the possibility of another operation but finally decided it might do more harm than good. They decided on radiation treatment. Experts at Boston's Lahey Clinic sent him to New Orleans where renowned cancer specialist Dr. Alton Ochsner would take Chennault as a patient. Ochsner—knowing Chennault would want the truth—told him he had six months to live.

The radiation treatments made him nauseated and he began to lose weight, but because they had always done so in the past, the family flew to Taiwan where they spent Christmas 1957 together.

Back in the States, he drove around the Revolutionary War battlefields of New England with Tom Corcoran and discussed the possibility of Anna living in Washington after he was gone. He was concerned that Anna, as his sole heir, might have trouble with the ownership of land and other property in the South.

Corcoran promised to look after the legal affairs of Anna and the children and to see that she was launched on a professional career in Washington—or elsewhere. Chennault was considerably relieved.

On January 13, 1958, his diary entry noted:

"No breakfast this morning. Bronchoscopy started at 09:30, finished at 10:10. Not much pain, but anesthetic unpleasant. Dr. Lewis very good indeed. Still coughing up blood, but not as much. Received many letters, telegrams and flowers. Many callers, but Dr. Ochsner allowed no visitors."[1]

From Walter Reed, Chennault wrote to the officers of the Fourteenth Air Force Association on the eve of its annual convention on March 4:

> It is a matter of deep regret that I cannot attend the dinner with you tonight. I recall the very pleasant and in fact inspiring dinner we enjoyed together last year.
>
> This dinner is particularly notable since it is the 15th anniversary of the activation of the 14th Air Force. The occasion recalls to my mind the difficult conditions under which we lived and fought 15 years ago. I recall also the fortitude and perseverance which all of you displayed in overcoming all difficulties and dangers. Nor can I forget that some of you made the last great sacrifice in carrying out your duties in China. It is these recollections which I am sure are shared by all of you and now bind us together in an association of mutual respect and friendship.
>
> Both Anna and I are looking forward to meeting and dining with you in San Francisco in August.
>
>   C. L. Chennault

The X-ray therapy at Walter Reed Hospital was giving him a fever and that interfered with his answering the many letters he was receiving from all over the world. Friends and former comrades, hearing of the news of his cancer, wrote from England, Taiwan, and from all over the United States.

Through the efforts of Corcoran, Joe Alsop, a number of high-ranking Air

Force generals, and a Louisiana congressman, considerable political and military pressure was exerted upon the Administration and, on July 15, President Eisenhower requested Congress to promote Chennault to lieutenant general. Chennault, by now frail and with skin drawn tight over his fevered face, was no longer interested in the long-delayed promotion.

Anna wrote to the members of the Fourteenth Air Force Association from New Orleans where Chennault had been moved back to Ochsner Foundation Hospital:

Dear Friends:

We enjoy hearing from you and appreciate your writing to us. During the past six months we have spent most of our time in the hospitals— Walter Reed of Washington and Ochsner Foundation of New Orleans. We have been at Ochsner almost one month at this time. General Chennault's condition has shown no improvement after three operations and he has been suffering from pain since last month. He weighs only 140 pounds—his weight was 180 two years ago—and depends entirely on tube feeding. All the doctors agree that he is a tough guy and will carry on his fight against this dreadful disease bravely, however the future looks quite dim from here. The problem is: how long can we keep him under this condition before the new medicine comes out? It has been heartbreaking to be caught in the middle of a crisis and don't know which way to turn. But we are not giving up hope and faith. My job is to be with him and help him to fight this battle the best I can. I do hope and pray that we will be able to attend the convention in S.F. Please ask all his "boys" to write to the "Old Man" for I know he will be happy to hear from each of you. . . .

Old friends began to visit him as they learned of his condition. Madame Chiang came to the hospital room and he tried to speak but was too weak.

"Don't try to talk, Colonel," she said, using his old familiar rank by which she had known him so long. "This time let me do the talking."

On July 27, 1958, Claire Lee Chennault died in the sixty-seventh year of his life.

Epilogue

The Associated Press, from New Orleans, wrote:

Lt. Gen. Claire Lee Chennault, whose Flying Tigers helped sweep Japanese aircraft from China skies during World War II, died today. He was 67. Death came to the leathery-faced flying leader two weeks after Rep. Herbert (D-Louisiana) sped a bill through Congress making Chennault a lieutenant general. It received unanimous approval in both houses July 18, and was signed by President Eisenhower that night.

Chennault's funeral was held in Washington several days later. His sons and daughters came and pallbearers included ex-AVG pilots Tex Hill, Ed Rector, Dick Rossi, and Chennault's oldest son Colonel John S. Chennault. Hundreds of Fourteenth Air Force men traveled to the service from all over the United States.

The funeral was attended by ambassadors, governors, generals, and members of Congress. The casket was drawn by horses down the tree-shaded lanes of Arlington Cemetery to the slow beat of drums and his body was buried on a grassy hill overlooking the Tomb of the Unknown Soldier.

Walking beside the casket were Generals Albert Wedemeyer, George Kenney, Curtis LeMay, Carl Spaatz, Nathan Twining, and, representing the United States Air Force, General Charles Stone.

Madame Chiang sat with Anna Chennault at the graveside service.

The gravestone lists Chennault's medals and decorations and on the rear of the stone is a pair of Chinese Air Force pilot's wings and Chinese characters that read "The Tomb of General Chennault"—the only Chinese inscription in Arlington Cemetery.

On November 14, 1958, Lake Charles Air Force Base in Louisiana was renamed Chennault Air Force Base.

In Taipei, Taiwan—in April 1960—a life-sized bust of Chennault was unveiled in the square near the Capitol building. It was the first statue of a foreigner ever erected by Chinese on their own soil.

APPENDIX

Below are the total amounts due the individual pilots covered by the above letters—confirmations complete through July 6, 1942.

NAMES	AMOUNT REQUESTED	NAMES	AMOUNT REQUESTED
Adkins, F. W.	$500.00	Laughlin, C. H.	2600.00
Bacon, N. R.	1750.00	Lawlor, F. L.	4250.00
Bartelt, P. R.	3500.00	Layher, R. F.	416.67
Bartling, W. E.	3633.33	Liebolt, E. J.	133.33
Bishop, L. S.	2600.00	Little, R. L.	5276.18
Blackburn, J. E.	1000.00	McGarry, W. D.	5142.85
Bolster, H. R.	500.00	McMillian, G. B.	2041.66
Bond, C. R.	4383.33	Merritt, K. T.	500.00
Boyington, G.	1750.00	Mickelson, E. I.	133.33
Bright, J. G.	3000.00	Moss, R. C.	2000.00
Brouk, R. R.	1750.00	Mott, R. D.	1000.00
Brown, C. K.	133.33	Neale, R. H.	7776.18
Burgard, G. T.	5392.85	Newkirk, J. V. K.	5250.00
Cole, T. J.	500.00	Older, C. H.	5041.66
Cross, J. D.	133.33	Olson, A. E.	500.00
Dean, J. J.	1633.33	Overend, E. F.	2916.66
Donovan, J. T.	2000.00	Petach, J. R., Jr.	1991.67
Dupouy, P. S.	1750.00	Prescott, R. W.	2642.85
Farrell, J. W.	500.00	Raines, R. J.	1600.00
Geselbracht, H. M.	750.00	Rector, E. F.	3258.33
Greene, P. J.	1000.00	Reed, W. N.	5250.00
Groh, C. G.	1000.00	Ricketts, F. I.	600.00
Gunvordahl, R. N.	500.00	Rosbert, C. J.	2276.18
Hastey, R. L.	500.00	Rossi, J. R.	3142.85
Haywood, T. C., Jr.	2541.66	Sandell, R. J.	2633.33
Hedman, R. P.	2416.66	Sawyer, C. W.	1133.33
Hill, D. L.	5625.00	Schiel, F.	3500.00
Hodges, F. S.	500.00	Shapard, Van	500.00
Hoffman, L.	133.33	Shilling, E. E.	375.00
Howard, J. H.	3166.67	Smith, R. H.	2750.00
Jernstedt, K. A.	5250.00	Smith, R. T.	4366.66
Jones, T. A.	2000.00	Wolf, F. E.	1133.33
Keeton, R. B.	1250.00	Wright, P.	1325.00
Kuykendall, M. W.	500.00	GRAND TOTAL	$146,999.87

NOTES

CHAPTER 5

1. Fairbank Report to Dr. Lauchlin Currie, 1942.
2. Ibid.
3. Ibid.

CHAPTER SIX

1. Fairbank Report to Dr. Lauchlin Currie, 1942.
2. Ibid.

CHAPTER SEVEN

1. Chennault, *Way of a Fighter*, p. 113.
2. Hotz, et al., *With General Chennault*, p. 106.

CHAPTER EIGHT

1. Hotz, et al., *With General Chennault*, p. 38.

CHAPTER NINE

1. Chennault Papers.
2. Ibid.
3. Ibid.
4. Ibid.
5. Ibid.

CHAPTER TEN

1. Chennault Papers.
2. Ibid.
3. Ibid.
4. Ibid.

CHAPTER ELEVEN

1. Stilwell Papers.
2. Ibid.
3. Chennault, *Way of a Fighter*, p. 170.
4. Stilwell Papers.

CHAPTER TWELVE

1. Letter from Patterson to Sebie Smith, 1982.
2. Letter from William Pawley to Chennault, March 16, 1942, Chennault Papers.
3. Chennault Papers.
4. Ibid.
5. Ibid.
6. Ibid.
7. Ibid.
8. Ibid.
9. Ibid.
10. Ibid.
11. Ibid.
12. Ibid.
13. Ibid.
14. Ibid.
15. Ibid.

CHAPTER THIRTEEN

1. Chennault Papers.
2. Chennault, *Way of a Fighter*, p. 169.
3. Stilwell Papers.
4. Ibid.
5. Chennault, op. cit., p. 160.
6. Chennault Papers.
7. Stilwell Papers.

8. Chennault Papers.
9. Ibid.
10. Ibid.
11. Ibid.
12. Ibid.
13. Ibid.
14. Ibid.
15. Ibid.
16. Ibid.
17. Ibid.
18. Ibid.
19. Ibid.
20. Ibid.
21. Stilwell Papers.

CHAPTER FOURTEEN

1. Chennault Papers.
2. Ibid.
3. Ibid.
4. Ibid.
5. Ibid.
6. Ibid.
7. Ibid.
8. Ibid.
9. Ibid.
10. Ibid.
11. Ibid.
12. Ibid.
13. Ibid.
14. Ibid.
15. Ibid.
16. Ibid.
17. Ibid.

CHAPTER FIFTEEN

1. Craven, The Army Air Forces in World War II, p. 406.
2. Chennault Papers.
3. Ibid.

CHAPTER SIXTEEN

1. Chennault Papers.
2. Ibid.
3. Chennault, Way of a Fighter, p. 182.
4. New York Times, October 5, 1942.
5. Chennault Papers.

CHAPTER SEVENTEEN

1. Chennault Papers.
2. Romanus and Sunderland, Stilwell's Mission to China, p. 255.

CHAPTER EIGHTEEN

1. Stilwell Papers.
2. Ibid.
3. Ibid.
4. Letter to Marshall, March 8, 1943, Romanus and Sunderland, Stilwell's Mission to China, p. 282.
5. Stilwell, ed. Theodore White, The Stilwell Papers, p. 206.
6. Chennault, Way of a Fighter, p. 218.
7. Romanus and Sunderland, op. cit., p. 321.
8. Chennault, op. cit., p. 218.
9. Stilwell, ed. Theodore White, op. cit., p. 206.
10. Romanus and Sunderland, op. cit., p. 324.
11. Letter from Marshall, May 3, 1943, Stilwell Papers.

CHAPTER NINETEEN

1. Chennault, Way of a Fighter, p. 222.
2. Ibid.
3. Vincent, Fire and Fall Back, p. 211.
4. Romanus and Sunderland, Stilwell's Mission to China, p. 345.
5. Ibid.
6. Ibid.
7. Ibid.
8. Interview with Tom Trumbull, Chennault Papers.

CHAPTER TWENTY

1. Romanus and Sunderland, Stilwell's Mission to China, p. 367.
2. Ibid, p. 389.
3. Romanus and Sunderland, Stilwell's Command Problems, p. 23.
4. Craven, The Army Air Forces in World War II, p. 20.
5. Ibid., p. 21.

6. Chennault, *Way of a Fighter,* p. 226.
7. Craven, op. cit., p. 27.
8. Chennault Papers.
9. Ibid.
10. Letter from Arnold to Chennault, February 25, Chennault Papers.
11. Letter, March 30, Chennault Papers.

CHAPTER TWENTY-ONE

1. Chennault, *Way of a Fighter,* p. 236.
2. Romanus and Sunderland, *Stilwell's Command Problems,* p. 312.
3. Ibid., p. 312.
4. Ibid., p. 315.
5. Ibid., p. 315.
6. Ibid., p. 316.
7. Ibid., p. 316.
8. Chennault, op. cit., p. 286.
9. Romanus and Sunderland, op. cit., p. 322.
10. Chennault, op. cit., p. 287.
11. Romanus and Sunderland, op. cit., p. 326.
12. Ibid., p. 326.

CHAPTER TWENTY-TWO

1. Chennault, *Way of a Fighter,* p. 294.
2. Craven, *The Army Air Forces in World War II,* Vol. 5, p. 102.
3. Ibid., p. 38.
4. Ibid., p. 38.
5. Ibid., p. 207.
6. Ibid., p. 218.

CHAPTER TWENTY-THREE

1. Vincent, *Fire and Fall Back,* p. 316.
2. Letter from Arnold to Chennault, Chennault Papers.
3. Chennault, *Way of a Fighter,* p. 306.
4. Romanus and Sunderland, *Stilwell's Command Problems,* p. 374.
5. Ibid., p. 376.
6. Vincent, op. cit., p. 173.

7. Romanus and Sunderland, op. cit., p. 377.
8. Ibid., p. 380.
9. Ibid., p. 386.
10. Ibid., p. 409.
11. Ibid., p. 379.

CHAPTER TWENTY-FOUR

1. Tuchman, *Stilwell and the American Experience in China,* p. 470.
2. Romanus and Sunderland, *Stilwell's Command Problems,* p. 431.
3. Stilwell Papers, p. 331.
4. Romanus and Sunderland, op. cit., p. 445.
5. Ibid., p. 442.
6. Ibid., p. 447.
7. Lohbeck, *Patrick J. Hurley,* p. 296.
8. Stilwell Papers, p. 346.
9. Craven, *The Army Air Forces in World War II,* p. 406.

CHAPTER TWENTY-FIVE

1. Romanus and Sunderland, *Time Runs Out in CBI,* p. 15.
2. Craven, *The Army Air Forces in World War II,* p. 256.
3. Chennault, *Way of a Fighter,* p. 575.
4. Ibid., p. 330.
5. Ibid., pp. 336–37.

CHAPTER TWENTY-SIX

1. Romanus and Sunderland, *Time Runs Out in CBI,* p. 252.
2. Craven, *The Army Air Forces in World War II,* p. 270.
3. Chennault, *Way of a Fighter,* pp. 349–50.

CHAPTER TWENTY-SEVEN

1. Chennault, *Way of a Fighter,* pp. 356–57.
2. Willauer Papers, January 15, 1946.
3. H. T. Samson letter, April 16, 1946, Chennault Papers.
4. Chennault, op. cit., p. x.
5. Wedemeyer, *Wedemeyer Reports!,*

p. 348; Kubeck, *How the Far East Was Lost,* p. 627.

6. Lattimore to Truman, June 10, 1945; Senate Judiciary Committee, *Hearings on the Institute of Pacific Relations.*
7. U. S. Congress, Hearings of the Committee on Armed Services and the Committee on Foreign Relations of the Senate, *Military Situation in the Far East,* Part 3, p. 2460.
8. Lohbeck, *Patrick J. Hurley,* p. 430.
9. Wedemeyer, op. cit., p. 19.
10. U. S. Department of State, *United States Relations with China,* p. 608.
11. Testimony of Dean Acheson, June 4, 1951.

CHAPTER TWENTY-EIGHT

1. Leary, *Perilous Missions,* p. 19.
2. Edward Souder, *The History of CAT,* p. 73.
3. Chennault, *Way of a Fighter,* p. 361.
4. Truman, *Memoirs: Years of Decisions,* pp. ii, 84.
5. Chennault, op. cit., pp. xiii, xiv.
6. U. S. Department of State, *United States Relations with China,* p. 212.
7. Chennault, op. cit., p. xvi.
8. Kubeck, *How the Far East Was Lost,* p. 388.
9. Chennault, op. cit., p. xvii.
10. Kubeck, op. cit., p. 339.

CHAPTER TWENTY-NINE

1. Louise Willauer letter, June 25, 1967.
2. Ibid.
3. Letter from Whiting Willauer to Louise Willauer, September 7, 1947.
4. Letter from Louise Willauer to parents, 1947.

CHAPTER THIRTY

1. Chennault Papers.
2. Leary, *Perilous Missions,* p. 57.
3. Ibid., p. 59.
4. Ibid., p. 65.

CHAPTER THIRTY-ONE

1. Leary, *Perilous Missions,* p. 68.
2. Ibid., p. 72.
3. Kubeck, *How the Far East Was Lost,* p. 413.
4. Bullitt letter, August 28, 1949, U. S. Congress, Senate Judiciary Committee (Internal Security Subcommittee), *Hearings on the Institute of Pacific Relations,* p. 4533.
5. Stuart, "How the Communists Got China," *U. S. News and World Report,* October 1954.
6. Chennault Papers.
7. Ibid.
8. Leary, op. cit., p. 80.
9. Ibid., p. 94.

CHAPTER THIRTY-TWO

1. U. S. Congress, Hearings of the Committee on Armed Services and the Committee on Foreign Relations of the Senate, *Military Situation in the Far East,* Part 5, p. 3589.
2. U. S. Congress, Committee on Foreign Relations, *A Decade of American Foreign Policy,* p. 728.
3. *Department of State Bulletin,* March 27, 1950, p. 469.
4. Leary, *Perilous Missions,* p. 102.
5. Ibid.
6. Ibid., p. 106.
7. Ibid., p. 107.
8. Ibid., p. 133.
9. Ibid., p. 142.
10. Ibid., p. 171.

CHAPTER THIRTY-THREE

1. Leary, *Perilous Missions,* p. 181.
2. Ibid., p. 193.
3. Ibid., p. 203.
4. Ibid., p. 205.
5. Ibid., p. 206.
6. Ibid., p. 213.

CHAPTER THIRTY-FOUR

1. Anna Chennault, *A Thousand Springs,* p. 299.

BIBLIOGRAPHY

Printed Sources

U. S. Department of State (Far Eastern Series 30). *United States Relations with China, 1944–49.* (White Paper). Washington: Government Printing Office, 1949.

U. S. Department of State. *A Decade of American Foreign Policy, 1941–1949.* Washington: Government Printing Office, 1950.

———. *Bulletins,* 1949–50.

———. *Papers Relating to the Foreign Relations of the United States, China, 1942.* Washington: Government Printing Office, 1956.

———. *Peace and War: United States Foreign Policy, 1931–1941.* Washington: Government Printing Office, 1943.

U. S. Congress, Senate:

Committee on Foreign Relations. *Investigation of United States Far Eastern Policy,* 3 vols., December 1946.

Committee on the Judiciary. *Report for the Year 1954.* 83rd Cong., 2nd Sess. Washington: Government Printing Office, 1955.

———. *Report on Internal Security for the Year 1956.* 84th Cong., 2nd Sess. Washington: Government Printing Office, 1957.

Subcommittee on Foreign Relations. *Nomination of Philip C. Jessup Hearings.* 82nd Cong., 1st Sess. Washington: Government Printing Office, 1951.

Committee on Armed Services. *Nomination of General of the Army George C. Marshall to be Secretary of Defense, Hearings.* 82nd Cong. 2nd Sess. Washington: Government Printing Office, 1950

Committee on Armed Services and the Committee on Foreign Relations of the Senate. *Military Situation in the Far East, Hearings,* 5 parts. 82nd Cong., 1st Sess. Washington: Government Printing Office, 1951.

Committee on the Judiciary, (Internal Security Subcommittee). *Institute of Pacific Relations, Hearings,* 15 parts. 82nd Cong., 1st Sess. Washington: Government Printing Office, 1951.

Committee on Foreign Relations. *A Decade of American Foreign Policy: Basic Documents, 1941–1949.* Washington: Government Printing Office, 1950.

U. S. Congress, House of Representatives:

Committee on Foreign Affairs. *National and International Movements,* Supplement III, "Communism in China." Washington: Government Printing Office, 1948.

Committee on Un-American Activities. *Language as a Communist Weapon.* 86th Cong., 1st Sess. Washington: Government Printing Office, 1956.

Committee on Un-American Activities. *International Communism: Consultation with Major General Claire Lee Chennault.* 85th Cong., 2nd Sess. Washington: Government Printing Office, 1949.

Unofficial Collections of Documents, Letters, Speeches:
China Presents Her Case to the United Nations. Chinese Delegation to the United Nations, New York: 1949.

Archives and Manuscript Collections:
Chennault Papers, Hoover Institution, Stanford, California (microfilm copy at Library of Congress).
Stilwell Papers, Hoover Institution, Stanford, California.
Willauer Papers, Princeton University Library, Princeton, New Jersey.
National Archives, Army Records (now Modern Military Records Division).
Office of the Chief of Military History. (Interviews recorded by its historians.)
Fourteenth Air Force Archives, Maxwell Field, Alabama.

Books and Magazines
Alsop, Joseph. "Why We Lost China," *Saturday Evening Post,* January 7, 14, 21, 1950.
Barrett, Colonel David D. "Dixie Mission: The United States Army Observer Group to Yenan, 1944." *China Research Monographs,* No. 6, Center for Chinese Studies, University of California, Berkeley, September 1970.
Belden, Jack. *Retreat with Stilwell.* New York: Knopf, 1943.
Bond, Charles. *A Flying Tiger's Diary.* College Station, Texas: Texas A & M University Press, 1984.
Chennault, Anna. *A Thousand Springs.* Middlebury, Vt.: Paul S. Eriksson, 1962.
Chennault, Claire Lee, ed. Robert B. Hotz. *Way of a Fighter: The Memoirs of Claire Lee Chennault.* New York: Putnam, 1949.
Craven, Wesley Frank. *The Army Air Forces in World War II.* Office of Air Force History, Washington, D.C. Chicago: University of Chicago Press, 1953.
Finney, Charles G. *The Old China Hands.* New York: Doubleday, 1961.
Frillman, Paul, and Graham Peck. *China: The Remembered Life.* Boston: Houghton Mifflin, 1968.
Hahn, Emily. *The Soong Sisters.* Garden City, N.Y.: Doubleday, 1943.
Greenlaw, Olga. *The Lady and the Tigers.* New York: E. P. Dutton, 1943.
Hotz, Robert, with the assistance of George L. Paxton and others. *With General Chennault: The Story of the Flying Tigers.* New York: Coward-McCann, 1943.
Kubeck, Dr. Anthony. *How the Far East Was Lost.* Chicago: Regnery, 1963.
Leary, William M. *The Dragon's Wings.* Athens: University of Georgia Press, 1976.
————. *Perilous Missions.* Tuscaloosa: University of Alabama Press, 1984.
Leonard, Royal. *I Flew for China.* New York: Doubleday, 1942.
Lohbeck, Don. *Patrick J. Hurley.* Chicago: Regnery, 1956.
Miles, Vice Admiral Milton E. *A Different Kind of War.* New York: Doubleday, 1967.
Romanus, Charles, and Riley Sunderland. *Stilwell's Command Problems.* Washington, D.C.: Department of the Army, Historical Division, 1956.
————. *Stilwell's Mission to China.* Washington, D.C.: Department of the Army, Historical Division, 1953.
————. *Time Runs Out in CBI.* Washington, D.C.: Department of the Army, Historical Division, 1959.
Rosholt, Malcolm. *Flight in the China Air Space 1910–1950.* Amherst, Wis.: Palmer Publications, 1984.

Scott, Robert Lee, Jr. *Flying Tiger: Chennault of China.* New York: Doubleday, 1959.

Stilwell, Joseph W., ed. Theodore White. *The Stilwell Papers.* New York: Sloane, 1948.

Stuart, John Leighton. "How the Communists Got China," *U. S. News and World Report,* October 1954.

Truman, Harry S. *Memoirs: Years of Decisions,* Vol. I. Garden City, N.Y.: Doubleday, 1955.

Tuchman, Barbara W. *Stilwell and the American Experience in China.* New York: Macmillan, 1971.

Vincent, Clinton D. *Fire and Fall Back.* San Antonio, Tex.: Barnes Press, 1975.

Wedemeyer, Albert C. *Wedemeyer Reports!* New York: Holt, 1958.

White Paper. *See* U. S. Department of State.

INDEX

CHENNAULT'S CHINA
1937 - 57

MILES 400
KM 400

NINGHSIA

KANSU
Lanchow

TSINGHAI

TIBET

MEKONG R.
YANGTZE R.
YELLOW R.

SZECHWAN
Kwanghan
Nancheng • Chengtu
• Chungking

SIKIANG

HIMALAYAS
NEPAL
BHUTAN
BRAHMAPUTRA R.
ASSAM VALLEY
Chabua
Ledo
LEDO ROAD
CHINDWIN R.
SALWEEN R.
THE HUMP

KWEICHOW
Kweiyang
Tzukung
Kütsing
Yunnanyi
Kunming
Chengkung

Mogaung
Myitkyina
Bhamo
Paoshan
Tengchung
Lungling
YUNNAN
Wenshan
Mengtzu
Lao-kai

GANGES R.
INDIA
Imphal
Calcutta
Indaw
Shwebo •
Mandalay
Lashio
BURMA ROAD
Yüankiang
RED R.
Hanoi
Haiphon

Maymyo
Laihka
Dienbienphu
FRENCH INDO CHINA

BURMA
Yenangyaung
Magwe
IRRAWADDY R.
SALWEEN R.
Toungoo

BAY OF BENGAL

LAOS
MEKONG R.

Rangoon
Moulmein
THAILAND

palacios